WHEN THE PARTY'S OVER
The Politics of Fiscal Squeeze in Perspective

PROCEEDINGS OF THE BRITISH ACADEMY · 197

WHEN THE PARTY'S OVER
The Politics of Fiscal Squeeze
in Perspective

Edited by
CHRISTOPHER HOOD
DAVID HEALD
ROZANA HIMAZ

Published for THE BRITISH ACADEMY
by OXFORD UNIVERSITY PRESS

Oxford University Press, Great Clarendon Street, Oxford OX2 6DP

British Library Cataloguing in Publication Data
Data available

Library of Congress Cataloging in Publication Data
Data available

Typeset by
New Leaf Design, Scarborough, North Yorkshire
Printed in Great Britain
on acid free paper by
TJ International Ltd, Padstow, Cornwall

ISBN: 978–0–19–726573–4
ISSN: 0068–1202

Contents

Part III: Conclusion

Figures and Tables

Tables

Notes on Contributors

Sebastián Dellepiane-Avellaneda is Lecturer in the School of Government and Public Policy at the University of Strathclyde, Glasgow. He has undertaken teaching and research in Essex, Dublin, Antwerp and Maastricht. His research interests include the politics of economic policy, governance and development, and research methodology. He has published several articles on monetary and fiscal politics in the *British Journal of Political Science* and in *European Political Science*. He is currently working on a collaborative project on 'The political economy of the European periphery' for a book to be published by Oxford University Press.

Chris Eichbaum is Reader in Government in the School of Government, and an Associate Dean in the Victoria Business School, Victoria University of Wellington. He has held public service positions in both the Australian Commonwealth and the New Zealand Public Service, and has worked as an adviser to ministers and prime ministers in New Zealand. In 2013 he completed a five-year term as a non-executive director on the board of the Reserve Bank of New Zealand. With Richard Shaw he is co-author of *Public Policy in New Zealand: Institutions, Processes and Outcomes*, 3rd edn (Auckland: Pearson Education New Zealand, 2011) and co-editor of *Partisan Appointees and Public Servants: An International Analysis of the Role of the Political Adviser* (Cheltenham: Edward Elgar, 2010).

Robert Gregory is Emeritus Professor of Politics in the School of Government, Victoria University of Wellington. He is a graduate of that university, and of the John F. Kennedy School of Government, Harvard University. He was a Visiting Professor in the then Department of Public and Social Administration, City University of Hong Kong, 2010–11. He has published widely in the areas of public administration and management, and public policy, with particular reference to issues of institutional and individual accountability and responsibility. He also worked for twelve years with the former New Zealand Broadcasting Corporation.

Niamh Hardiman is Senior Lecturer in the School of Politics and International Relations at University College Dublin. Before this she was Fellow and Tutor in Politics for a number of years at Somerville College, Oxford, and she worked for a time in the Economic and Social Research Institute in Dublin. She is currently working on a joint-authored book on the political economy of the European periphery, to be published by Oxford University Press. She is the editor of *Irish Governance in Crisis* (Manchester: MUP, 2012). She is a member of the blog collective Crooked Timber (www.crookedtimber.org).

David Heald is Professor of Accountancy at the University of Aberdeen Business School. His research interests focus on public sector accounting reform, public expenditure management and control, fiscal transparency, public audit and financing devolved governments. He has had extensive policy involvement, including as a member of the Financial Reporting Advisory Board to HM Treasury (2004–09) and specialist adviser on government accounting and public expenditure to the Treasury Committee of the House of Commons (1989–2010). He is working on a Leverhulme Trust project on 'The architecture, governance and substance of UK public audit' (2012–15). This 'Fiscal Squeeze' book renews his collaboration with Christopher Hood, with whom he co-edited *Transparency: The Key to Better Governance?* (OUP for the British Academy, 2006).

Rozana Himaz is Lecturer in Economics at Queen's College, Oxford. Since 2011 she has been a researcher for the ESRC-funded project 'When the Party's Over: The Politics of Austerity in Public Services', headed by Professor Christopher Hood, at the Department of Politics and International Relations, Oxford. She has taught micro, macro and quantitative economics at several universities including the London School of Economics, Cambridge and Oxford. She has also worked as a researcher for the Young Lives project (Department of International Development, Oxford), at the Institute of Policy Studies in Sri Lanka, and as a consultant for the World Bank and the International Labour Organization. Her research interests lie in the empirical analysis of issues pertaining to welfare and public policy.

Christopher Hood CBE FBA has been Gladstone Professor of Government, All Souls College, Oxford since 2001. He specialises in the study of executive government, regulation and public sector reform. He has been writing on the subject of cutback management for over thirty years, currently holds an ESRC Professorial Fellowship and combines academic work with public engagement.

Walter Kickert is Professor of Public Management at Erasmus University Rotterdam. He specialises in public governance, management, organisation and administrative reform, especially in Europe. Among his publications are *Managing Complex Networks* (London: Sage, 1997) and *The Study of Public*

Management in Europe and the US (London: Routledge, 2008). His most recent research theme is the current fiscal crisis and budget cutbacks in Europe. Until 2011 he was deputy editor of the journal *Public Administration*. In 2012 he was awarded the Routledge prize for public management research.

Anders Lindbom is Professor in Political Science at Uppsala University, Sweden. His research has focused particularly on welfare state reform and political decision-making. He has published articles in many journals including *Journal of Public Policy*, *Governance*, *Journal of European Public Policy*, *Scandinavian Political Studies* and *Journal of European Social Policy*. Lately he has been doing research on why Social Democrats sometimes conduct large-scale privatisations and whether voters punish incumbents for welfare retrenchment at the next election.

Martin Lodge is Professor of Political Science and Public Policy at the Department of Government and the Centre for Analysis of Risk and Regulation at the London School of Economics. His research interests are in executive politics and regulation. He is also an editor of one of the oldest academic journals in the field, *Public Administration.*

Alasdair Roberts is the Jerome L. Rappaport Professor of Law and Public Policy at Suffolk University Law School, Boston, Massachusetts. He writes extensively on problems of governance, law and public policy. His most recent books are *America's First Great Depression* (Ithaca NY: Cornell University Press, 2012) and *The Logic of Discipline: Global Capitalism and the Architecture of Government* (Oxford: OUP, 2010). He was elected a fellow of the US National Academy of Public Administration in 2007 and appointed a public member of the Administrative Conference of the United States in 2010. He is also an Honorary Senior Research Fellow of the School of Public Policy, University College London and co-editor of the journal *Governance*.

Donald J. Savoie holds the Canada Research Chair in Public Administration and Governance at the Université de Moncton. He has published numerous books on public policy, public administration and governance, and his work has won prizes in Canada, the United States and Europe. He was elected a Fellow of Canada's National Academy and awarded several honorary degrees from Canadian universities. His latest book is *Whatever Happened to the Music Teacher? How Government Decides and Why* (Montreal & Kingston: McGill-Queen's University Press, 2013).

Kai Wegrich is Professor of Public Policy and Administration at the Hertie School of Governance, Berlin. He is European editor of *Public Administration* and co-editor (with Martin Lodge) of the book series Executive Politics and Governance (Palgrave). He is also co-chair of the permanent study group on Performance in the Public Sector of the European Group of Public Administration (EGPA). His research interests are in executive politics, public management and regulation.

Preface and Acknowledgements

This book is an exercise in mixing and bridging, since it brings together politics and economics, the past and the present, quantitative and qualitative analysis.

It brings together politics and economics because we set out to produce a book that would concentrate on the political analysis of what we here call fiscal squeeze (for reasons we explain in Chapter 1), but still engage seriously with the voluminous literature on political economy. It brings together the past and the present because, at a time when dramatic fiscal pressures were central to politics in many countries in the aftermath of the great financial crash of 2008, we wanted to analyse past cases of fiscal squeeze in different places to see what, if anything, they had in common. And it brings together quantitative and qualitative analysis because, at a time when there are plenty of books of essays on the general subject of the politics of austerity, we wanted to focus more specifically on fiscal squeeze. This book combines systematic analytic comparison with a set of descriptive case studies and thereby engages carefully with the available published numbers while exploring what lies behind them.

The bridging and mixing took all of us to the edge of our intellectual comfort zones if not beyond, but the aim of the book was to produce jointly what we could not have achieved on our own, namely a pooling of expertise in the history and fiscal politics of different countries, a combination of disciplinary backgrounds (in economics, public finance accounting and political science), and also a mixing of different academic generations.

The ancient Goths are said to have discussed all important matters twice, once drunk and once sober. All of our discussions were of course conducted with the utmost sobriety, but we have discussed the underlying issues of this book much more than twice, and the thousand-plus emails we exchanged as all the chapters went through successive drafts are only part of the deliberation that went into this book. The central ideas of the book were successively refined as a result of discussion in two conferences a year apart (one a backroom affair in Oxford in the wet and cold April of 2012, the other a large-scale conference in central London in the hottest week of 2013), plus numerous online and face-to-face editorial discussions.

Nietzsche said all theory is autobiography, and certainly this book has taken shape against a period of several years in which the politics of fiscal squeeze was seldom out of the headlines, with endless debates over matters such as who should suffer how much 'austerity', whether unelected economists should rule the world, and whether the neo-liberalism of recent decades was a busted flush in a new world of severe fiscal pressure. We tried to maintain a measure of academic distance in order to put the present and the recent past into perspective, but the politics of fiscal squeeze was happening all around us as we talked academic concepts beneath the Gothic pinnacles of All Souls College, Oxford and the classical columns and scrolls of the British Academy's building in London's Carlton House Terrace.

This project has been a long time in the making and we have many debts to acknowledge—institutional and personal, intellectual and material. The project would have been impossible without the financial support provided by the Economic and Social Research Council that paid for the time we needed to develop and refine the concepts, bring the participating scholars together, and carry out the detailed comparative analysis and one of the case studies. It would have been very much more difficult without the generosity of All Souls College, Oxford, in hosting a vital 'backroom event' to discuss cases and concepts at an early stage in the spring of 2012. And the project was helped enormously by the support it received from the British Academy, whose Events and Prizes Committee accepted a proposal from us for a British Academy conference in the summer of 2013 to present and discuss drafts of the papers that became the chapters for this book, and whose Publications Committee later accepted the collected volume for publication in this series.

Vital as such institutional support is, a project like this needs help from specific individuals too, and we are particularly grateful to James Rivington of the British Academy for helpful advice and encouragement throughout the process, to Angela Pusey and Penny Collins for so capably organising the British Academy conference that led up to this book, and to Brigid Hamilton-Jones for helping us develop and present the book for publication. More specifically, we wish to thank: Emma Anderson for event organisation, pulling the typescript together and preparing the index; Janet English for project-managing the book's production; and Susan Milligan for her meticulous copy-editing.

But a book like this needs more than financial and logistical help, important as that is. We have had a great deal of intellectual guidance, not only from the insights and advice we gained from the contributors (without them there would have been no book) but also from those who helped us to shape this analysis before, during and after the British Academy conference, including Lucy Barnes, Sir Christopher Foster, Maura Francese, Andrew Gamble, Patrick Le Galès, Lord (Gus) O'Donnell, Christopher Pollitt, Rt Hon. John Redwood MP, Rt Hon. Peter Riddell, Lord (Nick) Stern and Daniel Tarschys.

We are deeply grateful also to three anonymous referees for the British Academy who assessed the draft of each chapter for the book and made helpful suggestions for improvement, and to the many participants in the British Academy conference who offered valuable suggestions and comments.

Christopher Hood, David Heald and Rozana Himaz
December 2013

Part I
Introduction

1

The Politics of Fiscal Squeeze

DAVID HEALD AND CHRISTOPHER HOOD

Putting the Politics of Fiscal Squeeze into Perspective

IT IS COMMONLY IMPLIED THAT THE GREAT FINANCIAL CRASH of 2008 and the dramatic policy changes that followed in many countries were unique in the history of the world. Many have commented on the sheer scale of the financial pressures on many governments in terms of deficit and debt and on the drastic monetary responses by central banks, setting their official lending rates at historic lows and printing money on an unprecedented scale (see, for example, Swagel 2009; Greenspan *et al.* 2010; Reinhart & Rogoff 2011).

We do not want to underplay the significance or the dramatic nature of those adjustments. But even so, historical comparisons are instructive. For example, the fiscal travails of the early United States in the early 19th century (when half of the states then in the Union had to default over their debts, mass protests had to be contained, and new unpopular taxes imposed in the middle of an international trade slump) merit some attention by those who think there are no parallels to the Eurozone debt crisis of the early 2010s (Roberts 2012: 204). Indeed, the experience of the Ottoman Empire after it defaulted on loan repayments to its foreign creditors in 1875 goes far beyond anything witnessed in the Eurozone countries in the 2010s so far (see Birdal 2010: 6–10). In that case, a large independent (ostensibly private) bureaucracy run by the Empire's European creditors was set up by the Decree of Muharrem issued by Sultan Abdülhamid II in 1881 to collect taxes that were paid directly to those creditors. Even in more recent times, experiences such as that of Mexico in 1995 in consequence of its so-called 'Tequila' crisis can provide some partial parallels to the problems experienced by crisis-hit countries in the 2010s. The currency slumped by almost 50 per cent after a pre-election spending splurge in 1994 had been financed by debt indexed to US dollars, with GDP then falling by some 7 per cent and industrial wages by 30 per cent in a single year, leading to a hasty 'bailout' (arguably mainly benefiting international creditors) organised by the United States, the IMF and the Bank for International Settlements (Humphrey 2000).

Proceedings of the British Academy, **197**, 3–25. © The British Academy 2014.

Of course there is always something unique about the circumstances of any given time. But even so, comparisons across space and time, both in the aftermath of major financial crises and in other conditions, can help us understand what we here call 'fiscal squeeze', explore the politics behind such processes and see what if anything they have in common. That is what this book aims to do. But first we need to explain why this book focuses on *fiscal squeeze*, why it is the *politics* of fiscal squeeze we want to focus on, and what we mean by putting fiscal squeeze into *perspective*.

Why *Fiscal Squeeze*?

This book is mainly concerned with efforts made by politicians and governments to correct the public finances by raising taxes or cutting spending or a mixture of the two. We put spending and taxes into the foreground and monetary policy into the background. But of course we recognise that the two types of policy overlap, for example when governments use inflation as a tax, or use default or devaluation as a way to deal with debt problems, as has often happened historically.

In this book we use the term 'fiscal squeeze' to denote political effort put into reining in public spending and/or raising taxes. Given that starting point, Table 1.1 indicates three basic possible varieties of fiscal squeeze, in terms of effort put into increasing revenue, cutting spending, or both at the same time. The possible types are three rather than four, because cell (1) of the table, with effort going into neither raising revenue nor cutting spending, does not constitute a 'squeeze'. We will later elaborate this very basic typology by adding subcategories, and it is worth noting that revenue-only fiscal squeezes (cell (3) of the table) seem to be extremely rare, at least in modern democracies.

We use the term fiscal squeeze because many of the terms used in the prevailing literature are ambiguous, politically loaded or have a technical meaning that refers to financial outcomes rather than political effort. For example, the term 'fiscal adjustment' is often used in practice by international econocrats as a euphemism for higher taxes and/or spending cuts, but it often means attempts to change spending relative to GDP, which is a measure of financial outcome rather than political effort.

Table 1.1.   Some basic types of fiscal squeeze.

Effort going into revenue increases	Effort going into expenditure cuts	
	No	Yes
No	(1)	(2)
Yes	(3)	(4)

The same goes for 'fiscal consolidation', which similarly is often used as a technical-sounding euphemism for the same sort of measures. But it is also used more strictly to denote a reduction in the fiscal deficit (the difference between total revenue and spending or 'primary balance'—the balance struck before taking into account interest payments on the public debt). And both fiscal adjustment and fiscal consolidation in the more technical sense are financial outcomes that can come about as a result of economic growth rather than painful belt-tightening measures by governments. Contrariwise, those belt-tightening measures do not necessarily lead to fiscal consolidation if the overall economy contracts significantly, for example as a result of an international slump.

The term 'austerity' is perhaps closer to denoting the political effort that this book concentrates on, but it is ambiguous for several reasons. It is often used to denote what we here call fiscal squeeze, but it is sometimes used as a non-technical synonym for fiscal adjustment or fiscal consolidation. Moreover, it has recently come to denote a policy position associated with faster rather than slower attempts to correct fiscal deficits, and with an emphasis on correcting such deficits through spending cuts rather than tax increases, in the context of an economic slowdown or recession. Mark Blyth's (2013) attack on austerity as a what-to-do doctrine, and his account of its intellectual history and links to contemporary neo-liberalism more generally, is a telling recent example of this usage of the term.

But that is only a particular subset of what we here call fiscal squeeze.[1] So, in contrast to the normative associations (positive or negative) that 'austerity' has acquired, and in contrast to the financial outcomes that fiscal adjustment and consolidation tend to denote, we use fiscal squeeze as a neutral term to denote those fiscal changes that reflect political effort put into belt-tightening or loss imposition (i.e. spending cuts or tax increases imposed by governments, or both), irrespective of whether or not those measures reflect any particular doctrine or result in fiscal consolidation in the technical sense of deficit reduction.

It follows that fiscal squeeze is harder to measure than economic or financial outcome indicators, since the extent of the effort it denotes is not directly measured by financial outcome numbers, for at least three reasons. One is that economic outcome data tend to focus on *implemented* spending cuts or revenue increases, whereas in politics, *announcement* is often important as well as implementation. Another is that, as already noted, financial outcomes can

---

[1] There are other terms that could also be considered. For example, the term 'cutback management', used by some academics in the 1980s (for instance Dunsire & Hood 1989), is less euphemistic and circumlocutory than 'fiscal adjustment' or 'fiscal consolidation' and embraces much of what we are concerned with here, but covers only spending reductions or containment rather than what happens to taxes, charges or similar measures.

change for reasons unrelated to political effort, for example if revenues rise in an economic recovery as a result of higher incomes rather than by politicians putting tax rates up.

In particular, policies such as income taxes and welfare spending often act as 'automatic stabilisers' that dampen fluctuations in real GDP. For instance, when GDP falls in a recession, the budget deficit tends to increase as a result of falling tax revenue and increased welfare spending, which in turn keeps aggregate demand and national income higher than it would otherwise have been. Similarly during a boom, budget deficits often reduce as tax revenue rises and welfare spending falls. Such effects do not occur equally in all times and places, dependent on the extent of welfare entitlements and of obligations to balance spending and revenue in the short term. But where they apply, these effects are 'automatic' in that they occur without explicit government intervention, and hence an assessment of the political effort going into fiscal squeeze has to take into account the extent to which effort goes into overriding the cyclical effect of such stabilisers, as we do in our quantitative analysis in the next chapter.

A third reason why political effort involved in cutting spending or raising taxes (or both) is not automatically represented by reported deficit and debt numbers is that such effort depends heavily on context. A key part of that context is the preferences of political leaders and their core supporters as well as those of the voters. For example, it seems likely that in early 1976 Harold Wilson's Labour government in the UK expended more political effort in persuading its fractious and divided governing party even to accept a (short-lived) policy of holding public expenditure constant than did Jean Chrétien's Liberal government in Canada two decades later in substantially cutting federal spending in very different political circumstances. In principle, public spending cuts may require less political effort from 'Tea Party' style politicians who are committed to shrinking the state and whose core supporters have the same preferences, than in cases where government leaders find themselves applying policies that go against their own publicly expressed preferences and/or the preferences of their core party supporters.

Against that, however, is the so-called 'Nixon goes to China' phenomenon, often observable in politics (see for example Cukierman & Tommasi 1998). This phenomenon is named after the episode in 1972 when a Republican US President (Richard Nixon) who had hitherto maintained a strong anti-Communist stance initiated a rapprochement between the United States and the People's Republic of China. As in that example, leaders who have declared preferences in a particular policy direction can sometimes win over core party supporters and voters more generally with lower political effort when they move in the opposite direction (by imposing spending cuts and/or tax increases) and represent that move as unavoidable, at least as a short-term expedient. The extra political effort involved in changing their own established stance may in turn mean lower political effort for political leaders in winning over voters or supporters. An analogy could be drawn with the amount of braking effort needed to slow or stop a vehicle going down a steep slope or at high speed, as compared to that needed when travelling uphill or at low speed; the extent of braking effort (as represented by the extent of decelerative force) is only imperfectly measured by how long it takes the vehicle to stop or indeed whether it stops at all. In that example, gradient and previous speed are the equivalent of political context, and that is why financial or economic outcome data can only be a rough proxy for the extent of the political effort put into restraining spending and/or raising taxes. As the poet Robert Burns more pithily put it, 'What's done we partly may compute, / But know not what's resisted.'[2]

Table 1.2 accordingly aims to bring out what a spectrum of *political* cost or effort might look like for tax increases and spending cuts. At the low end of expected political costs, it identifies situations where governments concentrate on 'inertia politics' or maintaining the status quo in the sense of existing tax or spending plans and resisting calls for tax cuts or spending increases or both. Higher expected political costs apply where governments impose losses through spending cuts or tax increases that are low in visibility, salience or

Table 1.2. Fiscal squeeze and political effort: indicative examples of the spectrum of political effort.

Fiscal instrument	Expected political cost or effort level		
	Fairly low (Mainly inertia strategies)	Medium (Imposition of less visible and salient losses)	Fairly high (Imposition of visible and salient losses)
Taxation	Resistance to pressure for tax cuts	Imposition of 'stealth taxes' (e.g. use of fiscal drag, fees or charges that are not formally counted as 'taxes', such as parking fines)	Imposition of visible tax rises or levying new taxes on key voters or funders
	Acceptance of tax rises or new taxes already in the pipeline	Imposition of taxes or tax rises that do not hit key voters, funders or supporters	Breaking key election promises over taxes
Spending	Resistance to pressure for spending increases	'Stealth cuts' (e.g. non-indexation of benefits, increases in qualifying periods)	Imposition of visible cuts in spending of high salience to key voters or funders
	Taking advantage of spending programmes already scheduled to end	Cuts in spending of low salience to key voters, funders or supporters (e.g. benefits to non-voters abroad or spending cuts targeted at opposition heartland areas)	Breaking key election promises over spending

[2] 'Address to the Unco Guid' (Burns, [1786] 2009: 18).

impact on their key voters, supporters or funders, for example in imposing high nominal tax rates on wealth or income far above the median-voter level. At the top end of expected political costs are situations where governments impose losses through spending cuts or tax increases that are high in visibility, salience or impact on their key voters, supporters or funders. We do not claim that such distinctions are always easy to draw, that they are readily represented by standard statistical measures, or even that the measures indicated in each of the columns of Table 1.2 will always represent low, medium or high political costs, given the issue of variable context mentioned earlier. The table merely aims to provide a point of departure for thinking about what political effort or costs mean in fiscal squeeze.

Given that fiscal squeeze, as defined earlier, can only be indirectly measured, we identify fiscal squeezes in this book in two ways. One is by qualitative judgements based on study of the politics of the time in a set of different places, for the case studies we introduce later. The other is by taking reported aggregates of spending and revenue as a rough proxy for political effort. For that second approach based on proxy measures, we go beyond the simple 'yes'/'no' classifications in Table 1.1 to identify two types of spending squeeze and two types of revenue squeeze. They are:

- 'soft' expenditure squeezes, when either (a) government spending falls relative to GDP, but such expenditure does not fall in constant-price terms or (b) expenditure falls in constant-price terms but not relative to GDP;
- 'hard' expenditure squeezes, when government spending falls both relative to GDP and in constant-price terms;
- 'soft' revenue squeezes, when either (a) tax revenues rise relative to GDP but such revenues do not rise in constant-price terms or (b) tax revenues rise in constant-price terms but not relative to GDP;
- 'hard' revenue squeezes, when tax revenues rise both relative to GDP and in constant-price terms.

We postpone all discussion of the technical issues involved in making these distinctions to Chapter 2, but we note here that when put together, those four types make multiple possible combinations, to which we return in the final chapter.

Why the *Politics* of Fiscal Squeeze?

Of course fiscal squeeze can be approached from many different perspectives. Economics tends to focus on assessing the best policies to be pursued by governments facing fiscal difficulties. Sociology and cultural studies tend to concentrate on the lived experience of fiscal squeeze, such as jokes, cartoons, graffiti or music. This book is centrally concerned with understanding the politics and political economy of fiscal squeeze—who gets what, how losses are imposed, who gets the credit and who gets the blame, and (relatedly) what, if any, longer-term political (or broader social) consequences follow from episodes of fiscal squeeze.

Fiscal crisis, pressure and contraction figured large in the political economy literature of the 1970s and 1980s in the wake of the economic and financial difficulties experienced by Western economies at that time (such as oil price shocks, 'staglation' and de-industrialisation). For example, public policy scholars Richard Rose and Guy Peters (1978) asked *Can Government Go Bankrupt?* (then as now, the answer is both yes and no). Marxist scholar James O'Connor (1973) in his much-quoted *Fiscal Crisis of the State* modified the traditional Marxist theory of the state to argue that the state's role in supporting capital accumulation would increasingly come into conflict with its role in legitimating the capitalist system. From a very different intellectual perspective, public choice scholars James Buchanan and Richard Wagner (1977) in their *Democracy in Deficit: The Political Legacy of Lord Keynes*, argued that runaway government spending was the result of Keynesian ideas combined (fatally in their view) with democratic processes.

The administrative politics of spending cutbacks also figured large in the literature of that period. For example, Daniel Tarschys (1985) highlighted in a comparative analysis the way 'hard choices' tended to be decentralised within executive government systems through 'frames, envelopes, caps, ceilings and cheese-slicers'. Observing OECD experience, Tørben Beck Jørgensen (1987) analysed 'stages' of spending cutbacks as fiscal pressure continued over time (running from initial 'decrementalist' strategies, through 'managerial' remodelling to 'strategic' cutbacks). Peter de Leon (1983) analysed the politics of 'policy termination' from a US perspective (arguing that ideology was the commonest reason for policy termination, but that cost reductions and attempts to correct for programme inefficiencies also played a part). Andrew Dunsire and Christopher Hood (1989) analysed bureaucratic winners and losers in UK central government in the 1980s against a range of theories of the bureaucratic politics of cutbacks.

Many of those themes re-emerged in academic and public debate as pressures for fiscal squeeze developed in the aftermath of the financial crisis of the late 2000s (see, for example, 't Hart & Tindall 2009; Bermeo & Pontusson 2012; Bartels & Bermeo 2013; Streeck & Schäfer 2013). This book picks up on three issues that are more or less explicit in much of this literature, namely whether there is something special about the politics of fiscal squeeze, whether fiscal squeeze is a political blame magnet or a credit-claiming opportunity, and whether fiscal squeeze is highly consequential for political development or just one of those short-term 'sugar rushes' in politics whose effect quickly wears off.

Fiscal Squeeze as a Special Style of Politics

The first proposition is that there is something different, and perhaps especially challenging, about the politics of fiscal squeeze as compared to other kinds of politics. That, after all, is the assumption that led Aaron Wildavsky (1980) and others to conclude that only constitutionally entrenched limits on government spending could counter the 'normal' upward pressures on public spending in modern democracies (as reflected in an extensive but contested literature on the politics of long-term growth in public spending and taxation (Peacock & Wiseman 1961; Hood 1991)). Likewise, Alasdair Roberts (2012) sees US state politics in the aftermath of the financial crashes of the 1830s and 1840s as harsher, more brutal, less rewarding, even more violent than in more expansionary times:

> Politics was not an easy craft during the First Great Depression ... Attention was seized by the ... fundamental task of combating forces that were pulling political and social structures apart ... Statesmen were occupied more than usual with the politics of denial: that is, explaining to powerful and angry constituencies why they had to be denied benefits or liberties, or why they were required to shoulder new burdens (Roberts 2012: 209–10).

The assumption here, chiming with well-known ideas about asymmetric preferences over losses and gains developed by Daniel Kahneman and Amos Tversky (1979) and others, is that loss imposition, where there are few 'goodies' to spread around, is more difficult and painful than distributional politics in times of plenty. From this perspective, we might expect fiscal squeeze politics to be markedly different from the politics of more expansionary times, for example in producing crises (that is, moments when political pressure is increased, usually as a result of disaster or political scandal (Tama 2011: 8)), abnormal 'Nixon goes to China' moments, and other departures from politics-as-normal.

The idea that fiscal squeeze presents challenges for democratic politics rests on plausible enough assumptions that raising taxes and reining in spending necessarily creates losers and that the imposition of such losses on significant numbers of voters makes fiscal squeeze politics a 'difficult craft'. Loss imposition may not involve high political costs when (a) 'maleficiary' voters are diffused or losses hit those with a low propensity to vote, or (b) the stakes are low. But when high-stakes losses are imposed on mobilised groups, it is plausible to assume that such policies will strain established conventions and ties (for example to mainstream political parties), and perhaps even democratic 'politics' itself, as opposed to rule by technocrats or other groups ostensibly outside the 'political class'.

Against such claims, however, a contrasting 'null hypothesis' is that the politics of fiscal squeeze is no more, or less, different from the politics of fiscal expansion than (say) railway politics is from arts and media politics. One way of framing such a null hypothesis is to suggest that episodes of fiscal squeeze do not necessarily share major political characteristics, by analogy with the famous first sentence of Leo Tolstoy's *Anna Karenina*, which states that (in contrast to happy families) 'every unhappy family is unhappy in its own way'.[3] A slightly different basis for a null hypothesis—that there is nothing particularly special about fiscal squeeze—would be the proposition that all politics, about fiscal squeeze or anything else, involves clashes among contradictory worldviews (such as small-state individualism and those who favour various forms of collectivism), battles over who wins and who loses, and struggles by interest groups to protect their positions and by political actors to gain credit and avoid blame. It may be just another arena for observing the practice of 'heresthetic', that is, the pursuit of political strategies to open up new cleavages that change where majorities lie (McLean 2002), for example by dividing voters in low-paid employment from voters who are welfare claimants. From that perspective it might be argued that all politics is inherently about relativities, whether on the upside in good times or on the downside in bad times, and that the absolute level of resources is much less of the essence than the 'who gets what, when, how'[4] of whatever resources are available at any given point in time.

Fiscal Squeeze as a Political Blame Magnet or a Credit-Claiming Opportunity

Closely related to that first issue about what if anything is special about the politics of fiscal squeeze is the issue of how credit-claiming and blame-avoidance play out when governments are imposing losses rather than distributing gains. The post-2008 Eurozone crisis produced frequent repetition of an aphorism attributed to Jean-Claude Juncker, long-serving prime minister of Luxembourg and leader of the Euro group during a period of deep crisis in the currency union, namely that 'we [politicians in government] all know what to do; we just don't know how to get re-elected after we have done it'.[5] In the

---

[3] Of course, by the end of the book, several years and many pages later, Tolstoy reached a different conclusion.

[4] Harold Lasswell's (1936) famous definition of politics.

[5] *The Economist*, 15 March 2007, 'The Quest for Prosperity'. Later Juncker produced an addendum: 'For a long time, we didn't know what to do, and we still weren't re-elected' (*Der Spiegel*, interview with Jean-Claude Juncker, 11 March 2013). Prime minister of Luxembourg from 1995 to 2013, Juncker was chosen as President of the European Commission in June 2014.

same sort of spirit, it is said that in the 1980s the IMF's Fiscal Affairs Department had a 'rule of thumb' that the practical maximum of fiscal effort to be expected from governments was a 1 percentage point reduction of public expenditure relative to GDP each year.[6]

The implication of the much-quoted Juncker comment is that heightened distributional conflict (as tax burdens rise and/or government funding shrinks, raising the stakes in rival claims for resources) will tend to put the political 'blame game' into overdrive, with stronger pressure on incumbent office-holders of all kinds to shift or avoid the blame. The political science literature on blame avoidance stems in modern times from the work of Kent Weaver in the 1980s (Weaver 1986; 1988), which was later developed by other scholars, including Richard Ellis (1994), Raanan Sulitzeanu-Kenan (2007) and Christopher Hood (2002; 2011). From that perspective, if 'blame games' are accentuated during periods of fiscal squeeze, we could expect to see a number of developments in organisational arrangements, presentational strategy and policy design. Central or federal governments might delegate more fiscal responsibilities to lower levels of government, passing the political pain down the line or assigning responsibility for making painful choices to technocrats rather than elected politicians.[7] Political spin machines might be more active in orchestrating diversionary tactics or battening down the hatches when efforts to blame predecessors in office or inexorable outside forces reach their limits. Policymakers might develop more defensive approaches to policy, for example by making spending cuts or tax hikes that affect key voters harder to identify (such as by lengthening qualifying periods for benefits or letting third parties impose 'administration charges' that do not officially count as taxes).

But while those who follow the line of thought summed up by the Juncker aphorism see politicians who preside over fiscal squeezes in government as facing almost impossible blame-avoidance pressures, another line of analysis has tended to focus on the credit-claiming opportunities that successful handling of fiscal squeeze may offer to an incumbent government. In particular, Alberto Alesina and his colleagues have argued in numerous papers that successful pursuit of fiscal consolidation and adjustment (rather than courting voters with higher expenditure and lower taxes) can indeed allow incumbent parties to secure re-election, rather than face punishment at the polls by disappointed voters (Alesina *et al.* 2010). But Larry Bartels' (2013) comparative study of election results in periods of economic crisis in the 1930s and more

---

[6] Lord (Nick) Stern, who was a Visiting Fellow in the IMF's Fiscal Affairs Department in the 1980s, recalled this unwritten working rule in his opening remarks to the 2013 British Academy Conference at which the papers that form this book were first presented.

[7] This would align with depoliticisation initiatives even in good times, such as in central banking and economic regulation, designed to distance elected politicians from key decisions (Flinders 2005).

recent times concluded that outgoing governments tended systematically to lose elections in those circumstances.

Can these two approaches be reconciled? What if anything explains why some democratic governments (such as that of Canada in the 1990s) are able to implement fiscal squeezes and comfortably secure re-election, while in other cases (such as that of Ireland in the 1980s) governments pursuing such policies experience electoral defeats? Is it just some 'political leadership' x-factor, or are there other ways of explaining why fiscal squeeze sometimes seems to be a 'curse' for incumbent politicians but not at other times? There are several possible ways of explaining that. One possibility is that the politics of inertia offers more blame-avoiding opportunities than the politics of initiative (as argued by Rose & Karran 1987 and Rose 1990). If so we might expect governing parties that 'inherit' fiscal squeeze policies they can blame on their predecessors to experience a lesser degree of punishment by voters than those who both plan and carry through fiscal squeezes. A second possibility is that blame directed at governments may depend on constitutional and institutional arrangements, with division-of-powers and multiple-veto-point structures making it harder for voters to allocate blame to governments than in simpler structures (Anderson 1995).

More generally, blame outcomes might possibly vary according to the depth and provenance of fiscal squeezes. For example, it seems plausible to argue that there is more scope for blame to be attributed to outside forces— such as international bodies, financial markets, foreign governments—for those fiscal squeezes that occur during times of fiscal crisis (as in the case where currencies suddenly collapse or international credit is obtainable only at punitive rates or not at all) and can be represented as resulting from economic *force majeure* (or 'exogenous' forces in the jargon of social science). More problematic for blame avoidance may be those kinds of fiscal squeeze that occur during times of fiscal *stress* but not fiscal *crisis* and/or that seem to come from (endogenous) forces inside the political system, for example when tax revolts drive governments into cutting public spending. From a blame-avoidance perspective we might therefore expect apparently 'exogenous' pressures for fiscal squeeze to be played up or exaggerated by those domestic political players who favour spending cuts (or possibly tax rises) as a way to tackle long-standing political and institutional problems they see as stemming from an over-extended public sector.

A further aspect that may help to shape the politics of blame is the depth of fiscal squeezes. At the end of the previous section, discussing proxy measures for the political effort put into fiscal squeeze, we distinguished between 'hard' and 'soft' squeezes in expenditure and revenue in terms of whether these items changed both relative to GDP and in constant-price terms, or only in relation to one of these criteria. Of course, as already mentioned, politics is about relativities as well as absolute levels of spending. But if all else is equal we might expect squeezes that were 'hard' in those terms to be a greater magnet for blame.

Table 1.3 puts those two sets of distinctions together—that is, whether fiscal squeeze is triggered mostly by exogenous or endogenous pressures and whether, based on realised outcomes, it is 'hard' or 'soft'. As we go from exogenous to endogenous and from soft to hard types of fiscal squeeze, we might expect the blame risk faced by incumbent parties pursuing fiscal squeeze policies to increase. So the cases in the bottom right-hand cell (4) of Table 1.3— namely fiscal squeezes that are hard and endogenous—are particularly interesting for political analysis. How, if at all, can incumbents in government pursuing endogenous hard-squeeze fiscal policies shift or share the blame for the losses they impose on voters?

Stretching the concept of credit and blame beyond the issue of the electoral fortunes and political reputations of the political actors involved in fiscal squeeze are intriguing questions about who wins and loses the longer-term 'narrative' of fiscal squeeze events: for example, which policies come to be portrayed as successful 'best-practice' cases in the world of international econocrats, and which are written off as failures (Mauro 2011). This aspect of credit and blame reflects the interplay between expertise and politics, in terms of which studies or policy examples command widespread attention and which are ignored. Some countries' policies are presented as 'poster children', model cases to be emulated elsewhere, while others are ignored, and indeed, as we will see later, what can be dubbed a 'poster child' at one point in time can turn into a 'problem child' at another. The same goes for the credit and blame attached to experts and academics. For example, when the 2008 global financial crisis started to produce fiscal crises, political decision-makers looking for reputable evidence to support fiscal squeeze policies (Summers 2013) seized upon and lauded the (later much criticised) work of Reinhart & Rogoff (2010)[8] and also Alesina & Ardagna's (1998; 2009) theory of 'expansionary fiscal contraction'. A few years later those opposed to fiscal squeeze seized upon IMF research (Blanchard & Leigh 2012) that found that its previous estimates of fiscal multipliers had been too low (Portes 2012). So the 'credit and blame' game over fiscal squeeze goes well beyond the immediate party political battles. Narrative construction (Kahneman & Tversky 1984; Entman 1993; Riessman 1993) is central to the political framing of fiscal squeeze,

---

[8] In an OECD working paper, Égert (2012) was unable to reproduce the 90 per cent threshold on the debt/GDP ratio (above which growth is said to be damaged), which had attracted much political and official attention as confirming the urgent necessity of fiscal squeeze, notwithstanding the recession. Data errors were later argued to have compromised the Reinhart & Rogoff results (Herndon *et al.* 2013).

Table 1.3. Four types of fiscal squeeze politics.

Realised outcome	Type of trigger	
	Exogenous (squeeze triggered by outside forces)	Endogenous (squeeze triggered by internal developments)
Soft	**1**	**2**
	Scope for external blame: high Type of loss imposition: relative	Scope for external blame: low Type of loss imposition: relative
Hard	**3**	**4**
	Scope for external blame: high Type of loss imposition: absolute	Scope for external blame: low Type of loss imposition: absolute

with the technical debates sometimes proxy wars between competing visions about the scale and scope of the state.

Fiscal Squeeze as a Critical Historical Juncture or a Political Sugar Rush

Related again to the issue of how the politics of credit and blame plays out during fiscal squeeze is a question about the longer-term political and social consequences of such squeezes. The rhetoric of political debate during battles over spending cuts or tax increases tends to be full of fervent claims by proponents and opponents about the likely effects of such policies (whether beneficial, deleterious, or regrettable but necessary). Proponents present them as vital medicine for preventing collapse and improving social conditions in the medium or long term, while opponents present them as likely to unwind fundamental social compacts and unleash deep and irreversible social damage. Both sets of arguments tend to play up the 'never-the-same-again' consequentiality of such policies, and critics of fiscal squeeze naturally tend to highlight those groups and institutions who can be portrayed as winners and losers (for instance, federal or national governments versus local or state governments, technocrats versus elected politicians, private sector employees versus public servants, the employed relative to the unemployed) and to suggest that those losses will not be reversible.

Nor are such disputes confined to the politicians of the day. Some scholars and historians have made similar claims about episodes of fiscal squeeze as representing what historical institutionalists term 'critical junctures': landmark events or decisive forks in the road that are deeply consequential for policies and institutions long into the future (Cappoccia & Kelemen 2007). For example, Alasdair Roberts (2012), in his account of the United States' financial crisis and later fiscal squeeze in the first half of the 19th century, sees major long-term institutional developments, such as the strengthening of the executive relative to the legislature and the development of modern bureaucratic policing, as flowing from that episode. Robert Skidelsky (1967: 386–7) attributes the way the UK's 1929–31 Labour government handled the challenges of fiscal squeeze as 'determining' the politics of the subsequent decade, in particular by helping 'to create and confirm a mood of national self-doubt, of pessimism regarding the future, in which appeasement could flourish'. The implication is that some years later it will be easy to trace fundamental longer-term changes in politics and society to significant episodes of fiscal squeeze.

The alternative null hypothesis to that vision of fiscal squeeze as highly consequential in the long term is that such episodes, albeit much quarrelled over in the short term, tend to be 'blips' or political 'sugar rushes', quickly reversed in a longer-term pattern of government growth in spending and taxing. The implication is that after those episodes, spending starts to rise as soon as immediate pressure for restraint fades, normal party political competition resumes under the usual rules of the game, and path dependency in the main lines of policy development hardly changes in the long term.

Such questions of consequentiality are central to the politics of fiscal squeeze, but are typically easier to ask than to answer. That is partly because political effort will typically go into muddying the distributional effects of fiscal squeeze policies. But it is also because cause and effect are always difficult to establish definitively in history and social science. Claims about the long-term effects of such squeezes on the electoral fortunes of political parties associated with them, on broader public attitudes to egalitarianism, 'big government' or redistributive state spending and even constitutional or major institutional changes, are easier to make than to prove at a standard that would satisfy a criminal court. Counterfactuals (like Robert Fogel's (1964) famous attempt to imagine how 19th-century America might have developed without railways) can always be contested and it is easy to fall into the *post hoc, ergo propter hoc* fallacy (that is, that if B follows A, A must have caused B). That is part of the reason why consequentiality is so debatable.

The standard scientific way of dealing with this classic problem is by methods of sensitivity analysis and 'consilience' (a term which comes from Whewell (1840) and means putting together different strands of evidence and seeing if they point in the same direction). And when we apply that sort of approach, as we shall see later, we find that in some cases fiscal squeezes do not seem to constitute critical junctures; in other cases we can more confidently attribute significant political and social consequences to them; and in others again the links are debatable.

That in turn raises the question: if fiscal squeeze sometimes seems to be consequential and sometimes not, what accounts for that? Could it be that (like public service reform, argued by scholars such as Chapman & Greenaway (1980)) fiscal squeeze only produces long-term consequences if the 'austerity' agenda somehow connects with other pressures for major changes in political direction? After all, advocates of deep reductions in public spending have always existed, independent of whether there is a current fiscal problem. For example, Tanzi & Schuknecht (2000) judged desirable a return to the public expenditure levels of *circa* 1960 (when industrialised countries averaged below 30 per cent of GDP); they also commended the *circa* 20 per cent ratio of newly industrialised countries, doubting the value of recent redistributive activity beyond 'core activities'. But financial crises can sometimes give renewed traction to such views. The same can go for other policy changes, for example when the UK's fiscal squeeze under a Labour government in the late 1970s paved the way for subsequent decisive changes in political direction under the Conservative government led by Margaret Thatcher,[9] with implications not only for the UK but also for other countries to which privatisation, deregulation and marketisation were exported.

What Does it Mean to Put Fiscal Squeeze into *Perspective*?

This book is primarily an exercise in comparative public policy rather than one of the many 'how to do it' guides to fiscal management that have emerged since the late 2000s, and its aim is to put fiscal squeeze into perspective. Putting the politics of fiscal squeeze into perspective means at least three things. First, we need to understand episodes of squeeze against the background of what else was happening within the society concerned (for example, whether there was an accompanying financial crisis) and what was happening in the wider world. Second, we need to look at episodes of fiscal squeeze with the benefit of hindsight, looking at what happened afterwards to see whether the squeezes had the effects claimed of them. And third, we need to compare fiscal squeezes with one another to see what, if any, common patterns they display. We do that partly by comparing aggregate data for the nine country episodes in Chapter 2 on as consistent a basis as possible, given the range of the cases in space and time. But we also need to look at the more qualitative political story behind those numbers, to explore how the politics worked and how blame was attributed, deflected or avoided.

The purpose of careful contextualisation is to try to pin down the specific contingencies that shape the process and effects of fiscal squeeze—an obvious point but one often neglected by policy advocates looking for models whose success can be replicated elsewhere. For example, those policy advocates who at the outset of the current era of fiscal squeeze after 2008 saw the 1980s and 1990s policies of Canada, Sweden and Ireland as models to follow ignored features of those experiences that were distinctive to each country (such as the

---

[9] Gamble (1988) characterised the shift as towards the free market and the strong state, with the latter making the former possible.

lack of mainstream opposition in Canada) or to the era in which they occurred (such as a benign international environment in the mid-1990s), and that is an error that careful contextualisation can help us to limit if not avoid. History tends to be written by winners and spinners, so it is important to look critically at cases that have become 'poster children' as against those not so sanctified or considered as 'basket cases', to see how far claims of transferable 'best practice' can be justified (OECD 2011).

Our Nine Cases

This book aims to combine a 'spreadsheet' approach to comparing fiscal squeeze with qualitative accounts of a set of country episodes intended to explore the politics behind the reported numbers and to explore what if any medium- or long-term consequences might plausibly be attributed to those various squeezes.

The conventional econometric way of selecting cases for comparative studies of fiscal consolidation is to identify episodes using *ex post* data relating to reported financial aggregates and GDP outcomes, using stipulated statistical cut-off points. But, as we have already pointed out (and the same point has been made by numerous critics of the standard econometric outcome-based approach, for example by Dellepiane-Avellaneda 2010), fiscal squeeze— defined as pronounced political effort on the part of governments to improve their public finances—is harder to put into numbers, since political effort is not always translated into outcomes reflected in economic data. Fiscal squeeze may or may not lead to fiscal consolidation, and fiscal consolidation can occur with or without fiscal squeeze.

We chose our cases here on a quite different basis. We restricted them to a small enough number (nine) to be explored qualitatively within a book-length study. We chose cases that involved different state types and that took place sufficiently far back in time to allow us to explore what happened afterwards and assess the consequences of fiscal squeeze at least ten years after the event. Instead of basing our cases on deficit-reduction-based analysis, we chose cases that involved *both* substantial cuts in expenditure or revenue increases (as measured by outcome data) *and* fiscal squeeze in the sense of political effort (as judged by country specialists). All of those cases involve fiscal adjustments that can justifiably be described as large and unusual in that country's experience, involving dramatic packages designed to restore fiscal health. Where they differed was in the relative proportions of spending reductions and tax increases that went into the fiscal squeeze, the mixes of monetary policy and changes in market regulation that accompanied them, and in the international economic context in which they occurred: for example, whether currency devaluation was possible and whether key trading partners were growing strongly or suffering from comparable difficulties.

Finally, within those limits we chose cases that are puzzling or contested in some way. By 'puzzling or contested', we mean cases that (i) appear to go contrary to stereotype or involve a major change of path for governments and institutions; (ii) have acquired a 'poster child' or role-model status in the recent what-to-do policy literature that merits a more critical assessment; and/or (iii) would not necessarily be picked up by the standard methodology of the *ex post* approach. Table 1.4 summarises how the cases we discuss here can be rated on those three criteria.

Thus Alasdair Roberts in this volume analyses the fiscal squeeze following from state government defaults in the United States in the early 19th century, a case hitherto seldom discussed in the fiscal consolidation literature, but which left a profound constitutional and institutional legacy and has strong relevance to many of the issues now being discussed concerning the fiscal

Table 1.4. Nine cases of fiscal squeeze that are puzzling or problematic.

Case	Decades of hindsight	Counters stereotype or seems to involve change in path?	International 'poster child' meriting closer or more critical assessment?	Problematic for conventional *ex post* selection approach?
United States 1840s	18	Perhaps[a]	No	Yes[b]
United Kingdom 1920s	9	Perhaps[c]	No	Yes[b d]
Netherlands 1980s	2.5	Yes[e]	No	Yes[f]
Ireland 1980s	2.5	No	Yes	No
New Zealand 1990s	2	No	Yes	No
Canada 1990s	1.5	No	Yes	No
Sweden 1990s	1.5	Yes[g]	Yes	No
Germany 1990s–2000s	1	Yes[h]	Yes	No
Argentina 1990s–2000s	1	Perhaps	No	Perhaps[i j]

[a] Because the case has been little discussed and goes against contemporary assumptions about US hegemony.

[b] Because the case dates from before the time of modern national accounts.

[c] Because deep spending cuts were made to a budget already in balance.

[d] Because the case is not picked up by *ex post* deficit-reduction analysis.

[e] Because the country changed from a 'Scandinavian' to a more conventional Northern European fiscal profile over the 1980s.

[f] Because the squeeze in local government spending does not show up in conventional national-level numbers.

[g] Because the squeeze involved significant cutbacks in welfare entitlements in an archetypical welfare state.

[h] Because a major squeeze took place in a political system often characterised as slow-moving, with multiple veto points and consequent 'joint decision trap' features.

[i] Because currency collapse and default produces only one year of unambiguous spending cutbacks.

[j] Because the political effort prior to 2003 is not reflected in fiscal outcomes.

politics of the Eurozone. Christopher Hood and Rozana Himaz analyse the 1922 'Geddes Axe' in the UK—a case nowadays often considered more as a 'problem child' than a 'poster child', in which the deepest cuts in UK civil spending in the last ninety years were made from a budget already in balance and in the middle of a deep recession. Walter Kickert explores cuts in spending by Dutch local authorities (which provide an important part of the Dutch public services) in the 1980s—a case which barely registers as a 'fiscal consolidation' since the local cuts are masked within overall national figures, and which reflects a process of fiscal repositioning over the 1980s that took the country from public expenditure/GDP ratios quite close to Scandinavian levels to levels more in line with non-Scandinavian Northern Europe. Niamh Hardiman analyses the severe fiscal squeeze in Ireland in the late 1980s (which made it a 'poster child' of expenditure-led fiscal adjustment and immediately preceded Ireland's much-vaunted 'Celtic Tiger' period) and compares it to the ferocious fiscal squeeze applied in Ireland, under external supervision, two decades later, after it became an early casualty of the Eurozone crisis of the late 2000s.

Of the five more recent cases, those of New Zealand, Canada and Sweden in the 1990s (analysed here respectively by Robert Gregory and Chris Eichbaum, Donald Savoie, and Anders Lindbom) have been extensively canvassed as role models, both by international organisations and by those centrally involved in these country episodes, and so merit a careful reassessment more than a decade after the event. These cases bring out the very different political structures and situations in which fiscal squeezes can take place—for example, virtually no mainstream opposition in the Canadian case as against a precarious coalition in Sweden; a federal structure with provinces to be squeezed through unfunded mandates in Canada as against a highly centralised unitary system in New Zealand. They also bring out the often undiscussed fact that all of these 'poster child' squeezes took place in the context of a relatively benign international economic environment. The German fiscal squeeze some years after unification (analysed by Martin Lodge and Kai Wegrich) is also a 'poster child' case, as a much-cited example of successful adjustment at the core of the Eurozone. It is also politically significant because it goes against the conventional characterisation of the German political system that might be expected to militate against decisive and 'hard' fiscal squeeze. The most recent case in this collection, that of Argentina as it went through the throes of default and devaluation, is analysed here by Sebastián Dellepiane-Avellaneda. Again, this case involved massive political effort to correct the public finances (after deep currency crisis followed by default and the drying up of foreign credit) but it barely shows up as 'fiscal consolidation' on conventional measures because GDP was falling by more than public spending.

Of course this analytic approach to case selection does not constitute a representative sample in the conventional analytic sense, does not match fiscal squeeze episodes with non-episodes in the style of randomised controlled trials (often seen as the 'gold standard' for policy analysis and social science more generally (Cartwright & Hardie 2012)), and falls a long way short of the massive datasets used by scholars in some other comparative studies. But it allows us to look at data much more critically than such studies can normally do, and shows up the limitations of the available documentary data in what it can tell us about 'fiscal squeeze' rather than taking the conventional point of departure which assumes that officially reported numbers of financial aggregates are necessarily valid and reliable bases for elaborate statistical analysis. And while this approach necessarily allows only limited positive generalisations, it does provide us with a basis for disconfirmation of commonly asserted propositions, on the 'black swan' principle that it only takes one negative case to undermine generalising claims.

The Plan of the Book

Comparisons across space and time can never be perfect, as already noted. But even with all the inevitable limitations discussed in the previous section, a comparison of the politics of fiscal squeeze across nine cases of democratic government in different times and places can improve our understanding of the three analytic questions that we posed earlier, namely whether there is something fundamental that distinguishes fiscal squeeze from other types of politics, how episodes of fiscal squeeze affect credit and blame, and what, if any, medium- or long-term consequences for politics and the society more generally these episodes leave behind.

To help throw light on those analytic questions, each of the country chapters and the comparative data analysis in Chapter 2 explore what seems to have prompted fiscal squeeze in each particular case, how the process of fiscal squeeze worked and what, if any, longer-term political and other social consequences can be traced in retrospect to the squeeze episode. The first issue, of what prompts fiscal squeeze, can help us to assess whether such episodes all seem to be prompted by the same standard set of economic or financial circumstances—such as debt and/or deficit levels—that make fiscal squeeze 'inevitable', and how far politics plays into the decision to squeeze. The second issue, of how the process of fiscal squeeze works, can help throw light on whether and how far there is something distinctive about the politics of fiscal squeeze, for example whether and how governments crafted their policies in the light of constitutional or public-order challenges, and whether fiscal squeeze produced political crisis or was handled by some version of

politics-as-normal. The third question, of what the political and social consequences of fiscal squeeze were in the short, medium and long term, can help
to throw light both on the politics of credit and blame and on the 'consequentiality' questions discussed earlier. Were spending cuts and tax increases
reversed and, if so, over what time period? How did the process affect intergovernmental relations, and with what consequences? Who were the long-
term winners and losers from the process and what were the political and
electoral effects in terms of political blame and credit accruing to political
parties and their leaders? Is it possible to identify broader social consequences
of fiscal squeeze, such as changes in the power of elites, threats to civil peace
or even threats to democratic government?

We return to these questions in the final chapter, where we also discuss
what if anything today's policymakers can learn from a contextual analysis of
yesterday's fiscal squeezes.

References

Alesina, A. & Ardagna, S. (1998), 'Tales of Fiscal Adjustment: Why They Can be
	Expansionary', *Economic Policy*, 13(27): 488–545.
Alesina, A. & Ardagna, S. (2009), *Large Changes in Fiscal Policy: Taxes Versus
	Spending*, Working Paper 15438 (Cambridge MA, National Bureau of Economic
	Research) (revised 5 December 2011).
Alesina, A., Carloni, D. & Lecce, G. (2010), 'The Electoral Consequences of Large
	Fiscal Adjustments' (Boston, Harvard University), later republished in A. Alesina
	& F. Giavazzi (eds), *Fiscal Policy after the Financial Crisis* (Chicago, University of
	Chicago Press for the National Bureau of Economic Research, 2013), 531–70.
Anderson, C. (1995), *Blaming the Government: Citizens and the Economy in Five
	European Democracies* (London, M.E. Sharpe).
Bartels, L. (2013), 'Ideology and Retrospection in Electoral Responses to the Great
	Recession', in Bartels & Bermeo (2013), 185–223.
Bartels, L. & Bermeo, N. (eds) (2013), *Mass Politics in Tough Times: Opinions, Votes,
	and Protest in the Great Recession* (Oxford, Oxford University Press).
Bermeo, N. & Pontusson, J. (eds) (2012), *Coping with Crisis: Government Reactions to
	the Great Recession* (New York, Russell Sage Foundation).
Birdal, M. (2010), *The Political Economy of Ottoman Public Debt: Insolvency and
	European Financial Control in the Late Nineteenth Century* (London, I.B. Taurus).
Blanchard, O. & Leigh, D. (2012), 'Box 1.1: Are we Underestimating Short-Term
	Fiscal Multipliers?', in IMF, *World Economic Outlook, October 2012: Coping with
	High Debt and Sluggish Growth* (Washington DC, International Monetary Fund),
	41–3.
Blyth, M. (2013), *Austerity: The History of a Dangerous Idea* (New York, Oxford
	University Press).
Buchanan, J. & Wagner, R. (1977), *Democracy in Deficit: The Political Legacy of Lord
	Keynes* (New York, Academic Press).

Burns, R. ([1786] 2009), *The Best Laid Schemes: Selected Poetry and Prose of Robert Burns*, ed. R. Crawford & C. MacLachlan (Princeton, Princeton University Press).

Cappoccia, G. & Kelemen, R.D. (2007), 'The Study of Critical Junctures: Time, Narrative and Counterfactuals in Historical Institutionalism', *World Politics*, 59: 341–69.

Cartwright, N. & Hardie, J. (2012), *Evidence-Based Policy: A Practical Guide to Doing it Better* (Oxford, Oxford University Press).

Chapman, R. & Greenaway, R. (1980), *The Dynamics of Administrative Reform* (London, Croom Helm).

Cukierman, A. & Tommasi, M. (1998), 'Why Does it Take a Nixon to Go to China?', *American Economic Review*, 88(1): 180–97.

de Leon, P. (1983), 'Policy Evaluation and Program Termination', *Review of Policy Research*, 2(4): 631–47.

Dellepiane-Avellaneda, S. (2010), 'Review Article: The Politics of Fiscal Policy in Europe', *European Political Science*, 9(4): 454–63.

Dunsire, A. & Hood, C. (1989), *Cutback Management in Public Bureaucracies: Popular Theories and Observed Outcomes in Whitehall* (Cambridge, Cambridge University Press).

Égert, B. (2012), *Public Debt, Economic Growth and Non-Linear Effects: Myth or Reality?*, OECD Economics Department Working Papers, No. 993 (Paris, OECD).

Ellis, R. (1994), *Presidential Lightning Rods: The Politics of Blame Avoidance* (Kansas, Kansas University Press).

Entman, R.M. (1993), 'Framing: Toward Clarification of a Fractured Paradigm', *Journal of Communication*, 43(4): 51–8.

Flinders, M. (2005), 'Depoliticisation: The Domestic Antecedents of New Labour's Statecraft', *British Journal of Politics and International Relations*, 7(4): 526–44.

Fogel, R. (1964), *Railroads and American Economic Growth: Essays in Econometric History* (Baltimore, Johns Hopkins University Press).

Gamble, A. (1988), *The Free Economy and the Strong State: The Politics of Thatcherism* (Basingstoke, Macmillan).

Greenspan, A.N., Mankiw, G. & Stein, J. (2010), 'The Crisis' [with Comments and Discussion], *Brookings Papers on Economic Activity*, Issue 1 (Spring): 201–61.

Herndon, T., Ash, M. & Pollin, R. (2013), *Does High Public Debt Consistently Stifle Economic Growth? A Critique of Reinhart and Rogoff*, Working Paper No. 322 (Amherst MA, Political Economy Research Institute, University of Massachusetts).

Hood, C. (1991), 'Stabilization and Cutbacks: A Catastrophe for Government Growth Theory?', *Journal of Theoretical Politics*, 3(1): 37–63.

Hood, C. (2002), 'The Risk Game and the Blame Game', *Government and Opposition*, 37(1): 15–37.

Hood, C. (2011), *The Blame Game: Spin, Bureaucracy, and Self-Preservation in Government* (Princeton, Princeton University Press).

Humphrey, B. (2000), 'The Post-NAFTA Mexican Peso Crisis: Bailout or Aid? Isolationism or Globalization?', *Hinckley Journal of Politics*, 2 (Spring): 33–40.

Jørgensen, T. Beck (1987), *Models of Retrenchment Behavior*, Working Paper No. 24 (Brussels, International Institute of Administrative Sciences).

Kahneman, D. & Tversky, A. (1979), 'Prospect Theory: An Analysis of Decisions under Risk', *Econometrica*, 47: 263–91.

Kahneman, D. & Tversky, A. (1984), 'Choices, Frames and Values', *American Psychologist*, 39(4): 341–50.

Lasswell, H. (1936), *Politics: Who Gets What, When, How* (New York, McGraw Hill).

Mauro, P. (2011), *Chipping Away at Public Debt: Sources of Failure and Keys to Success in Fiscal Adjustment* (Hoboken NJ, Wiley).

McLean, I. (2002), 'William H. Riker and the Invention of Heresthetic(s)', *British Journal of Political Science*, 32(3): 535–58.

O'Connor, J. (1973), *The Fiscal Crisis of the State* (New York, St. Martin's Press).

OECD (2011), *Restoring Public Finances*, OECD Working Party of Senior Budget Officials, Public Governance and Territorial Development Directorate (Paris, OECD).

Peacock, A.T. & Wiseman, J. (1961), *The Growth of Public Expenditure in the United Kingdom* (Princeton, Princeton University Press for the National Bureau of Economic Research).

Portes, J. (2012), 'More on Multipliers: Why Does It Matter?', NIESR blog on 12 October, http://niesr.ac.uk/blog/more-multipliers-why-does-it-matter#. UbJPAeVwYdU (accessed 12 December 2013).

Reinhart, C.M. & Rogoff, K.S. (2010), 'Growth in a Time of Debt', *American Economic Review*, 100(2): 573–8.

Reinhart, C.M. & Rogoff, K.S. (2011), 'From Financial Crash to Debt Crisis', *American Economic Review*, 101(5): 1676–1706.

Riessman, C.K. (1993), *Narrative Analysis* (Thousand Oaks CA, Sage).

Roberts, A. (2012), *America's First Great Depression: Economic Crisis and Political Disorder after the Panic of 1837* (Ithaca NY, Cornell University Press).

Rose, R. (1990), 'Inheritance before Choice in Public Policy', *Journal of Theoretical Politics*, 2(3): 263–91.

Rose, R. & Karran, T. (1987), *Taxation by Political Inertia* (London, Allen and Unwin).

Rose, R. & Peters, B.G. (1978), *Can Government Go Bankrupt?* (New York, Basic Books).

Skidelsky, R. (1967), *Politicians and the Slump: The Labour Government of 1929–31* (London, Macmillan).

Streeck, W. & Schäfer, A. (eds) (2013), *Politics in the Age of Austerity* (London, Polity).

Sulitzeanu-Kenan, R. (2007), 'Scything the Grass: Agenda-Setting Consequences of Appointing Public Inquiries in the UK. A Longitudinal Analysis', *Policy and Politics*, 35(4): 629–50.

Summers, L. (2013), 'The Buck Does Not Stop with Reinhart and Rogoff: Political Leaders Pushing Austerity Made Their Choice, Then Cast About for Intellectual Buttresses', *Financial Times*, 6 May.

Swagel, P. (2009), 'The Financial Crisis: An Inside View', *Brookings Papers on Economic Activity*, Issue 1 (Spring): 1–78.

Tama, J. (2011), *Terrorism and National Security Reform: How Commissions Can Drive Change During Crises* (Cambridge, Cambridge University Press).

Tanzi, V. & Schuknecht, L. (2000), *Public Spending in the 20th Century: A Global Perspective* (Cambridge, Cambridge University Press).

Tarschys, D. (1985), 'Curbing Public Expenditure: Current Trends', *Journal of Public Policy*, 5(1): 23–67.

't Hart, P. & Tindall, K. (eds) (2009), *Framing the Global Economic Downturn: Crisis Rhetoric and the Politics of Recessions* (Canberra, ANU Press).

Weaver, R.K. (1986), 'The Politics of Blame Avoidance', *Journal of Public Policy*, 6(4): 371–98.

Weaver, R.K. (1988), *Automatic Government: The Politics of Indexation* (Washington DC, Brookings).

Whewell, W. (1840), *The Philosophy of the Inductive Sciences: Founded upon their History* (London, J.W. Parker and Cambridge, J. & J.J. Deighton; 2nd edn, reprinted 2007, Whitefish MT, Kessinger Publishing).

Wildavsky, A. (1980), *How to Limit Government Spending* (Berkeley, University of California Press).

2

Comparing Fiscal Squeezes Across Nine Country Cases

ROZANA HIMAZ AND CHRISTOPHER HOOD

THIS CHAPTER BRINGS TOGETHER SOME INDICATIVE NUMBERS for the nine cases of fiscal squeeze considered in this book, on the basis of available published documentary data. Its aim is to use such numbers to identify episodes of 'hard' and 'soft' fiscal squeeze and explore what light those numbers can shed on the questions raised in Chapter 1 about what leads up to, accompanies and follows from fiscal squeezes.

As explained in Chapter 1, any analysis based on standard published financial data is necessarily limited in what it can say about the politics of fiscal squeeze, for at least four reasons. First, as the previous chapter noted, since we conceive 'fiscal squeeze' as the political effort that goes into cutting spending or raising taxes, it cannot be directly measured by conventional economic and financial indicators. Such indicators can only provide proxies for such effort, which is assessed more directly in the qualitative chapters. Second, the standard data available report *realised* outcomes, that is, when spending actually fell or revenue rose, rather than plans or budgets, though the latter are also obviously important for the politics of fiscal squeeze, as noted in the previous chapter. Third, the standard figures available in international databases relate to the national level, whereas in two of our cases the analysis of the qualitative chapters focuses on what happened at state or local government level. Even for the national level, IMF and OECD data can yield different results in some cases, due to differences in definitions, conventions and sources, and two of our cases go back before the days of modern national accounting, so we have to go on retrospective approximations derived by economic historians. Fourth, exactly what constitutes an 'episode' of fiscal squeeze—when it starts or ends, or both—can be contestable, as noted in the previous chapter and several of the chapters that follow.

Without losing sight of those unavoidable limitations, this chapter explores three main things. First, we characterise and compare the nine 'squeezes', in terms of how severe were real changes in spending or revenue and changes in those items relative to GDP, how long the squeezes lasted, and

Proceedings of the British Academy, **197**, 27–51. © The British Academy 2014.

whether they were accompanied by major reforms. Second, to establish similarity or difference in initial conditions, we compare what was happening in each country and in the international environment in the year before the squeeze began, in terms of a set of economic and political/governmental indicators. Third, to explore the effect of fiscal squeezes, we compare what happened in each of those episodes in the public finances, in the economy more widely and in political outcomes.

Identifying and Comparing Fiscal Squeezes

In Chapter 1 we explained that we identify fiscal squeezes in this book in two ways. One, to be applied in the nine chapters that follow, takes the form of qualitative judgements based on study of the politics of the time. The other, to be developed in this chapter, takes reported aggregates of spending and revenue as rough proxies of political effort. For this second approach, as also explained in Chapter 1, we distinguish between 'soft' and 'hard' squeezes as indicating different levels of 'squeezedness', making four basic types as follows:

- 'soft' expenditure squeezes, when either (a) government spending falls relative to GDP, but such expenditure does not fall in constant prices or (b) expenditure falls in constant prices but not relative to GDP;
- 'hard' expenditure squeezes, when government spending falls both relative to GDP and in constant prices;
- 'soft' revenue squeezes, when either (a) tax revenues rise relative to GDP but such revenues do not rise in constant prices or (b) tax revenues rise in constant prices but not relative to GDP;
- 'hard' revenue squeezes, when tax revenues rise both relative to GDP and in constant prices.

From these four basic types of squeeze (on financial outcome data) there are at least 16 possible combinations, to which we will return in Chapter 12. Squeezes can apply to revenue or expenditure, they can be soft or hard as defined above, they can be single or double (depending on whether only one fiscal element is squeezed or both are), and they can be hybrid if a hard squeeze on one dimension (revenue or expenditure) is accompanied by a soft squeeze on the other.

However, going from these logical possibilities to categorising and comparing empirical cases means we unavoidably have to make judgements on at least three issues, namely (i) what thresholds or cut-offs to set for identifying squeeze; (ii) how or whether to allow for cyclical economic variations; and (iii) what starting point to take for the analysis.

Thresholds

Identifying four basic types of squeeze provides an analytic starting point but does not of itself establish exactly the point at which squeeze begins. For example, if government spending in a given country rises by 0.001 percentage points of GDP in time period A and falls by 0.001 percentage points in time period B, does that mean period B should be counted as a soft expenditure squeeze according to the definitions given earlier? In that extreme example, clearly not: any reported difference between periods A and B is probably within the range of measurement error and even if not, such a tiny alteration would suggest no real difference between the two time periods. That sort of threshold issue arises in any categorisation exercise, whether we are sorting eggs into different sizes or fiscal episodes, and there is no hard and fast answer as to where the threshold or cut-off point should be set.

For the ratio measures (that is, changes in expenditure and revenue relative to GDP), we took as our starting point the observation, noted in the previous chapter, that the Fiscal Division of the IMF at one time commonly thought that a reduction of spending as a percentage of GDP by 1 percentage point a year represented the upper bound of what was normally feasible and practicable. In line with that, if IMF or equivalent expenditure and GDP data showed that expenditure as a percentage of GDP fell compared to the previous year, and that such a fall was sustained over at least two years with an average annual fall of 1 percentage point or more, we counted that as a squeeze episode, with the start of the episode defined as occurring in the first year of the fall and the end of the episode as the year just before that falling trend was reversed.[1] In addition to that, we took a single year as a squeeze episode only if expenditure fell relative to GDP by substantially more than that (i.e. at least 2 percentage points). We applied the same threshold to revenue, but in reverse, with a rise in revenue of at least 1 percentage point relative to GDP over a period of at least two years taken as marking the threshold of squeeze.

Such a threshold for defining squeeze 'episodes' provides a convenient starting point and broadly follows the conventional literature on fiscal consolidation. But threshold or cut-off issues also arise for our levels measure of

---

[1] Of course, complications arise where the ratio followed a 'down-up-down pattern', with an 'in between year' where expenditure as a ratio of GDP rose before falling again in the subsequent year (as happened in Germany in 1999 and the USA in 1841). For the purposes of this analysis, that 'in between' year was counted as part of the episode if the rise in the ratio of spending to GDP was very small, i.e. around 0.1 percentage points compared to the previous year, and/or was followed by a substantial fall in the ratio of expenditure in the subsequent year (more than 2 percentage points, rounded to the nearest unit).

spending falls or revenue increases in constant-price terms.[2] Here we took any constant price percentage fall in expenditure or rise in revenue as meaningfully describing a squeeze. But this definition can be refined as discussed below.

Cyclical Effects

A second issue to be faced in identifying fiscal squeezes is whether and how far to take cyclical effects into account. Chapter 1 noted that tax revenue tends to fall in economic downturns and to rise in economic upturns (and government spending tends to change in the opposite direction where public welfare benefits are available to those who are unemployed or on low incomes). So if all else is equal, raising tax revenue or cutting spending in a recession might be thought to demand more political effort than doing so in a boom. To identify episodes of fiscal adjustment, the IMF literature on fiscal consolidation sometimes uses cyclically adjusted figures, taking account of the 'output gap' (actual GDP less potential GDP, the standard measure of how far economies are performing below their potential). The difficulty is that cyclical corrections of that type are 'notoriously imperfect and arbitrary to some extent' (Alesina & Ardagna 2012: 5) even for relatively recent cases, and even more so for cases such as that of the United States in the early 19th century.

We did not directly use such cyclically adjusted figures but did use estimations of the sensitivity of revenue and expenditure to the output gap to see how much difference accounting for cyclical changes in revenue and expenditure made to the definition of fiscal squeeze episodes in practice. To do that, we took into account estimates of the elasticity of spending and revenue to the output gap for several of our nine country cases (Girouard and André 2005), which was less than −0.5 for expenditure and around 1 for revenue. When a percentage fall in expenditure relative to a percentage rise in the output gap was greater than 1 and when a rise in revenue was correspondingly greater than 1, we could plausibly assume that such changes exceeded the normal cyclical response of expenditure and revenue to changes in the output gap and therefore represented political effort. If expenditure fell or revenue rose as the output gap fell, that too is taken to represent political effort.

---

[2] The issue of the appropriate deflator to use to arrive at constant-price measures also arises. We used the GDP deflator to calculate expenditure and revenue in constant prices. That reflects an (of course contestable) assumption that price changes measured by the GDP deflator are a meaningful measure for this purpose. Concerns expressed by Baumol (1967) about 'unbalanced technological progress', where certain types of public sector costs may have a long-standing tendency to rise faster than general prices, were not taken into account for this analysis.

The Analytic Point of Departure

Any analysis unavoidably has to start from somewhere. So we began here by taking IMF data wherever it was available.[3] We also began with the most conventional approach in the fiscal consolidation literature of looking at revenue and expenditure relative to GDP to define 'episodes' of squeeze as occurring when the ratio of expenditure to GDP fell over a period of two years or more with an average annual fall of 1 percentage point or more (or fell in a single year by at least 2 percentage points), as explained earlier. We then looked to see what difference it made to the existence and periodisation of a fiscal squeeze for our nine cases when we used other measures, namely constant-price measures rather than ratios, revenue rather than expenditure, cyclically adjusted measures rather than unadjusted ones, OECD data rather than IMF data (where available), and the qualitative judgements of the nine country experts who wrote the chapters which follow.

Table 2.1 reports how the nine cases compare according to whether we identify fiscal squeeze episodes on the basis of revenue or expenditure, ratios to GDP or constant-price changes, aggregate outcome data or the qualitative judgements of country experts. As described earlier, we also calculated cyclically adjusted measures for revenue and spending where output gap data were available, but these cyclically adjusted figures did not in fact produce results very different from the unadjusted figures as to the existence and length of fiscal squeezes, so the latter were used for greater simplicity. We also looked at cases where both IMF and OECD data were available to see if they led to very different conclusions about the timing of fiscal squeeze episodes, and found they did not.[4]

As can be seen from Table 2.1, looking at expenditure cuts in constant-price terms for the most part does not show a radically different periodisation of fiscal squeeze episodes, although for the United States, New Zealand and Sweden the constant-price expenditure-based episodes occur for much shorter periods than the ratio-based episodes. The same goes for establishing the existence of episodes, although the case of the Netherlands barely registers as a fiscal squeeze at all in terms of spending in constant prices (with such spending only falling in a single year, 1988, and by less than 1 per cent).

---

[3] We used IMF data as a starting point because for six of the nine countries IMF data were available for the relevant period, whereas OECD data were available only for five countries. In cases such as Sweden, IMF and OECD data for general government expenditure differ (reflecting different definitions, conventions and sources), so using IMF data wherever possible made for greater consistency.

[4] The only two cases in which timings of fiscal squeeze episodes differed as between IMF and OECD data were those of New Zealand and Sweden, and out of those the only striking difference is between the timing of the New Zealand episode in absolute-spending terms, which began a year earlier and ended three years earlier on OECD than on IMF data.

Table 2.1. Comparing alternative ways of defining expenditure squeeze 'episodes'.

		Expenditure-based		Revenue-based		Qualitative (approx.)
		Ratio	Constant price	Ratio	Constant price	
USA	Period	1838–43	1838–40, 1843	No episode	No episode	1837–1840s
	Depth*	−1.8	−29.7, −50.1			High
UK	Period	1923–25	1923–24	No episode	No episode	1922–24
	Depth*	−9.0	−18.8			High
New Zealand	Period	1992–97	1992–93, 1995	No episode	1993–95	1991–99
	Depth*	−11.4	−9.6, −0.2		12.9	High
Netherlands	Period	1983–89	1989	No episode	1981–89	1982–89
	Depth*	−5.3	−0.7		15.1	Medium
Ireland	Period	1987–89	1983, 1987–89	No episode	1981–85, 1987–88	1984–89
	Depth*	−12.2	−0.3, −11.6		20.0, 9.2	High
Germany	Period	1996–2000	1995–96, 1999	No episode	1992, 1994–2000	1990s
	Depth*	−9.8	−9.2, −2.7		4.7, 17.6	Medium
Sweden	Period	1993–2000	1993–97	No episode	1995–2001	1990–97
	Depth*	−15.5	−3.5		25	Medium
Canada	Period	1993–97	1994–97	No episode	1990–2000	1994–97
	Depth*	−9.5	−4.4		35.9	High
Argentina	Period	2003	2003	2003–04	1997–98, 2000, 2003–10	1999–02: Medium/high
	Depth*	−8.2	−15.0	6.0	19.5, 0.3, 112	2003: Low

* For all definitions of episodes apart from the last column: (a) when expenditure is expressed as a ratio, the depth is the cumulative percentage point fall over the episode; (b) when expenditure is expressed as an absolute value, depth is the total percentage fall in real expenditure over the episode. The revenue-based definition is the exact opposite, with a 'rise in revenue' replacing 'fall in expenditure'. Note that depth for a particular country under the two categories 'ratio' and 'constant price' cannot be compared because the former is the percentage point fall, while the latter is the percentage fall. For the last column, 'depth' reflects a qualitative judgement about the extent of political effort during the qualitatively defined episode, using the criteria outlined in Chapter 1, Table 1.2.

Sources: USA: Carter *et al.* (2006). UK: Mitchell (1988), ch. 11. All other countries: World Economic Outlook Database, October 2012; OECD database no. 91, April 2012.

Table 2.1 also shows fiscal squeeze episodes defined in terms of revenue rising as a proportion of GDP and in constant-price terms. In several cases, such episodes overlap the episodes defined on the basis of constant-price expenditure reductions, but as the table shows, there is only one revenue squeeze episode among the nine cases in the basis of the ratio measure (that of Argentina in 2003–04) and in the case of Ireland the measure of revenue rises in constant-price terms indicates a fiscal squeeze starting much earlier than the episode as defined by expenditure falls, consistent with Niamh Hardiman's analysis in Chapter 7.

The right-hand column of Table 2.1 represents our interpretation of the timing and severity of each squeeze based on the accounts given by the country experts who wrote the case study chapters in this book, and who had case knowledge of when governments planned or announced fiscal squeezes, as well as when squeezes were implemented. The estimate of depth into 'high', 'medium' and 'low' represents our interpretation, based on a reading of the case chapters, of the political effort going into each squeeze. Low, medium and high here reflect the spectrum of estimated political effort (running respectively from mainly inertia strategies through imposition of less salient and visible losses, to imposition of visible and salient losses) that was presented in Table 1.2 of the previous chapter. It should be stressed that these categories are not the same as the hard/soft distinction of fiscal squeezes, which, as already stated, refers only to the realised financial outcome as an indirect measure of political effort.

Except in the cases of Argentina, Ireland and Sweden, the episodes as represented in the right-hand column of Table 2.1 start a year before the episodes based on financial outcome data. The disparity is not surprising because those judgements include the point at which squeezes were planned or announced. That estimated political effort mostly shows up in the financial outcome data after a lag of about a year. But in the case of Argentina, discussed in Chapter 11, governments made many unsuccessful attempts at squeezing, which only appeared in the outcome data after the currency was devalued in 2002. Similarly, the qualitative definition of the 'squeeze' episode for Ireland reflects efforts to increase revenue in the mid-1980s, and that for Sweden reflects efforts to reform pensions and taxation before 1994.

What the analysis of Table 2.1 shows is that we have to be careful not to 'reify' fiscal squeezes and to be aware that such episodes differ in timing and depth depending on whether we use expenditure or revenue as the starting point, whether we focus mainly on ratios or on levels, and whether we focus on qualitative judgements that include plans and budgets or on reported data on financial outcomes. Nevertheless, this analysis also shows that it is meaningful to categorise all of these nine cases as a fiscal squeeze in at least one important sense. Table 2.2 accordingly summarises the nine cases on seven financial aggregates, indicates the time period of the squeeze as derived from the ratio of expenditure to GDP, and indicates the type of squeeze each case represents on the basis of financial outcome data, referring back to combinations of the four 'soft'/'hard' types as defined earlier. That is:

- a 'hard' squeeze denotes a squeeze on revenue or expenditure both in constant prices and relative to GDP;
- a 'soft' squeeze denotes a squeeze on revenue or expenditure in constant prices or relative to GDP but not both;
- a 'double' squeeze denotes a squeeze on both revenue and expenditure;
- a 'single' squeeze denotes a squeeze on expenditure or revenue but not both;
- a 'hybrid' squeeze refers to a squeeze that is soft on one dimension (revenue or spending) but hard on the other.

Table 2.2 shows that in most of the nine cases expenditure cuts went well beyond the '1 per cent a year' rule of thumb referred to earlier, and in seven of them expenditure fell markedly in real terms as well as relative to GDP, representing cases of what in the previous chapter we called 'hard' fiscal squeezes on the expenditure side.[5] In the other two cases, expenditure growth fell behind GDP growth but spending did not fall in real terms, representing what we termed 'soft' fiscal squeezes. As can be seen, the sharpest percentage point falls, in terms of annual averages (column 5 of Table 2.2), came in Argentina (8.5 per cent) and Ireland (4.1 per cent). The cuts reported for the USA may seem relatively small compared to the other cases at 1.8 per cent of GDP, but the scale of those spending reductions look rather different if one notes that reported expenditure fell by no less than 72 per cent from 2.5 per cent of GDP in 1837 to 0.7 per cent of GDP in 1843, and that expenditure in constant prices more than halved by the end of the seven-year episode compared to the beginning. Table 2.2 also shows that in most cases the deficit reduced over the episode (though it slightly increased in the UK as a result of revenue falling more sharply than expenditure, indicating a squeeze on the expenditure but not the revenue side), and that in a number of cases (Canada, Germany and Argentina) the deficit reduction was achieved by revenue increases as well as relative or absolute reductions in expenditure.

As for the classification of types of squeezes in the right-hand column of Table 2.2, the Swedish case is the only one of our nine in which classification of the squeeze in these terms is highly sensitive to the measures used. If we go on the expenditure ratio measure, the squeeze episode runs from 1993 to 2000

---

[5] Such falls in real expenditure were larger than could plausibly be attributed to business cycle effects, since the percentage fall in such expenditure was more than the change in the output gap, at least for some of the years, for New Zealand, Germany, Canada and Ireland.

Table 2.2. Nine fiscal squeeze episodes compared.

Country and period of squeeze on the basis of expenditure as a ratio of GDP	Total % point fall in expenditure/ GDP over the episode[a]	% change in expenditure in constant prices[b]	% change in revenue in constant prices[b]	Average annual % point change expenditure/ GDP[c]	Average annual % point change in revenue/ GDP[d]	Deficit adjustment per year[e]	% of deficit adjustment due to cut in expenditures[f]	Type of squeeze on financial outcome data
USA 1838–43[g]	−1.8	−61.5	−59.5	−0.3	−0.2	0.1	287.0	Single (expenditure) hard squeeze
UK 1923–5	−9.0	−16.3	−22.2	−3.0	−3.9	−0.6	−566.0	Single (expenditure) hard squeeze
New Zealand 1992–97	−11.3	−9.9	7.8	−1.6	−0.9	0.9	177.7	Hybrid squeeze
Netherlands 1983–89	−5.3	10.9	12.8	−0.8	−0.6	0.2	−400.6	Double soft squeeze
Ireland 1987–89	−12.2	−11.6	6.5	−4.1	−0.7	3.3	−124.2	Hybrid squeeze
Germany 1996–2000	−9.8	−9.8	13.6	−1.9	0.3	2.1	90.5	Hybrid squeeze
Sweden 1993–2000	−15.5	−0.0	22.6	−1.9	−0.6	1.5	126.6	Double soft squeeze[h]
Canada 1993–97	−9.5	−4.0	16.3	−1.9	−0.0	1.8	105.0	Hybrid squeeze
Argentina 2003	−8.5	−15.0	23.0	−8.5	3.0	11.5	73.9	Double hard squeeze

[a] The total fall is calculated relative to the expenditure to GDP ratio in the year immediately preceding the squeeze. In all cases apart from New Zealand and the USA, expenditure figures refer to general government expenditure and all expenditure apart from that for the USA includes debt charges.

[b] Total change in expenditure (or revenue as the case may be) in constant price terms is calculated relative to expenditure (or revenue) in the year immediately before the start of the episode as defined here. GDP deflators are used to calculate constant-price values.

[c] The total percentage point change in expenditure as a ratio of GDP over the episode, divided by the number of years the episode lasted.

[d] The total percentage point change in revenue as a ratio of GDP over the episode divided by the number of years the episode lasted.

[e] The deficit (revenue–expenditure) adjustment per year is the cumulative fiscal adjustment divided by the number of years the episode lasted.

[f] The percentage of deficit adjustment attributable to spending cuts, calculated for the relevant period in each country as Cumulative change in expenditure/Cumulative change in deficit. The number exceeds 100 in some cases because of falls in revenue.

[g] GDP estimates for the USA at the time vary widely according to source. The ratios here use GDP as given in Carter *et al.* (2006), series Ca9, pp. 3–23. However, when three of the four alternative estimates of GDP given in the same source document are used, the percentage point fall in expenditure as a ratio of GDP indicates double digit values (12%) and the corresponding annual fall is over 2 percentage points of GDP. Similar numbers are observed for revenue as a ratio of GDP.

[h] This case is the only one in the set whose classification is highly sensitive to the measures used—see discussion in text.

Sources: USA: Carter *et al.* (2006). UK: Mitchell (1988), ch. 11. Argentina, New Zealand, Germany, Sweden, Canada and Ireland: IMF World Economic Outlook Database, October 2012. The Netherlands: OECD database No. 91, April 2012. GDP deflator data taken from IMF World Economic Outlook, April 2012.

with an overall fall of −0.4 per cent in real expenditure over the period, which works out as an annual fall of 0.0 per cent in constant-price terms and would thus count as a case of soft spending squeeze. But if we had taken spending in constant prices as the baseline for defining an episode of fiscal squeeze (as in column 3 of Table 2.1), the Swedish episode would run from 1993 to 1997,[6] with an annual fall in real expenditure over these of about 0.7 per cent, and this could thus be considered a hard expenditure squeeze for those years.

Triggers and Prompts for Fiscal Squeeze

To understand how far politics played into these nine episodes of fiscal squeeze—taking into account the different possible periodisations of fiscal squeeze shown for some of the cases in Table 2.1—it is instructive to see how far a common set of key economic conditions preceded those episodes. Accordingly, on the basis of the ratio-of-expenditure-to-GDP measure of fiscal squeeze shown in Table 2.2, Table 2.3 provides an indication of preceding economic conditions by comparing budget and current account deficits, national debt levels, and whether the domestic economy was going through a notable financial crisis such as the collapse of an asset price bubble in the year before the squeeze. We also present some indicators of what was happening in the world economy, including OECD average rates of expenditure and deficits (government budget and current account) and whether there was a global recession or an event that caused particular economic hardship such as a currency crisis or oil price hike.

Even looking at the raw numbers collated in Table 2.3, we can see some striking variations. For example, in the case of the UK in the 1920s the budget deficit was very low but the national debt was very high (well over 100 per cent of GDP), whereas for New Zealand in the 1990s it was the other way round. The cases also appear to have had massively different levels of national debt relative to GDP in the year before the start of the relevant expenditure squeeze. Some of these squeeze episodes began in a relatively stable or benign international economic environment (such as the cases of Germany, Sweden, Canada and Ireland (in the 1980s)), while for others (USA, UK, New Zealand, the Netherlands) international conditions were far from stable or benign. These differences remain if we define fiscal squeezes according to the constant-price spending levels measure shown in Table 2.1, and the conclusions are the same.

---

[6] If we use a cyclically adjusted definition of spending cuts in constant-price terms, as defined earlier, the Swedish episode would run from 1996 to 1997 (when expenditure in constant prices fell by some 2 per cent over the period), as is pointed out by Anders Lindbom in Chapter 9 of this volume.

Table 2.3. Nine expenditure squeeze episodes: domestic and international economic conditions in the year before the squeeze.

Episode	Domestic conditions						International conditions		
	National debt % GDP (DEBT)[a]	Budget deficit % GDP (DEFICIT)	Expenditure % GDP (EXPEN)	Current account deficit % GDP (CURR)	Domestic financial crisis[b]	Global recession / financial crisis (WORLD)	Budget deficit (OECD average)[c]	Expenditure (OECD average)[c]	Current account deficit (OECD average)[c]
USA[d] 1838–43	0.2	−0.8	2.1[d]	n/a	Yes	Yes	n/a	n/a	n/a
UK 1923–25	170.0	−0.5	35.5	4.3	No	Yes	n/a	n/a	n/a
New Zealand 1992–97	50.0	−4.5	42.2	−4.4	No	Yes	−2.9	42.3	−0.6
Netherlands 1983–89	26.7	−6.1	59.6	2.7	No	Yes	−5.0	41.6	−6.0
Ireland 1987–89	108.2	−12.0	52.0	−3.0	No	No	−5.0	41.1	−0.2
Germany 1996–2000	37.9	−9.5	54.8	−1.1	No	No	−4.8	42.6	0.1
Sweden 1993–2000	17.7	−8.9	67.2	−2.8	No	No	−4.6	42.3	−0.4
Canada 1993–97	59.1	−9.1	53.2	−3.7	No	No	−4.6	42.3	0.4
Argentina 2003	164.9	−15.9	38.9	9.0	Yes	No	−3.3	40.3	−1.1

Note: For DEBT, DEFICIT, etc. see Appendix B, Table 2.9.

[a] The sources and definitions for public debt in this column vary widely and cannot be compared between countries. The figure for Sweden is general government net debt for 1993 rather than 1992, due to unavailability of data in the IMF source used.

[b] The financial crises are the financial panic in the USA after the asset price bubble burst in 1837 and the Argentine crisis consisting of default on debt in 2001 and de-linking of the Argentinian peso from the US dollar the following year.

[c] All in terms of % of GDP. Note that OECD average for expenditure taken from the OECD database is not strictly comparable with the individual expenditure percentages reported for Ireland, Argentina and New Zealand since the latter numbers are taken from the IMF database and there may be definitional differences.

[d] Nominal GDP figures unavailable for the pre-1840 period. Estimates for the GDP for the 1830–40 period have been extrapolated backwards using data from 1840 to 1850, assuming linearity. US data pertain to Federal Government finances.

Sources: USA: Carter *et al.* (2006). UK: Mitchell (1988), ch. 11. Argentina, New Zealand, Germany, Canada, Sweden, Ireland: IMF World Economic Outlook Database, October 2012. National debt data (for all countries, apart from UK, Netherlands and USA): IMF database, October 2012. National debt UK taken from UK Debt Management Office official website http://www.dmo.gov.uk/. All other data from the OECD database no. 91, April 2012.

If, as is suggested by Table 2.3, there is no single set of economic conditions that precede fiscal squeeze in these cases, what about the politics? Does it take 'strong government' to initiate a spending squeeze in a democracy, given that (as was pointed out in the previous chapter) such squeezes necessarily involve imposing losses on at least some voters and that there is likely to be a political blame risk associated with cutting public spending? Here the political science literature points in somewhat different directions, insofar as one well-known line of argument (notably Lijphart 1999) suggests that it takes 'majoritarian' systems to achieve the kind of changes in policy direction that cannot readily be achieved by consensus decision-making, while another line of argument (for example, Anderson 1995) holds that citizens find it harder to assign blame for unpopular economic decisions where powers and responsibilities are divided across different institutions and veto players. So are expenditure squeezes more likely to happen when a powerful government with a cohesive party and a strong popular mandate commands all the levers of fiscal power— or when there is no single strong source of power and a number of weaker players are more likely to be able to share or pass the blame among themselves?

To explore that issue, the first three rows of Table 2.4 are indicators of 'government strength' in each of the nine cases at the time when the various expenditure squeezes began, with 'government' here referring to the party or parties that planned or initiated cuts in spending that later materialised.

The first row concerns the number of 'veto players' in the domestic political system at the time—as represented by whether the governmental system was presidential or parliamentary and whether government was held by a single party or a coalition.[7] With more than one key veto player, we might expect 'blame deflection' among the parties for the losses imposed by fiscal squeeze to be more possible, but also that decisive action might be more easily blocked.

The second row in Table 2.4 concerns how cohesive, 'strong' or otherwise the government was in a legislative sense at the outset of the relevant fiscal squeeze in the nine cases. What we are trying to capture here is how likely it is that prime ministers or government chief executives can count on support in the legislature, or alternatively how high the propensity to 'rebel' is within the legislature. This indicator is drawn from the first four rows of numerical variables at the bottom of Table 2.4, which represent indicators from the World Bank's Database of Political Institutions 2012,[8] supplemented by relevant literature to estimate the values for those cases (such as that of the USA in the 1830s) not included in that database.

---

[7] Other possible sources of veto points, not included in this analysis, include whether the central bank was independent or not, and whether government was federal or unitary.

[8] See http://econ.worldbank.org/ and Beck *et al.* (2001). See Appendix A for political variable definitions.

Table 2.4. Nine expenditure squeeze episodes: veto points, legislative coherence of government, popular support and political orientation of government at the outset of the squeeze.

	USA	UK	NZ	Netherlands	Ireland	Germany	Sweden	Canada	Argentina
Institutional veto points[a]	1	1	0	1	1	1	1	0	1
Legislative strength[b]	0	1	1	1	1	1	0	1	1
Popular strength[c]	1	1	0	1	0	0	0	0	0
Orientation (predominantly right or centre-right government)[d]	No	Yes	Yes	Yes	Yes	Yes	Yes	No	Yes
Variables used to support definitions above									
Allhouse	n/a	n/a	1	0	0	0	0	0	0
Numgov/Totalseats	n/a	n/a	0.6	0.7	0.5	0.5	0.5	0.6	0.4
Govfrac	n/a	n/a	0	0.6	0.3	0.4	0.7	0	0
Oppfrac	n/a	n/a	0.1	0.6	0.1	0.4	0.4	0.6	0.4
Numvote	50.8	55.9	47.9	70.2	48.5	48.4	37.7	41.2	37.4

Note: For political variables Allhouse, Numgov etc. see Appendix A.

[a] Institutional veto points: Coded as 1 if the government system was presidential (rather than parliamentary) or if the government was a coalition. A government was counted as a coalition if Govfrac > 0.

[b] Legislative strength: Coded as 1 if Allhouse = 1 *or* Numgov/totalseats ≥ 0.50 *or* if Govfrac − Oppfrac ≥ 0.50 *or* Govfrac − Oppfrac ≤ −0.3 when Govfrac = 0 *or* Govfrac − Oppfrac ≤ 0.3 when Govfrac > 0.

[c] Popular strength: Coded as 1 if the vote share of all government parties was greater than 50%, i.e. if Numvote ≥ 50%.

[d] Orientation: Coded as 1 if the predominant political orientation of the parties in central government that planned or initiated the fall in expenditure was right or centre-right according to the standards of the time.

Source: Own calculations using Beck *et al.* (2001).

For this analysis we divide 'strength' into three components, namely the existence or otherwise of a working majority in the legislature,[9] control of both houses of the legislature[10] and whether or not the government party or parties were considerably less fractionalised than the opposition parties in the legislature at the time when the fiscal squeeze began.[11] Legislative strength in Table 2.4 is coded as strong (= 1) if any of those conditions representing the probability of support or rebellion held true and 0 otherwise.

Another indicator of government strength, given in the third row of Table 2.4, concerns the extent of popular support (i.e. from the voters at large, not the legislature) commanded by the party or parties in government at the previous general or legislative election. This measure of 'strength' is based on the total share of votes gained by all government parties presented as variable 'numvote' later in the table. For this purpose we code the incumbent party or parties at the start of the expenditure squeeze as popular (1) if their share of the popular vote at the preceding general election was greater than 50 per cent.

The fourth row in Table 2.4 looks at the orientation of the government, in terms of whether the parties at central government level that planned the subsequent fall in spending were predominantly right or centre-right according to the standards of the time. Apart from the USA and Canada, all of those governments were right or centre-right, but in several cases the governments that carried those expenditure squeezes were of a different political composition.

As with the economic factors shown in Table 2.3, the raw indicators in Table 2.4 show that these nine governments embarked on expenditure squeezes from positions of varying legislative strength and institutional vetoes, and again those conclusions do not essentially alter when the squeeze is measured in terms of levels of spending in constant prices rather than as a ratio of GDP.

Tables 2.3 and 2.4 provide some relevant pointers to the degree of variation in initial economic and political conditions. Table 2.5 brings those two elements together into a qualitative comparative analysis (Ragin 1987) designed to explore the proposition that countries about to enter a 'hard' expenditure squeeze (as defined earlier) could be expected to display a common set of unfavourable economic conditions (namely, historically high national debt, budget deficit, current account deficits and domestic financial

[9] Counted as 'strong' if Numgov/Totalseats ≥ 0.50, and 'weak' if not.

[10] Counted as strong if the party of the prime minister or chief executive has a working majority in all the houses of the legislature (as represented by the variable 'Allhouse') and 'weak' if not.

[11] Counted as 'strong' if on the World Bank's indicators of fractionalisation of government and opposition parties, the government parties are considerably less fractionalised than the opposition parties, specifically if Govfrac – Oppfrac ≤ 0.30 when Govfrac > 0, such that there is a 30 per cent or greater chance that two randomly picked deputies from opposition members of the legislature belong to different parties than applies to deputies from government members of the legislature.

Table 2.5. Initial economic and political conditions associated with hard and soft expenditure squeezes.

	Initial economic and political conditions								Expenditure squeeze outcome
High debt	High budget deficit	High current account deficit	Domestic financial crisis	Strong government	Popular government	Institutional veto points	Orientation 'right' or centre-right		
(D)	(B)	(C)	(F)	(S)	(P)	(V)	(R)		
0	0	1	1	0	1	1	0	USA	Hard
0	1	0	0	1	0	1	1	Germany	Hard
0	1	0	0	1	0	0	0	Canada	Hard
1	0	0	0	1	1	1	1	UK	Hard
1	1	0	0	1	0	0	1	Ireland	Hard
1	1	0	0	1	0	0	1	New Zealand	Hard
1	1	0	1	1	0	1	1	Argentina	Hard
0	1	0	0	0	1	1	1	Netherlands	Soft
0	1	0	0	0	0	1	1	Sweden	Soft

crisis) and also a common set of political conditions in terms of government legislative strength and popular support and the existence or otherwise of substantial veto points.

Table 2.5 therefore consolidates the information from Tables 2.3 and 2.4 about initial economic and political conditions into the form of a 'truth table' designed to explore which if any of these conditions are sufficient to precede a 'hard' or 'soft' expenditure squeeze. The groupings in Table 2.5 are based on analysing the pre-squeeze economic indicators relative to the conditions of each country at the time and coding them in each case as 0 or 1, to show whether indicators such as debt levels were high or low relative to that country's experience at that particular time. So the first three columns in Table 2.5 are based on taking the level of each of the relevant indicators in the year before the expenditure squeeze episode relative to their values in the 20-year period around that episode,[12] coding them as 1 if their pre-squeeze values lay in the top 10 per cent (or bottom 10 per cent, as the case may be) and 0 if not. That 10 per cent cut-off level is, of course, arbitrary, but is intended to pick up cases where the value of those pre-squeeze economic indicators was notably higher or lower than at other times over the 20-year period.[13] The three columns in Table 2.5 relating to political conditions use the coding shown in Table 2.4. When we put those two sets of indicators together, each row in the table indicates the configuration of initial conditions applying to each country case.[14]

What is striking from Table 2.5 is the variety of patterns shown by these nine cases for the economic indicators, and for the political indicators the only common feature associated with 'hard' expenditure squeeze (leaving aside the US case, where the squeeze considered here is mainly at state government level) is that of 'strong government' in a legislative sense. From these nine cases we draw the general conclusion (following on from what was said in the previous chapter) that hard expenditure squeeze in these cases was associated with governments that were strong in a legislative sense, but that such squeezes can develop in a range of economic circumstances and particularly that historically high levels of debt and/or deficit were not invariably present in the run-up to fiscal squeeze.

In the jargon of Qualitative Comparative Analysis (QCA), the so-called 'least parsimonious solution' (that is, the one that includes every possible combination) to the question about what economic and political conditions are sufficient for a 'hard' expenditure squeeze can be written as:

---

[12] The 20 years included the squeeze periods themselves.
[13] See Table 2.9, Appendix B for details.
[14] See Appendix B for details.

dbCFsPVr + dBcfSpVR + dBcfSpvr + DbcfSPVR + DBcfSpVR +
DBcfSpvR + DBcfFSpVR → Hard (1)

In solution (1) above, a capital letter, such as D or B, refers to the presence of a condition. Thus D refers to high debts being prevalent and B high budget deficit. A lower case letter, such as d or b, refers to the condition not holding. Thus d refers to a situation where debts are not high and b where budget deficits are not high. What this equation says is that each of those seven configurations is sufficient to precede a hard expenditure squeeze.

When it comes to 'soft' expenditure squeeze, the least parsimonious solution to the question of what economic and political conditions precede such a squeeze can be written as:

dBcfSPVR + dBcfspVR → Soft (2)

There are no contradictory configurations between solutions (1) and (2) (i.e. there are no rows of the truth table that lead to both 'hard' and 'soft' outcomes). We cannot simplify (1) any further, and can conclude that for these nine country cases, there are seven different paths to the 'hard' outcome, with no two cases having the same initial conditions.

Whereas there are no common economic conditions that are sufficient for hard expenditure squeezes in these nine cases, the presence of governments with a high degree of legislative strength is sufficient to precede hard expenditure squeezes in all cases (apart from the US case, for which we only have federal data in Table 2.4), partially in line with the idea mentioned earlier that 'strong' governments might be best placed to apply such loss-imposing policies on some voters. But the same does not apply to strong popular support and the absence of veto points. In the next section we will explore whether those strong governments experienced correspondingly strong blame from voters.

Economic and Political Impacts and Consequences of Expenditure Squeezes

Chapter 1 noted that in the mainstream econocratic literature about 'fiscal adjustment' and 'consolidation', the outcome indicators that get most attention are economic and financial, particularly in terms of debt and expenditure levels. For example, Alesina & Ardagna (2012) focus on deficit and debt levels following episodes of expenditure cuts, defining an outcome as successful if in the three years after the 'tight' year, the ratio of the primary deficit to GDP is on average at least 2 percentage points below its level in the tight year, or if in the three years after the year of adjustment, the debt-to-GDP ratio is at least 5 percentage points below its level in the year before the start of the adjustment year.

Such measures assume, of course, that deficit and debt reduction are the essential reasons for fiscal squeezes, and we have already shown that that did not apply for all of the nine cases considered here. Table 2.6 gives the change in deficits and debt levels as well as some other economic indicators in the year after the end of the nine fiscal squeezes, compared to the beginning. The table then assesses whether the squeeze was a 'success' or not, as shown in columns 7 to 9.

Given the basis on which these cases were selected, it is not surprising that Table 2.6 shows a substantial reduction in spending relative to GDP in most of them (notably Sweden, New Zealand and Ireland). According to Alesina & Ardagna's (2012) financial criteria for 'success' in terms of debt and deficit reduction relative to GDP as mentioned earlier, budget deficit reductions are observable for six of the cases (but not those of the UK, Germany or the Netherlands), and debt reductions are also observable for six of the cases, the exceptions being the USA, Germany and the Netherlands. As between the start and end of the expenditure squeeze, unemployment levels also fell in most cases. The current account deficit improved for four of the nine cases, namely, Germany, Sweden, Canada and Ireland.

Table 2.7 suggests that incumbent parties or leaders lost vote share in the short term as a result of voter punishment in more than half of these cases for which an election occurred within the expenditure squeeze episode or up to two years after the episode ended, and in over half of those cases those incumbents also lost office. But the table also shows that nearly half of the cases were exceptions to that pattern (for example, Jean Chrétien's Liberal government in Canada in the 1990s). Indeed, in the Argentine case the real political upsets came during the period of economic turmoil associated with default and devaluation (when the UCR party President Fernando de la Rúa abruptly resigned in 2001 amid violent unrest, and the country had three presidents in ten days), rather than after the fiscal squeeze as measured here. It may be that economic performance or changes in living standards help to explain the difference between 'yeses' and 'nos' in the sixth column of Table 2.7. The table also suggests that planning and initiating an expenditure squeeze had higher electoral cost than simply implementing it.

Again a truth table can help to systematise these conclusions. Table 2.8 accordingly uses some of the information on pre-squeeze political conditions from Table 2.4, and about the nature of the expenditure squeezes from Table 2.2, to explore how such factors relate to the electoral outcome immediately after the squeeze was implemented. Table 2.8 excludes the case of Argentina in 2003 because the incumbent government at the time was an appointed interim government rather than an elected one.

Table 2.6. Economic performance in the year after the end of expenditure squeezes, compared to the beginning.

	Change in unemployment rate[a]	Percentage point change in national debt as a % of GDP[b]	Percentage point change in budget deficit as a % of GDP[c]	Percentage point change expenditure as a % of GDP	Percentage point change in current Account deficit as a % of GDP	Success with respect to debt reduction[d]	Success with respect to deficit reduction[e]	Success with respect to expenditure reduction[f]
USA 1838-43	—	1.1	1.1	-0.9	n/a	No	Yes	Yes
UK 1923-5	-1.0	5.0	-0.9	-7.2	-3.2	Yes	No	Yes
New Zealand 1992-97	-2.9	-27.7	4.6	-11.0	-0.6	Yes	Yes	Yes
Netherlands 1983-89	-3.1	7.2	0.9	-4.8	-1.1	No	No	Yes
Ireland 1987-89	-4.1	-14.9	21.0	-10.4	1.6	Yes	Yes	Yes
Germany 1996-2000	-1.1	4.5	8.7	-7.3	1.1	No	No	Yes
Sweden 1993-2000	-0.7	-16.0	10.4	-15.5	7.6	Yes	Yes	Yes
Canada 1993-97	-3.0	1.7	9.2	-9.4	2.4	Yes	Yes	Yes
Argentina 2003	-8.9	-37.9	13.8	-7.0	-7.3	Yes	Yes	Yes

[a] The change in unemployment is calculated as the rate in the year after the episode *less* the rate in the year before the start year.

[b] Change in debt as a ratio of GDP is calculated as a percentage point change in the ratios at the end and compared to beginning. A negative figure indicates that debt increased.

[c] Change in deficit as a ratio of GDP is calculated as a percentage point change in the ratios at the end and compared to beginning. A negative figure indicates that deficit increased.

[d] Squeeze 'successful' if in the three years after the tight year, the ratio of the primary deficit to GDP was on average at least 2 percentage points below its level in the tight year.

[e] Squeeze 'successful' if in the three years after the year of adjustment, the debt-to-GDP ratio was at least 5 percentage points below its level in the adjustment year.

[f] Squeeze 'successful' if in the eight years after the *end* of adjustment, the expenditure-to-GDP ratio was at least 5 percentage points below its level in the year before the start of the adjustment year. This criterion is not meaningful in the case of the USA, where expenditure was under 3 per cent of GDP during the 1837–51 period. However, it is coded 'yes' because expenditure as a percentage of GDP fell by around 20% from 2.1% in 1837 to about 1.7% in 1851.

Source: Own calculation using the following data sources: USA: Carter *et al.* (2006). UK: Mitchell (1988), ch. 11. Argentina, New Zealand, Germany, Canada, Sweden, Ireland: IMF World Economic Outlook Database, October 2012. National debt data (for all countries, apart from UK, Netherlands and USA): IMF database, October 2012. National debt UK taken from UK Debt Management Office official website http://www.dmo.gov.uk/. All other data from the OECD database no. 91, April 2012.

Table 2.7. Nine expenditure squeezes compared: the political aftermath.

Case	General election years[a]	Did incumbent plan or initiate squeeze?	Did incumbent implement squeeze?	Change in vote share of incumbents[b]	Did incumbents lose office at election?[c]	Were there constitutional or major institutional changes?
USA 1838–43	1840	Yes	Yes	-4.0	Yes	Yes
	1844	Yes	Yes	-4.8	Yes	
UK 1923–25	1923	Partly	Yes	-0.5	Yes	No
	1924	No	Yes	2.6	Yes	
New Zealand 1992–97	1993	Yes	Yes	-12.8	No	Yes
	1996	Yes	Yes	-1.2	Partly	
Netherlands 1983–89	1986	Yes	Yes	2.9	Yes	No
	1989	No	Yes	0.7	No	
Ireland 1987–89	1987	Yes	No	-12.1	Yes	No
	1989	No	Yes	-0.1	Partly	
Germany 1996–2000	1998	Yes	Yes	-6.3	Yes	No
	2002	Yes	Yes	-2.4	No	
Sweden 1993–2000	1994	Yes	Yes	0.5	Yes	No
	1998	No	Yes	-8.1	No	
	2002	No	No	3.4	No	
Canada 1993–97	1997	Yes	Yes	2.7	No	No
Argentina 2003	2003[d]	No	Yes	n/a	n/a	No

[a] The elections considered are those that occurred within the expenditure squeeze episodes or within two years after those episodes ended.
[b] Entries for the USA and Argentina reflect votes in presidential rather than congressional elections. Numbers refer to the percentage point change in the votes gained by the incumbent party relative to the previous election. If the incumbent government was a coalition, the vote share reported is that for the party to which the incumbent chief executive (i.e. president or prime minister) belonged.
[c] 'Partly' denotes episodes in which the previous incumbents had to share office with a coalition partner after the election, as in New Zealand after the 1996 election and in Ireland after the 1989 election.
[d] From January 2002, an interim government was in power.

Table 2.8. Political context, nature of expenditure squeeze and outcome at first election.

Political context during the first year squeeze was implemented					Expenditure squeeze outcome
Hard squeeze (H)	Orientation (R)	Strong government (S)	Institutional veto points (V)		Lost office at first election after implementing squeeze
1	1	1	0	NZ	0
1	0	1	0	CAN	0
1	1	1	1	UK, GER, IRE	1
1	0	0	1	USA	1
0	1	1	1	NED	1
0	1	0	1	SWE	1

The 'least parsimonious solution' to the question about what political conditions and what type of expenditure squeeze are sufficient for a party losing office at the first election after implementing the squeeze can be written as:

$$HRSV + HrsV + hRSV + hRsV \rightarrow \text{Lose office}$$

This specification can be written more parsimoniously as:

$$V \rightarrow \text{Lose office}$$

This says that having institutional veto points, either due to having a presidential system or a coalition government, is sufficient for the party to lose office after implementing a fiscal squeeze, regardless of whether it is hard or soft. When it comes to not losing office, the least parsimonious solution

$$HRSv + HrSv \rightarrow \text{Not lose office}$$

can be simplified as:

$$HSv \rightarrow \text{Not lose office}$$

That is, a hard expenditure squeeze implemented by a strong government that is not a coalition is sufficient for not losing office, in this analysis.

As for constitutional and major institutional changes introduced in the aftermath of expenditure squeezes, the most unambiguous case of such developments is the debt limitation and balanced-budget rules introduced in the case of the United States. New Zealand's shift from its former 'majoritarian' first-past-the-post electoral system to a form of proportional representation in 1993 may well have been at least partially produced by the expenditure squeeze of that time, but in that case it seems to have been only part of a broader electoral reaction against two successive single-party governments pushing radical policy changes through New Zealand's unicameral legislature after winning only a plurality at the polls. That relative absence of major constitutional and institutional change after these nine cases of expenditure squeeze is notable, given the idea introduced in Chapter 1 that fiscal squeezes might be expected to be high-consequence events for democratic politics and to produce long-term effects in the political system.

Conclusions

Chapter 1 distinguished between the economics and the politics of fiscal squeeze. It also distinguished (in Table 1.3) between exogenous and endogenous fiscal squeezes (that is, those which came about through pressure from outside as against domestic political pressures) and between hard and soft squeezes on expenditure and/or revenue. We suggested that from a blame-avoidance perspective, the hard endogenous variety would be the ones most likely to put pressure on incumbents and perhaps on the political system more widely.

The comparison of the nine cases here suggests three main conclusions. First, there is no set of preceding economic and financial conditions that is common to all the nine cases of expenditure squeeze considered here, and certainly not to the seven cases of 'hard' expenditure squeeze. That conclusion emerges from the analysis of Tables 2.3 and 2.5, and it suggests either that expenditure squeezes come in different economic varieties or that economic factors are mediated through politics, or both.

Second, it was suggested earlier that governments were more likely to be in a position to apply loss-imposing policies on voters where they commanded reliable support in the legislature and did not face institutionalised 'veto players', but that blame-avoidance might be more readily achieved when responsibility-attribution by voters was more limited. What this analysis shows is that the hard expenditure squeezes in all but one case were applied by governments with comfortable legislative majorities, but that such squeezes were by no means confined to 'majoritarian' governments: many of the hard spending squeezers were coalitions. But the hypothesis that strong governments implementing hard expenditure squeezes will experience correspondingly strong blame from voters in the first available post-squeeze election is not invariably supported by this analysis. The three strongest governments (on the measures reported in Table 2.4) implementing hard squeezes all secured re-election post-squeeze in spite of lowish popular support, whereas coalitions applying hard squeezes failed to do in some cases, such as that of Germany.

Third, among these nine cases, instances of constitutional or major institutional change only came in the aftermath of 'hard' expenditure squeezes. But they occurred after only a minority of such squeezes, and in contrast to the notion that 'hard' and 'endogenous' squeezes would present the biggest challenges to incumbent parties trying to hold on to office, the only cases of incumbents securing re-election are found in precisely that category.

Appendix A

Political Variables

All political variables used in Table 2.4 and its notes are extracted from the World Bank's Database of Political Indicators 2012 (updated January 2013). See Beck *et al.* (2001).

Allhouse: Records whether the party or parties of the executive has an absolute majority in the houses that have lawmaking powers (appointed upper houses are considered to be controlled by the executive).

Numgov: Records the total number of seats held by all government parties.

Totalseats: Records total seats in the legislature, or in the case of bicameral legislatures, total seats in the lower house.

Govfrac: Records the probability that two deputies picked at random from among the government parties will belong to different parties.

Oppfrac: Records the probability that two deputies picked at random from among the opposition parties will belong to different parties.

Numvote: Records the total share of the popular vote gained by all government parties.

Appendix B

Table 2.9 shows the cut-off values used to code whether the economic conditions DEBT, DEFICIT, EXPEN and CURR lie within the 'particularly poor' dichotomous category.

All cut-off values are calculated using data for 20 years around expenditure squeeze episodes (including within-squeeze years), for each country separately. The cut-off is the 90th percentile, values above which lie the top 10 per cent of the data. If the relevant value in Table 2.3 lay above the cut-off value (for positive values) or below the cut-off (for negative values), it was coded as 1 in the truth table and 0 otherwise.

'CURR' is intended to proxy and contextualise a country's external trade performance. Apart from current account balance used in Table 2.9, we also consider two other indicators of trade performance:

1 The growth rate in export volume relative to the growth of the country's export market, representing potential export growth if the country's market shares are unchanged (OECD Economic Outlook database inventory, Annex Table 53). We define growth in export performance as being particularly poor if the respective values lay in the bottom 10 per cent of export growth during the reference period.

2 The competitiveness index from the OECD database that relates unit labour costs to weighted labour costs in competitor countries. We define a country's competitiveness as low if it lay in the lowest 10 per cent during the reference period. For all the countries, if at least two of the three external trade performance indicators we use were outside the cut-off point, CURR was coded as 1 in Table 2.5.

Table 2.9. Cut-off values for initial economic conditions (values above which lie the top 10%).

	EXPEN	DEF	DEBT	CURR
USA	n/a	n/a	n/a	n/a
UK	33.4	−2.6	170.0	−0.9
NZ	39.9	−4.4	46.5	−6.4
Netherlands	58.7	−5.4	49.6	2.0
Ireland	26.3	−11.1	107.4	−9.6
Germany	49.3	−4.1	53.5	−1.3
Sweden	68.3	−8.9	24.6	−2.7
Canada	52.0	−8.3	67.8	−3.7
Argentina	37.9	−6.0	139.4	−4.2

Note: EXPEN: Expenditure as a percentage of GDP; DEF: Budget deficit (revenue minus expenditure) as a percentage of GDP; DEBT: Debt as a percentage of GDP; CURR: Current account deficit as a percentage of GDP.

Source: Author calculations. The Netherlands data are from OECD database No. 91, April 2012; UK data from Mitchell (1988). All other data from IMF World Economic Outlook Database, October 2012.

References

Alesina, A. & Ardagna, S. (2012), *The Design of Fiscal Adjustments*, NBER Working Paper 18423 (Cambridge MA, National Bureau of Economic Research).

Anderson, C.J. (1995), *Blaming the Government: Citizens and the Economy in Five European Democracies* (Armonk NY, Sharpe).

Baumol, W.J. (1967), 'The Macroeconomics of Unbalanced Growth: The Anatomy of Urban Crisis', *American Economic Review*, 57: 415–26.

Beck, T., Clarke, G., Groff, A., Keefer, P. & Walsh, P. (2001), 'New Tools in Comparative Political Economy: The Database of Political Institutions', *World Bank Economic Review*, 15(1): 165–76.

Carter, S., Gartner, S.S., Haines, M., Olmsted, A., Sutch, R. & Wright, G. (2006), *Historical Statistics of the United States: Millennial Edition* (Cambridge, Cambridge University Press), http://hsus.cambridge.org/ (accessed 10 June 2012).

Girouard, N. & André, C. (2005), *Measuring Cyclically-Adjusted Budget Balances for the OECD Countries*, OECD Working Paper No. 434.

Lijphart, A. (1999), *Patterns of Democracy: Government Forms and Performance in Thirty-Six Countries* (New Haven, Yale University Press).

Mitchell, B.R. (1988), *British Historical Statistics* (Cambridge, Cambridge University Press).

Ragin, C.C. (1987), *The Comparative Method: Moving Beyond Qualitative and Quantitative Strategies* (Berkeley, University of California Press).

Part II
Case Studies

3

Managing Fiscal Squeeze after the United States' Panic of 1837

ALASDAIR ROBERTS

National Crisis and Fiscal Squeeze[1]

IN 1836–39, THE UNITED STATES SUFFERED A FINANCIAL SECTOR COLLAPSE that plunged the nation into a severe economic crisis. This was well before the advent of national income accounting, and as a result we have no precise measure of how bad economic conditions became. Economic historians who have attempted to make retrospective estimates of growth rates suggest that the trough of the crisis was 1840–42. It is possible that in the worst years the economy still grew by 1 or 2 per cent—although this would still have been a substantial setback for a developing country that was accustomed to annual GDP growth of perhaps 5 per cent (see Chapter 2, Table 2.1).

However, the significance of the economic crisis of the early 1840s cannot be gauged by looking narrowly at GDP alone. The economic shock was powerful enough to cause widespread disorder, unprecedented political instability, and deep tensions in relations between the United States and the United Kingdom. The political strains were so intense that some Americans questioned whether the country could hold itself together. These political and diplomatic woes arose primarily because of the damage that was done to national and state finances during the crisis, and the way in which politicians managed the politics of fiscal squeeze.

The American economy had been booming in the mid-1830s. British cotton mills had an extraordinary appetite for American cotton, and as a result the plantations of the American south were expanding rapidly, driving growth in other sections of the country as well. There was rampant speculation in land throughout the country. This was encouraged by the easy credit offered by a loosely regulated banking industry and the massive influx of capital from Britain. State governments added fuel to the bubble by borrowing cheap

---

[1] Readers should refer to Roberts (2012) for discussion of the broader economic and political difficulties of this period, rather than the fiscal squeeze which is the subject of this chapter.

Proceedings of the British Academy, **197**, 55–72. © The British Academy 2014.

money in London to finance new canals, turnpikes and railroads. This economic bubble collapsed in phases between the spring of 1836 and December 1839. Federal policies that were intended to restrain land speculation may have contributed to the collapse. However, external factors were also at play. The British economy slowed and demand for American cotton weakened. The Bank of England also made stop-and-start decisions about interest rates that caused a series of panics among American financiers. The American financial sector finally collapsed at the end of 1839. Foreign and domestic commerce tumbled soon after.

The revenues of state and federal governments also evaporated, prompting legislators at both levels to begin wrestling with an extraordinary project of fiscal squeeze. At the state level, the challenge was servicing a massive amount of foreign debt. At first, the main response was default. By 1842, one third of American states were in default on British loans, and many state legislators were advocating the outright repudiation of those obligations. This exacerbated diplomatic and military tensions between the United States and the United Kingdom. Meanwhile, the decline in federal revenues caused the unravelling of a compact that had been forged between northern and southern states in better times a decade earlier. The short-term effect of fiscal squeeze was an increase in partisanship and legislative gridlock in Washington.

But the long-term consequences of fiscal squeeze were different. Strategies of managing fiscal squeeze shifted substantially during the crisis. By the end of the crisis, many state governments had resumed payments on their debts; developed new methods of collecting taxes; and adopted constitutional restrictions on deficit financing. Meanwhile, federal politicians had undertaken a painful renegotiation of federal tax policies and—in sharp contrast to the trend of policy in state legislatures—adopted a more pragmatic attitude about debt financing of federal expenditures. Neither of these changes was accomplished easily. Electoral volatility increased markedly during this period. Still, the effect of the crisis was to produce a transformation in the American constitutional order whose effects are still obvious today.

The States' Fiscal Squeeze

To understand the character of the twin fiscal crises of the 1840s, two preconceptions about American politics must be put aside. The first is the notion that the most important aspects of political conflict are played out at the federal rather than the state level. The second is the notion that American politicians of the 19th century conformed to a restrictive, laissez-faire view regarding the role of government in economic development. Until the financial crisis of 1836–39, American state governments sought to encourage economic development in two ways. The first was through the construction of 'internal improvements'—what we now call transportation infrastructure. State governments financed and built roads, canals and railroads, which they considered to be essential to settlement and trade. The second mode of state action was through state-supported or state-owned banks. Operating with capital that was provided by state government, these banks provided credit to facilitate commerce and support expansion by farmers and plantation owners.

Federal policy—or more precisely, confusion in federal policy—encouraged state action. The federal government had a lukewarm attitude towards support of internal improvements, because it was seen to set a dangerous precedent for intervention in the internal affairs of the southern states. Inaction at the centre meant that pressure for governmental support of economic development was directed principally towards state capitals. State activism was also encouraged by ready access to foreign capital. Borrowing abroad was politically easier than financing through taxation. The spectacular success of New York State's toll-financed Erie Canal, and the apparently unstoppable boom in real estate, seemed to prove that state loans could be repaid with transportation revenues and banking profits. European investors, tantalised by the promise of high returns backed by government guarantees, eagerly purchased state bonds. In just three years—1836 to 1838—American states accumulated obligations roughly equal to the combined national debt of Russia, Prussia and the Netherlands.

Cheap foreign credit fuelled extensive, uncoordinated and rivalrous state action. Pennsylvania, worried that the Erie Canal would give New York State a predominant role in managing trade with the interior, borrowed heavily to build its own network of roads, canals and railroads from Philadelphia in the east to Pittsburgh in the west. Maryland, fearing competition from Pennsylvania, launched its own projects to connect its eastern shore with the Ohio River. Indiana adopted a scheme to cover the state with a lattice-work of canals, roads and railroads, which it called the Mammoth plan. Illinois followed with a comparable plan a few months later. Mississippi established two state banks, capitalised with borrowed money, to promote agricultural development; Arkansas soon followed, and so did Florida Territory. There was no sense that legislators were taking a significant risk in establishing these banks. Capital was being borrowed in London at 5 per cent, and lent to entrepreneurs in the states at 8 per cent. State banks, like the toll-financed canals and turnpikes, seemed to be machines for printing money.

The financial collapse brought an end to these illusions. As the cotton business and land bubble collapsed, state-owned banks (like many others) became insolvent. The decline in trade also meant less traffic on canals, turnpikes and railroads. The first effort at fiscal squeeze consisted of an attempt to curb losses by calling an immediate halt to the construction of new projects.

Some states tried to hoard cash by paying contractors with state-issued scrip. Neither of these measures could do much to avoid the hard reality: that there was no longer enough revenue to make the payments that were coming due on state debt. By 1841, for example, the state of Maryland had interest obligations of $600,000 a year, while it earned only $50,000 from its canal and railroad holdings.

This led to the next form of fiscal squeeze: a wave of state defaults. Michigan and Indiana were the first to default, in July 1841. Maryland, Arkansas and Illinois followed in October 1841. Four months later, in February 1842, Mississippi and Florida Territory fell. Pennsylvania followed in the autumn of 1842, and Louisiana in January 1843. By that time nine state or territorial governments, responsible for two-thirds of all the American government debt in private hands, were routinely missing interest payments, attempting to sidestep creditors, or threatening to repudiate their obligations entirely.

These defaults provoked outrage in London. British investors had been persuaded that state-issued debt was essentially riskless. After default, many Americans attempted to correct this understanding. American bonds had been paying 5 or 6 per cent while British government bonds were paying only 3: obviously the premium was a compensation for added risk. But British investors could point to the representations made by distinguished Americans in the years before collapse. Massachusetts senator Daniel Webster visited London to bolster the market for American bonds in the summer of 1839. Default, he had assured investors, 'would be an open violation of public faith, which would be followed by the penalty of dishonor and disgrace; a penalty that no state would be likely to incur' (McGrane 1935: 22).

The wrath of British investors was intense. Americans in London were banned from clubs, chastised at dinner parties and mocked in the newspapers. 'There is an opinion pretty current among discerning persons in England', the poet William Wordsworth wrote to an American friend, 'that Republics are not to be trusted in money concerns, I suppose because the sense of honour is more obtuse, the responsibility being divided among so many' (Wordsworth 1851: 2.356–7). Investors' anger was stoked by the lack of any immediate remedy against the states. The doctrine of sovereign immunity, entrenched in the US Constitution, made it impossible to seek redress in American courts. The British government also refused to take up the investors' complaints. The federal government of the United States was no more helpful. American diplomats rebuffed investors, insisting that central authorities would not 'be held, in any wise, or to any extent, responsible for any default, actual or eventual' (McGrane 1935: 243).

The defaulting states found themselves in an extraordinary position. They were free to do as they wished. Obviously it would be difficult to borrow in the future if they treated their current creditors badly. But if they failed to honour their debts, there would be no sanction from American courts or any other part of American government. In many states there were legislators who argued for outright repudiation of state debt. In some places the case for repudiation was bolstered by evidence that legislators had been manipulated by bankers eager to make a profit on the handling of state debt. Many Americans also harboured a long-standing resentment against Britain's exploitation of its economic and military power. 'The doctrine of repudiating state debts is spreading rapidly,' a prominent Philadelphia merchant wrote in his diary at the end of 1841. '[It] is spoken of openly and boldly defended by many presses and leading politicians' (Fisher 1952: 224).

Remarkably, though, most of the defaulting states chose to honour their debt. Only two states—Mississippi and Florida—opted for outright repudiation of all debt. (A third, Arkansas, was practically in this camp as well, refusing to acknowledge its liabilities until after the Civil War.) Two states, Louisiana and Michigan, repudiated some but not all of their obligations. All of the other states—Pennsylvania, Illinois, Indiana and Maryland—resumed payments to all bondholders between 1845 and 1848. But it should not be thought that this was an easy choice. It followed only from a prolonged—and for British investors, frustrating—debate about the proper course of action. The period was marked by a sharp increase in electoral volatility in many states. The historian Reginald McGrane (1924: 145) observes that the crisis that began in the late 1830s 'loosened the political moorings of the country'.

British investors were not mere spectators of the wrangling in state capitals. Leading British banks hired American agents to persuade reluctant state politicians. There were rumours of bribes and campaign contributions to friendly legislators. The Boston agent for Barings Bank launched 'a campaign of propaganda' (Hidy 1949: 293), hiring prominent authors to write articles against repudiation and paying editors to publish them. Some of these agents despaired about their work. 'You are little aware of the corrupt morals of the low, stealthy, base intriguing politician of the west,' two agents wrote from Illinois to London in 1845. 'The demagogues are numerous … You must expect from them every species of intrigue, falsehood, and baseness' (McGrane 1935: 123–5).

There were practical reasons for the recalcitrance of many state politicians. Even if they agreed in principle that state debts should be honoured, there was the question of how the money necessary to make payments would be obtained. There was no hope of generating enough money from tolls or bank profits. But states had no other dependable source of revenue. Some had experimented with property taxes, but these were deeply unpopular. In Maryland, for example, property taxes in the state had been completely abolished in 1824. Marylanders who wanted to repay state debts had to overcome popular hostility to the idea of direct taxation and then construct, almost from scratch, the capacity to collect taxes. Initial attempts by the Maryland legislature to impose a property tax in the wake of default failed because of the refusal of local officials to collect it. State legislators eventually took the responsibility for collecting taxes into their own hands and raised the penalties for non-compliance.

The shift in tax policy was not unique to Maryland. In Pennsylvania, too, 'the state was embarrassed by its inability to collect the taxes that were levied … the central treasury [lacked] machinery for the collection of direct taxes' (Garver 1919: 41). This began to change after the Pennsylvania legislature adopted tougher legislation in 1844. Indeed, there was a broad shift in policy regarding property taxes across the United States. The crisis of the 1840s 'altered citizens' expectations and realities regarding the incidence of taxation', John Wallis (2000: 34) argues. The idea that states could pursue a 'tax-free system of finance' (Wallenstein 1987: 49)—dependent only on tolls and enterprise profits—was abandoned.

State policies changed in other important ways. The wave of defaults provoked a reconsideration of the wisdom of state activism in the pursuit of economic development. States had been seized by euphoria as they launched their improvement schemes at the height of the boom. When Indiana approved its Mammoth Internal Improvement Act in 1836, 'There was a general rejoicing; every pane of glass in the city was illuminated; and the population turned out on the streets as upon a great holiday' (Fowler 1850: 1.675). Only a few years later, many Americans took a more cautious view about the capacity of democratically elected legislatures to make sensible decisions about large plans for public improvement. Some now recognised the capacity of voters to be 'inflamed with the internal improvement fever' (Sutton 1849: 768). Others recognised the tendency of legislatures to produce grandiose schemes as a result of 'bargain and intrigue, log-rolling and corruption' (Fowler 1850: 1.682).

The democratic process was seen to have its weaknesses, and so corrective measures were thought necessary. Between 1842 and 1852, the legislatures of twelve states organised conventions to overhaul their state constitutions so that the debacle of the late 1830s would not be repeated. Indiana flatly prohibited any kind of borrowing except in cases of invasion or insurrection, or to pay the interest on state debt. California proscribed borrowing for special projects unless the authorising law provided 'ways and means' for repaying the debt, and was approved in a popular referendum. The reformed Maryland constitution prohibited state involvement 'in the construction of works of internal improvement, or in any enterprise which shall involve the faith or credit of the State'. The New York Constitution of 1846 barred state guarantees for the debt of private corporations.

Attitudes about the management of fiscal squeeze at the state level had changed profoundly during the crisis of the 1840s. Indeed, the crisis triggered a significant shift in the American constitutional order. Most states— including many that had never defaulted in the 1840s—eventually adopted constitutions that restricted their ability to borrow and promote economic development through investment in public enterprises. These rules proved to be extraordinarily robust. During the current economic crisis, for example, some critics have complained about the inability of states to pursue stimulative fiscal policies because of anti-deficit rules that are entrenched in state constitutions. (Indeed, these rules actually aggravate economic slowdowns, by requiring cuts in state government expenditure because of declining tax revenues. This places the burden of stimulating the US economy primarily on the US federal government.) These critics are confronting one legacy of the crisis of the 1840s.

The adoption of these constitutional restrictions required a significant change in popular attitudes about the democratic process—a change that was even more profound than the shift in opinion about direct taxation. In the 1820s and 1830s there had been a powerful surge towards democratisation in the United States. Most states abolished property restrictions on voting, and popular participation in elections grew dramatically. One-quarter of white males actually voted in the presidential election of 1824, but four-fifths actually voted in the election of 1840. It was an era marked by optimism about the capacity of mass electorates to govern themselves intelligently. 'We have an abiding faith in the virtue, intelligence, and full capacity for self-government, of the great mass of the people,' said the *Democratic Review* in 1838. 'We are opposed to all self-styled "wholesome restraints" on the free action of the popular opinion and will' (*Democratic Review* 1838: 2).

The drive within constitutional conventions to establish limits on borrowing and state involvement in internal improvements was understood as a challenge to this faith. In Indiana, a critic of restriction complained that it was 'palpably subversive of the self-evident principle that the will of the majority must govern' (Fowler 1850: 1.673). 'The people are the source of power,' agreed an Iowa delegate. 'If the people send foolish men here to represent them and make laws for them, who will spend their money for them unnecessarily, it is their business, not ours' (Lord 1857: 1.267). By the end of the 1840s, however, this had become a minority view. The weight of opinion now ran in favour of constraining popular sovereignty. Constitutional restrictions might be 'shackles upon the power of the legislature', a delegate to Kentucky's constitutional convention conceded, but they were demanded by experience (Sutton 1849: 762). 'Self-government is no longer a theory, it has been demonstrated,' agreed John Pettit, a delegate to the Indiana constitutional convention. 'It is to prevent the evils resulting from excitement and passion, that we take our calmer and quieter hours to bind ourselves and our fellow man' (Fowler 1850: 1.660).

The Federal Fiscal Squeeze

The central government of the United States also confronted a fiscal crisis during the early 1840s. But the federal crisis was different in character to that of many states. The central government was not at risk of default. In fact, it began the crisis almost entirely free of debt. This was the result of policy and good fortune. The country had ended war with Britain in 1815 with a substantial national debt. But successive presidents pursued a common policy of reducing the debt as quickly as possible. 'The total extinguishment of the debt', said John Quincy Adams, was 'a fundamental maxim in the system of public credit of the United States' (*Niles' Register* 1832: 248). High tariffs on imported manufactures provided the means with which the debt would be repaid. Andrew Jackson, President from 1829 to 1837, firmly resisted pressure from legislators to divert tariff revenue towards internal improvements, insisting that was a matter for the states alone. Jackson's supporters held a gala banquet in Washington in 1835 to celebrate the elimination of federal obligations.

In the mid-1830s, federal revenues were also enhanced because of the economic boom. The total revenue intake in 1836, $50 million, was twice what it had been in 1830, and much in excess of federal expenditures, which amounted to only $30 million. But the impression of fiscal health may have been illusory. Federal revenues were buoyed because the government was selling a major asset, consisting of land in southern and western states. In 1835–36 the federal government sold an expanse equal to the whole of England, and earned more from land sales than it did from the tariff. Revenues of the Post Office Department, the biggest part of the federal establishment, were buoyed by the boom as well, and in the mid-1830s its income also exceeded its expenditure by a healthy margin.

The robust health of the federal Treasury made it easier for the nation's leaders to manage tensions within the union. The sharpest division was between the northern and southern states, and centred on the question of tariffs. The tariffs adopted immediately after the War of 1812 had enjoyed broad support throughout the country. But southern support for tariffs declined as they were raised throughout the 1820s and 1830s. Southerners began to see a sharp distinction between the economic interests of North and South. The nascent manufacturing sector of northern states benefited from protection. But the southern states had no significant industries, and depended on open access to the British market. Southern resentment over tariffs mounted.

By the midpoint of Andrew Jackson's first term as president, this resentment had reached the flashpoint. Virginia congressman Charles C. Johnston came to Washington in December 1831 convinced that the next session of Congress 'would form a crisis in which the political destiny of this Government would be determined, either for evil, or for good, for years to come' (Johnston 1921: 202). John Quincy Adams warned northerners that 'they must relieve the South or fight them' (Peterson 1982: 25). Congress attempted to conciliate. A new law that lowered tariffs in 1832 undermined militancy in many southern states, but not in South Carolina, where a state convention declared the tariff laws to be unconstitutional and threatened to secede if the federal government attempted to enforce them.

Jackson replied with a combination of threats and concessions. Congress approved an expansion of the president's power to use force to collect federal taxes in South Carolina. But it also endorsed his request for a further reduction in federal tariffs. In March 1833 Congress adopted legislation that promised a gradual but substantial reduction of duties on imported goods, until all of the increases of the previous decade had been wiped away. These concessions defused the conflict in South Carolina. Southerners understood that by the date fixed in the 1833 law—30 June 1842—relief from protective tariffs would finally be delivered. This compromise on tariffs, so vital to the preservation of peace within the union, was made possible by the health of the federal Treasury. Of course there were manufacturing interests that sought protection regardless of how the revenue was used. But their capacity to make a public case for tariffs was weakened by the reality of a massive surplus. Supporters of protection were compelled to justify 'the oppression of drawing money out of the pockets of the people for nothing, merely to accumulate it in the treasury' (Gales & Seaton 1833: 8.484).

To a lesser degree, the surplus also helped to ease tensions between seaboard and frontier states. As we have seen, the great need in the frontier states was for transportation infrastructure. President Jackson had come down firmly against federal involvement in the construction of such internal improvements, fearing that it would lead to an unhealthy expansion of central authority. However, federal legislators took some of the sting away from Jacksonian strictures by adopting another policy—a commitment to distribute the federal surplus among the states. In June 1836, Congress passed legislation promising that the federal surplus available on 1 January 1837 would be divided and paid in four instalments to the states. Technically, the Treasury retained power to retrieve the money deposited with states, but this was widely understood as a pretence to avoid the appearance of pure distribution, which Jackson seemed more likely to veto.

Added to this new policy was one improvement that lay unambiguously within the federal sphere: an expansion of the Post Office Department. The department had an importance which is analogous to that of the internet today. It was the country's central nervous system: the conduit by which business was done, news carried and politics managed. And while the department enjoyed profits, Congress enthusiastically expanded its responsibilities. The Post Office Department's routes increased by 40 per cent, from 113,000 miles to 156,000 miles, between 1835 and 1840—particularly in rural and frontier areas. The postal network grew more in those five years than it had in the previous seventeen.

During the 1830s, federal politicians crafted a delicate compact that held together the major sections of a fractious union. The amount of money that was involved in this informal compact was not particularly large by modern standards. In 1837, federal revenues might have been 3 per cent of GDP. But this is the wrong way to judge the significance of the compact, for two reasons. The first is that Americans of 1837 would have compared the scale of revenues to their experience of the preceding five decades. From this point of view the amounts involved were very substantial. And the second reason is that the compact was not merely about money. It was also a declaration about the importance of the three sections—North, South and West—within the union. If one section attempted to renegotiate the compact, it would be construed by other sections not merely as a fiscal adjustment, but as a statement about power and status within the federal system.

The compact was negotiated on the assumption that the federal Treasury would enjoy continued good health. But the financial crisis of 1836–39 quickly brought an end to the demand for federal lands. Receipts from the sale of lands in 1840 were one-eighth of what they had been in 1836. As trade seized up, tariff revenue also became unreliable. Income from postal services softened too, and the Post Office Department ran a succession of large deficits after 1838. This was not wholly the result of economic troubles. The department faced competition from private carriers who, unburdened by costly rural and frontier routes, offered better rates to customers on the urbanised east coast. Existing law purported to give the Post Office a monopoly over mail delivery and in 1840 the financially troubled department attempted, for the first time, to prosecute its competitors. The results were devastating for the Post Office. Courts interpreted the law so narrowly that the ban on competition was effectively gutted, and customers flocked to private carriers.

The shift in federal finances happened with stunning rapidity (see Figure 3.1), and federal politicians became preoccupied with the problems of fiscal squeeze. The first casualty of the collapsing Treasury was the policy on distribution of the federal surplus to the states. The Treasury had calculated at the start of 1837 that $37 million was available for distribution, and by the autumn of 1837, three of the promised four instalments had been paid to the states. The fourth payment was due in October 1837. By that time it was clear that the federal government was unable to pay its ordinary expenses, much less the $9 million still due to state governments. Congress quickly revised the distribution law to delay payment of the fourth instalment until 1839. But it was obvious by late 1838 that the federal government still lacked the ability to pay, and Congress postponed the last payment indefinitely.

State governments, convinced that the federal government would continue payouts, were caught flatfooted. In December 1837 the Governor of Pennsylvania had urged the state legislature to increase appropriations even though Congress had just deferred payment. The legislature increased spending and obtained a loan that was to be repaid in 1839 out of the anticipated proceeds of the fourth instalment. When Congress deferred the instalment indefinitely, Pennsylvania was left with an uncovered liability equal to one-third of its total current expenditures. Indiana, Michigan, Mississippi and New York also borrowed against the anticipated fourth instalment. Many state politicians accused the federal government of a breach of faith.

In fact, though, the federal finances were in a miserable condition. In May 1838, President Martin Van Buren told Congress that there was only $216,000 in the Treasury: enough to finance government operations for two days. The

Figure 3.1. US federal government revenue and expenditure, 1820–50.
Source: Historical Statistics of the United States.

hard reality was that the United States government would have to borrow to meet its obligations. This was a difficult pill for the Democratic president to swallow. Van Buren's predecessor, Andrew Jackson, had made the elimination of the federal debt a major plank in party policy. At first the Van Buren administration asked Congress to finance the deficit by issuing treasury notes—small denomination paper that could be given to creditors instead of cash. Hardened Democrats were prepared to argue that, so long as the country was relying on treasury notes alone, it still had no national debt. Treasury notes, it was said, were only a stop-gap to bridge a temporary decline in revenues.

Congress narrowly approved the issue of treasury notes in 1837. When conditions did not improve significantly in 1838, the Van Buren administration called for another issue, and Congress again relented. 'Here now, is another emergency—another unexpected crisis,' said Senator William Prescott. 'I believe the treasury habitually exists in a state of emergency—in a critical condition' (*Niles' Register* 1838: 262). This was not far from the truth. The Treasury routinely overestimated how much revenue it was likely to collect in the coming year, and then sought short-term financing to cover the deficiency. New issues of treasury notes were approved in 1839, 1840 and 1841. In that year, spending exceeded revenue by almost 60 per cent.

After March 1841 the Whigs claimed control of the presidency as well as the House and Senate. The pretence of Democratic finance—that the federal government merely had short-term financing gaps, which could be bridged by treasury notes—was now abandoned. Congress authorised a $12 million loan in July 1841 and another $5 million loan in April 1842. By 1843, the federal debt was back to $33 million, roughly what it had been in the early years of Jackson's presidency. 'The brilliant prospect that had been held out, of the extinction of the national debt—which had been the fond vision of Jackson's administration—was shattered' (Turner & Craven 1965: 464–5). But if the practice of deficit financing was now clearly re-established, there were limits to how far it could be pursued. American financial markets were deeply unsettled and domestic demand for federal bonds was weak. European investors had even less appetite for federal bonds. The federal government was now paying for the sins of the defaulting states. Federal agents were humiliated when they attempted to sell bonds in Europe in 1842. A story circulated in London about what the US agents had been told by the financier James de Rothschild. 'You may tell your government', said Rothschild, 'that you have seen the man who is at the head of the finances of Europe, and that he has told you that you cannot borrow a dollar' (Ferguson 1998: 374).

Federal politicians also pursued the tactic of restraining expenditures. But the entire system of budgeting conspired against them. Estimates about amounts needed in the coming year were initially produced by bureaus within the five executive departments (State, Treasury, Post Office, Army and Navy). It was generally acknowledged that bureaus had incentives to inflate their requirements—to 'make them larger than is necessary', as President James Polk later said, 'calculating that they will be cut down and reduced by Congress' (White 1954: 81). Bureau heads sent their requests to cabinet secretaries, who were so short-staffed that they could do little but tally the requests and send the total directly to Congress. There was no central review of proposed spending for the whole of government by the Treasury department, and no presidential budget as we know it today. Eventually, in 1845, President James Polk asserted his right to review departmental estimates before they were sent to Congress, but even then Polk lacked much capacity to judge whether the requests were reasonable.

Congress did little better in scrutinising expenditures. The House of Representatives established a special Committee on Retrenchment to search for savings. It was chaired by a Virginia Democrat, Thomas Gilmer, who took his assignment so seriously that he became known in Washington as Retrenchment Gilmer. 'Retrenchment fever ran high,' John Quincy Adams recalled (Adams 1876: 95). But budget hawks in Congress were stymied by their inability to discern where reductions were possible. When the Retrenchment Committee asked departments to identify possible savings in 1842, 'the response was a general request for more clerks' (White 1954: 151).

The Post Office presented particular challenges for advocates of retrenchment. By the early 1840s it was dependent on subsidies from general revenues, and beset by competition from private carriers. There was deep resistance within Congress to a reversal of the expansion that had been undertaken in 1836–40. But neither was there an appetite for continued subsidies. One possible remedy was strengthening the statutory ban on competition from private carriers, but advocates of private enterprise baulked at tightening the government's 'odious monopoly' over postal services (*Hunt's Merchants' Magazine* 1844: 524). After several years of prevarication, Congress acted. Unwilling to countenance a substantial reduction of postal routes, it gave the Post Office the monopoly on letter mail which it continues to enjoy today. The suppression of private competition would 'put an end to all interference with the revenues of the department', promised the author of the 1845 legislation, Democratic Senator William Merrick (Gales & Seaton 1844: Document 137, p. 10). By 1848 the Post Office Department was again producing surpluses.

Most of the reduction in federal expenditure was borne by the army and navy, and in particular the army, which saw its budget cut in half between 1838 and 1842. But the pursuit of economies in defence was complicated by problems of internal security and foreign policy. The army was struggling to contain Indian resistance in the south and restrain conflicts between Americans in northern states and British colonists in Canada. It was also obvious that a larger navy was necessary to protect the American merchant fleet and advance national ambitions for expansion in the Pacific, where Britain was once again the main rival. Competition between the United States and the United Kingdom became more acrimonious in the early 1840s, in large part because disputes over default had corroded goodwill between the two countries. Congress was torn between the desire for retrenchment and the desire to check British ambitions through the expansion of American military capabilities.

There were other areas in which Congress faced pressure for increased expenditure. Distressed state governments were appealing to Washington for help. Proposals that the federal government should assume the debts of defaulting states were rebuffed. But another idea—that of distributing the now-diminished flow of revenue from land sales among the states—enjoyed more success. In the autumn of 1841, Congress adopted a law promising a resumption of the policy of distribution. It was heralded as 'a relief measure to the indebted states', who once again tallied the amounts to be received from Washington in the following year (*Democratic Review* 1841: 207).

The national capital now began the main drama of the federal fiscal crisis: the unravelling of promises about tariff reform that had been made a decade earlier. The law that had been adopted in 1833 to appease South Carolina and other southern states specified the exact date on which federal tariffs would be sharply reduced: 30 June 1842. Many Americans 'looked upon [the tariff law of 1833] as a sort of temporary appendix to the Constitution, and consequently sacred' (Bourne 1885: 18). But by late 1841, circumstances had changed radically. Northern manufacturers had been prospering in 1833, but in 1841 they were suffering badly and unwilling to give up tariff protection. And the federal government itself was distressed. It could not meet its ordinary expenses—as well as the newly made promises of distribution to the states—if tariffs were lowered as the 1833 law proposed.

By early 1842 it was clear that the compact of 1833 would have to be re-negotiated. All of the sectional tensions that had been suppressed in good times were now inflamed. In New York, in April 1842, thousands of workers rallied against the planned reduction of federal tariffs. In the South, meanwhile, politicians railed against northern treachery. 'We have patiently waited,' said South Carolina senator John C. Calhoun. 'And now that the time has arrived ... [the manufacturers] coolly and openly violate every provision in our favor' (Calhoun 1874: 104). At the same time, western legislators appealed for preservation of the policy of distribution. Federal aid, said Abraham Lincoln, an Illinois legislator, was essential 'in the midst of our almost insupportable difficulties' (Nicolay & Hay 1894: 249).

The atmosphere in Washington became toxic. As in the states, controversy over economic and fiscal policies had contributed to unprecedented electoral volatility and a corrosion of goodwill. Legislators appeared to be incapable of crafting a replacement for the compact of 1833. Disgust with the 'confusion and tumult' in the Congress pervaded the popular press (*Alexandria Gazette* 1842). The *Baltimore Clipper* asked whether members of the national legislature 'can really possess American hearts—there being, apparently, so total an indifference to the interests of the country' (*Baltimore Clipper* 1842). 'The unsettled state of the tariff question' was causing transatlantic trade to seize up, aggravating economic stagnation on both sides of the ocean (*Preston Chronicle* 1842).

The deadline of 30 June 1842 approached rapidly. A few weeks before the deadline, a coalition of northern and western legislators succeeded in passing legislation that deferred the scheduled reduction in tariffs for one month, while reaffirming Washington's commitment to the policy of distribution. President John Tyler, sympathetic to southern sentiments, vetoed the bill and instructed federal officials to reduce tariffs as the 1833 law required. The enraged coalition of legislators sent Tyler another bill in August, permanently setting high tariffs and affirming the policy of distribution. Tyler once again vetoed the bill. In Congress, there was agitation for Tyler's impeachment. Finally, in late August, Congress approved a bill that Tyler was prepared to sign. It abandoned the compact of 1833 by raising tariffs, but also abandoned the policy of distribution. The bill passed with a majority of one vote in the House of Representatives and one vote in the Senate. Northern representatives voted overwhelmingly for the law, while the South voted overwhelmingly against.

In the north, the new tariff law was credited with breathing new life into the ailing economy. 'The Tariff of 1842 is doing wonders for us,' wrote Calvin Colton, a protectionist pamphleteer (Colton 1844: 122). But southerners fumed. In December 1842 the South Carolina legislature approved a resolution condemning the tariff law and warning that it might turn again to nullification. In July 1844 the South Carolina politician Robert Rhett, later a member of the confederate Congress, called for secession. The 1833 compromise 'was in fact a treaty, made between belligerent parties with arms in their hands', said South Carolina Governor James Hammond. This treaty had been broken by the 1842 law and there was no reasonable ground, he concluded, for believing that the federal government would ever repeal it. 'Our state is bound ... to adopt such measures as will bring all her moral, constitutional, and if necessary, her physical resources in direct array against a policy ... which impoverishes our country, revolutionizes our government, and overthrows our liberties' (Houston 1896: 155).

Southern anger was reduced after the inauguration of Democratic President James Polk in March 1845. The Polk administration introduced modest reductions in federal tariffs in 1846. The administration underestimated the subsequent loss in revenue, and at the same time launched an unexpectedly expensive war with Mexico, so that in 1847 the United States had the largest federal deficit in its history. This was more easily financed as overseas investors fled from the unrest that seized Europe in 1848. The American economy was also reawakening, spurred by the discovery of gold and silver in the territory of California, acquired as a result of the war with Mexico. This marked the end of the crisis of the 1840s. Still, the federal fiscal crisis had given evidence of the sectional divisions that would plunge the country into civil war a few years later.

The Legacy of Two Crises

Fiscal troubles were not the only major problem confronting American politicians during the hard years that followed the financial crisis of 1836–39. The United States and the United Kingdom also clashed repeatedly as the two countries sought to consolidate or expand their spheres of influence—along the New York State and Maine borders, in the Oregon Territory, in the Sandwich Islands, and even in Texas. Each of these territorial conflicts threatened to escalate into war. There were troubles at home as well: an uprising by disenfranchised workers in Rhode Island; violent agrarian protests in upstate New York; and rioting in major cities of the north-east. The nation was also seized with an acrimonious debate about whether to re-establish a central bank for the United States. That struggle also provoked two presidential vetoes and a break between the Whig president, Tyler, and leading Whigs in Congress.

All of these questions crowded the political agenda and were tightly intertwined. Consequently it should not be surprising that politicians in Washington and state capitals were sometimes slow in confronting the new fiscal realities. And there were other factors that made the politics of fiscal squeeze less manageable. The first was the simple truth that the politics of retrenchment was more difficult than the politics of expansion: dividing losses in a period of economic decline was harder than dividing gains in a period of growth. The negotiation of new compacts about the allocation of national resources, better suited to new circumstances, took time. Settled ideas—about popular sovereignty, the role of government in economic affairs, the obligations of sections of the nation to one another—had to be reconsidered, and new ideas advanced to take their place. This process of adjustment was made even more complicated because of the general decay in societal trust that followed as understandings of all kinds—financial, political, diplomatic—unravelled.

The process of adjustment was difficult and long. Nonetheless, it is evident that the American political class *did* adjust. The politics of fiscal squeeze changed over time. This was most obvious at the state level. The dream of a 'tax-free system of finance' was definitively abandoned, and new understandings about methods of financing government and the role of government in economic development were entrenched in law. In a sense, state legislators were reconciling the idea of popular sovereignty to the realities of international finance—or more precisely, constraining popular sovereignty to fit the realities of a world in which capital flowed freely across national and sub-national borders.

There was evidence of learning at the federal level as well, although not so clearly as at the state level. Eventually, federal politicians acknowledged new fiscal realities and renegotiated policies on taxation and aid to the states. There were the early signs of the trend towards centralisation of budgetary authority within the executive branch, and a more vigorous assertion of presidential power through the use of the veto. And there was also evidence of a new pragmatism in Washington about the morality of deficit financing, and the relationship between the central government and international capital. The crisis had effected a curious inversion of attitudes about debt financing by state and federal governments. In 1837, state governments were borrowing liberally overseas, while federal politicians boasted about their parsimony. By 1848, it was the federal government that was borrowing overseas, while state governments adopted constitutional prohibitions on deficit spending. The foundations of the modern American fiscal system had been established.

References

Adams, John Quincy (1876), *Memoirs of John Quincy Adams*, xi (Philadelphia, J.B. Lippincott & Co.).

Alexandria Gazette (1842), 'The Exchequer Plan', *Alexandria Gazette*, 19 February.

Baltimore Clipper (1842), 'Important Papers', *Baltimore Clipper*, 15 March.

Bourne, Edward G. (1885), *The History of the Surplus Revenue of 1837* (New York, G.P. Putnam's Sons).

Calhoun, John C. (1874), *The Works of John C. Calhoun* (New York, D. Appleton & Co.).

Colton, Calvin (1844), *The Junius Tracts* (New York, Greeley & McElrath).

Democratic Review (1838), 'Introduction', *Democratic Review*, 1(1): 1–15.

Democratic Review (1841), 'Monthly Financial and Commercial Article', *Democratic Review*, 9(38): 203–8.

Ferguson, Niall (1998), *The House of Rothschild: Money's Prophets, 1798–1848* (New York, Viking).

Fisher, Sidney George (1952), 'The Diaries of Sidney George Fisher', *Pennsylvania Magazine of History and Biography*, 76(2): 177–220.

Fowler, H. (ed.) (1850), *Report of the Debates and Proceedings of the Convention for the Revision of the Constitution of the State of Indiana*, 2 vols (Indianapolis, A.H. Brown, Printer).

Gales & Seaton (1833), *Register of Debates in Congress* (Washington DC, Gales & Seaton).

Gales & Seaton (1844), *Public Documents of the Senate for the First Session of the Twenty-Eighth Congress* (Washington DC, Gales & Seaton).

Garver, Frederic B. (1919), *The Subvention in the State Finances of Pennsylvania* (Menasha WI, George Banta Publishing Company).

Hidy, Ralph (1949), *The House of Baring in American Trade and Finance* (Cambridge MA, Harvard University Press).

Houston, David (1896), *A Critical Study of Nullification in South Carolina* (New York, Longmans, Green & Co.).

Hunt's Merchants' Magazine (1844), 'The Post Office Department', *Hunt's Merchants' Magazine*, 11 (December): 522–39.

Johnston, Charles C. (1921), 'Letter from Charles C. Johnston to John B. Floyd', *William and Mary Quarterly*, 2nd series, 1(3): 201–6.

Lord, W. Blair (1857), *Debates of the Constitutional Convention of the State of Iowa*, 2 vols (Davenport IA, Luse, Lane & Co.).

McGrane, Reginald (1924), *The Panic of 1837* (Chicago, University of Chicago Press).

McGrane, Reginald (1935), *Foreign Bondholders and American State Debts* (New York, Macmillan).

Nicolay, John & Hay, John (eds) (1894), *Abraham Lincoln: Complete Works* (New York, The Century Company).

Niles' Register (1832), 'Report on the Tariff', *Niles' Register*, 42(14): 248–57.

Niles' Register (1838), *Niles' Register*, 54 (23 June): 262.

Peterson, Merrill D. (1982), *Olive Branch and Sword: The Compromise of 1833* (Baton Rouge LA, Louisiana State University Press).

Preston Chronicle (1842), *Preston Chronicle* (6 August): 1.

Roberts, Alasdair (2012), *America's First Great Depression: Economic Crisis and Political Disorder after the Panic of 1837* (Ithaca NY, Cornell University Press).

Sutton, B. (1849), *Debates and Proceedings of the Convention for the Revision of the Constitution of the State of Kentucky* (Frankfort KY, A.G. Hodges & Co.).

Turner, Frederick Jackson & Craven, Avery (1965), *The United States, 1830–1850* (New York, Norton).

Wallenstein, Peter (1987), *From Slave South to New South: Public Policy in Nineteenth-Century Georgia* (Chapel Hill NC, University of North Carolina Press).

Wallis, John J. (2000), 'State Constitutional Reform and the Structure of Government Finance in the Nineteenth Century', in J.C. Heckelman, J.C. Moorhouse & R.M. Whaples (eds), *Public Choice Interpretations of American Economic History* (Boston, Kluwer Academic Publishers), 33–52.

White, Leonard (1954), *The Jacksonians: A Study in Administrative History, 1829–1861* (New York, Macmillan).

Wordsworth, Christopher (ed.) (1851), *Memoirs of William Wordsworth* (Boston, Ticknor, Reed & Fields).

4

The UK Geddes Axe of the 1920s in Perspective

CHRISTOPHER HOOD AND ROZANA HIMAZ

Introduction: Why the Geddes Axe is a Distinctive Case for the Politics of Fiscal Squeeze

THE 'GEDDES AXE' OF 1922 (named after a businessman turned civil servant turned politician who chaired a special committee in 1921–22 to recommend deep cuts in public spending), is an unusual and distinctive case of fiscal squeeze in at least four ways.

First, spending cuts are often preceded and indeed triggered by large budget deficits But in the UK in 1922, heavy spending cuts were applied to a budget that was already in balance.

Second, while the UK government was certainly experiencing fiscal *stress* at that time, because it had to refinance a large amount of short-term debt incurred during World War I, there was not an acute fiscal *crisis* in the sense that spending cuts were forced by dramatic developments in the currency or securities markets. Rather, the cuts seem to have been triggered by a form of tax revolt against the level of income, capital and consumption taxes, all of which had been raised sharply in World War I and remained at historically high levels after the war. Domestic political pressure to cut taxes was the immediate trigger for the spending cuts. The Geddes Axe thus represents a fiscal squeeze with a strong endogenous element, in the language of the introductory chapter.

Third, the cuts recommended by the Geddes Committee were actually implemented, in contrast to many proposals for reductions in public spending. Indeed, as will be shown later, the cuts implemented were even greater than those recommended by the Geddes Committee.

Fourth, the Geddes Axe cuts were deep both by cross-national standards (as shown in Chapter 2) and by the standards of later cutbacks in the UK, making this case a clear instance of hard fiscal squeeze, in the terminology of the introductory chapter, at least as far as spending reductions are concerned.

Proceedings of the British Academy, **197**, 73–92. © The British Academy 2014.

The Geddes Axe cuts were preceded by sharp tax increases in 1921, which together with deep cuts in defence spending between 1919 and 1921 led the budget to swing from a large deficit (29 per cent of GDP in 1919) to a surplus of 3 per cent in 1921. The Geddes Axe spending cuts were followed by tax cuts and indeed (consistent with the 'tax revolt' point made earlier), revenue fell by more than spending between 1923 and 1925. That means that this case is one of fiscal squeeze only on the expenditure side.

Figure 4.1 puts the story into longer-term historical perspective by comparing what happened to spending and revenue during the Geddes Axe period with what happened before and over the subsequent eight decades.

Table 4.1 tells the story in a slightly different way, comparing several episodes of UK expenditure cutbacks and revenue increases between 1900 and 2010, both as ratios of GDP and in constant prices. It shows that the total percentage point fall in expenditure as a ratio of GDP between 1923 and 1925 was 9.0, compared to 1922, implying an annual average expenditure reduction of 3.0 percentage points. It also shows that expenditure fell in constant-price terms over the period by over 16 per cent. The only other times that expenditure cuts were larger than this were during the post-World Wars I and II demobilisation periods, when expenditure fell respectively by 6.9 and 6.3 percentage points annually, but it is important to stress that those cuts were in both cases concentrated exclusively on defence. Thus the Geddes Axe cuts were undoubtedly severe compared to other fiscal squeeze episodes in the UK, amounting to the third-largest annual cuts over the whole century

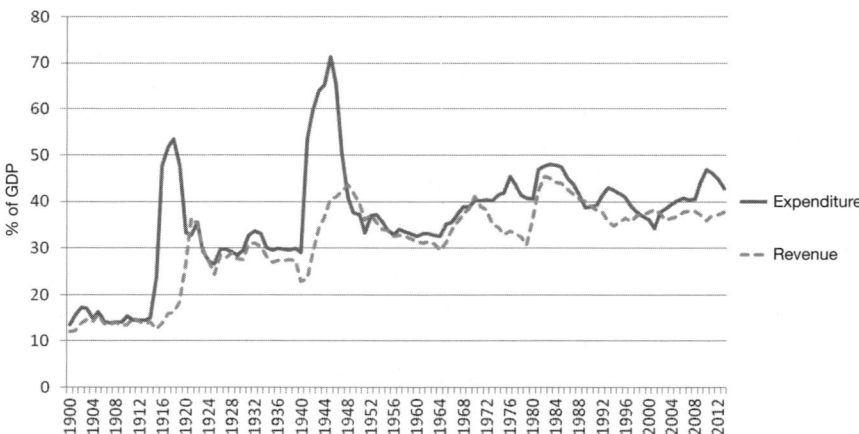

Figure 4.1. Total UK government expenditure and revenue as a percentage of GDP, 1900–2013. *Source:* 1900–80 based on Mitchell (1988), ch. 11, tables 4, 12, 13, 15, 16 and ch. 16; 1981–2012 based on the Public Finances Databank, 27 January 2014, Office for Budget Responsibility, UK.

Table 4.1. Episodes[a] of UK expenditure cutbacks and revenue increases, 1900–2013.

	Percentage point change as a ratio of GDP		Percentage change in constant prices 2008=100	
	Total over the episode	Average per year	Total over the episode	Average per year
Expenditure				
1919–21 post-WW I	−20.6	−6.9	−54.6	−18.1
1923–25 Geddes Axe	−9.0	−3.0	−16.3	−5.4
1933–35	−4.2	−1.4	−2.4	−0.8
1946–51 post-WW II	−38.0	−6.3	−50.5	−8.4
1954–56	−4.3	−1.4	−3.4	−1.2
1977–80	−4.8	−1.2	−5.0	−1.2
1984–89	−9.3	−1.6	+0.2	0.0
1994–2001	−8.8	−1.1	+6.4	+0.8
2011–13[b]	−4.2	−1.4	−6.3	−2.1
Revenue				
1916–21	23.8	3.9	114.5	19.1
1926	4.0	4.0	10.8	10.8
1931	3.3	3.3	6.4	6.4
1942–48	20.2	2.9	67.4	9.6
1965–70	11.6	1.9	60.2	10.0
1980–82	10.6	3.5	31.5	10.5

[a] 'Episodes' are here defined as sustained falls in expenditure or rises in revenue, where the average annual fall (or rise) as a ratio of GDP is no less than 1 percentage point of GDP. For more details see definition in Chapter 2 of this volume.

[b] This episode was ongoing at the time of writing.

Source: 1920–80 based on Mitchell (1988), chs 11 and 16; 1981–2010 based on the Public Finances Databank, 27 January 2014, Office for Budget Responsibility, UK.

between 1910 and 2010, and the largest of all if postwar cuts concentrated entirely on military demobilisation are excluded.

Given the two last-mentioned features of the Geddes cuts, those expenditure reductions had some sustained effect on debt-to-GDP levels. UK national debt as a ratio of GDP was 180 in 1923 and fell to 175 in 1926, thus meeting Alesina & Perotti's (1996) condition for a 'successful' contraction (namely if in the three years after the 'tight' year, the ratio of the primary deficit to GDP is on average at least 2 percentage points below its level in the tight year or, three years after the adjustment, the debt-to-GDP ratio falls to 5 percentage points below the level in the tight year).

These four distinctive features may help to explain why the Geddes Axe became a legend in British politics. The Geddes cuts came on top of deep postwar reductions in defence spending and the axe again fell sharply on defence (making cuts that had to be reversed at the end of the subsequent decade in the run-up to World War II). But what was different about the

Geddes cuts was that they fell heavily on civil spending as well, striking hard at an expansionary programme of postwar reconstruction, on which a coalition of Liberals, Conservatives and a few from the Labour Party campaigning together had won the so-called 'coupon' election of 1918. Prominent among those plans were a 'homes for heroes' social housing programme and plans for educational expansion, which included a scheme for compulsory part-time education between the ages of 14 and 18. The Geddes Axe arguably had the short-term political effect of helping to delay the break-up of the coalition government elected in 1918 for a few months or perhaps more (by delaying the point at which the restive Conservatives opted to leave the coalition, which they finally did in 1922, after a by-election victory by an Independent Conservative had indicated that the Conservatives could win power on their own). Its longer-term effects are more debatable, as will be shown later.

What was the Trigger for Reversing the Expansionary Policies of Postwar Reconstruction?

So what was the political trigger for this notable squeeze on spending, sharply braking the expansionary policies of post-World War I reconstruction? Severe economic problems coinciding with looming difficulties in financing short-term government debt and strongly entrenched beliefs in the Treasury that the only way to stabilise the economy was to return the currency to the gold standard, all seem to have played a part. But the proximate trigger seems to have been political and electoral, in the form of electoral challenges to the governing coalition.

An economic crisis developed as an inflationary boom immediately after World War I abruptly gave way to recession and mass unemployment. Having been only 2 per cent in 1920, unemployment doubled in the three months between December 1920 and March 1921 and rose to over two million in June 1921, reaching 11.3 per cent in that year—the third-highest unemployment rate recorded over the whole period 1920–2010.

With urgent political pressures for effort to revive trade and restore full employment, leading figures in the government saw public spending cuts rather than fiscal expansion as the necessary response. It must be recalled that this episode of fiscal squeeze took place before the days of Keynesian economics or modern ideas of structural adjustment and automatic stabilisers, as discussed in Chapters 1 and 2. Indeed, UK policy for financing government spending at that time followed the so-called 'McKenna Rule', which included a commitment to balance non-defence expenditure and revenue year by year (Daunton 2002; Nason and Vahey 2007). Indeed, on top of such prevailing attitudes and practices, spending cutbacks were seen as a way to reduce unemployment. The prime minister's private secretary, Thomas Jones, wrote, 'The first thought was of public economy' (Jones 1969: 124). David Lloyd George, the prime minister, said in a vote-of-confidence debate the following year that the international security problems created or left unresolved by the war had left countries 'over-burdened by taxation'. Moreover, Lloyd George declared in the same debate, the restoration of prewar international trade links was hampered by financial problems:

> But before trade can be fully restored you must be able to establish everywhere the convertibility of currency into gold or its equivalent ... In order to achieve that, one of the first considerations is to induce the nations to balance their budgets ... (HC Deb. 3 April 1922 Vol. 152 cc1885–996).

On top of such beliefs that the way to restore international trade was to restore the gold standard were difficulties in refinancing government debt (hugely inflated by war) in a recession. Overall government debt stood at some 150 per cent of GDP in 1921, and Andrew McDonald (1989: 654–5) points out that 'failure to reborrow the huge burden of short-term debt could at any time have overthrown the whole of the Treasury's strategy. In March 1921, the state not only had a floating debt of £1,275m, but nearly 14 per cent of its other internal debt was due to mature within the next three years.' So the Treasury had to keep interest rates high to be sure of re-borrowing the debt, which increased the pressure of debt interest on the budget, even with various privatisation measures in 1920–21 and 1921–22 to pay down specific debt obligations (McDonald ibid.). So in the short term the main focus of financial management had to be on conversion and re-borrowing of debt rather than debt redemption, particularly since payments on large debts to the USA incurred during World War I were due to start in 1922–23.

Such economic and financial problems, together with the then received ideas as to how to deal with them, were undoubtedly important background factors in prompting this severe squeeze on spending. But the immediate trigger for the Geddes Axe seems to have been political and electoral, in the form of a tax revolt. In 1921 a media-led campaign for cutting 'government waste' to enable taxes to be cut successfully challenged the coalition government in by-elections. The campaign mobilised a constituency for public spending reductions accompanied by tax cuts among financially 'squeezed' southern English middle-class voters on whom the coalition government (and particularly its members from the Conservative Party) depended for its re-election.

There was a political constituency to be mobilised for lower taxes and reduced spending, because taxes rose very sharply in the wartime period between 1913 and 1919, as shown by Figure 4.2. The standard rate of income tax rose fourfold over that time, to 30 per cent. And anyone living on a fixed income from investments would have seen a fall of approximately two-thirds in the purchasing power of their income over that period, together with a reduction in the value of their assets of about 30 per cent. Tax on profit had also risen sharply during the war, and remained high in the early 1920s. Immediately before World War I, in 1913, average tax on profit was around 5 per cent. During the war, to raise revenue, an Excess Profits Duty (EPD, a form of corporate tax) was introduced, with a tax rate on profits that rose from 13 to 26 per cent between 1916 and 1918. EPD was formally abolished in 1921, but replaced with taxes on profits that continued to be high, at 25 per cent in 1921 (Nason & Vahey 2012).

It was against that background that an 'Anti-Waste League' was set up by a powerful press baron, Lord Rothermere, in January 1921. Designed to appeal to middle-class voters who felt taxes were too high, the League won three by-elections against coalition Conservative candidates in southern England in 1921 and also had the effect of causing Liberal and Conservative candidates in other elections to declare themselves as 'Anti-Waste'. The first of those victories occurred in January 1921, when an Anti-Waste candidate (Sir Thomas Poison) defeated the Conservative coalition candidate by a large majority in a previously Conservative-held seat, and in June of that year the League won two other by-elections against Conservative Unionist candidates in Westminster St George's and Hertford (the latter had previously been held by an independent MP, but the Anti-Waste League candidate in the by-election won a large majority over the Conservative coalition candidate in a straight fight). The electoral losses and the continuing threat to their electoral

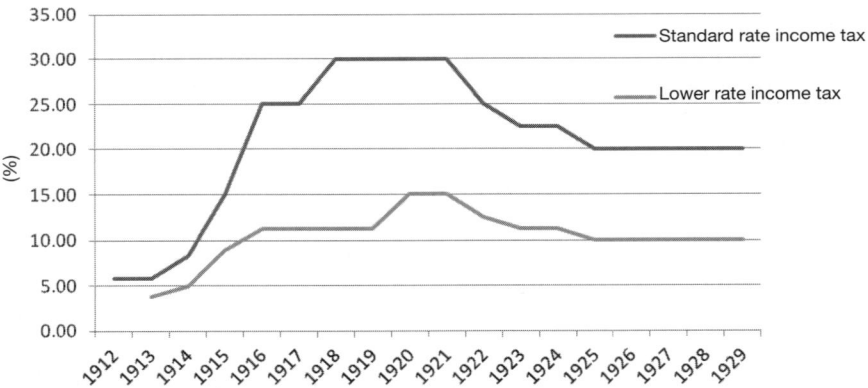

Figure 4.2. Standard and lower rates of UK income tax, 1912–29.
Source: Personal correspondence, Prof. Roger Middleton, Co-editor of British Historical Statistics Project, University of Bristol.

base posed by the Anti-Waste League in their southern English seats[1] dismayed the Conservatives (the biggest party in the coalition) and panicked the Liberal prime minister (David Lloyd George) into switching from the expansionary policy of postwar reconstruction into a policy of spending cuts and tax reductions designed to outflank the Anti-Waste League politically and keep the Conservatives in the coalition. It was that tax-revolt electoral threat that appears to have been the immediate trigger for the formation of the Geddes Committee.

That political panic among the prime minister and cabinet over electoral losses strengthened the hand of the Treasury, which already wanted to cut back public spending and indeed had been engaged in 'fiscal consolidation' measures under the previous Conservative Chancellor of the Exchequer (Austen Chamberlain, who was replaced by the Liberal Robert Horne in 1920). The Treasury's immediate reason for wanting to cut public spending was to make it easier to refinance the public debt, as mentioned above. Its longer-term reason was the aspiration among senior Treasury officials to harden the currency and go back to the prewar gold standard.

How Did the Process of Fiscal Squeeze Work and What Changes were Effected?

The distinctive institutional arrangement employed for cutting down government spending in response to these challenges was a five-person 'Committee on National Expenditure', comprising a group of prominent businessmen (the sexist term is appropriate here: they were all men) headed by the retiring minister of transport, Sir Eric Geddes.[2] This committee was appointed in August 1921, hard on the heels of the Conservative by-election losses in the previous month, as noted above. Its formation was announced by the prime minister, though the committee was to advise the Chancellor of the Exchequer.[3] The committee worked in stages, delivering reports to the government at monthly intervals between December 1921 and February 1922, which were considered in cabinet committees before being published in February 1922.

Sir Eric Geddes (1875–1937), the chair, was one of Lloyd George's close political confidants, having worked with him since his days as Minister for

---

[1] For example, challengers from the Anti-Waste League threatened Conservative candidates in what were considered to be safe seats for the party in the Westminster Abbey and Lewisham West by-elections in August and September 1921 respectively, leading to narrow Conservative wins in both cases.

[2] The others were Lord Inchcape, Lord Faringdon, Sir Joseph (later Lord) Maclay and Sir Guy Granet. All were senior business figures with close connections with government or politics.

[3] The title of the UK's finance minister.

Munitions in World War I, first as a special civil servant (one of the 'men of push and go' Lloyd George recruited from business in World War I) and later as a political colleague in the cabinet (see Stevenson 1971: 225). The formal brief of his committee was to make recommendations to the Chancellor of the Exchequer 'for effecting forthwith all possible reductions in the National Expenditure on Supply Services, having regard especially to the present and prospective position of the revenue'. The target it was set by the Chancellor of the Exchequer in 1921 was to find £100 million of savings from total supply expenditure for the fiscal year 1922–23, on top of £75 million already broadly agreed between the Treasury and spending departments as a result of a request by the Treasury to all departments in May 1921 for proposals for cutbacks in spending of the order of 15 per cent of total spending.

Much of this £75 million in 'savings' offered by departments arose from falls in prices and wages or the ending of special war-related spending. Indicating just how 'low-hanging' this fruit was, the Geddes Committee commented: 'The reductions in estimates shown in response to your [i.e. the Treasury's] circular are … by no means fully the result of curtailment of activity, or of economical administration, and this point cannot be too fully brought out' (Committee on National Expenditure 1921: 3). Total planned supply expenditure for 1921–22 was £603 million, and the committee was being asked to find over 15 per cent of cutbacks from total spending, in addition to more than 10 per cent already agreed. So what was being aimed at was a single-step reduction in government spending from 1921–22 to 1922–23 of more than 27 per cent.

Both the composition of the committee and its role as an external body imposed into the normal process of bilateral bargaining between the Treasury and the spending departments were controversial. Both of those issues are illustrated by a comment made by the prime minister's private secretary, Thomas Jones (1969: 166), in a diary entry for 2 August 1921:

> Luncheon with P.M., Horne, and Hankey [Cabinet Secretary]. Some talk of the Geddes Economy Committee. I pretended … to deprecate these departures from constitutional precedent and to hint that the business of the Chancellor was to be one. P.M. chaffed me that what I really objected to was the personnel—millionaires, and that I would prefer to entrust the country's finances to a committee of Webb, Tawney, Cole and Arthur Greenwood.[4]

The underlying political arrangement was that any proposals for changes of 'policy' had to be approved by cabinet committees. The committee apparently worked virtually full-time from the time of its appointment in mid-1921 to the spring of 1922. It issued a first interim report less than five months after it had

---

[4] Names of prominent Labour or socialist figures of that time.

been appointed, in December 1921, and two further reports in early 1922. In the event, it fell slightly short of its target of £100 million of extra cutback proposals, recommending reductions of £87 million, of which £52 million was finally accepted by the cabinet. Even so, those are remarkable reductions in historical perspective, amounting to about 20 per cent of central government spending, when the 'Geddes' cuts are put together with those agreed between government departments and the Treasury in the summer of 1921.

So how did that process work, and how did the Geddes Committee propose to cut back public spending by such a large amount? The committee's first interim report analysed what could practically be cut and what was beyond the reach of 'economy', at least in the short run. In the latter category it put debt charges, payments that could only be unwound by legislation (such as road-building grants), pension obligations and various politically sensitive financial commitments to war veterans and the bereaved (notably war graves and training and resettlement grants to war veterans). The committee therefore concluded that most of the cuts had to be concentrated on three main classes of spending, namely defence, operations in the Middle East arising from World War I (mainly Palestine and Iraq, which had become British mandates under the League of Nations after the fall of the Ottoman Empire), and those items of other civilian expenditure that were not obligations imposed by statute, which could only be changed by primary legislation (Committee on National Expenditure 1921: 164–8).

Turning to the distribution of proposed cuts across policy domains, out of the £87 million of extra cuts recommended by the committee, over half (nearly £53 million) came from defence and war pensions. Almost a quarter of those proposed cuts (£18 million) came from education spending. Of that £18 million, some £10 million was targeted on elementary education, to be achieved by replacing a matching grant system to local government by cash rationing; raising the school entry age from five to six; closing schools in London with fewer than 100 pupils; increasing class sizes from 32 to 50; reductions in teachers' salaries; and cuts in administration spending. The other £8 million of proposed education cuts were targeted at higher education (that is, education above 14, the statutory school-leaving age at that time), with proposals for substantial increases in tuition fees; limiting free places for lower-income pupils to 25 per cent of the total; ceasing direct grants from central government to schools and colleges (instead, all spending was to go through local authorities); scrapping measures for developing Technical Schools that had been provided for in the 1918 Education Act (which had raised the school leaving age to 14 in England and Wales and provided for an extension of compulsory part-time education from 14 to 18); and cutting grants to universities by some 20 per cent (Committee on National Expenditure 1921: 103–23).

The remaining quarter of Geddes' proposed cuts, of £17 million or so, was distributed in smaller packages around the other civil departments. The committee ended its final report by saying that the remaining £13.5 million of its original target of £100 million could readily be achieved as a result of naval disarmament agreements that would reduce naval shipbuilding costs, by further reductions in naval and military spending, and by the effect of prices falling faster than the 1922–23 spending estimates had assumed (ibid.: 165–70).

In the event, the planned cuts agreed by the cabinet included £75 million that had been agreed before the Geddes Reports came out and a further £52 million out of the £87 million suggested by the Geddes Report. And those planned cuts worth £127 million agreed by the cabinet were not only implemented but exceeded, with overall cuts in civil expenditure between 1922 and 1923 totalling no less than £162 million in nominal terms at the central government level, as shown in Table 4.2. The cuts implemented in civil expenditure were dominated by social security, education, health, and operations in the Middle East, while defence spending fell by £80 million.

As Table 4.2 shows, the initial cuts went even deeper than those nominal terms reductions suggest, because of the effect of prices falling between 1922 and 1923, which meant that the Geddes cuts were still more impressive in constant-price terms than in current-cash terms. And as the top half of Table 4.3 shows, certain categories of civil expenditure at central government level such as social security spending continued to fall in nominal terms between 1923 and 1924, as did defence expenditure. Spending on civil service salaries also fell sharply between 1922 and 1923. Cuts made in white-collar civil service employment between 1920 and 1931 had the effect of reducing the number of civil service employees by one-third. Since the jobs of ex-servicemen in the civil service were protected, the job cuts were largely achieved by dismissing temporary staff who had been recruited during World War I, most of whom were women.

Table 4.2.   UK spending cuts between 1922 and 1923: planned versus actual (£m).

	Defence	Education	Social security	Health	Foreign	Pay	Total
Cuts already planned							75
Geddes recommendations	53	18		16			87
Nominal cuts	79	15	13	12	20	6	162
Real cuts (1922 prices)	85	16	14	13	22	7	176

Sources: Author calculations based on Committee on National Expenditure (1921), (1922a), (1922b); Mitchell (1988), ch. 11, table 4. GDP deflator figures for UK used to calculate 1922 prices taken from L.H. Officer & S.H. Williamson, 'What was the UK GDP then?', Measuring Worth 2014, http://www.measuringworth.com/ukgap (accessed March 2014).

The lower half of Table 4.3 expresses the change in expenditure (of both central and local government) in percentage point terms, when expressed as a proportion of GDP. The last column indicates overall central and local government expenditure, including debt charges (which were around £300 million each year over the period). The preceding columns indicate spending in the major policy domains that saw the sharpest falls. As can be seen, during the 1923–25 period, the sharpest fall was in social security spending (nearly 2 percentage points lower than 1922 levels, reflecting cuts in some of the social, welfare and pension provision introduced in the previous decade), followed by defence spending which saw a sharp drop of 1.7 percentage points and education (0.5 percentage points). The strategy of concentrating on types of

Table 4.3. Actual outcomes for six categories of spending, UK 1921–26.

| Year | Defence | Debt charges | Civil expenditure[a] | | | | | Total civil | Total[b] overall |
			Social security	Health	Education	Consular	Salaries		
Nominal values: central government (£m)									
1921	292	340	110	72	59	5	18	478	1181
1922	190	320	96	73	65	32	17	465	1070
1923	111	320	83	61	50	12	11	303	812
1924	106	310	72	60	48	18	12	258	749
1925	115	310	71	65	49	7	9	245	751
1926	120	320	70	65	49	8	11	264	776
Percentage point fall between years: general government[c]									
1921–22	−1.5	0.4	1.3	0.2	0.7	0.6	0	0.8	2.8
1922–23	−1.6	0.3	−1.2	−0.2	−0.3	−0.4	−0.1	−3.2	−6.1
1923–24	−0.1	−0.3	−0.8	−0.1	−0.1	0.1	0	−1.1	−2.3
1924–25	0.1	−0.3	0.1	0.0	−0.1	−0.3	−0.1	−0.6	−0.5
1925–26	0.2	0.6	0.9	0.1	0.3	0.0	0.1	0.7	3.2
Total fall 1923–25	−1.7	−0.3	−1.8	−0.3	−0.5	−0.5	−0.2	−4.9	−9.0

[a] In the top half of the table, civil expenditure at central government level comprised the sub-categories shown, plus works and buildings, law and justice, trade, industry and roads. In the bottom half, civil expenditure includes all central government expenditure (apart from debt charges, defence and costs of tax collection) and all local government expenditure.
[b] In the top half of the table total overall expenditure includes debt charges, civil expenditure, defence expenditure and costs of central government tax collection. In the bottom half, total overall expenditure comprises all of the above and where applicable spending at both local and central government levels.
[c] The percentage point fall is calculated as the difference between two years of the ratio of nominal expenditure as a percentage of GDP. For example, the percentage point fall in total expenditure between 1921 and 1922 (expressed as 1921–22 in column 1) is calculated thus:

$$\frac{expenditure_{1922}}{GDP_{1922}} \times 100 \quad - \quad \frac{expenditure_{1921}}{GDP_{1921}} \times 100$$

Source: Mitchell (1983), ch. 11, table 4 for central government and tables 12, 13, 15 and 16 for local authority expenditure; GDP data taken from ch. 16, table 5.

spending that could be cut without heavy-duty legislative changes meant the axe initially fell onto capital as well as current spending, but capital spending was restored relatively quickly, no doubt reflecting pressures to stimulate economic growth to counter mass unemployment.

Excluding debt charges, total expenditure fell by about 9 per cent of GDP over this period, and of these cuts, 7 percentage points were due to cuts at the central government level while 2 percentage points were at the local government level. Within the constraints applying to the Geddes Committee, as noted earlier, the cuts in central government spending were spread fairly widely across policy domains, whereas at local government level, by far the sharpest reduction was in housing expenditure. At that time, central government transfers to local government amounted to about 6 to 10 per cent of central government expenditure (compared to roughly 20 per cent today), and 2 per cent of GDP (compared to roughly 9 per cent today). These transfers fell by 0.5 per cent as a proportion of GDP over 1923–25, a fall similar to the reductions in several other categories of central government expenditure such as colonial and consular expenses. Thus, in sharp contrast to spending cuts in other periods in the UK and in some of the other country cases in this volume where 'unfunded mandates' to lower levels of government were a key feature of fiscal squeeze, the Geddes cuts did not fall more heavily on local than on central expenditure.

Within the political process that this remarkable squeeze on public spending involved, the main opposition to the Geddes recommendations seems to have come from the education departments and the Admiralty. The latter issued what a senior Treasury civil servant (P.J. Grigg) described as 'a flaming attack' on the Geddes proposals for cuts in naval spending, probably egged on by Winston Churchill (then Colonial Secretary), who had chaired the cabinet committee that considered the proposals for defence cuts (Grigg 1948: 77). As far as the proposed cuts in education were concerned, a letter from Sir Rupert Howarth of the Cabinet Office to Thomas Jones on 12 January 1922 about the consideration of the Geddes proposals by a cabinet committee chaired by Austen Chamberlain (the Conservative leader within the coalition government) indicates the political friction the Geddes proposals had caused:

> As things have turned out there is very little trouble from the Civil Departments other than the Board of Education. The Ministry of Health will bring their Estimates down to the Geddes figure, accepting in the main the Geddes proposals ... The Ministry of Labour also acquiesce in the recommendations of the Geddes Committee in so far, of course, as those recommendations consist in referring the various highly contentious questions to expert Committees for examination ...

> The Board of Education problem stands on quite a different footing. In reply
> to the Geddes cut of … £18 millions in all, Mr. Fisher[5] offers for England and
> Wales a cut of about £2½ millions for 1922–23 and some comparatively
> insignificant reductions in subsequent years. The whole difficulty boils down to
> the question of teaching cost and any very large economies can only be realised
> either by reducing the number of teachers or reducing the pay of teachers or by
> a combination of the two methods. It is strongly represented that to throw a
> large number of teachers on to the unemployment market would be politically
> a blunder and morally a crime. On the other hand the teachers say that their pay
> should not be reduced unless the pay of other Government servants is also
> correspondingly reduced … (Jones 1969: 191–2)

In response to this opposition, the prime minister agreed to drop the
Geddes proposals for cuts in teachers' pay and it was apparently understood
that Herbert Fisher would not publicly advocate larger classes but would try
to reduce numbers of teachers in the more heavily staffed districts by between
4,000 and 6,000, and could expect the suspended provisions of his 1918
Education Act to be reintroduced in better economic circumstances (ibid.:
192). In the event, less than one-third of the Geddes proposals for £18 million
cuts in the education budget were realised (see Peden 2000: 169).

The Board of Education was not alone in resisting the cuts. An example
of some of the other resistance within government was a mighty battle
between the Treasury and the British Museum, which although not a 'big
ticket' item in total public expenditure, absorbed roughly half the total public
funding going to museums and galleries at that time. The Geddes Committee
wished to avoid cutting the 'purchase grant' (that is, the budget for acquisitions)
and so proposed that admission fees should be charged at the Museum on
four days each week, with three 'free days' and free passes for bona fide students (Committee on National Expenditure 1922b: 89). The idea had come
from Treasury observation of what other museums and galleries were doing
and the Treasury was trying to make it a general rule for all museums and
galleries, arguing that the only alternative to admission fees was to cut grant
funding. If the British Museum successfully resisted this policy, the Treasury
feared it would not be able to hold the line with the other museums and
galleries.

But that was just what the British Museum did do, in a long-drawn-out
war of attrition which it eventually won. Its Director, Sir Frederick Kenyon,
resisted the plan on two grounds. One was to claim that primary legislation
would be needed to make the change, since the 1753 Act under which the

---

[5] Herbert A.L. Fisher, (Liberal) President of the Board of Education for England and Wales,
who had been the architect of the 1918 'Fisher' Education Act, many of the provisions of which
were suspended by the cutbacks.

British Museum Trustees operated required them to give 'free access to all studious and curious persons'. Argument about that issue went on for a year, after which the Treasury Solicitor concluded (in March 1923) that legislation would be needed to alter the requirements of the 1753 Act, whereas legislation was not needed for other museums and galleries to impose admission fees. Kenyon's other line of defence was to argue that the fees policy would be inherently damaging:

> The Trustees ... strongly deprecate the imposition of a fee for admission on four days in the week, as suggested. They consider that it would seriously restrict the service which the Museum renders to national education and culture, and that the restriction would operate mainly at the cost of the poorer classes. They think it would be most regrettable to break the tradition of over a hundred and sixty years' free service to the education and intellectual refreshment of the people, for the sake of so small a sum as is estimated to be received from the change (letter 16.3.1922, Treasury File T160, National Archives).

The Treasury resisted such arguments and put a clause empowering the British Museum's Trustees to make regulations imposing charges for admission into an omnibus Fees (Increase) Bill the following year, introduced by the then Conservative Chancellor of the Exchequer (Stanley Baldwin). But the Treasury lost even that fight. There was a vigorous debate at the second reading stage of the bill (7 March 1923), a hard-fought battle in the Standing Committee when the clause (no. 9) relevant to the British Museum was approved by a single vote (20 March), only for the clause to be withdrawn two days later at the report stage (a late stage in the legislation) after it was revealed that to realise extra revenue of some £6,000 per year, the necessary turnstiles would cost about £500 to install and at least one more person would probably need to be employed to collect the fees.

That saga was only one of the many battles that followed from the Geddes Report, even after the cabinet committees had watered down the Geddes proposals (for example, accepting only £16 million of Geddes proposals for a cut of £21 million in naval spending, £10 million out of the proposals for £20 million cuts in army expenditure, £2.5 million out of the proposals for £5 million cuts in air force spending, and £11.7 million out of Geddes proposals for £22.7 million cuts in social services spending (Higgs 1922: 257)). But the cuts sufficed to deliver the tax reductions that the government thought it needed to outflank the Anti-Waste League. So in his May 1922 budget the Liberal Chancellor of the Exchequer duly announced a cut of income tax rates by approximately one-sixteenth (to take effect in 1923), cuts of about one-third in some politically salient indirect taxes (notably those on tea, coffee, cocoa and chicory) and cuts in postal and telephone charges. The Liberal–Conservative government accordingly survived until October of that year, when in the course of another political crisis (the Chanak crisis[6]) Conservative MPs led by Stanley Baldwin overwhelmingly voted to pull out of the coalition, rejecting the views of their leader, Austen Chamberlain.

What were the Economic, Social and Political Consequences of Fiscal Squeeze in the Short, Medium and Long Term?

Andrew McDonald (1989: 651) sees the Geddes Committee as a case of 'the politics of gesture', designed to send public and political signals for short-term political benefit. H.A.L. Fisher, the President of the Board of Education (for England and Wales) also saw the Geddes Committee as 'a sop to anti-waste' (in his diary entry for 2 August 1921, quoted in Kinnear 1973: 24). We have suggested that it was the electoral threat to the coalition government (and particularly to the Conservatives) in 1921 that triggered the Geddes Axe to outflank the Anti-Waste League and pave the way for tax cuts. It can be argued that the Geddes Axe was more than a 'gesture' or 'sop', but its long-term effects are surprisingly elusive, even nearly a century after the event.

As we have seen, the Geddes Committee's specific proposals for cutbacks were considerably watered down in cabinet (even though the sum of the cuts eventually achieved exceeded what Geddes proposed), and many of the Committee's more radical proposals for cutbacks did not survive the political process in 1921–22. For example, its recommendation for a unified Ministry of Defence (Committee on National Expenditure 1921: 8) did not come about until 1964. Its proposals for dismantling national public sector pay agreements (McDonald 1989: 673), for example in the police, where standardised rates of pay throughout Great Britain had been introduced in 1919, and for radically altering the financing of the national health insurance system by pushing most of the funding onto private or independent insurers, have never been implemented. Over ninety years later these items still present significant political challenges to would-be budget-cutters.

In the medium term, the Geddes Committee was in some ways the model for the identically named Committee on National Expenditure appointed a decade later by the Labour Chancellor of the Exchequer (Philip Snowden) in a deep financial crisis in 1931 and chaired by Sir George May, with nominees from each of the three political parties. But the outcome of the May Committee was quite different. In contrast to the Geddes Committee, the

---

[6] When Lloyd George (in the absence of the Conservative Foreign Secretary, Lord Curzon) threatened to declare war on Turkey as Turkish troops advanced on the Dardanelles neutral zone then guarded by British and French troops.

May Committee split on party lines, with the Labour minority calling for a mixture of wage cuts and higher taxes on investors, and the Conservative and Liberal majority arguing that fiscal squeeze should concentrate on spending cuts, in particular on public services and rates of unemployment benefit. That issue split the Labour cabinet and led in August 1931 to the formation of a National Coalition government led by the Labour leader, causing a long split in the Labour Party. Moreover, even with cuts in unemployment benefit, public spending was cut by much less in the early 1930s than it had been a decade earlier, as is shown in Figure 4.1 and Table 4.1 above.

As shown earlier, clear losers from the Geddes Axe included those in the defence world, recipients of social security, housing subsidies and welfare spending, and women in the civil service. The losers also included those who would have benefited from the 1918 (and 1921) plan to extend post-14 technical education and some of the other measures envisaged by those Acts.

Indeed, in addition to creating individual losers, it could be argued that the suspension of the 1918 Education Act's provisions for 14–18 technical education had a broader social effect in contributing to a decline in British performance relative to competitor countries in continental Europe (particularly Germany) and thus exacerbated a long-term weakness in UK economic competitiveness. But such claims are difficult to assess. Some, such as Barnard (1947: 274), see the Geddes cuts as the main obstacle to the implementation of those plans, but others have offered different interpretations. For instance, Curtis (1948: 246 and 251–7) argued that important factors other than funding hampered the development of technical education, such as resistance by employers and the lack of trained teachers. Moreover, even after the attempt to resume the 1918 plans for technical education by the UK's first Labour government during its brief period of power in 1924, a 1926 report (the Hadow Report) expressed concern that parents and teachers tended to regard technical education as inferior to academic education of the kind provided by grammar schools. Even after such technical education was eventually reintroduced formally in the UK in the 1944 Education Act, such cultural concerns remained (and indeed are often said to continue to this day). The impact of the Geddes Axe on post-14 education (relative to those other cultural and logistical factors) may therefore not be as clear-cut as it might at first appear.

Could there also have been a medium- or long-term collective loss created by the Geddes cuts, in the sense that cutting government spending during a recession—the exact opposite of the now conventional Keynesian remedy for counter-cyclical fiscal policy—probably exacerbated the unemployment that 'retrenchment' was supposed to mitigate? It does seem likely that the Geddes Axe exacerbated the UK's sluggish economic performance at that time, although it has been argued (for instance by Temin 1976 and Eichengreen

1992) that it was the overvalued exchange rate which the Geddes Axe helped to prop up, together with contractionary monetary shocks, that were the strongest influences on the UK's poor economic performance in the 1920s. It might also be argued that the strategy of tax cuts the Geddes Axe was intended to facilitate, instead of going too far, did not go far enough. While income tax rates were cut to please middle-class voters, as shown in Figure 4.2 above, there were no commensurate reductions on taxes on profits, such as the corporate tax. Nason & Vahey (2007) show that tax on profit, which had increased sharply during World War I, remained higher than average taxes on labour or consumption after the war. They argue that these levies are likely to have had a negative impact on investment, growth, economic performance and unemployment during the interwar period, suggesting that the tax-cutting medicine associated with the Geddes cuts may have been insufficiently rather than excessively applied.

The long-term military effects of the Geddes Axe are hard to assess as well. From the late 1930s it has often been claimed that 'Treasury tight-fistedness' and the restraint on defence spending by successive governments in the interwar years left the UK militarily unprepared for war with a rearmed Nazi Germany in 1939. It has been said that a lack of up-to-date equipment and materiel contributed to military failures in the early years of World War II, such that the British army was defeated in France and the UK itself only narrowly avoided defeat and invasion (see, for example, Wheeler-Bennett 1948; Barnett 1970). But to the extent that such well-known claims are true, it could be argued that the real problem lay not so much in the Geddes cuts of the early 1920s as in the continuation of spending restraint into the years between 1933 and 1938 (when Germany spent three times as much on defence as the UK, overtaking the UK as an air power in the mid-1930s (see Peden 1979: 7)). After all, the advice given to the Geddes Committee (reflecting a cabinet decision of 1919) that the UK would not be involved in any great war over the following ten years proved to be prescient and accurate, was still being upheld by Winston Churchill as Chancellor of the Exchequer in 1928, and was only officially abandoned in 1932 after Japan's invasion of Manchuria (Peden ibid.).

So if there was an unpreparedness problem that left the UK as a state perilously close to defeat and occupation in the late 1930s, it might more plausibly be attributed to the Treasury's continuing insistence on matching defence spending to the country's economic and financial resources after the 'ten-year rule' was abandoned in 1932 than to the Geddes cuts of the early and mid-1920s. Moreover, it seems at least doubtful whether retaining more World War I military technology and establishments would have helped either to deter or defeat Germany's military rearmament efforts of the 1930s. The more plausible charge against Geddes would thus be of initiating a mindset towards military spending that went on too long, and of leading to a situation in which by 1933 (when German rearmament began in earnest) the British army had little post-1918 equipment, the air force was only the fifth among the world's air powers, and though the navy remained the largest in the world up to World War II, many of its ships were obsolete as a result of spending restraints which precluded building up to the limits allowed by international arms-limitation treaties at that time (Peden 1979: 5–6). But even then, a more vigorous reversal of the Geddes policy after 1932 could arguably have made the UK more adequately prepared for war in 1939.[7]

Finally, what of the party political effects of these major spending cuts? Were the incumbent parties punished by voters at the polls, in line with the retrospective voting ideas discussed in Chapter 1? Answering that question is trickier than it might seem, for two reasons. First, identifying 'incumbents' is complicated, because in this case the cuts were originally approved by a coalition government consisting of part of the Liberal Party and most of the Conservatives, then implemented mainly by Conservatives (with a brief period of minority Labour government in 1924). So is it the 'incumbents' who originated the cuts programme that are to count, or the 'incumbents' who implemented it, and if it is the first, which parties in a coalition government are to be counted? Second, as we have shown, this is a case of an expenditure-only fiscal squeeze, where deep cuts in public spending were matched by tax cuts and falls in revenue. Therefore, retrospectively minded voters faced the choice of whether to punish incumbents for spending cuts or to reward them for tax cuts, and it is plausible to argue that punishment for spending cuts might apply more to Liberal than Conservative incumbents, while reward for tax cuts might apply more to the latter.

Table 4.4 summarises the fate of the parties in UK general elections from 1922 to 1924, and shows that the 1922 election outcome precisely fits that expectation. The part of the Liberal Party that had been in the coalition government (then called the National Liberals, under David Lloyd George) did indeed suffer electoral punishment and the prime minister himself lost his seat, while the part of the Liberal Party that not been in the government did not, and the Conservatives do seem to have been rewarded. After that election, most of the Liberals re-formed into a single party under a different leader and the reunited party fared better in the subsequent election, only to suffer a catastrophic decline in its vote after it precipitated the fall of the first

---

[7] Much less examined than the issue of military preparedness for World War II is the possible effect of the heavy cuts effected by the Geddes Axe on spending in Iraq and particularly Palestine, where the absence of effective policing in the 1920s may well have played a contributory part in the rise of Zionism, and all the long-term consequences flowing from that. We are indebted to Jeremy Thomas for making this point at the British Academy conference at which this paper was first presented.

Table 4.4.   UK general election results 1922–24.

Date and parties competing (incumbents italic)	Seats	Share of total vote	Change in number of seats	Change in share of votes (%)	Incumbent prime minister
1922					
Conservative	*345*	*38.2*	*+10*	*+5.6*	
National Liberals	*62*	*11.6*	*−71*	*−2.0*	*David Lloyd George*
Liberal	54	17.5	+26	+5.4	
Labour	142	29.5	+79	+7.3	
Others	12	3.2	+2	−2.1	
1923					
Conservative	*258*	*38.1*	*−87*	*−0.1*	*Stanley Baldwin*
Liberal	159	29.6	+105	+12.1	
Labour	191	30.5	+79	+7.3	
Others	7	1.8	−5	−1.4	
1924					
Conservative	419	51.9	+161	+13.8	
Liberal	40	30.9	−119	+1.3	
Labour	*151*	*38.2*	*−40*	*+7.7*	*Ramsay MacDonald*
Others	4	0.8	−5	−1.0	

Source: Butler & Butler (2010), ch. 4.

Labour government in 1924. It thus seems plausible to argue that the 1922 election fits the blame hypothesis set out in Chapter 1 and that the biggest long-term political loser from the Geddes Axe was the Liberal Party, which was thereafter out of government at central level (other than as a minor partner in the 1931 National Government and the World War II coalition) until 2010.

In short, the messy party political picture that applied to the UK in the 1920s may have made blame attribution by the voters more difficult than the UK's common stereotype as a two-party majoritarian system might suggest, and in this case the spending cuts were accompanied by tax cuts which the 1921 victories of the Anti-Waste League had shown to matter to key voters in the south of England. Given that both punishment for spending cuts and reward for tax cuts were at stake in the 1922 election, it is consistent with the retrospective voting hypothesis that the party that was more likely to be rewarded for tax cuts (the Conservatives) was not obviously punished by voters for its role in the Geddes Axe, at least until those cuts had begun to bite, while the party that was more likely to be punished for spending cuts (the National Liberals) was the main short-term loser after the Geddes Axe, and the Liberal Party as a whole seems to have been the main long-term loser.

Almost a century after the Geddes Axe, it remains an important case of 'fiscal squeeze' (specifically in the form of major spending cuts) both in the UK and internationally. But its long-term effects remain elusive.

References

Alesina, A. & Perotti, R. (1996), *Fiscal Adjustments in OECD Countries: Composition and Macroeconomic Effects*, NBER Working Paper 5730 (Cambridge MA, National Bureau of Economic Research).

Barnard, H.C. (1947), *A Short History of English Education, 1760–1944* (London, University of London Press).

Barnett, C. (1970), *Britain and her Army, 1509–1970: A Military, Political and Social Survey* (London, Allen Lane).

Butler, D. & Butler, G. (2010), *British Political Facts, 1900–1985* (Basingstoke, Macmillan).

Committee on National Expenditure (1921), *First Interim Report of Committee on National Expenditure*, Cmd 1581 (London, HMSO).

Committee on National Expenditure (1922a), *Second Interim Report of Committee on National Expenditure*, Cmd 1582 (London, HMSO).

Committee on National Expenditure (1922b), *Third Report of Committee on National Expenditure*, Cmd 1589 (London, HMSO).

Curtis, S.J. (1948), *History of Education in Great Britain* (London, University of London Press).

Daunton, M. (2002), *The Politics of Taxation in Britain, 1914–1979* (Cambridge, Cambridge University Press).

Eichengreen, B. (1992), *Golden Fetters: The Gold Standard and the Great Depression 1919–1939* (New York, Oxford University Press).

Grigg, P.J. (1948), *Prejudice and Judgement* (London, Jonathan Cape).

Higgs, H. (1922), 'The Geddes Reports and the Budget', *Economic Journal*, 32(126): 251–64.

Jones, T.J. (1969), *Whitehall Diary*, ed. K. Morgan, i (1916–1925) (London, Oxford University Press).

Kinnear, M. (1973), *The Fall of Lloyd George* (London, Macmillan).

McDonald, A. (1989), 'The Geddes Committee and the Formulation of Public Expenditure Policy, 1921–22', *The Historical Journal*, 32(2): 643–74.

Mitchell, B.R. (1988), *British Historical Statistics* (Cambridge, Cambridge University Press).

Nason, J.M. & Vahey, S.P. (2007), 'The McKenna Rule and UK World War I Finance', *American Economic Review*, 97(2): 290–4.

Nason, J.M. & Vahey, S.P. (2012), 'UK World War I and Interwar Data for Business Cycle and Growth Analysis', *Cliometrica*, 6(2): 115–42.

Peden, G. (1979), *British Rearmament and the Treasury: 1932–1939* (Edinburgh, Scottish Academic Press).

Peden, G. (2000), *The Treasury and British Public Policy 1906–1959* (Oxford, Oxford University Press).

Stevenson, F. (1971), *Lloyd George: A Diary*, ed. A.J.P. Taylor (London, Harper & Row).

Temin, P. (1976), *Did Monetary Forces Cause the Great Depression?* (New York, W.W. Norton).

Wheeler-Bennett, Sir J. (1948), *Munich: Prologue to Tragedy* (London, Macmillan).

5

Carpe Diem! New Zealand's Fiscal Squeeze, 1990–1993: Economic Problems, Welfare Reform and Political Consequences

ROBERT GREGORY AND CHRIS EICHBAUM

The Lead-Up

New Zealand's fourth Labour government was elected to office in July 1984 after a snap election called by the National Party prime minister, Sir Robert Muldoon. Since coming to office in 1975, Muldoon—as both prime minister and minister of finance—had presided over rising 'stagflation' and burgeoning fiscal deficits, before in 1982 instituting a full wages and prices freeze. Although the new Labour government faced a fiscal deficit of 9 per cent of GDP, New Zealand was in no danger of defaulting on its growing overseas debt, and no 'bailout' from the International Monetary Fund was sought. Instead, led by prime minister David Lange, and finance minister Roger Douglas, the government devalued the New Zealand dollar by 20 per cent, before floating it, deregulated the finance sector, and abolished foreign exchange controls. It rapidly withdrew agricultural subsidies, and progressively removed import protections for the manufacturing sector. To help overcome the fiscal deficit, the government lowered the marginal rates on personal income tax, from 66 per cent progressively to 33 per cent, while introducing a 10 per cent goods and services tax (GST), raising this to 12.5 per cent in 1989. All these policies were collectively and eponymously labelled 'Rogernomics'.

The government imposed on income earners receiving the universal national superannuation a surtax of 20 per cent on other taxable income over a low threshold. Unemployment doubled under the Labour government, to 7.5 per cent by mid-1989, and the average period of unemployment increased threefold, with most new jobs being part-time ones. The introduction of the Public Finance Act 1989 (PFA) saw New Zealand become the first government

Proceedings of the British Academy, **197**, 93–114. © The British Academy 2014.

to move from cash to accrual accounting, using generally accepted accounting practice (GAAP).

In keeping with the general growth of the economy, the fiscal deficit dropped to a more sustainable level of just under 2 per cent in 1987–88. Net government expenditure as a percentage of GDP rose from just on 36 per cent in 1984–85 to more than 39 per cent five years later.

The government overwhelmingly won re-election in August 1987. However, following months of highly publicised political in-fighting between Lange and Douglas in the late 1980s, the Labour Party suffered its heaviest electoral defeat since first winning office in 1935. It lost 27 seats from its 1987 parliamentary majority, in a 13 per cent electoral swing against it in the 1990 election. The National Party, led by 55-year-old Jim Bolger, swept into power with 48 per cent of the vote and 67 seats in the 97-seat parliament—its highest ever number of seats, either in absolute or percentage terms.

The National Party campaigned on a platform promising a 'Decent Society' to repair the damage that it claimed 'Rogernomics' had been inflicting on New Zealand society.

Reforming the Welfare State

The day after winning the election, Bolger met with Treasury officials, who revealed to him what he later described as an 'unmitigated mess of extraordinary proportions', and a 'massive poisoned chalice' for the new government (Radio New Zealand 2013). As a result of underperforming loans following the global share market crash of October 1987, the country's largest commercial bank, the Bank of New Zealand (BNZ), had been bailed out by the Labour government in 1989 with a $610 million recapitalisation (Hunt 2009). The new government found that it had to substantially extend this rescue process, and was also informed that the $89 million fiscal surplus forecast in the Labour government's 1990 budget had instead turned out to be a $3.3 billion deficit of 3.5 per cent of GDP, forecast to balloon out to 4.8 per cent of GDP for 1991–92, and to 6.3 per cent of GDP for 1992–93. In this New Zealand case, therefore, the ensuing fiscal squeeze stemmed from a mix of exogenous and endogenous factors.[1]

The political opportunities thrown up by the BNZ crisis were not lost on the new minister of finance, the first woman in New Zealand to hold the job,

---

[1] The fiscal blowout resulted from the rapidly deepening recession in the months following the Labour government's budget in July 1990. Moreover, spending decisions taken by the cabinet since this budget had been built into the baselines for departmental allocations, meaning higher aggregate spending in both the current and future years (McKinnon 2003: 348).

40-year-old Ruth Richardson. She later observed that the BNZ rescue package 'added to the sense of crisis that enveloped the early weeks of our government, which could only add impetus to my agenda. The episode was also excellent propaganda value for the government. As Roger Douglas knew only too well, a crisis inherited from your predecessor can give you a flying start in terms of impetus and goodwill' (Richardson 1995: 76).

Before entering parliament in 1981, Richardson had been a lawyer in the department of justice and the peak lobby organisation Federated Farmers. As the opposition's finance spokesperson, she had been a strong supporter of the radical economic policies adopted by the Lange government, and had developed firm libertarian instincts. These were largely in keeping with a strong political mood of the times in Anglophone democracies. The then secretary to the Treasury, Graham Scott, later described her as 'really the only genuinely ideological Minister of Finance I worked for' (McKinnon 2003: 349). On the other hand, incoming prime minister Bolger—a sheep and cattle farmer before entering parliament in 1972—was much more pragmatically centrist in his politics.

At the core of Richardson's ideology was the belief that the welfare state had become too much of an economic burden, and that it should be radically revamped, in order to foster greater individual responsibility and less reliance on the state. She saw herself as being on 'a moral mission' (James 2007). Little in the fiscal situation she faced in 1990–91 demanded that she use social welfare reform as the main lever of fiscal management, and indeed the previous government had resisted taking this path.

Richardson immediately flew to New York, where she persuaded Standard & Poor's to give New Zealand a single downgrade rather than the double one which the rating agency had intended. In this endeavour she may have been assisted by the fact that the deficit as a proportion of GDP was actually no worse, and a great deal better, than those that preceding New Zealand governments had been running in the early to mid-1980s (see Figure 5.1).

Whatever the case, it clearly suited the government's political purposes to depict the fiscal position as a crisis. Thus, in an 'Economic and Social Initiative' (ESI), announced to parliament on 19 December 1990, Bolger and Richardson recast the new government's programme as one of desperate urgency. Some key election commitments—including the popular promise to remove the sur-tax on national superannuation—would not now be kept. In Richardson's words, 'Keeping our promises would make our fiscal task even harder. Failing to keep our promises would cause huge political fallout. The scene was set for the loss of moral authority that would dog the government for the whole of its first term in office' (Richardson 1995: 79).

Welfare spending would bear the brunt of expenditure cuts, by reducing the level of some benefits, the complete abolition of others, and the tightening

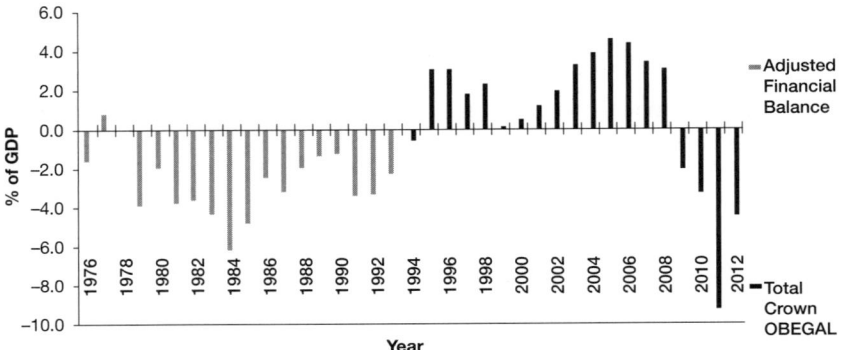

Figure 5.1. Core government surplus and deficit as a percentage of GDP, New Zealand 1976–2012.
Note: The graph uses two different series because of changes in government accounting practices from 1994. OBEGAL is the Operating Balance of Expenditure Before Gains and Losses. Adjusted Financial Balance is the financial balance without non-forecast items and extraordinary receipts.
Source: New Zealand Treasury (2012) Fiscal Time Series: Historical Fiscal Indicators 1972–2012. Year End 2012 Update, http://www.treasury.govt.nz/government/data

of eligibility requirements. Targeting would replace universality, and incentives to work would be produced by reductions in social spending replacement rates. Income support entitlements would be cut back by between 2.9 per cent and 24.7 per cent from 1 April 1991, in order to save $1.275 billion or about 1.7 per cent of GDP in transfer payments in the new government's first fiscal year. The effect of these cuts was worsened by the government's decision to abandon its election promise to increase the rates by 4.9 per cent to help offset consumer inflation. In addition, significant expenditure reductions were also made in health and education, and in housing assistance.

The ESI also presaged the end of a long-standing system of industrial conciliation and arbitration. The National government's subsequent Employment Contracts Act 1991 (ECA) abolished collective bargaining, and greatly weakened the trade union movement (Walsh & Brosnan 1999). The inevitable logic—particularly at the margins of the labour market—would see wages fall and conditions of employment deteriorate.

On 30 July 1991, Ruth Richardson became the first woman anywhere in the Western world to present a budget, which she had impulsively heralded as the 'Mother of All Budgets'.[2] In delivering it, she argued that its strategic aim

---

[2] This was a word play on Saddam Hussein's contemporary 'Mother of All Battles'. Bolger greatly regretted this appellation, fed to Richardson by a journalist: 'the term … became one of extreme derision. All the PR coaching and colourful packaging [of the budget] was thus destroyed by a single throwaway line' (Bolger 1998: 116).

was 'to transform New Zealand from a declining, debt-ridden country into a dynamic, enterprising and prosperous nation'. She lamented 'decades of chronic overspending by the state', proclaiming that 'The redesign of the welfare state is integral to our strategy for growth ... The only sustainable welfare state is one that is fair and affordable. Our current system is neither' (New Zealand Parliamentary Debates, 517, 1991: 3254–3255).

At this time the level of New Zealand's public expenditure as a proportion of GDP was about 40 per cent, broadly in line with the OECD average, and much less than in other welfare states like Denmark and Norway. Nor were the country's benefit levels high by international standards (Stephens 1999). As Blyth (2013: 211) observes, 'Mere facts will (sometimes) not be allowed to get in the way of a good ideology.' So Richardson's budget, together with the ESI, reduced the disposable incomes of most beneficiaries, in some cases by up to 30 per cent. They provided the foundation for what Boston (1999: 4) described as 'the most radical social policy changes in 60 years'. According to Richardson (1995: 87), 'To me, the role of government was not to redistribute income, but to provide a guaranteed minimum of income and services for those unable to look after themselves.'

The ESI and the 1991 budget thus introduced a major shift in the targeting of healthcare services, tertiary education student funding, and welfare benefits. It promoted a strategic move from welfare to 'workfare', with up to six-month stand-down periods for unemployed people seeking a benefit. A long-standing universal family benefit was abolished, subsidies for consultations with doctors were cut, and charges for medical prescriptions were increased threefold. State housing rentals were to be raised to market levels in three annual increments, partly compensated for by a cash supplement for low-income families.

As had been promised during the National Party's election campaign, income tax was not raised, but those on higher incomes were required to pay more for their health services. In preparing the departmental estimates, a total of $600 million—close to the cost of the BNZ bailout—was to be saved by allowing no compensation for increases in departmental input costs, by requiring all new policy initiatives to be funded by reallocating resources from within departmental budgets, and by cuts offered up by departments.

The 1991 budget not only kept the superannuation surtax in place but it also subjected the universal pension to income testing, with a 'free zone' of $80 per week and an effective marginal tax rate of 93 per cent. The subsequent political outcry from the growing numbers of well-off people over the age of 60 induced the government to reconsider its position, in what has been called a 'less than edifying demonstration of policy-making' (McKinnon 2003: 355). Consequently, it raised the surtax from 20 to 25 cents in the dollar, taking effect from 1 April 1992. In addition, the surtax now cut in at a substantially lower level of earnings, superannuation inflation adjustments were deferred for two years, and the age of eligibility for national super-annuation was to be increased progressively over 10 years from 60 to 65. Those aged between 60 and 64 who were unemployed or without other income were required to live on the unemployment benefit.

Short-Term Outcomes

Squeezing Welfare Beneficiaries

The ESI and the 1991 budget together stayed the growth in nominal and real core government spending during the recession of 1990–93 (see Figure 5.2).[3] It is significant to note that core government expenditure as a proportion of GDP fell from just over 40 per cent in 1991 to 38 per cent in 1993, and to 32 per cent in 1996.

In the midst of this recession the unemployment rate reached 11 per cent in 1991, with almost 16 per cent of the working-age population receiving a welfare benefit that year. Central to the squeeze were the reductions in the value of welfare payments for the unemployed, sole parents, and individuals

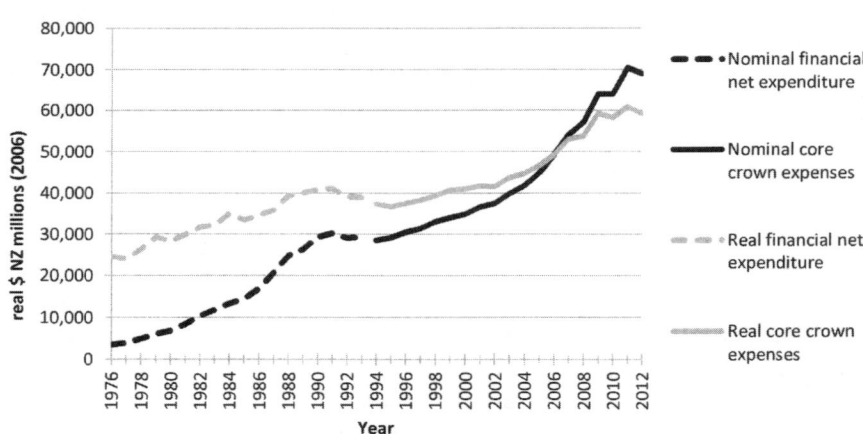

Figure 5.2. Nominal and real core New Zealand government expenditure, 1976–2012.
Source: New Zealand Treasury (2012) Fiscal Time Series: Historical Fiscal Indicators 1972–2012. Year End 2012 Update, http://www.treasury.govt.nz/government/data

---

[3] 'Core' government refers to public service departments and ministries, parliamentary offices, national superannuation, and the Reserve Bank of New Zealand (RBNZ, the central bank). It does not include crown entities, state-owned enterprises, or local government.

who were unable to work because of sickness. The average value of these weekly welfare payments dropped in real terms from $246 in 1990 to $221 in 1993, before rising to $225 three years later. Expenditure was also reduced by the rise in the age of eligibility for national superannuation. Overall social security and welfare expenditure as a proportion of GDP declined from 14.1 per cent in 1991 to 12.8 per cent by 1996, having remained quite stable from 1990 to 1994 (see Figure 5.3).

Stronger economic growth rates from 1993 to 1995, averaging nearly 5 per cent per annum, saw welfare payments decline and tax revenues increase, leading to an operating surplus of 3 to 4 per cent of GDP in the mid-1990s. In fact, through the decade of the 1990s, New Zealand's rate of economic growth per capita was similar to the OECD average. Little of this surplus was used for any projected 'social dividend'. Instead, the government maintained a tight fiscal rein, to enable it to retire public debt and then to deliver tax cuts before the 1996 general election.

The post-1993 economic recovery raised employment rates among sole parents, and reduced the numbers and average time on the unemployment benefit. But by 1997–98 economic performance was again in decline, partly due to the Asian financial crisis, and to two serious droughts in New Zealand. In the meantime, under its targeting agreement with the government, the RBNZ had brought inflation down to around 2 per cent by the mid-1990s, from about 19 per cent in the late 1980s. Mortgage rates dropped from 15.5 per cent in 1991 to 7.5 per cent by 1994. In sum, there is good evidence to

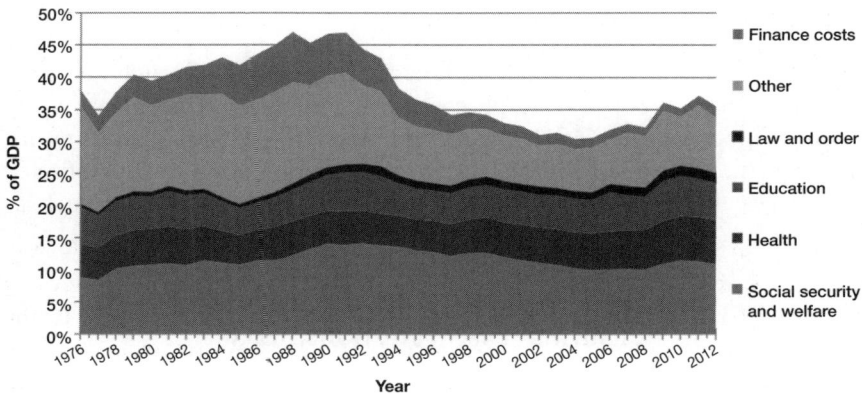

Figure 5.3.   Components of core government expenditure as a percentage of GDP, New Zealand 1976–2012.
Note: From 1994 there was a different method of measuring government expenditure.
Source: New Zealand Treasury (2012) Fiscal Time Series: Historical Fiscal Indicators 1972–2012. Year End 2012 Update, http://www.treasury.govt.nz/government/data

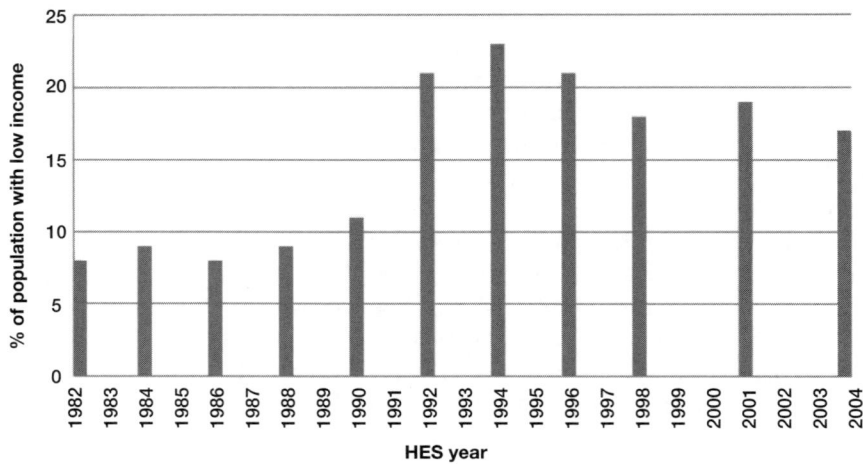

Figure 5.4. Percentage of population with low incomes, New Zealand 1982–2004.
Note: The measure is the proportion of households with equivalised after-housing costs disposable incomes less than 60% of the housing adjusted median in 1998 (adjusted for inflation). HES = Household Economic Survey.
Source: Perry (2013).

show that, in the shorter term at least, the ESI and the 1991 budget were effective in dealing with the fiscal circumstances that spawned them.

However, the social costs were heavy. The rate of New Zealanders on low incomes almost doubled between 1990 and 1992, with a further increase to 1994 (see Figure 5.4). A comprehensive academic analysis at the end of the decade argued that the reforms failed or fell short in many important respects, intensifying poverty and social exclusion, and imposing new economic costs on adversely affected individuals and on the government, through new prisons and a growing police force, and with rising numbers of people receiving income support (Boston *et al.* 1999a: 301). According to two commentators, 'The benefit cuts caused considerable poverty among beneficiaries, reflected in a large surge in demand for assistance from private charities such as food-banks' (Dalziel & Lattimore 2001: 68).[4]

Ensuring 'Fiscal Responsibility'

The fact that the rapidly deteriorating fiscal situation was not known to the public during the 1990 election campaign provided the impetus for increased

---

[4] Kelsey (1997: 292) records that Salvation Army food parcel assistance increased by 76 per cent in the first three months of 1991, 432 per cent in 1992, and 30 per cent in 1993—a more than tenfold increase over three years.

transparency in the management of the public accounts. In a report to parliament the following year, the chief ombudsman argued that 'the public interest is not served by the way in which the release of financial and economic information is arranged or withheld by the Government and officials to meet political objectives' (Chief Ombudsman 1991: 10). He suggested that in the period before a general election 'an authenticated non-political survey of the state of the economy' should be published 'for all to see and understand'. This idea was taken up by the government, with Ruth Richardson being the driving force behind the introduction of the Fiscal Responsibility Act 1994 (FRA), which was widely heralded as groundbreaking legislation among Western countries. Coming on top of the adoption of GAAP, the FRA made it hard for any government to increase expenditure without confronting the politically challenging task of increasing tax.

The Act required governments to adopt a medium- to long-term approach to fiscal policy, rather than focusing on short-term political considerations, and to ensure that comprehensive information about the government's fiscal intentions was made publicly available.[5] It also laid out five principles of responsible fiscal management, binding on a minister of finance: (1) government debt to be maintained at prudent levels; (2) operating expenses not to exceed operating revenue on average, over a reasonable period of time; (3) a positive value of crown net worth to be maintained to provide a buffer against adverse shocks; (4) all fiscal risks to be prudently managed; and (5) the level and stability of tax rates to be reasonably predictable for future years. (What constituted a 'prudent' level of crown debt was not specified, being left up to governments to determine and publicly explain.)

The FRA, along with the politically 'independent' RBNZ, were considered by Treasury and other econocratic proponents to be the pillars of New Zealand's new 'economic constitution', designed to ensure that macroeconomic management was 'politics-proofed' (McKinnon 2003: 357–8). (Events have since confirmed the naïvety of this aspiration.)

Political Pushback: Changing the Electoral System

Critics were quick to label Ruth Richardson's strategic revision of the welfare state 'Ruthanasia', while supporters were convinced of its courageous fidelity to the soundest principles of fiscal management. As it turned out, Richardson was minister of finance in what was to be the last New Zealand government to be swept into office with a large majority under the first-past-the-post

---

[5] The Labour-led coalition government had parliament repeal the FRA in 2004, incorporating its provisions in the PFA instead.

(FPP) electoral system, which had been in place since 1914. She had seized the opportunity provided by National Party's landslide win in 1990 to push forward her plan for radical welfare reform.

The 1991 budget did not of itself foment a popular drive for change in the electoral system. It would be fairer to say that it was widely seen as the latest example of egregious political deceit and abuse of executive power, which stretched at least as far back as the time of the autocratic Muldoon. But National's election slogan of a 'Decent Society' did not seem to fit well with what the 1991 budget delivered, no matter how alarming the fiscal deficit was seen to be.

The desire for electoral change was impelled by increasingly popular concern over the concentration of power in the hands of the political executive— New Zealand's counterpart of the 'elective dictatorship' that Lord Hailsham had earlier identified in Britain (*The Listener*, 21 October 1976: 496–500). In New Zealand, this concentration of power was even greater, given the country's unitary system of government, and a unicameral parliament. Especially till the parliamentary Labour party disintegrated in the late 1980s, the Lange government had prided itself on its strategy of 'crashing through' its programme of radical reforms—'give opponents so many targets at once they won't know which to shoot at'—in the face of any opposition. The mood of the times was well depicted by Mulgan (1992: 16), who observed that in New Zealand, 'Politicians as a class have reached new depths of public contempt … There is widespread public anger and contempt for what is seen as blatant dishonesty and deception.'

There had also been a growing sense of electoral unfairness under FPP. In the 1981 election the Social Credit Party had gained just on 21 per cent of the vote, which gave it only two seats in parliament. Three years later the New Zealand Party had won more than 12 per cent of the vote, with a nil return in seats.

Neither of the two main political parties, which had since 1936 been able to swap the baubles of office between them under FPP, wanted a change to proportional representation. Nevertheless, soon after assuming office, Lange's government had set up a Royal Commission on the Electoral System, which in 1985 recommended that the country change to proportional representation by adopting the German Mixed Member Proportional (MMP) model. During the 1987 election Lange had casually promised that his government would hold a referendum on the matter were it to be re-elected. It did win the election, emphatically, but no such referendum was held.

For his part, Bolger was personally opposed to proportional representation, preferring instead the re-establishment of an upper chamber, which had been abolished by general parliamentary agreement in 1950. Nevertheless, during the 1990 election campaign he also promised that a referendum would be held on the question of proportionality, and having been widely seen to have turned his back on the promise of a 'Decent Society' (especially the undertaking to remove the superannuation surtax), he felt that he could not also renege on the referendum commitment.

In the event, 85 per cent of those who voted in the 1992 non-binding referendum opted for electoral change, with more than 70 per cent of valid votes being cast in favour of the MMP alternative (the other options being Single Transferable Vote, Supplementary Member, and Preferential Voting). In a binding referendum held at the time of the 1993 election, 54 per cent of those who voted opted for a change to MMP as against retaining FPP.[6]

The 1993 election itself was almost disastrous for the National government, which had campaigned on a 'Spirit of Recovery' platform. It lost 17 seats in the House, with its popular vote dropping from 48 per cent in 1990 to 35 per cent. Its majority of seats fell from 37 to just one, with Labour securing 45, and the left-wing Alliance and the centrist New Zealand First (NZF) party two each.[7] (The National Party's electoral support did not, in fact, fully recover until the 2005 election.)

Most of the blame for this electoral turnaround fell upon Ruth Richardson. She received little credit for her role in promoting the FRA, with the real pain of benefit cuts far outweighing seemingly abstract appeals to responsible fiscal practice. Consequently, Bolger removed her from the finance portfolio, giving the job to the more conservative Bill Birch, a close personal friend. As minister of labour, Birch had been responsible for the introduction of the contentious ECA, but he was also known to have clashed with Richardson in caucus and cabinet over her radical welfare reforms.

Bolger offered Richardson other leading portfolios, which she refused, preferring to retreat to the backbenches. The following year she resigned from parliament, embarrassing her party colleagues by forcing a by-election, which had it been lost by National, might have brought down the government. As it was, the National candidate won only narrowly what had for many years been a safe seat for the party, with the Alliance party candidate a close second.

In 1996, the first MMP election saw the emergence of a centre-right majority coalition government of the National Party and the NZF party, holding a one-seat majority in the new parliament. National had gained 34 per cent of the vote, Labour 28 per cent, and NZF 13 per cent, which gave it 17 seats in the new parliament.

---

[6] The prospect that a change to MMP would mean 120 rather than 99 MPs reduced the proportional system's appeal. Also, the pro-FPP lobby was more strongly financed than its opposition in the lead-up to the referendum.

[7] The Alliance party, a coalition of groups to the left of the Labour Party, had been formed in 1991.

NZF was thus the 'kingmaker' party. It had been founded only in 1993 by a former National Party minister, Winston Peters, who had been sacked from the cabinet by prime minister Bolger in 1991. Peters was now deputy prime minister to Bolger, and was also given the newly created portfolio of Treasurer, senior to the finance portfolio held by Birch. Peters' main electoral constituency comprised middle-aged and more elderly voters ('grey power') angry at the retention and strengthening of the surtax regime on national superannuation. One of the major concessions Peters secured from his coalition partner was the abolition of this tax, which occurred in April 1998. In the meantime, growing numbers of National Party members of parliament had become disenchanted by what they saw as Peters' restrictive influence on government policymaking.

In December 1997, a caucus coup saw Bolger ousted as prime minister in favour of transport minister Jenny Shipley, a close friend and ally of Richardson. Shipley, who as minister of social welfare during the term of the first Bolger government had been responsible for the implementation of the welfare cuts, thus became New Zealand's first female prime minister. Bolger retired from parliament in 1998, being appointed New Zealand's ambassador to the United States.

Peters and Shipley found it impossible to cooperate, and the coalition government broke up in 1998. The remnants of the Shipley-led government managed to survive until the 1999 election, which produced a centre-left minority coalition government led by Labour's Helen Clark, partnered by the Alliance, and supported in parliament on crucial votes by the Green Party.

In sum, from 1990 New Zealanders experienced a decade of political twists and turns, highlighted by a major constitutional change. Much of this originated in Richardson's opportunistic reform of the welfare state. In the event, this ended her own political career, and ultimately also led to Bolger's political demise. If examined in the context of the blame game possibilities outlined by Heald and Hood in Chapter 1 of this volume, the Bolger–Richardson policy initiative of 'hard' fiscal squeeze, which they portrayed as an essential response to an inherited fiscal crisis, did not protect the National government from the almost terminal political blame directed by voters in New Zealand's unitary Westminster parliamentary system.

Longer-Run Outcomes

Economic Performance

Nearly two and a half decades on, it is difficult to trace current circumstances directly back to the National government's response to the 1991 fiscal deficit.

There are too many intervening variables, both exogenous and endogenous. Nevertheless, in outlining some present-day conditions, it is not unreasonable to see that response as a significantly influential progenitor.

It is generally agreed among New Zealand commentators that the country's economic performance over the past twenty years or so has been steady if unspectacular (apart from the success in maintaining both low inflation and low unemployment). The country's real per capita GDP growth has averaged 0.5 per cent below the OECD median, with current account deficits averaging 5 per cent of GDP—about the sixth-largest, relative to GDP, in the OECD (Wheeler 2013: 3). New Zealand's quest to achieve and maintain levels of per capita GDP in the top half of the OECD league table continues to be an underlying aim of New Zealand macroeconomic management, together with that of achieving and maintaining a fiscal surplus. However, the OECD has reported that 'New Zealand is falling further behind in its ambition to catch up with OECD living standards, in particular Australia's, by 2025' (OECD 2011: 9). Net long-term emigration to Australia especially, largely by skilled and semi-skilled New Zealanders seeking more attractive wages and conditions, has increased markedly in the past few years.[8] More positively, New Zealand's ratio of government debt-to-GDP declined progressively from a high point of 62.4 per cent in 1994 to 17.4 per cent in 2008, before climbing again in recent years.

The programme of economic deregulation pursued by the fourth Labour government, 1984–90, brought the country into a globalised and increasingly interdependent world of trade, capital and knowledge flows; and the National government's ESI and 1991 budget together constituted the first serious attempt to reassess the priorities and means of welfare spending. Yet they could not alter the fact of New Zealand's vulnerability as a small trading nation, far away from some of its main export markets—a country once described by *The Economist* as 'the last bus stop on the planet' (McKinnon 2003: 417). According to the Governor of the RBNZ, 'The OECD and IMF believe size and distance, which limit economies of scale and market opportunities, account for around three quarters of the gap in [New Zealand's] per capita income compared to the OECD average' (Wheeler 2013: 4).

Whatever the case, since the near loss of office by the National government in 1993, and the later advent of MMP, commentators of opposing ideological persuasions have argued about whether the country's longer-term economic performance was impeded by the reforms of the 1980s and early 1990s, or whether a loss of political nerve has since prevented the adoption of further market-led policies that would have enhanced performance.

---

[8] For example, during 2011–12, the net figure was just on 44,300, an increase of 32.5 per cent over the previous year.

Rising Income Inequality

New Zealand's egalitarian tradition strongly influenced the politics of macro-economic management throughout most of the last century (Fischer 2012; Lipson 2011). This ethos was built on, and in turn maintained, largely compressed relativities in wage and salary structures, and high levels of social mobility. While there were several occasions in the decades after World War II when governments of both the centre-left and the centre-right sought greater fiscal stringency at times of economic strain, with some people gaining and others losing, by and large few lost so badly that they could not reasonably be supported by the welfare state, while none gained so much that their apparent privilege fostered any widespread politics of envy. From the 1980s, however, the increasing effects of globalisation, and other factors—such as the demographics of emigration and immigration—placed this ethos under growing strain. The fiscal squeeze programme of the early 1990s ensured, wittingly or not, that this impetus was sustained through the 1990s, and well beyond (Rashbrooke 2013).

Although income inequality has generally risen across most OECD countries since the mid-1980s, between 1985 and 2008 the rise in New Zealand's Gini coefficient was larger than in all countries except Sweden, undoubtedly reflecting a lower 'starting point' for these countries with strong egalitarian traditions (OECD 2011). In absolute terms, New Zealand's score was 0.26 in 1988, rising to a peak of 0.34 by 2011. The sharpest increase occurred between 1988 and 1990, followed by a more gradual but consistent rise over the ensuing 11 years (see Figure 5.5). One leading political commentator, himself not unsympathetic to the approach taken by Richardson in her budget, later commented that 'in [New Zealand] in the 1980s inegalitarianism came particularly swiftly and with particular intensity and Ruth Richardson jammed her foot on the accelerator' (James 2007).

Those people comprising the wealthiest 1 per cent of the population have not grown as wealthy, proportionately, as have those in the top 1 per cent in many other OECD countries (OECD 2011), but those who were already on lower income levels in New Zealand have become increasingly worse off.

A marked rise in income inequality as measured by the Gini coefficient is one thing; the social attitudes that sustain an egalitarian tradition are another. A 2010 survey found that 62 per cent of respondents believed that income differences in New Zealand were too large, and that the gap between high-paid and low-paid occupations was too big and increasing (Massey University 2010). However, in the same survey, 40 per cent, as compared with 50 per cent in 1992, agreed that it was the government's responsibility to close the income gap; while about 50 per cent favoured people on higher incomes paying a larger share of taxes than those on lower incomes—a reduction from 70 per

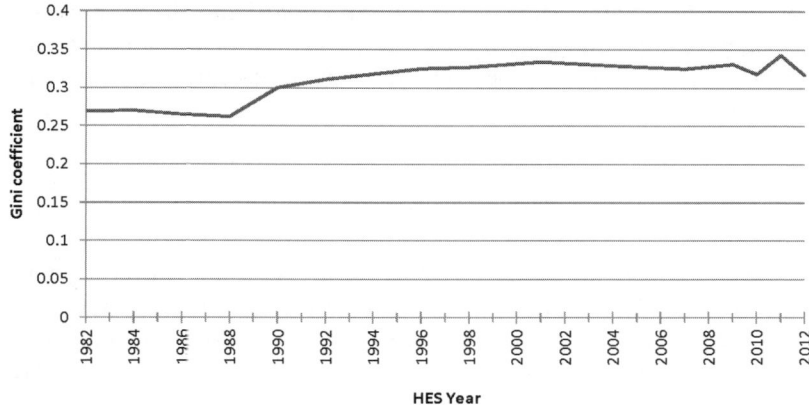

Figure 5.5.   New Zealand Gini coefficient, 1982–2012.
Note: Gini coefficient of equivalised disposable household income of individuals, using the OECD equivalence scale. HES = Household Economic Survey.
Source: Perry (2013), adjusted for data corrections in Perry (2014).

cent in 1992 and 60 per cent in 1999. (The authors of the survey suggest that this decline may partly reflect the attitudinal effects of 'fiscal creep'.)

The survey also showed, however, that 80 per cent of New Zealanders consider themselves to be 'middle-class'. Fifty-five per cent of respondents believed New Zealand *ought* to be a society with most people in the middle, and only 37 per cent perceived that there was a small elite, with most people at the bottom. The latter result is a marked change from the early 1990s, when 62 per cent of respondents saw it that way. Nor was age an important predictor of attitudes to social inequality.

A New Zealand Values Survey, conducted in 2004–05, found that respondents were evenly divided between believing that New Zealand should have more or less income inequality, and that more were in favour of individual responsibility than collective responsibility in ensuring that everyone was provided for (Carroll *et al.* 2011). For his part, Barber (2011) has found that increasing inequality in New Zealand has been accompanied by 'worsening social outcomes', including mental health problems, obesity, teenage pregnancies, and a lower life expectancy compared to that in more egalitarian countries. On the other hand, there remain high levels of social trust, and 'New Zealanders generally share an underlying sense of fairness and appear willing to support a range of policies to reduce income inequalities' (Barber 2011: 68).

Finally, research by Humpage (2011), using four main sources of survey data, found that the number of people agreeing that New Zealand was an unequal society actually decreased during the 1990s; and the proportion of people between 1993 and 2005 who agreed that government should redistribute income and wealth from the 'rich' to 'ordinary' people declined from 49 per cent to 29 per cent.

Pressing Social Issues

As it is, New Zealand faces some pressing social issues, not entirely or mainly because of the global financial crisis and subsequent recession. Youth unemployment, especially, is high. In 2012, New Zealand's Children's Commissioner established a working group to investigate the causes of and possible remedies for rising rates of child poverty and poverty-related illnesses among New Zealand children. A report by the working group shows a dramatic increase in child poverty rates in the early 1990s (see Figure 5.6).[9]

In this multicultural society, unemployment rates among Maori and Pasifika people have consistently been three times higher than for the

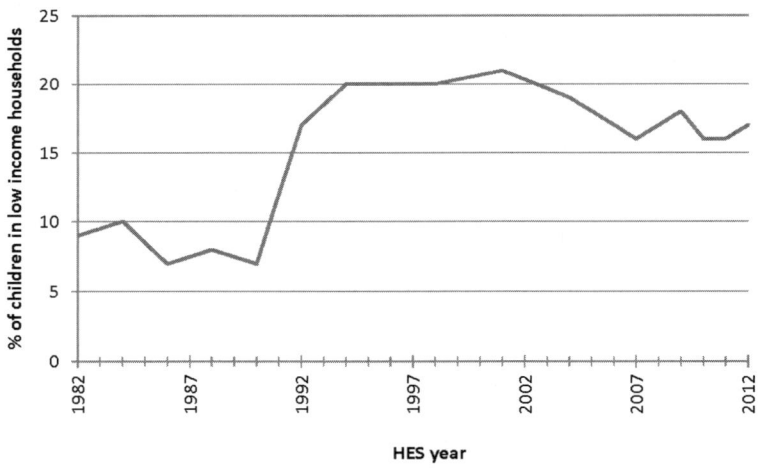

Figure 5.6.   Trends in child poverty rates, New Zealand 1982–2012.
Note: The measure is the proportion of households with equivalised after-housing costs disposable incomes less than 50% of the housing adjusted median in 1998 (adjusted for inflation). HES = Household Economic Survey.
Source: Report of the Expert Advisory Group on Solutions to Child Poverty (2012). Original source: Perry (2013), adjusted for data corrections in Perry (2014). See too Boston & Chapple (2014).

[9] However, Carter *et al.* (2013) argue that the relationship between trends in income inequality and poverty in New Zealand is not straightforward.

European population over the past 15 years, and their populations are growing at a faster rate (Spoonley & Bedford 2012). Moreover, wealthier people are much less likely to be held to account for white-collar tax evasion than poorer people are to be convicted of welfare fraud (Marriott 2012).

Violent offences against children have also risen sharply. On top of this, a 2013 United Nations Children's Fund (UNICEF 2013) report on the state of children in the world's most advanced economies found that New Zealand had one of the highest rates of children not in any form of education, training or employment, and that the country fell behind poorer nations on many of the measures. What is notable about this UNICEF report is that the countries leading the way in child wellbeing are those which have often been regarded as similar to New Zealand in their commitment to social welfare: the Netherlands, Sweden, Norway, Finland and Iceland.

Although New Zealand's education system is considered to be performing well, ranking seventh among 65 countries on OECD measures, between 2010 and 2011 the achievement gap between the country's lowest- and highest-decile schools increased to nearly 32 per cent, despite a fall in the rate for the latter.[10] The gap in reading performance between New Zealand students from different socio-economic backgrounds is the widest among all OECD countries.

In New Zealand it was for many decades widely believed that the government had a prime social responsibility to ensure affordable housing for citizens. Consequently, rates of home ownership were among the highest in the world. By 2013, however, housing prices had risen to levels well beyond the reach of increasing numbers of people, thus further reinforcing inequality.

Ironically, four years after her 1991 budget, Ruth Richardson herself observed that 'We are increasingly becoming two societies: the mainstream of New Zealanders who are taking advantage of the new economic opportunities, and an underclass still trapped in a cycle of dependency' (Richardson 1995: 198). It is not difficult to argue that her budget contributed substantially to the continuing growth of this underclass.

Deregulation: The 'Leaky Homes' Crisis and Other Disasters

Like its predecessor, the Bolger government of 1990–93 was attracted to rolling back what it saw as an overly 'interventionist' state. Accordingly, it introduced the Building Act 1991, which came into force three years later.

---

[10] Lower-decile schools draw students from poorer areas, and receive proportionately more government funding than higher-decile schools, which are generally sited in more affluent localities.

This legislation largely deregulated the building industry, instituting instead a 'performance-based' regime, founded on the expectation that commercial competition and professional norms would maintain and enhance construction standards (Mumford 2010). The main upshot, however, was a building and financial disaster that continues to be played out. Between 1994 and 2005, thousands of homes were constructed that proved later to be uninhabitable because they were inadequately insulated from the weather, and were subject to internal rot. The financial costs were in 2009 officially estimated to be about $11.3 billion, but experts that year also suggested that up to 89,000 homes could fail, at a total cost of some $23 billion, not including government costs (PriceWaterhouseCoopers 2009). About 64 per cent of the costs are being borne by the home owners themselves, 26 per cent by local councils, and 10 per cent by the central government.

In addition, a new Health and Safety in Employment Act 1992 (HSEA) left it to employers to self-regulate the working conditions of their employees. Consequently, official inspectorate capacity was greatly reduced over time, a factor which contributed significantly to a 2010 gas explosion that killed 29 men working in a coal mine (Report of the Royal Commission on the Pike River Coal Mine Tragedy 2012).[11] The HSEA required employers to maintain safe working environments through 'good faith' cooperation with those doing the work. In the decades after the Act's inception, however, New Zealand's safety standards dropped markedly, especially in comparison with Canada, Australia and Britain. The Cave Creek tragedy of April 1995, in which 14 people were killed when a wilderness viewing platform collapsed, was partly attributable to a regulatory failure and a departmental culture of 'doing more with less' (Gregory 1998).

Conclusion: Firm Intentions and Mixed Outcomes

The ESI and the 1991 budget together constituted a determined challenge to the shape of the welfare state that had been developed by New Zealand's first Labour government in the 1930s and 1940s. Based heavily on ideological perspectives, and propagated as being essential in dealing with a dramatic and unexpected fiscal crisis, they arose from a political opportunity generated by a combination of exogenous shocks and endogenous structural problems in the New Zealand economy. The two instruments brought about a turning point in New Zealand's social history, effectively challenging the structure of welfarism in ways that have since withstood the test of time and changing political fortunes. Although the Bolger government dropped some aspects of

---

[11] The government established in 2013 a stand-alone crown agency, WorkSafe New Zealand, to regulate occupational health and safety.

its proposed changes to national superannuation soon after Richardson had delivered her budget, it stuck determinedly with its programme for several years, losing swathes of political support from many superannuitants who had previously backed the National Party.

A case of 'hard' fiscal squeeze, its impact on welfare beneficiaries, in particular, was severe. It enhanced and sustained wider economic and political forces which transformed New Zealand into a much less egalitarian society than it was in the early 1980s, as gauged by income distribution, if not entirely by social attitudes. An uglier face of New Zealand society is today more apparent than it might otherwise have become, just as a huge amount of human trauma was generated by the ideologically based deregulation of the building industry and the softening of controls over occupational health and safety. However, New Zealand's fiscal deficit of 3.5 per cent of GDP in 1990 had become a surplus of 3 per cent of GDP by 1996, and most of the other macroeconomic indicators were in a healthy state. The overall outcome was therefore mixed: an appreciable improvement in macroeconomic performance (sustained until the late 1990s), accompanied by an enduring rise in income inequality with inter-generational social consequences.

The policies implemented between 1990 and 1993 also shifted the political centre towards the right. New Zealanders, although they remain strongly committed to sustaining the state's dominant role in public health, education and welfare, are today less committed than in earlier times to ensuring that the government carries the main responsibility for closing the substantial income gap that grew from the late 1980s and through the 1990s. Policy options that were once central to the maintenance of New Zealand's 20th-century welfare state—such as higher taxes and universal benefits—are today much less politically viable.

In the shorter term, the ESI and the 1991 budget, and in particular the broken electoral promises which they embodied, boosted what had already been high levels of public mistrust of politicians. These factors contributed, perhaps decisively, to the subsequent change to proportional representation, which has brought parliament into the centre of the governing process. As Malone (2008: 232) has observed, 'MMP has produced a significant rebalancing of the constitution. The obligation on ministers to consult within and between multiple parties and to accommodate the policy preferences of those parties … has significantly restricted executive power.'

Finally, the Fiscal Responsibility Act, probably Ruth Richardson's most widely admired achievement, made New Zealand a front-runner in the international quest for greater fiscal transparency.[12]

---

[12] The 2012 Open Budget Index ranked New Zealand in first place, with a score of 93/100. The 18 OECD countries included had an average score of 72/100.

Note. The authors thank David Rea, Research Fellow in the Institute for Governance and Policy Studies, at the School of Government, Victoria University of Wellington; and Nila Panko, PhD student in the Health Services Research Centre, School of Government, Victoria University of Wellington, for their invaluable help in compiling and interpreting data for this chapter.

References

Barber, P. (2011), 'How to Get Closer Together: Impacts of Income Inequality and Policy Responses', *Policy Quarterly*, 7(4): 62–8.

Blyth, M. (2013), 'Paradigms and Paradox: The Politics of Economic Ideas in Two Moments of Crisis', *Governance*, 26(2): 197–215.

Bolger, J. (1998), *Bolger: A View From the Top—My Seven Years as Prime Minister* (Auckland, Viking).

Boston, J. (1999), 'New Zealand's Welfare State in Transition', in Boston *et al.* (1999b), 3–19.

Boston, J., & Chapple, S. (2014), *Child Poverty in New Zealand* (Wellington, Bridget Williams Books).

Boston, J., Dalziel, P. & St John, S. (1999a), 'Rebuilding an Effective Welfare State', in Boston *et al.* (1999b), 301–36.

Boston, J., Dalziel, P. & St John, S. (eds) (1999b), *Redesigning the Welfare State in New Zealand: Problems, Policies, Prospects* (Auckland, Oxford University Press).

Carroll, P., Casswell, S., Huakau, J., Howden-Chapman, P. & Perry, P. (2011), 'The Widening Gap: Perceptions of Poverty and Income Inequalities and Implications for Health and Social Outcomes', *Social Policy Journal of New Zealand*, 37: 111–22.

Carter, K., Gunasekara, F. & Blakely, T. (2013), 'The Relationship Between Trends in Income Inequalities and Poverty in New Zealand', *Policy Quarterly*, 9(2): 24–9.

Chief Ombudsman (1991), Prime Ministerial Briefing Papers Including Bank of New Zealand Data: Report of the Chief Ombudsman, *Appendix to the Journals of the House of Representatives, 1991–1993*, Vol. IA (Wellington).

Dalziel, P. & Lattimore, R. (2001), *The New Zealand Macroeconomy: A Briefing on the Reforms and Their Legacy*, 4th edn (Auckland, Oxford University Press).

Fischer, D. (2012), *Fairness and Freedom: A History of Two Open Societies: New Zealand and the United States* (New York, Oxford University Press).

Gregory, R. (1998), 'Political Responsibility for Bureaucratic Incompetence: Tragedy at Cave Creek', *Public Administration*, 76(3): 519–38.

Humpage, L. (2011), 'Neo-Liberal Reform and Attitudes Towards Social Citizenship: A Review of New Zealand Public Opinion Data 1987–2005', *Social Policy Journal of New Zealand*, 37: 83–96.

Hunt, C. (2009), 'Banking Crises in New Zealand: An Historical Perspective', *Reserve Bank of New Zealand Bulletin*, 72: 26–41.

James, C. (2007), 'Ruth Amid the Alien Corn', paper to the Victoria University Politics Programme and Stout Centre conference on 'The Bolger Years', 28 April.

Kelsey, J. (1997), *The New Zealand Experiment: A World Model for Structural Adjustment?* (Auckland, Auckland University Press).

Lipson, L. (2011), *The Politics of Equality: New Zealand's Adventures in Democracy*, introduction by J. Johansson (Wellington, Victoria University Press).

Malone, R. (2008), *Rebalancing the Constitution: The Challenge of Government Law-Making Under MMP* (Wellington, Institute of Policy Studies).

Marriott, L. (2012), 'Tax Crime and Punishment in New Zealand', *British Tax Review*, issue 5: 623–56.

Massey University (2010), *Social Inequality in New Zealand: International Social Survey Programme* (School of Communication, Journalism & Marketing).

McKinnon, M. (2003), *Treasury: The New Zealand Treasury, 1840–2000* (Auckland, Auckland University Press).

Mulgan, R. (1992), 'The Principles of Rogerpolitics', *Public Sector*, 15: 16–17.

Mumford, P. (2010), 'Enhancing Performance-Based Regulation: Lessons from New Zealand's Building Control System', unpublished PhD thesis, Victoria University of Wellington.

OECD (2011), 'Executive Summary', in *OECD Economic Surveys: New Zealand 2011* (Paris, OECD Publishing), http://www.oecd.org/newzealand/economicsurveyof-newzealand2011.htm (accessed 18 April 2013).

Perry, B. (2013), *Household Incomes in New Zealand: Trends in Indicators of Inequality and Hardship 1982–2012* (Wellington, Ministry of Social Development).

Perry, B. (2014), *Household Incomes in New Zealand: Trends in Indicators of Inequality and Hardship 1982–2012—Revised Tables and Figures, 27 February 2014* (Wellington, Ministry of Social Development).

PriceWaterhouseCoopers (2009), *Department of Building and Housing: Weathertightness—Estimating the Cost* (Wellington), http://www.dbh.govt.nz/UserFiles/File/News/WHRS/pdf/PWC-weathertightness-estimating-cost-full-report.pdf (accessed 18 April 2013).

Radio New Zealand (2013), 'Sunday Morning': Interview with Jim Bolger, by Chris Laidlaw, 28 April, www.radionz.co.nz/national/programmes/sunday (accessed 29 April 2013).

Rashbrooke, M. (ed.) (2013), *Inequality: A New Zealand Crisis* (Wellington, Bridget Williams Books).

Report of the Expert Advisory Group on Solutions to Child Poverty (2012), *Solutions to Child Poverty in New Zealand: Evidence for Action* (Wellington, Children's Commissioner), http://www.occ.org.nz/assets/Uploads/EAG/Final-report/Final-report-Solutions-to-child-poverty-evidence-for-action.pdf (accessed 10 February 2014).

Report of the Royal Commission on the Pike River Coal Mine Tragedy (2012), http://pikeriver.royalcommission.govt.nz/Final-Report (accessed 18 April 2013).

Richardson, R. (1995), *Making a Difference* (Christchurch, Shoal Bay Press).

Spoonley, P. & Bedford, R. (2012), *Welcome to Our World? Immigration and the Reshaping of New Zealand* (Auckland, Dunmore Publishing).

Stephens, R. (1999), 'Poverty, Family Finances and Social Security', in Boston *et al.* (1999b), 238–59.

UNICEF (United Nations Children's Fund) (2013), *Child Well-Being in Rich Countries: A Comparative Overview*, www.unicef-irc.org/Report-Card-11/ (accessed 18 April 2013).

Walsh, P. & Brosnan, P. (1999), 'Redesigning Industrial Relations: The Employment Contracts Act and its Consequences', in Boston *et al.* (1999b), 117–33.

Wheeler, G. (2013), *Improving New Zealand's Economic Growth*, speech to Canterbury Employers' Chamber of Commerce (Christchurch), http://www.rbnz.govt.nz/research_and_publications/speeches/2013/5124358.pdf (accessed 11 February 2014).

6

Fiscal Squeeze in Dutch Municipalities in the 1980s: Cutback Measures and Public Management Reforms

WALTER KICKERT

Introduction

THIS CHAPTER ANALYSES HOW DUTCH LOCAL GOVERNMENT handled fiscal squeeze in the 1980s. The two oil shocks of the 1970s produced a worldwide major economic crisis, which in numerous Western states led to increasing debts and budget deficits. A decline in economic activity caused a fall in state revenues while also leading to increasing public expenditures, especially in unemployment benefits and social security. Budget cuts, downsizing and retrenchment of public services took place in most Western welfare states, including the Netherlands. In the 1980s increasing welfare obligations, together with cutbacks on municipal revenues imposed by national government, had a major impact on Dutch local government. Substantial expenditure cutbacks became imperative in order to avoid impending budget imbalances. At the time the widely shared perception was that Dutch municipalities were confronted with a massive and severe fiscal crisis. This chapter will show that in hindsight this dramatic impression deserves nuancing.

In the terminology used in this book there was a moderate fiscal squeeze in the Netherlands in the period 1983–89, at the general government level. But over a third of the general government expenditure comprised spending at the municipal level, and the municipal-level trends in revenue and expenditure were noticeably different from those at central government level. Figure 6.1, drawn from retrospectively constructed data to be explained later, indicates expenditure cuts of about 2.4 percentage points of GDP in the 1982–85 period at the central level. But at municipal level the spending squeeze was much sharper, at around 6 percentage points, and occurred slightly later, in the period from 1986 to 1990.

Proceedings of the British Academy, **197**, 115–137. © The British Academy 2014.

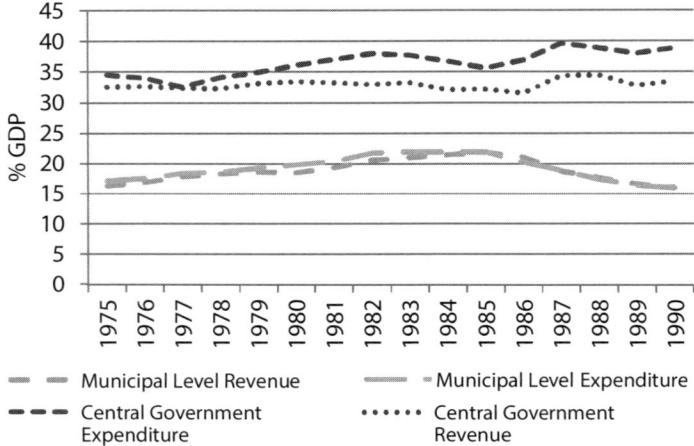

Figure 6.1.   Revenue and expenditure at central government and municipal level, Netherlands 1975–90.

Notes: Central Government Expenditure (revenue) is here calculated as General Government Expenditure (revenue) *less* Municipal Level Expenditure (revenue). It includes both current and capital expenditure.

Source: Municipal Level Expenditure and Revenue: Central Bureau of Statistics (CBS), Netherlands, http://statline.cbs.nl/StatWeb/publication/?DM=SLNL&PA=37385&D1=57-65&D2= 76-101&HDR=T&STB=G1&VW=T; General Government Expenditure and Revenue: OECD Economic Outlook, No 93, June 2013.

There are several reasons why the pressure on the Dutch Municipal Fund in the 1980s and the way local government responded to that pressure is a significant case for the understanding of the politics of fiscal squeeze.

First, it is an internationally remarkable case because fiscal consolidation was undertaken by local authorities with few tax-raising powers of their own. In contrast to decentralised and federal states where local government collects significant own revenues, such as the Scandinavian states, Germany and the Swiss cantons, Dutch local government had had very few independent own sources of income: taxes and levies were only around 5 per cent of total municipal revenue throughout the 1980s. Local income was predominantly provided by national government, which in the 1980s one-sidedly imposed income cutbacks of an unprecedented magnitude. Not only was the decline in local revenues exogenous, the same applied to the increase in expenditures, especially in social security, which was mainly due to rising unemployment. Moreover, Dutch local government was legally obliged to have a balanced budget. Substantial and structural (that is, more than temporary) imbalance between local expenditures and revenues was prohibited by law, so local government was obliged to solve an externally inflicted fiscal problem. They stood with their backs to the wall. It was a tough challenge to address such fiscal pressures within timescales measured in financial years.

Secondly, the Dutch local fiscal consolidation in the 1980s was associated with an internationally well-known early case of adoption of New Public Management (NPM). Over this period Dutch local governments not only tackled their fiscal problems by cutbacks, retrenchments and other short-term measures to balance the budget, but also reformed their broader financial management system. Fiscal consolidation was followed by NPM-type measures in Dutch local government. Many Dutch municipalities opted for a business-style financial management system, a reform trend that progressively extended to more and more municipalities over a period of more than a decade. This widespread introduction of business-style management, result-orientation and client-awareness in Dutch municipalities gained an internationally renowned reputation as it was embraced in the early 1990s as a guiding exemplar for German local government reform ('neues Steuerungsmodell') and in the mid-1990s for Switzerland's NPM-like reforms ('wirkungsorientierter Verwaltungsreform').

Thirdly, the Dutch local experiences with fiscal squeeze are internationally worth noticing as they may have had another longer-term side-effect. Not only did the fiscal squeeze lead to NPM-type reforms, but the NPM reforms in the longer run led to counter-effects. In the 1990s Dutch local politicians started to realise that the technocratic and managerial NPM-style of government was predominantly intra-organisational and inward-oriented, and that the external outward-orientation towards citizens and community had been neglected. A quest for new forms of local democracy followed, leading to measures for increased participation, involvement and cooperation of citizens and social groups in local policymaking. In public opinion and the press, the prevailing technocratic and managerial style of the governing national politicians in the 2000s was claimed to be an important factor in the enormous popularity of the outsider-populist Pim Fortuyn and the subsequent electoral upsurge of populist political parties.

This chapter first considers the causes of the fiscal squeeze in the 1980s, that is, the decrease in municipal revenues and increase in expenditures in the context of the legal requirement to balance budgets. The main revenue source considered is the Municipal Fund, a block grant from central government which was introduced in the 1920s when a number of specific local taxes were abolished. This is because Municipal Fund spending is better documented from surviving records, unlike the 'other income' category of spending. Secondly we describe the municipal responses to the fiscal squeeze, that is, what cutback measures and strategies were employed. In that section we distinguish between the cutback measures and strategies, and the linked reform of the financial management system. Thirdly we consider some empirical evidence about the causes and effects of public management reform, and finally we also consider longer-term effects that went beyond management reform, that is, developments in local democracy in the 1990s.

The chapter uses two different sources of data. To indicate some long-term trends we use data from the Central Bureau of Statistics in the Netherlands (CBS), which are consistent over time, but are constructed retrospectively using recent accounting conventions, meaning that these numbers sometimes differ from numbers actually reported in the 1980s and the categories are different.[1] To track the fiscal squeeze of the 1980s, we therefore have to complement those retrospective CBS data with data from contemporary sources such as Jacobs (1986) and the Miljoenennota (budget documents).

Causes of Fiscal Squeeze: The Requirement to Balance Municipal Budgets Together with a Decrease in Incomes and Increase in Expenditure

The national government had practised anti-cyclical Keynesian policy in the second half of the 1970s, resulting in mounting budget deficits. Budget cuts at the national level only genuinely commenced in the 1980s. Still, deficits, as shown in Figure 6.1, kept on rising as the deviation between expenditure and revenue widened in the 1980s. In contrast, local government in the Netherlands was legally prohibited from having an unbalanced budget (in an accrual accounting system). The law stated that if a municipality had a 'substantial and structural (i.e. more than temporary) imbalance between expenditures and revenues', it was placed under the strict legal tutelage of the provincial authority. Every single major expenditure was thenceforth to be approved by the province, and a stringent financial regime was instituted, the so-called 'Article 12' of the Municipal Act (Havermans 1984). In former times a supplementary budget for Article 12 municipalities at least partially compensated for the painful regime of stringent legal constraints. Since the fiscal crisis of the late 1970s numerous municipalities were compelled to make an appeal for Article 12 status. The supplementary Article 12 budget then became distributed over so many cities that it hardly yielded a sizeable alleviation any more. In such straitened circumstances municipalities had no option but to balance their budgets themselves.

---

[1] For the most part, overall movements in expenditure and revenue do not differ drastically from one version of the CBS data to another, but there are data breaks caused by changes in accounting conventions, notably before and after a change in 2004, which meant that financial transactions (lending) and internal transactions (e.g. internal interest, addition to own reserves) were no longer included.

Because of the legal obligation to balance the local budget, the annual reports on municipal finances (*ex ante* budgets and *ex post* accounts) of the Central Bureau of Statistics do not show systematic deviations between revenue and expenditure. Although municipalities in their multi-year budget forecast did announce the danger of imminent severe deficits, their annual budgets were, as prescribed by law, balanced. The only way of reconstructing the size and extent of impending local budget imbalances (deficits) is to study the causes of the threatening deficits, that is, the decline in the various sources of local income and the rise in expenditures. We will therefore analyse the cutbacks in the general allocations from the Municipal Fund, and subsequently some specific allocations. We will then move on to analysing a particular type of expenditure that sharply increased at the time.

Municipal Incomes

Dutch municipalities have three sources of income: own incomes, general allocations and specific allocations. Figure 6.2 provides an indication of the development of these three sources of income. (The source of this data is Annual Budgets for the post-1987 period. Note that disaggregated income data is not available in the Annual Budgets for the 1980–86 period. This issue will be revisited later in this discussion.)

- *Own incomes*, namely (1) own taxes, the main one being property tax, plus other minor taxes (tourist tax, dog tax etc.) and (2) levies for sewerage and waste disposal, besides funeral charges, building permits etc. These own revenues at the time amounted to 8 to 10 per cent of total local authority incomes. Municipalities were legally constrained in their competence to augment such revenues. Moreover, local political parties were not eager to increase local taxation on their citizens, the more so as developments in local property taxes were closely and critically watched by the media.

- *General allocations* from the Municipal Fund, as mentioned earlier. This fund was allocated by national government to municipalities as a block grant. It was the budget part for which a municipality had financial autonomy to reach its own allocation decisions. These general allocations were substantially curtailed during the 1980s. Though the reduction was moderate in absolute terms, the reduction relative to GDP was more substantial, as shown above in Figure 6.1. The Municipal Fund also declined relative to specific grants from central government, thus reducing the extent of financial autonomy of local government. The Municipal Fund gradually recovered at the end of the 1980s when national government reached a covenant with municipalities about decentralisation.

- *Specific allocations*, the budgets allocated by national government (via the respective ministerial departments) to municipalities for specific services such as education, housing, policing etc. Local government had no financial autonomy to make its own allocation decisions and adjust these budgets or spend the money on other projects. The specific allocations from the various national departments were also substantially downsized in the 1980s, to the extent that many municipalities spent more on police, schools, education etc. than the sums they received from central government. In particular, rising local expenditures on social assistance for the unemployed became a heavy burden on the municipal budget (see below).

We cannot fully track what happened to these categories of funding over the whole of the 1980s, because disaggregated data, following the accounting norms of the time, are only available for the post-1987 period. But we can use the retrospective data constructed by the CBS based on 2004 accounting norms, to explore trends in different sources of local revenue throughout the 1980s. Although the categorisation of various revenue sources is not the same as what was operational in the 1980s, Figure 6.3 broadly confirms the trends discussed above. Own incomes stayed roughly constant over the 1980s at around 5 per cent of total income, 'other income' starts to dip from the mid-1980s, and Municipal Fund allocations show a drastic fall from around 20 per cent of total municipal income in the early 1980s to about 12 per cent in the mid-1980s. In constant price terms, the fall in Municipal Funds between 1981 and 1986 was about 25 per cent.

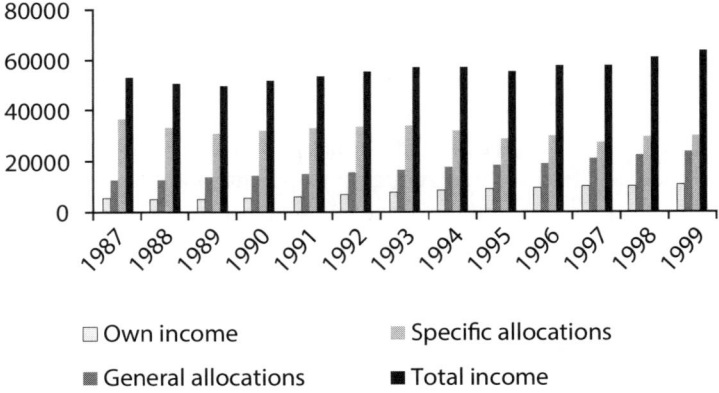

Figure 6.2. Sources of Dutch municipal income (million guilders).
Source: Annual Budgets 1987–99.

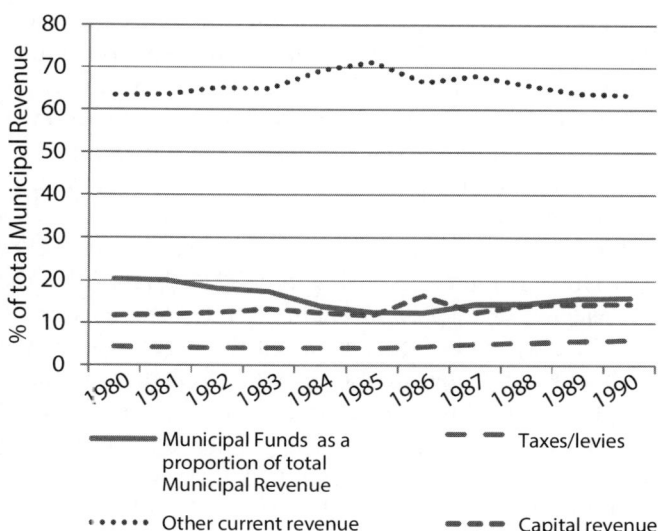

Figure 6.3.   Disaggregated Dutch municipal revenue sources.
Source: Central Bureau of Statistics (CBS).

Focusing on Municipal Funds, Table 6.1 shows how fiscal consolidation measures by national government resulted in an accumulation of cutbacks on the Municipal Fund from 1982 (the advent of the Christian–Liberal Lubbers-I government) to 1988.

These cuts appear to have been disproportionately large, compared to other cuts at the national level. But the issue of whether the budgetary pain was justly, reasonably and proportionately distributed between national and local government was contested. The coalition agreement of the Christian–Liberal

Table 6.1.   Accumulated cutbacks in the Dutch Municipal Fund (million guilders).

	1982	1983	1984	1985	1986	1987	1988
Spring budget 1982	47.6	122.6	156.2	185.1	185.1	185.1	185.1
Coalition agreement 1982		65.0	121.0	232.0	409.0	558.4	699.7
Benefit principle cuts		65.0	139.0	232.0	417.0	417.0	417.0
Further cutbacks 1984			60.0	88.0	118.0	118.0	118.0
Further cutbacks 1985				60.6	60.6	60.6	60.6
Further cutbacks 1986					50.0	50.0	50.0
Further cutbacks 1988							30.0
Total accumulated	47.6	252.6	476.2	797.7	1,239.7	1,389.1	1,560.4
Annual increase of cutbacks		205.0	223.6	321.5	442.0	149.4	171.3

Source: Jacobs (1986: 212).

Lubbers-I cabinet in 1982 announced that municipalities would have to make a 'reasonable contribution' to the consolidation of the nation's public finances. The Association of Dutch Municipalities, the Council for Municipal Finances, the Inter-provincial Consultation Body, and several parties in parliament accused the cabinet of imposing unreasonable, that is, more than proportionate, budgetary cuts. Parliament demanded that the cabinet deliver a White Paper on the proportion of (provinces and) municipalities in the budget cuts, the so-called 'proportionality paper' (Ministerie van Financiën 1984).

The Association of Dutch Municipalities (VNG) argued that the financial figures were evidence of disproportionality (VNG 1984; Jacobs 1986). They claimed that the local budget cuts exceeded the percentage of the national budget cuts that municipalities were supposed to realise according to the 1984 'proportionality paper'. Another argument was that since the early 1980s national government spending had exceeded the growth of the Municipal Fund. Figure 6.4, based on contemporary budget data, demonstrates the more than proportionate squeeze on the Municipal Fund compared to the national expenditures and to GDP.

In its 1984 'proportionality paper' the cabinet presented different figures, showing that the retrenchments at national, provincial and municipal level had remained almost proportional during that period. But specialists in public finance were aware that budget figures can be calculated, presented and interpreted in different ways (Jacobs 1986; Jochoms 1997). Indeed, for what they are worth, the retrospective CBS data on total expenditure at the municipal level, compared with total expenditure at central government level, indicate that cuts in central government spending were made earlier (between

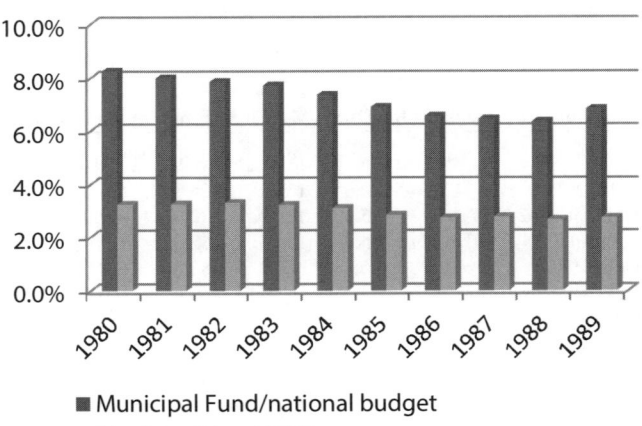

Figure 6.4. Comparative development of Dutch Municipal Fund.
Source: Annual Budgets 1980–90.

1982 and 1985) than those applying to local government, but that the local government cuts were much deeper than central government cuts after 1985.

The User-Pay Principle

Another contested issue at the time was the user-pay principle (or 'benefit principle', in Dutch parlance), a new cutback instrument introduced by the Lubbers-I cabinet, implying that the state should levy taxes or tariffs corresponding to the 'benefit' the citizen gained from the public goods and services that were delivered. The government argued that these 'benefit principle' cuts could be recouped by municipalities by incorporating them in the charges paid by local citizens for their services. These cuts (about a third of the total) should therefore be left out of the 'proportionality' debate, said the cabinet. The municipalities' counter-arguments were that they possessed legal autonomy in determining the price for their local services, that the cabinet's calculations of possible 'benefit cuts' were incorrect, and that national government itself had not accomplished its own planned user-pay programme (planned increases in school tuition, higher fares for public transport, tolls for bridges and motorways, and more, were not realised). Most municipalities in practice refrained from imposing 'benefit cuts' on their citizens and did not increase their tariffs, which increased the pressure on their budgets.

Increased Expenditures: General Assistance Act

The General Assistance Act, enacted in 1965 as the concluding piece in the social security system, provided assistance in case social insurance and other forms of social security failed to cover the needs of individual citizens or families. The maximum level of social assistance was 95 per cent of the legal net-minimum wage. The execution of the General Assistance Act was assigned to municipalities. The ministry of social affairs financed 90 per cent of the assistances while 10 per cent (as well as the organisational costs) was to be paid for by the municipalities themselves out of the general allocations from the Municipal Fund. This supposedly provided an incentive for efficient budget control by municipalities. Since the late 1970s municipalities were confronted with a sizeable growth of assistance expenditures, due to the worsening economic situation and increasing unemployment. Figure 6.5 shows that expenditure rose sharply in the early 1980s, only to stabilise in the late 1980s.

Not only did expenditure for social assistance grow in general, but it was very high in municipalities with high unemployment figures (Van der Staaij 1984: 43). Municipalities complained that the rise in social assistance expenditures was unprecedented and unpredictable. Because of the bad shape of the economy, municipalities were in no position to influence the growth in the

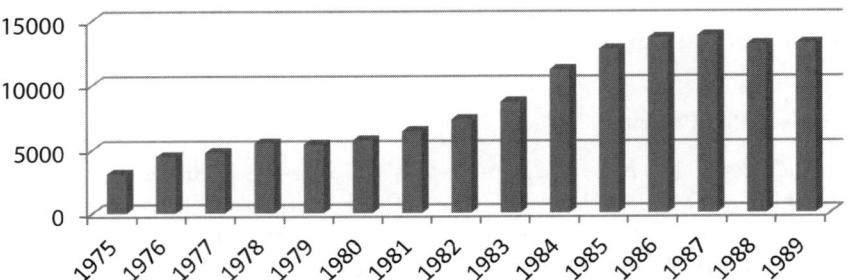

Figure 6.5. Budget of Dutch social assistance (million guilders).
Source: Annual Budgets 1975–89.

number of applications and recipients. The 10 per cent that municipalities had to contribute from their own funds had grown immensely, while at the same time the Municipal Fund incomes had diminished and the organisational costs were not compensated for at all.

During the parliamentary debate about the 1984 'proportionality paper', the government was asked to fully compensate the municipalities for the unforeseen increases in social assistance expenditures. The government decided to compensate for two-thirds of the increases in programme costs, adding 58.8 million guilders to the Municipal Fund. Furthermore, two-thirds of the increase in organisational costs was also compensated for, leading to another 26 million. Although municipalities were naturally happy to receive this compensation, the Association of Dutch Municipalities calculated that even with these compensations for unforeseen increases, the net result still was a substantial loss, some 515 million guilders in the period 1981–85, and that the compensation still did not cover two-thirds of the annual increases, as shown in Table 6.2.

Table 6.2. Increase in number of Social Assistance recipients, 1983–84.

	Number in 1983	Number in 1984	% of population
Nijmegen	10,471	12,476	8.8
Groningen	11,208	13,844	8.2
's-Hertogenbosch	5,892	6,988	7.8
Arnhem	7,886	9,277	7.2
Tilburg	8,943	10,259	6.7
Almelo	3,507	4,012	6.4
Helmond	3,043	3,434	5.7
Total for 7 municipalities	50,950	60,290	7.4
Total for Netherlands	456,756	533,201	3.7

Source: VNG, September 1984: 15.

Responses to Fiscal Squeeze:
Cutback Strategies and Financial Management Reform

As mentioned above, because of the legal obligation to balance budgets, the annual reports on municipal finances by the CBS could not and did not contain figures on municipal budget deficits. Yet the annual CBS reports reveal that, although the national total of expenditures equalled the total of revenues, municipalities switched expenditures from the current account to the capital account, funding current spending by cutting capital investment. In 1985 expenditures of 1,863 million guilders (1.4 per cent of the total of 132.7 billion expenditures) were transferred to the capital account. In 1986 2,209 million of the total expenditures of 130.9 billion (1.6 per cent) were transferred to the capital account (CBS 1986; 1987). These figures confirm the impression from other case studies that municipalities, at least at the start of the cutbacks, chose to cut procurement costs and capital reserves rather than personnel or services.

Not surprisingly, in the 1980s numerous publications on local cutbacks saw the light. The Association of Dutch Municipalities organised several seminars and conferences on the theme. Studies were carried out into cutbacks in specific policy areas and cities (Dijk 1988) or regions (Olieman 1986; Bentvelsen 1989). Here two in-depth case studies of local cutback measures and strategies will be considered (Heij 1985; Jochoms 1997).

Heij (1985) investigated a number of small, medium-sized and large municipalities as to the contents of their cutback measures and the strategies they deployed, and found that the strategy used to prepare the cutback measures differed between municipalities. In small municipalities the cutback operation was prepared by the financial division, whereas in larger municipalities the operation was prepared by the sector divisions in consultation with the respective aldermen (local councillors). A centralised preparation of cutbacks encountered objections and protests by the local officials, and the support of those officials for the implementation of the cutbacks was usually deemed indispensable.

By contrast, the content of the cutback measures showed similarities between municipalities. Although not always sharply distinct, some stages in the cutback process could be discerned. In the first stage municipalities appeared to cut 'low-hanging fruit' and 'frills' and to solve problems by cutting capital reserves. When these ad hoc measures were no longer sufficient, structural measures were taken to increase incomes or decrease expenditures by efficiency measures, downsizing and cutting tasks. Cutbacks were realised in investments rather than in personnel or material. Forced dismissals did not occur. Sectors such as police, education and social services were relatively spared. The extent of national government regulations and control of specific sectors to a large extent determined the flexibility of budget adjustments, and therefore the capacity for cutbacks. However, Heij's study covered only the early stages of municipal cutbacks. Later on the nationally imposed cutbacks intensified.

Different Approaches in Different Phases

Jochoms (1997) studied one large municipality for a period of over twenty years (1967–90). The study found that during the 1980s fiscal squeeze period the municipality seriously depleted its capital reserves to finance its budget deficits, to the extent that the reserves became negative, which was legally prohibited (Jochoms 1997: 319). Jochoms (ibid.) also found that the municipality managed to curb the growth in its expenditures from 7 to 4 million guilders, with retrenchments mounting up to the mid-1980s and peaking in 1987.

Jochoms' study discerned different phases in the municipality's approach to fiscal squeeze:

- *Phase 1: Denial of crisis (until 1982)*. The municipality had been confronted with budget deficits before and had always been able to get over it. In 1979 the political and administrative leadership was not convinced of the structural nature of the deficits and decided to take the risk of using the capital reserves. In 1980 and 1981 the deficit was again solved by using the capital reserve. Other financial-technical measures were taken, such as skipping the regular budget compensation for price inflation. Structural retrenchments did not take place. Voluntary and half-hearted attempts were made, but did not materialise.
- *Phase 2: Retrenchment policy (1982–83)*. Retrenchments on existing policies only commenced in 1982. A steering group was established, consisting of financial division heads and aldermen, who were to come up with multi-year proposals to the municipal council. The list consisted of increasing incomes and applications of the 'benefit principle', cutting the 'fat' off the budget, and efficiency measures. The budget 'frills' were cut off. At the end of 1982 a second cutback operation was needed. And in 1983 again two cutback operations had to be carried out. In this second phase the previous voluntary bottom-up approach was abandoned and a central steering group established. When time pressure intensified, decision-making became centralised in the hands of a few people. The decisions were mainly financial-technical. Political prioritising by the municipal council barely took place.

- *Phase 3: Political paradox (1984–85)*. The approach was changed. Politicians were to take the lead in determining the cuts, and the sector divisions were to elaborate the political priorities. The steering group determined the necessary size of sector cutbacks and the aldermen decided on the contents of the cuts. Three types of measures were distinguished: efficiency measures, measures to increase incomes and apply the user-pay principle, and task downsizing or cutting. The capital reserves cuts also continued. Politicians were not eager to diminish external services to the public. Internal efficiency measures turned out to be more acceptable.
- *Phase 4: Integration (1986–90)*. Whereas the 1986 budget contained a forecast imbalance of 3.3 million, the forecast 1987 budget imbalance suddenly exploded to a staggering 12.9 million. The rates for local property taxes and sewerage were increased. Staff cuts were planned. Still the political courage to downsize or cut external services to citizens was lacking. Increasing charges and efficiency were the favourite strategies.

It was only in the 1990s (after the period Jochoms investigated) that another more fundamental strategy emerged in the municipality, that is, discussions about its core tasks. From long-term, strategic and fundamental discussions the general local policy targets and aims were distilled and translated into core tasks to be carried out by the municipality. Non-core tasks could be privatised or hived off, but in the early 1990s such negative choices were not (yet) made (Jochoms 1997: 338).

The results from these case studies seem to confirm the conclusions of the cutback management literature of the 1980s (for a recent review see Raudla *et al.* 2013): the fundamental distinction between across-the-board strategies, such as cheese-slicing, decrementalism and equal misery on the one hand, and targeted or selective strategies on the other, involving political prioritising of tasks and taking selective decisions. The advantages of decremental strategies were that they were relatively quick and easy to carry out, they minimised conflicts since they avoided specifying victims, and they appealed to a common sense of justice and fairness of the cuts. Politicians did not have to stick their necks out by making explicit priorities in public service delivery.

Reform of the Financial Planning and Control System

The necessity of major cutbacks exposed the lack of effective overview of the financial means available. Municipal councils demanded better financial information to help them take decisions. Existing instruments for policy-making, planning and financial control—the usual cycle of policy plan, multiyear budget, annual budget, report and annual account—were considered inadequate for the far-reaching cutback decisions that had to be taken. Municipal councils had been overloaded with extensive annual budgets and accounts with large amounts of facts and figures that hardly provided them with insight and overview. The detailed figures in the budgets and accounts (the annual accounts being presented only several years later to the council) did not satisfactorily enable council members to influence policymaking. Less detail and more overview were desired. Another main point of criticism was the lack of insight into the factual implementation and realisation of policymaking, the outputs and outcomes of the decisions. Policy goals should be translated into specific and measurable tasks and results.

Several municipalities began to devise a better financial planning and control system (Kickert 2000). Following local initiatives in 1987 a project group was set up by the ministry of home affairs to devise and introduce a new system (in Dutch called *beleids- en beheersinstrumentarium*, abbreviated as BBI; Ministerie van Binnenlandse Zaken 1989). The BBI project formulated the following starting points:

- overall control by the council and aldermen;
- 'integral management' responsibilities for line managers;
- responsibilities for results based on task contracts;
- decentralisation of authority;
- periodic assessment of and accounting for results.

The new planning and control system was to consist of various phases:

- formulating a general policy programme and plan;
- deriving a specific product- and output-based budget from the general policy plan;
- presenting intermediate management reports based on products and outputs;
- presenting the annual report and accounts.

Aardema (2002) in his evaluation of the impact of the BBI showed that it was more than merely a new financial control instrument. It was a new approach to local governance, policymaking and control. The primary reason for the development of the new financial system was the fiscal stress that Dutch municipalities endured in the 1980s. The BBI project soon attracted dozens of municipalities volunteering to cooperate. It was widely publicised and seminars and conferences attracted many participants. In 1989 municipalities took over the lead from the ministry of home affairs and established a BBI foundation to continue the development of the new system. The objectives of BBI were not confined to mere financial management, but included a strengthening of the position of the municipal council, improvement of management and organisation, and better client-orientation. By the early 1990s a majority of Dutch municipalities were implementing BBI. The BBI project group continued to organise meetings, conferences and courses to disseminate the ideas, and even published a BBI magazine. Universities were involved in academic studies The BBI project was formally terminated in 1995. By that time the fiscal squeeze period was over, attention shifted from financial instruments to more strategic visions, and the objectives of the BBI project were broadened from purely financial to more administrative and organisational matters (Aardema 2002; Van Helden 1998).

Organisational Reform: The Divisionalised Business Model

Not only did the fiscal squeeze cause a major reform of the local financial planning and control system, it also led to a major reform of local organisational structure. The need to better facilitate decision-making on cutback measures demanded a better financial management system, and the new financial system demanded a reform of the administrative organisation. Accordingly, in the later 1980s many municipalities adopted a form of divisionalised business model (the so-called 'concern-division' model: Bekke & Hiemstra 1998; Camps 1996; Kickert 2000). The divisional business model with its small and lean corporate centre and relatively autonomous corporate divisions, which had become popular worldwide in the private corporate sector, the well-known decentralisation ideas of the management guru Peter Drucker, was translated to the Dutch public sector.

The responsibilities for both policymaking and execution were decentralised to the sector divisions. The number of sector divisions was reduced and merged with the policy staff of the central city management, to attain clear and consistent tasks. The sector divisions gained a high degree of autonomy by means of management contracts. 'Integral management' (both line and staff functions) was delegated to the line managers. Public tasks that primarily consisted of external direct services to the citizens became more client- and customer-oriented. New techniques such as the 'one-stop-shop' were introduced. ICT played an important role in the development of such new client-friendly reforms. Facilitating services such as catering and maintenance were often transformed into profit centres or completely privatised.

The central city management, now called 'concern staff', was supposed to be lean (De Vries 1995; Camps 1996; Bekke & Hiemstra 1998). As many tasks as possible were decentralised to the sector divisions. Only a limited number of tasks were considered to be appropriate for the corporate centre:

- overall planning and control: setting the overall frames for planning and control of the divisions, carrying out the audits, using the management reports;

- overall strategy: the long-term future strategic and cross-sector plans;
- policy coordination between and across the sector policies of the divisions.

Understandably, in the beginning the central staff concentrated on financial planning and control. The financial problem was, after all, the primary reason for all the changes. Only later did the strategic and long-term planning function really take shape.

The high degree of decentralisation of both policymaking and executive tasks to the sector divisions did bring with it a threat of 'sectoralisation' of the local administration. The weekly management team meeting, the gathering of the division managers presided over by the central city manager (in Dutch *gemeentesecretaris*, municipal secretary), was to fulfil the role of cross-sector coordination. The prime responsibility for coordination across the sector divisions' boundaries fell on the city manager and his or her slimmed down 'concern staff'. The perception of sector fragmentation of policymaking and organisation led many municipalities to rethink and elaborate the tasks of the centre and empower the coordination and strategic cross-sector functions. In some cities the central city manager was left with a role that was indeed lean and almost empty; in other cities he became an 'uncrowned King or Rasputin' (Korsten 1995).

Effects of NPM Reform: Empirical Studies

It is commonly assumed that Western governments adopted business-type management techniques because of financial stress. The argument is that governments with financial problems had an incentive to introduce techniques to improve effectiveness and especially efficiency of service delivery, which they believed were to be found in business management. This 'financial stress hypothesis' was put forward by Hood who illustrated it at a macro-level by comparing various OECD countries (Hood 1995).

Van Helden (2000) carried out a micro-level test of this hypothesis by studying eight municipalities in the Netherlands. Van Helden tested the hypothesis that the weaker the financial position of a municipality the more likely it was to adopt business-style planning and control instruments. The empirical test did not confirm the financial stress hypothesis. Only two out of the eight municipalities fitted with the hypothesis (Van Helden 2000). Further critical methodological scrutiny of his approach and data did not enable Van Helden to revise his refutation. This empirical refutation is remarkable, as the hypothesis is taken for granted all over the world. The empirical refutation implies that the introduction of managerial-style reforms had been relatively independent of the fiscal setting.

Another Dutch scholar of local government reform, Ter Bogt (2008a), concluded that economic-rational considerations alone did not fully explain the reforms. To assess how far factors such as economic rationality, mimicry, external legitimation and automatism played a part in the implementation of changes in management control (BBI) in Dutch municipalities and provinces, Ter Bogt (2008a; 2008b) conducted interviews with politicians and professional managers to get a general impression of the interviewees' perceptions of the nature and effects of changes. As to reasons for introducing management changes, the respondents not only mentioned economic reasons, such as improvement of performance, efficiency and effectiveness, but also political reasons such as volatility and uncertainty. Following this reform trend in other organisations was also mentioned. General and financial city managers attended MBA courses, and learned about and embraced business administration ideas, models and techniques. NPM was a worldwide trend, and local management reforms were a nationwide trend in Dutch municipalities. City managers regularly met each other, exchanged ideas about their respective reforms, and adopted each other's allegedly successful reform models (mimicry). Also mentioned in their responses was the need for formal compliance with new rules and regulations externally imposed by central government. Disappointments with reforms in the past were mentioned as a reason for further change (Ter Bogt 2008a).

As to the effects of the reforms, most interviewees mentioned that no systematic measurement of efficiency and effectiveness and effects of changes had taken place. The overall impression was that a combination of various management changes had resulted in slightly improved performance. Most interviewees found it difficult to specify clearly the effects of the introduction of accrual accounting systems and were rather negative about the effects of the output budgeting systems introduced in many municipalities by the BBI project. In 2002–03 central government had obliged local government to draw up outcome budgets (and also outcome annual reports) in addition to product budgets. The interviewees did not consider this reform, an obligation imposed by central government, to be a success. It was difficult to give clear definitions of the goals and aims of programmes. Performance measurement and benchmarking were also critically evaluated by interviewees. The experiences with quantitative performance measurement were disappointing, especially in the beginning. Only gradually was more useful performance information produced. But it helped to develop and encourage a more performance-oriented culture in their organisations. However, the reverse seemed true as well, as the interviewees also suggested that a more performance-oriented culture stimulated the use of performance information (Ter Bogt 2008b).

So not only was the commonly held assumption that fiscal stress accounted for the introduction of NPM-type reforms not validated, but the same applies to the widely shared view that NPM reforms lead to higher effectiveness and efficiency.

Effects beyond NPM: Local Democracy in the 1990s

When in the early 1990s German municipalities adopted the Tilburg model as the basis of their 'neues Steuerungsmodell' and when the Swiss in the mid-1990s came across the Tilburg case and incorporated it into their reforms of 'wirkungsorientierter Verwaltungsführung', some Dutch municipalities had already departed from this managerial model of reform, moving from an internal management-oriented view towards a more external citizen-oriented one. According to Hendriks & Tops (1997) the 1980s were the years when local government was orientated inwards upon its own functioning. External relations were tense, particularly because of the cutbacks. Cities tried to create business-style relations with their external partners. Output criteria were developed to determine the size of subsidies. Public–private partnerships became the new catchword for relations with private investors. But the criticism that local government 'lacked ears and eyes', that the adoption of private business-style models had gone too far, that citizens were more than clients and customers, could also be heard.

The four-yearly Dutch local elections of 1990 were a shock for local democracy. The average turnout dropped from 73 per cent to 62 per cent, and in some cities fell below the symbolic threshold of 50 per cent. Moreover, extreme right parties for the first time gained access to a number of city councils. Local politicians reacted by a 'search for the lost citizen', which, according to Hendriks & Tops (1997), consisted of two different approaches, namely an institutional approach and a process-oriented one. An institutional line can be recognised in renewed debates about directly elected mayors, alderman drawn from outside the city council, the use of local referendums and so on. Except for local referendums, which have indeed been held in a number of cities on specific local high-profile issues, these debates had little effect.

The second, process-oriented renewal of local decision-making was more noteworthy. In various ways citizens were given a more prominent role in the local decision-making processes. Alongside the traditional forms of citizen participation, new methods were introduced such as citizen polls, citizen panels and so on, and in particular new procedures for interactive decision-making. Local government had become more cautious and decided to involve citizens and other interest groups in the early stages of the planning of prestigious projects, such as a new city hall or concert hall. In cases of different and opposing interest groups, the role of local government in such decision-making processes shifted towards one of process architecture and process management. The main aim was that the process should yield some form of feasible compromise and consensus.

However, interactive decision-making could lead to major political tensions and conflicts. The formal authority of the officially elected politicians, who in principle have the ultimate say in decision-making, was at stake. The 'primacy of democratic politics', with policy decided by locally elected representatives, could be imperilled.

The search for alternative forms of democracy at the end of the 1990s also led to a legal restructuring of the local democratic system. The Municipal Act was changed into a so-called 'dualism' model in which the relationship between the city council and the College of Mayor and Aldermen became more separate (Korsten & Tops 1998).

Another remarkable development in Dutch local (and national) politics was the rise of populist parties in the 2000s. At the end of the 1990s a general shift in citizens' views on politics and government took place, in the form of an ever-increasing distrust of politics and government, which at the national level culminated in the sudden and unexpected popularity of the outsider-populist Pim Fortuyn in 2002 and the subsequent electoral success of right-wing populist parties, at both national and local level.

In a sense this right-wing popular party upsurge might possibly be a side-effect of public management—not in the direct sense that this electoral development could be related to the increasing dissatisfaction of citizens with the quality of public service management, but rather in a more indirect sense, that it followed a period in which politicians had assumed a rational-technocratic and managerial style. In particular, this was the period of Liberal and Social Democrat coalition cabinets, in which the two ideologically opposed parties had chosen purely pragmatic politics and compromise policymaking. This 'technocratic manager' attitude was symbolised in the person of the Labour Party leader at the time, Ad Melkert, who was brought down by Fortuyn publicly on TV during the 2002 election campaign. The 2002 general election, right after the murder of Fortuyn, resulted in the victory of his party, which then became a partner in the new (short-lived) coalition cabinet. The successful Fortuyn revolt and the many local post-Fortuyn populist parties frightened the local politicians. Local governments seemed paralysed and inertia reigned. Nobody dared to take any significant measures for fear of these popular protest parties. Though debatable and empirically unproven, this possible indirect link between public management and right-wing populist politics is a matter for consideration.

Summary and Conclusion

This chapter has shown that the fiscal squeeze in Dutch local government in the 1980s was caused by several factors. First, Dutch local government had a legal obligation to balance its budget. Secondly, we have shown that the decreases in municipal income were externally imposed cutback measures decided upon by national government, and that the budgetary pains were unevenly distributed between national and local government. Thirdly, we gave a few examples of increases in municipal expenditures, mainly due to the deteriorating economy and rising unemployment. The conclusion seems justified that municipalities were standing with their backs to the wall, and with their hands tied.

As national figures on local budget deficits and cutbacks did not exist, because of the legal obligation to balance budgets, cutback measures and strategies could only be analysed at the local level of individual municipalities. Studies showed that in the early stages of the fiscal squeeze municipalities 'solved' uncovered expenditure 'surpluses' by cutting capital reserves and adopting other financial-technical 'bookkeeping' measures. Then they turned to cutting the low-hanging fruit, the budget frills, and later on took efficiency measures and downsized some public services. In the beginning municipalities were not convinced of the urgency or structural nature of the fiscal problems. The usual initial resistance to change took place, that is, denial and defence. Only later did municipalities start to recognise the problem, adapt to the new situation, and move to the next stage of cost-efficiency measures and downsizing. Politicians were not eager to downsize the services to the citizens. Fundamental decision-making and political priority-setting only occurred at a late stage of the fiscal squeeze. Apparently, across-the-board measures, cheese-slicing, and other decremental strategies were more favoured than prioritising of public tasks and targeted or selective decision-making.

Although during the 1980s Dutch municipalities were deeply concerned with the cutbacks, and some municipalities were confronted with dozens of percentages of impending budget deficits, the national macro-figures reveal another picture. The steady rise of local incomes from the Municipal Fund during the 1970s flattened in the early 1980s and decreased in absolute terms in 1985 and 1986, but later again increased. The annual increase of cutbacks on the Municipal Fund was 1.6 per cent in 1983, peaked to 3.7 per cent in 1986 and decreased to 1.4 per cent in 1988. Even the accumulated cutbacks on the Municipal Fund over the 1982–88 period only amounted to 12.8 per cent. Combined with the decrease in specific allocations, total municipal incomes did decrease in the period 1987–89 but only by a few percentage points per year, and afterwards again increased. The impression, then widely shared by local politicians and officials as well as academics, that Dutch municipalities were confronted with massive and severe cuts, in hindsight seems somewhat exaggerated, and only in terms of multi-year accumulated cutbacks was the size of the fiscal squeeze considerable. Indeed, as Figure 6.1 at the outset of this chapter showed, fiscal squeeze in Dutch municipalities in the period 1982–89 seems to have been a 'soft' squeeze which produced fiscal consolidation and was undertaken in conditions of fiscal stress but not fiscal crisis.

Fiscal Squeeze and NPM Reforms

Dutch municipalities not only solved their budgetary problems with short-term measures like cutbacks, retrenchments and cost-efficiency, but also decided to fundamentally reform their financial management system. The fiscal squeeze was a key factor leading to a nationwide financial management reform in Dutch local government, encompassing more and more municipalities over a period of more than ten years.

Although it is commonly presumed that NPM-type reforms were introduced because of fiscal stress, this claimed causal relationship is doubtful. There is a marked difference between what was said by municipalities or their interest organisations about the fiscal squeeze and the BBI reform project, and the conclusions of academics based on careful empirical analysis. The latter studies, albeit few in number, refute the presumed causal link between fiscal stress and the adoption of BBI-type reforms. Reasons other than economic efficiency led to NPM-type reforms, such as following the allegedly successful reforms of other municipalities, and the formal compliance with new rules and regulations. It is remarkable that a hypothesis that is taken for granted all over the Western world was so clearly refuted in this case.

The other causal claims mentioned above about the effects of the squeeze are also problematic. The assumption that the inward-looking, intra-organisational, management-oriented type of reform was causally related to the later more outward-looking, citizen-oriented reform in the 1990s is also highly debatable. The 'search for the lost citizen' was rather triggered by alarming political events at the time. The quest for new and alternative forms of local democracy such as local referendums, citizen panels and polls, interactive decision-making and the like was a development that took place independently of NPM. And the assumption that the sudden and surprising upsurge of populist parties in the 2000s might have something to do with NPM is even more dubious. The populist Fortuyn was indeed the flamboyant opposite of the technocratic manager Melkert, but several other factors also explain the electoral success of populist parties.

History Repeated

The banking crisis of 2008 and subsequent economic crisis again resulted in a fiscal crisis which impelled the Dutch government in 2010 to undertake a fiscal squeeze that seriously affected municipalities. Moreover, the continuing crisis in the Eurozone after 2010 forced the Dutch government to take further successive cutback measures, including cutbacks imposed at local level. For Dutch municipalities this seems inevitably to lead to another period of fiscal squeeze and consolidation.

References

Aardema, H. (2002), *Doorwerking van BBI*, dissertation, Leusden, Bestuur en Management Consultants.

Bekke, A.J.G.M. & Hiemstra, J.M. (1998), 'Het Gemeentelijk Apparaat', Hoofdstuk 18, in A.F.A. Korsten & P.W. Tops, *Lokaal Bestuur in Nederland* (Alphen, Samsom).

Bentvelsen, T. (1989), *Financiële zorgen van gemeenten in de randstad* (Delft, Onderzoeksinstituut Technische Bestuurskunde, TU Delft).

Bogt, H.J. ter (2008a), 'Recent and Future Management Changes in Local Government: Continuous Focus on Rationality and Efficiency?', *Financial Accountability and Management*, 24: 31–57.

Bogt, H.J. ter (2008b), 'Management Accounting Change and New Public Management in Local Government', *Financial Accountability and Management*, 24: 209–41.

Camps, Th.W.A. (1996), 'De Levensduur van Gemeentelijke Organisatiemodellen', in *Is er nog Toekomst na het Sectorenmodel?* (Velp, Rijnconsult).

Centraal Bureau voor de Statistiek (CBS) (1986), *Statistiek der gemeentebegrotingen 1985* (The Hague, CBS).

Centraal Bureau voor de Statistiek (CBS) (1987), *Statistiek der gemeentebegrotingen 1986* (The Hague, CBS).

Dijk, S. (1988), *Het geld is op. Gemeentelijke bezuinigingen in Diemen*, Master's thesis, VU Amsterdam.

Havermans, A.J.E. (1984), *Artikel 12: Gemeenten*, dissertation, Katholieke Universiteit Nijmegen.

Heij, P.R. (1985), *Mogelijkheden en Onmogelijkheden van een Gemeentelijk Ombuigingsbeleid* (The Hague, IOO).

Helden, G.J. van (1998), 'A Review of the Policy and Management Instruments Project for Municipalities in the Netherlands', *Financial Accountability and Management*, 14: 85–104.

Helden G.J. van (2000), 'Is Financial Stress an Incentive for the Adoption of Businesslike Planning and Control in Local Government? A Comparative Study of Eight Dutch Municipalities', *Financial Accountability and Management*, 16: 83–100.

Hendriks, F. & Tops, P.W. (1997), 'Tussen democratisering en Verzakelijking. Trends in de hervorming van het lokaal bestuur in Nederland en Duitsland', *Bestuurswetenschappen*, 51: 190–217.

Hood, C. (1995), 'The "New Public Management" in the 1980s: Variations on a Theme', *Accounting, Organizations and Society*, 20: 93–109.

Jacobs, A.G.A. (1986), 'Nogmaals evenredigheid', *B&G*: 212–14.

Jochoms, Th. (1997), *Aan Facades Voorbij* (Delft, Eburon).

Kickert, W.J.M. (2000), *Public Management Reforms in The Netherlands* (Delft, Eburon).

Korsten, A.F.A. (1995), 'Das Tilburger Modell oder Tilburg als neues Mekka der öffentlichen Verwaltung', in R. Kleinfeld & A.F.A. Korsten (eds), *Konzern Stadt: Neue Steuerungsmodelle in den Kommunalverwaltungen* (Krefeld).

Korsten, A.F.A & Tops, P.W. (1998), *Lokaal Bestuur in Nederland* (Alphen, Samsom).

Ministerie van Binnenlandse Zaken (1989), Beleids- en Beheersinstrumentarium (BBI), Den Haag.

Ministerie van Financiën (1984), Evenredigheidsnota (April) (The Hague), TK 83–84, 18328, no. 2.

Olieman, R. (1986). *Gemeentelijke uitgaven versus gemeentelijke problemen. De situatie in de provincie Utrecht* (Rotterdam, Economisch geografisch instituut, Erasmus Universiteit Rotterdam).

Raudla, R., Kruusenberg, R. & Randma-Liiv, T. (2013), Literature review on cutback management (Tallinn, COCOPS paper, Tallinn University of Technology).

Staaij, D. van der (ed.) (1984), *Heroverwegen bij Gemeenten* (Alphen, Samsom).

Vereniging van Nederlandse Gemeenten (VNG) (1984), *Brief aan de Eerste en Tweede Kamer over gemeentefinanciën* (28 September) (The Hague).

Vries, K. de (1995), 'Organisatie vernieuwing in een middelgrote stad, besturen met het concernmodel', in *Handboek Management van Overheidsorganisaties* (Alphen, Samsom), G3120.

7

Repeating History: Fiscal Squeeze in Two Recessions in Ireland

NIAMH HARDIMAN

Introduction

IRELAND HAS BEEN TAKEN AS AN EXEMPLARY CASE OF FISCAL ADJUSTMENT, not once, but twice, in its recent history: first in the late 1980s, more recently in the implementation of a sharply contractionary policy mix after the crisis of 2008, underpinned by the terms of the international loan agreement negotiated in November 2010. History has in a sense repeated itself, first as tragedy, we might say, and then as tragedy again. In both cases, Ireland attracted international plaudits for the determined way in which it implemented fiscal consolidation measures. Indeed, since the experiences of the 1980s were followed by a return to growth within a few years, Ireland was one of the key cases on which the argument for 'expansionary fiscal contraction' was made.[1] The lessons from Ireland have therefore played an important role in shaping international conventional wisdom in the post-2008 period.

Critics of the 'expansionary fiscal contraction' hypothesis have shown that growth in the Irish economy in the late 1980s came about not as a result of fiscal consolidation—the biggest achievements in which followed, not preceded, the resumption of growth—but from factors such as the devaluation of 1986 which improved Ireland's international competitiveness position, and the 'Lawson boom' in the United Kingdom, which induced a sharp upturn in the demand for Irish exports. These conditions could not be replicated within the Eurozone, since currency devaluation was not possible and deflationary policy kept international demand conditions sluggish.

But a focus on the politics of fiscal squeeze shifts our attention to a number of other considerations that are usually excluded from discussions about the determinants of fiscal consolidation and its likely implications for growth. As Chapter 1 of this volume notes, the focus must be on governments' *ex ante* intentions. This may extend the time period to be studied backwards, beyond

---

[1] Additional references are included in an earlier draft of this paper, at Hardiman (2013).

Proceedings of the British Academy, **197**, 139–160. © The British Academy 2014.

that normally studied when the focus is on explaining successful outcomes. A second implication is that the policy mix involved in phases of fiscal squeeze might look different once we look at the political effort exerted over the whole period of interest. A third area that opens up for consideration is the political and electoral consequences of undertaking fiscal squeeze. Advocates of expansionary fiscal contraction argue that there is no electoral penalty for undertaking difficult fiscal squeezes (Alesina *et al.* 2011). Under certain circumstances, governments may indeed be able to persuade their own members and the electorate at large that a fiscal squeeze is necessary (Mauro 2011). But there is also evidence that governments that presided over tough fiscal decisions suffered electorally (Mulas-Granados 2004). All of these considerations suggest that we need to attend more closely than has hitherto been the case to the politics underlying phases of fiscal squeeze.

How the Politics of Fiscal Squeeze Set the Agenda in the 1980s

Most analyses of the fiscal corrections undertaken in Ireland during the 1980s focus narrowly on the period 1987–89, because this is the period during which an appreciable change occurred in the recorded deficit. But the size of the public debt was central to political debate for longer than that. Fiscal squeeze was a central issue in Irish public life from 1981 right through to 1989 and beyond.

Framing the Debate About Fiscal Squeeze

Understanding how this came about requires us to take a somewhat longer view of the trajectory of budgetary policy. Irish fiscal policy adhered to conservative principles for several decades following independence in 1922, under the guidance of the then fiscally orthodox Department of Finance. Governments were reluctant to permit budget deficits in any circumstances. The total tax take was small in comparative OECD context, and social services were poorly developed until some modernisation began in the late 1960s.

The departure from an orthodox fiscal stance was driven in large part by party political competition, and specifically by the terms on which the populist, centre-right Fianna Fáil party, then in opposition, contested the general election of 1977. Between 1973 and 1977, the government was formed by a coalition of the centre-right, fiscally orthodox Fine Gael party with the centre-left but much smaller Labour Party. This period saw the worst of the oil-price crisis, and the coalition had grown increasingly unpopular as it sought to manage stagflation without incurring large increases in debts or deficits. As in many other European countries at this time, the result was felt in rising unemployment. Fianna Fáil, the 'natural' party of government since the foundation of the state in 1922, was deeply anxious to return to power. The party committed itself to a series of expensive election pledges. It promised to restore prosperity and to boost employment through a sustained expansion in public spending, in what was to be the first sustained attempt at Keynesian stimulus measures. Fianna Fáil, if elected, would 'spend its way to full employment'. The party simultaneously proposed to abolish revenue instruments such as local domestic rates and car tax. It was elected with a landslide victory, and set up a new Department of Economic Planning and Development to oversee the government programme.

However, the main plank of the spending plan involved creating new public sector jobs. Additional spending commitments resulted from the Fianna Fáil government's attempts to broker two pay deals with the trade union movement and the employers' associations (the 'National Understandings' of 1979 and 1980). But in a highly open economy, with a currency pegged to sterling, the stimulus package tended to increase the consumption of exports, thereby worsening the trade deficit. Moreover, these measures had a pro-cyclical effect, taking effect as they did during a period of economic recovery, thus adding to public spending obligations during an upturn.

Official advisers in the Department of Finance and economic commentators alike warned about the growth of budget deficits. But leadership struggles within Fianna Fáil meant that the expansionary policy stance persisted into the early 1980s. During 1981 and 1982, efforts to address the growing budget deficit, conceived of as the Public Sector Borrowing Requirement, fell foul of volatile electoral politics: three general elections were held in an 18-month period. This is the period during which the public finances became a central issue in public debate. On the one side stood Fine Gael, the party of fiscal orthodoxy, under the leadership of Garret FitzGerald, whose father had been a prominent member of the government of the Irish Free State that was established in 1922. Fine Gael voiced increasingly urgent concern about the unsustainable debt dynamics. On the other side was Fianna Fáil, whose flamboyant and mysteriously wealthy leader Charles J. Haughey was still struggling to win a majority of seats in order to establish his own leadership over the party, and was therefore anxious to postpone having to take unpopular electoral decisions. The conflict between FitzGerald and Haughey was the stuff of many parliamentary set-pieces, dramatising in their style and personality, as much as in their politics, two contrasting strands in Irish public life.

It was not until late in 1982 that a stable new government was formed, and this held power until 1987. FitzGerald's Social Democratic-inflected preferences made it possible for Fine Gael to form a coalition with the much smaller

Labour Party (Mair 1987). But Labour had been taking a turn towards the left since 1969. The coalition was bound from the start to encounter difficulties in implementing the fiscal squeeze, the necessity of which Fine Gael was committed to, and to which the Labour Party had reluctantly assented.

The period after the return to government of Fianna Fáil in February 1987 is normally seen as the principal period of fiscal retrenchment. But in the framework of fiscal squeeze, this can be seen as just one moment of a much longer political effort. The politics of fiscal squeeze dominated every budget introduced by the Fine Gael–Labour coalition, starting with the tough budget that caused the short-lived government that had been elected in June 1981 to fall in January 1982. The most difficult years came in the first half of the 1980s, when it was not altogether clear that Ireland would be able to recover from the compounded problems of ever-rising debt and stalled growth, very high unemployment and mass emigration, along with ongoing uncertainty about the potential spillover of the Northern Ireland Troubles into the politics of the Republic. Moreover, a great deal of Ireland's public borrowing was held in foreign currency, so Ireland was vulnerable to shifting international interest and exchange rates.

Public spending net of debt service was rising, first as a consequence of the pro-cyclical spending boost of the late 1970s, and then because the demands on welfare spending grew as unemployment began to mount—from 8 per cent in 1980 to almost 17 per cent in 1985. Meanwhile, revenues had fallen in the late 1970s as a result of the budgetary give-aways promised in the 1977 election.

Tough Choices Between Tax Increases and Spending Cuts

This leads us to our second consideration, that is, the timing and composition of budgetary adjustment. The politics of fiscal effort that underlay the sustained budgetary squeeze of the 1980s throw the 'orthodox' story about Ireland's fiscal adjustment into question. The total public debt continued to accumulate until 1987, when it was about 112 per cent of GDP, after which it started to come down. However, even though the debt-to-GDP ratio was not stabilised in the first half of the 1980s, significant fiscal retrenchment had been undertaken during the lifetime of the Fine Gael–Labour coalition government. Between 1982 and 1986, on the key indicators of the time, the Exchequer Borrowing Requirement actually did fall by three points and the Public Sector Borrowing Requirement by more than five points (Honohan 1992: 290). Contrary to the standard account of Ireland's fiscal squeeze of the 1980s, 'most of the improvement in the fiscal balance was achieved through increases in tax revenues rather than expenditure cuts' (Honohan 1992: 312). In fact, the years in which the central government deficit showed its worst performance were 1982 and 1983. In those years, the total deficit stood at about 12.5 per cent of GDP. Revenues had been around 33 per cent of GDP during the 1970s, and accounted for 37 per cent of GDP in 1981, and this rose rapidly to 41 per cent in 1983, where it stabilised until 1988. These changes meant that the public finances almost reached a primary balance in 1985, and actually did so in 1988, as Figure 7.1 shows.

The reason why the coalition government relied more heavily on increased taxation than on spending cuts arises from the divergence in political priorities at the heart of the coalition government. Although both parties recognised that something had to be done, agreement over how precisely to address the deficit proved difficult to obtain. Emigration also picked up pace in the mid-1980s, disguising the true effects of job losses and underemployment. Even after the resumption of GDP growth in the late 1980s, a period of 'jobless growth' followed, with no appreciable change in employment rates until after 1994. This put sustained pressure on welfare expenditure, and on other categories of entitlement such as housing benefits. But while welfare payments—still set at low levels at this time—were not cut, other categories of public spending were indeed targeted. For example, an embargo on public sector recruitment was introduced, a controversial measure at a time when private sector employment was falling.

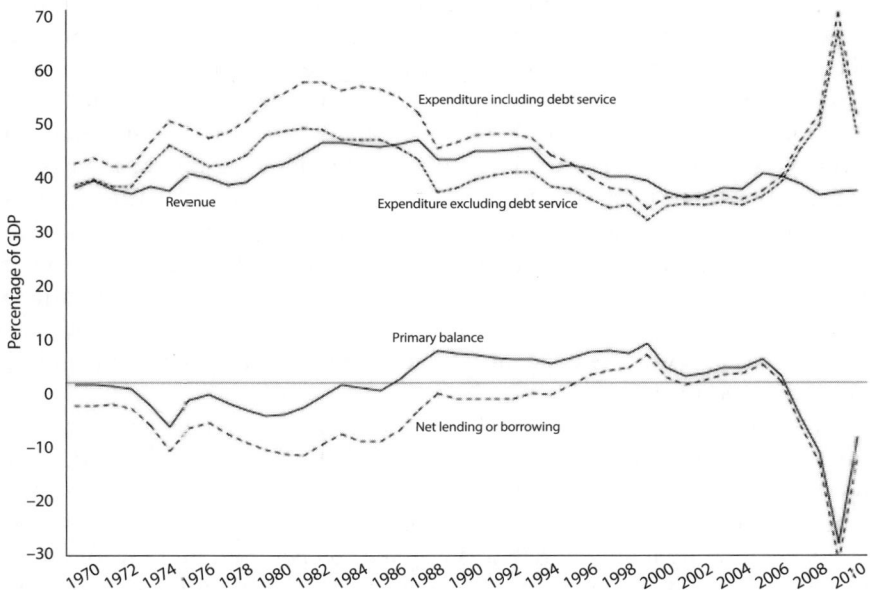

Figure 7.1.   Revenues, expenditure and primary balance as % GDP, Ireland 1970–2010.
Source: Central Statistics Office (2012); European Commission (2013).

Cabinet debates were famously prolonged and indecisive, not least because of the irreconcilability of party political preferences over how to address the ongoing fiscal crisis. But if forthright public spending cuts were contentious, so too were overt tax increases. Indeed, the short-lived coalition government of 1981–82 fell in February 1982 when an independent socialist ally vetoed the compromise budget package, an occasion memorialised as a vote against introducing a new indirect tax on children's shoes. So the question arises as to how much of the increase in total revenues was attributable to uncorrected fiscal drag at a time of high inflation—requiring little *ex ante* agreement on fiscal squeeze—and how much of it followed from more difficult budgetary innovation.

The question is perhaps not so easily resolvable in these terms, though. By the 1980s, over-reliance on fiscal drag as a revenue raiser had itself become highly politicised. Some of the largest street demonstrations ever seen in Ireland were held across the country in 1979 and 1980, organised by the trade union movement, to protest against what had come to be seen as an already very unfair income tax system. The Irish revenue system had evolved in a rather ad hoc manner over time, so the distributive consequences of tax increases were not well planned. Many categories of income and expenditure used in other countries were exempt in Ireland, particularly property and wealth. Corporation tax had been held at a low rate for many firms since the 1950s, as part of an economic development strategy based on promoting exports and attracting foreign direct investment. Groups such as farmers and the self-employed were able to avail themselves of advantages such as self-reported income and lagged tax payment. Tax administration was patchy and inefficient. The result was that ever-heavier tax burdens were imposed on employees earning ever-lower levels of income, since these were the easiest sources of revenue to target effectively. Pay-As-You-Earn (PAYE) and consolidated income and social insurance contributions had only been introduced in the early 1970s, and high inflation had pushed ever-larger numbers into the tax net. In 1965, the marginal tax rate of a single person on average industrial earnings was 31.5 per cent, and that of a single person on twice the average level of earnings was the same. In 1985, these rates were 56.3 per cent and 62 per cent respectively.

The coalition government was highly constrained in its policy options, but much of the agonising over budget policy was about how best to extract yet more revenue from a system that was already creaking, without damaging the labour market even further. In 1983/4, the number of tax bands was increased to six and the top marginal rate was raised to 65 per cent; and the following year the lowest rate of 25 per cent was abolished, leaving employees with a tax rate of 35 per cent on the lowest income tier. The distortions in the overall tax system only worsened as the fiscal crisis deepened. However, although Fine

Gael was by tradition a fiscally orthodox party, under the leadership of Garret FitzGerald it supported tilting the balance of the income tax increases in a somewhat progressive direction, and this made agreement with the Labour Party a little easier to achieve.

Paying the Political Price

This brings us to our third consideration, the political costs of engaging in tough fiscal squeeze, and the electoral penalties this may entail. The Fine Gael–Labour government performed poorly in the opinion polls as the date for the next general election drew nearer, and the centre-right, populist Fianna Fáil stepped up its attack. Fianna Fáil made increasing political capital out of the high income tax rates and the under-funding of what were still quite low-level social and health services. It stood on a platform of reversing the cuts that had already taken place. It also initiated talks with the trade union movement and employers' associations, with a view to trying to revive a negotiated stance on economic management.

The election results were disastrous for Fine Gael and for Labour, and the principal beneficiary was Fianna Fáil. Also benefiting was a new party, the fiscally conservative, socially liberal Progressive Democratic Party, which was a breakaway from Fianna Fáil but which also appealed to some disillusioned Fine Gael voters. But though Fianna Fáil was now the largest party, it did not command a majority in parliament. Labour was deeply unwilling at this time to consider a possible new coalition alliance with Fianna Fáil.

What was especially striking about the results of the 1987 election was that in a country with no strong left–right political cleavage, the class basis of support for parties was more strongly marked than previously. Fianna Fáil still won a large vote share across all social groups, but its support among working-class voters rose disproportionately, while its middle-class support base shrank. Meanwhile, Fine Gael's support among middle-class voters stayed fairly secure, while its ability to reach across class divisions, never very strong, became weaker. There was a strong core of support, mostly middle-class, for 'responsible' fiscal policies. But there was also a rising wave of social discontent, especially among the working class, for an end to spending constraints and redress of the high tax burden (Penniman & Farrell 1987; Sinnott 1995).

At first, it appeared that Ireland was about to enter another phase of electoral instability in which no party would be able to form a stable government. But two developments in the aftermath of the election changed the situation. First, with the prospect of forming a government in view, Fianna Fáil shifted its pre-election stance dramatically. It now accepted the case made by the outgoing government that the public finances had to be stabilised, since the total debt was still on an upward trajectory. Secondly, Fine Gael's new leader, Alan Dukes, committed the party to refrain from opposition to Fianna Fáil's budgetary measures for electoral advantage (as Fianna Fáil in opposition had consistently sought to do), provided Fianna Fáil adhered to a deficit-reducing strategy that Fine Gael could assent to. Fine Gael's so-called 'Tallaght Strategy' (named after the Dublin suburb where Dukes secured his reluctant party's acquiescence) gave Fianna Fáil considerable freedom of manoeuvre. But it proved electorally very costly to Fine Gael. The new minority Fianna Fáil government then went on to undertake a programme of fiscal consolidation more dramatic than anything of which the preceding government had been capable.

Fianna Fáil's policy mix between 1987 and 1992 differed from that of the preceding government in its willingness to undertake severe spending cuts. At the same time, it committed to a modest programme of reform in both tax composition and tax administration. A tax amnesty in 1988 signalled the start of a new era of tax enforcement. Employee tax rates were reduced, the base was broadened and the net widened, and new compliance measures were introduced. All this was made possible by a tripartite agreement negotiated in 1987, the Programme for National Recovery. This involved pay increases lower than the anticipated inflation rate, which would be offset by improvements in disposable income as a result of changes in the incidence and level of taxation.

The 1987 and subsequent pay–tax deals were later held to be pivotal to achieving fiscal stabilisation and consolidation (MacSharry & White 2000). But as Figure 7.1 shows, without the increase in revenues that had been achieved in the preceding years, the corresponding cuts in expenditure would have had to be very much more severe, or the new tax concessions much smaller, to achieve the fiscal consolidation the government was aiming for.

A corollary of the social partnership agreement was that the trade unions acquiesced to deep cuts in public spending, including not only an embargo on further public sector recruitment, but sharp cuts in spending on social services. Fianna Fáil also squeezed welfare spending in real terms, which the coalition government had not done—real welfare rates had remained constant between 1982 and 1987. Large cuts were made in the capital budget. In retrospect, many economic commentators noted that this was a mistake, and that squeezing investment in infrastructure had long-lasting damaging effects on growth as well as on the quality of services. But since the main target at the time was to reduce total borrowing, it was counted a successful strategy.

Fianna Fáil's public successes in bringing about improvements in the budgetary situation in the years after 1987 were only in part attributable to their new determination to stabilise the public finances. As noted earlier, international factors played a key role in facilitating deficit stabilisation during the 1980s. The parity between the Irish pound and sterling had been severed in 1979, and Ireland participated in the European Exchange Rate Mechanism (ERM) during the 1980s and 1990s, before entering European Monetary Union in 1999. In October 1986, the government managed a smooth devaluation of 8 per cent of the Irish pound against sterling. This meant that during the period of fiscal consolidation of the 1980s, the Irish government was able to take advantage of changes in exchange rates to adjust the distributive costs of fiscal management. During the ERM currency crisis of 1992, the Irish pound was further devalued by 9 per cent against the Deutschmark (Honohan & Conroy 1994).

Ireland's attempts to reduce its public deficit and regain control over its debt dynamics were also greatly assisted by an upturn in the international economy in the late 1980s. Devaluation, supported by domestic attempts to restrain costs, was making Irish goods and services more competitive. But the so-called Lawson boom in the United Kingdom made a significant difference to the capacity of Irish producers to benefit from domestic policy efforts. The importance of these international contextual factors has all too often been overlooked. Once the international framework is fully brought into focus, Ireland's model status as a case of 'expansionary fiscal contraction' becomes much less convincing.

The distributive effects of fiscal squeeze during the 1980s were mixed. Fine Gael and Labour, despite their urgent rhetoric about fiscal crisis, maintained real welfare rates, even at the height of the crisis and during the worst of the unemployment. Fianna Fáil, despite having campaigned on issues of social justice, imposed spending cuts that had more severe effects on the most economically and socially vulnerable. By 1989, though, it was already presiding over an economic upturn, and its inability to secure an overall majority again is attributable to voters' concerns over accountability and corruption scandals.

The electoral consequences of fiscal squeeze in Ireland provide scant endorsement for the expectation that governments will suffer no adverse effects. Both governments suffered large losses after their period in office. Fine Gael suffered all the more as it was credited with responsibility for endorsing Fianna Fáil-initiated hardship, because it provided external support for the minority Fianna Fáil government of 1987–89 without extracting visible concessions. The experience of fiscal crisis can be credited with giving rise to a new era in Irish electoral politics. The long Fianna Fáil hegemony had ended, and coalition governments appeared to have come to stay.

A Return to the Politics of Fiscal Squeeze Since 2008

The circumstances in which Irish governments found themselves required to engage in very tough fiscal squeeze once again, in the wake of the 2008 global economic crash, were very different from those of the 1980s. Ireland had been a member of the European Monetary Union since its inception in 1999. It could not secure competitiveness gains by devaluing its currency, and it was bound by the terms of the EU's Excessive Deficit Procedure. There was no external demand boost to stimulate domestic growth, and the fragility of the European banking sector as a whole constrained the availability of credit. Ireland was additionally encumbered by the terms of its own bank rescue decisions. The Fianna Fáil-led government had provided a blanket guarantee to six major domestic financial institutions in September 2008 in order to stabilise a worsening run on the banks, but the liabilities turned out to be considerably worse than anticipated (Clarke & Hardiman 2012). In November 2010, Ireland was obliged to enter a loan programme provided by the European Commission, the European Central Bank (ECB) and the International Monetary Fund (which became known as the 'Troika'). The bailout of the Irish banking sector was amongst the largest in comparative terms (Laeven & Valencia 2012: 20–1); but the home-grown fiscal mistakes made during the boom made their own large contribution to the severity of the debt and deficit problem.

From late 2010 onwards, although there was some domestic discretion over the details of how spending cuts and tax increases were to be implemented, the terms of the fiscal consolidation programme were set by the external lenders. Against this very different backdrop compared with the 1980s, it is striking that, this time round, there was extensive cross-party agreement on the principles and priorities of the extreme fiscal squeeze that was to be undertaken. The return to government of a Fine Gael–Labour coalition in February 2011 involved minimal changes in overall policy priorities. Once again, we might consider how the terms of debate about fiscal squeeze came to be shaped, and how the composition of adjustment between tax increases and spending cuts was arrived at, before we turn to the political costs of undertaking fiscal squeeze, and the electoral consequences for the parties involved.

Fiscal Squeeze as the Only Option

Ireland found itself in serious fiscal trouble early on in the course of the international crisis. Having been lauded for its super-normal growth experiences in the 1990s and 2000s, its crash proved to be one of the most severe among the developed economies. The immediate causes of Ireland's fiscal crisis, and the protracted experience of fiscal consolidation that began during 2008, were not due to excesses in the public finances prior to the crisis. Ireland's general public debt at the start of 2008 was 27.5 per cent of GDP. By the end of 2011 it stood at 108.2 per cent. Having run little or no deficit during the 2000s, the general government deficit rose to 7.3 per cent in 2008 and 14 per cent in 2009. The cost of bank recapitalisation resulted in a deficit of 31.2 per cent being recorded in 2010 (as Figure 7.1 shows), which drove up the public debt in subsequent years. But the government's own deficit was still considerable, at over 12 per cent in 2010, well outside the 3 per cent EMU rules.

How did Ireland end up in such dire straits, from such apparently virtuous fiscal performance in the preceding years? Three features of the Irish public finances combined to produce hidden vulnerabilities. First, the low interest rates available under EMU after 2000 resulted in a surge in borrowing, producing a large property bubble (Dellepiane et al. 2013). Government failed to control these unintended perverse consequences of monetary union, and indeed intensified them through incentivising construction and property speculation. Lax and even non-existent financial regulation permitted banks to become severely over-exposed, especially in the years between 2003 and 2007 (Clarke & Hardiman 2012). Secondly, the tax reforms that had started in the late 1980s, involving lower rates and broader bases, were not systematically pursued. Rather, tax cuts came to be valued for their own sake. Tax measures that were intended to be job-friendly relieved large numbers of lower-paid employees of any tax liabilities, so that by 2008, some 50 per cent of employees were outside the tax net altogether. This resulted in a continuous weakening of the state's revenue capacity, a vulnerability that only became fully apparent when the crisis hit. Thirdly, the surge of economic growth from 1994 to 2008 had given governments a new freedom to engage in public spending. They could do this without impairing EMU fiscal targets because the revenue stream was so buoyant. But after 2000, permanent public spending commitments, especially current spending on public sector pay and welfare transfers, were increasingly reliant on transient revenues from the property bubble. Thus when the international crisis erupted in Ireland, the public finances were unusually vulnerable.

Ireland's fiscal squeeze from 2008 onwards was harsh indeed. Between July 2008 and spring 2013, Ireland had nine episodes of fiscal adjustment. By 2014, the total adjustment has been estimated to total almost €30 billion, through a combination of spending cuts and increased taxation. The overall government deficit, which was 7.3 per cent GDP in 2008 and 14 per cent in 2009, was reduced somewhat to 13.1 per cent in 2011 and 7.6 per cent in 2012. Ireland was originally committed to getting the deficit to under 3 per cent by 2015, a timetable relaxed somewhat in spring 2013. GDP was estimated to have fallen some 18 per cent between 2007 and 2010 alone.

The context of the early adoption of fiscal retrenchment, and the unwavering commitment to this on the part of two successive governments, needs some explanation. After all, most developed economies adopted expansionary measures during 2008/9 in response to the global downturn; Ireland was an outlier (Dellepiane & Hardiman 2012). The explanation lies partly in the new information that was then coming to light about the true fragility of the public finances. Part of the explanation can also be found in economic analysts' retrospective understanding of the fiscal squeeze of the 1980s. The persistent weaknesses in Irish macroeconomic policymaking and implementation were coming under more intense scrutiny. Academic economists were increasingly vocal in their criticism of governments' tendency to engage in pro-cyclical fiscal policy (Bénétrix & Lane 2012; Lane 2010). The stimulus of the late 1970s had been followed by an unfortunately timed correction that worsened an already pronounced downturn. Again during the 'Celtic Tiger' period in the 1990s and 2000s, fiscal policy had been too expansionary, and many held that a fiscal squeeze could no longer be postponed in spite of the severe downturn. Prominent professional economists in Ireland argued that the difficulties experienced by the coalition government in pursuing fiscal squeeze between 1982 and 1987 had led to an excessive delay in stabilising the public finances; that this had had adverse consequences for lost output and had unnecessarily prolonged unemployment; and that these mistakes should not be repeated. And while Irish policy experts held no brief for 'expansionary fiscal contraction', there were few voices to counter the prevailing view that regaining 'national economic sovereignty' was a top priority, that the scope for fiscal stimulus was vanishingly small, and that closing the deficit quickly was the most defensible way to restore the conditions that would facilitate recovery (Kinsella & Leddin 2010).

Total government expenditure escalated rapidly from 42.8 per cent GDP in 2008 to 48.8 per cent in 2009. This was brought down to 44.1 per cent in 2012. But percentages can be misleading when both numerator and denominator are fluctuating. Total government expenditure continued to rise, from €77.1bn in 2008 to €78.4bn in 2009. By 2011 it had been brought down to €76.4bn, and to about €70bn in 2012. But meanwhile, revenues had plummeted from €63.9bn in 2008 to €55.9bn in 2009. New tax increases pushed this figure up somewhat to €57bn in 2012, and projections would have it at €63.1bn by 2015. The overall fiscal adjustment, in an economy with a GDP of €161,034bn in 2012, was estimated at almost €21bn between 2008 and 2011, a considerable fiscal effort.[2]

---

[2] GNP was €129,232bn in 2012. The gap between GNP and GDP in Ireland rose steadily from the 1980s onwards, due to the significance of the foreign-owned sector in the Irish economy; see Department of Finance (2012a: 12), Economic and Social Research Institute (2013). These

The Composition of Fiscal Adjustment

The composition of Irish fiscal adjustment after 2008 followed the 'orthodox' approach whereby priority is given to cutting expenditure over increasing revenues (Dellepiane & Hardiman 2012). The profile of fiscal adjustment is summarised in Table 7.1, which shows that the Irish strategy was based on securing about two-thirds of the fiscal effort through cutting spending, and one-third through raising taxes.

The first aim of fiscal squeeze was to prevent public spending from continuing the upward trajectory on which it was headed during the 2000s. It has been estimated that if no action had been undertaken, the deficit in 2011 would have grown to 20 per cent of GDP, and Ireland would have been heading for a debt-to-GDP ratio of 180 per cent GDP by 2014 or 2015 (Coffey 2011). Coffey estimated that between 2008 and 2011, 'almost €9bn of current expenditure cuts have been announced, but gross voted current expenditure is

Table 7.1.   Composition of Irish fiscal adjustment strategy, 2008–12.

Intervention	Key budgetary measures	Size of fiscal effort
July 2008: expenditure adjustments	Efficiency cuts	€1bn
October 2008: budget 2009	Income levy; spending cuts, including welfare	€2bn
February 2009: expenditure adjustments	Cuts to public sector pay as 'pension levy'; public sector pay increase stopped	€2.1bn (€1bn in 2010)
April 2009: supplementary budget	Tax increases esp. levy; €1.2bn current, €600m capital	€3.6bn, €1.8bn Total €5.4bn
December 2009: budget 2010	Spending cuts on all welfare, public sector pay and numbers; capital cuts; tax increases	€4.4bn
December 2010: budget 2011	Current cuts €2.1bn, capital cuts €1.9bn, other €0.7bn; tax increases €1.4bn	National Recovery Plan 2011–14 projects €10bn cuts, €5bn tax
December 2011: budget 2012	Current cuts €1.4bn, capital cuts €0.8bn; tax increases €1bn	€3.2bn
Adjustment 2008–11		€20.8bn
Projected overall adjustment 2008–14	65% expenditure 35% revenue	€29.6bn

Source: Department of Finance (2011); European Commission (2010); Budget documents 2009, 2010, 2010, 2011.

companies pay low rates of corporation tax on profits, sizeable proportions of which are repatriated. Consideration of the resources available for deployment in the Irish economy must take account of the implications of an FDI-led industrial policy for the politics of revenue and redistribution.

only €0.5bn lower than it was four years ago'. On the other hand, government was running to stand still on the revenue side, in the context of declining and depressed economic activity. Coffey noted that almost €8bn of revenue-raising measures were introduced over the period, but that revenue was actually €7.4bn less than it had been four years previously. Large spending cuts were announced, and significant tax increases were announced and implemented, but total revenues still fell far short of spending commitments.

That is not to say that the effects of spending cuts were not felt in a very real way. The first round of fiscal squeeze, in a small supplementary budget in July 2008, involved attempts at efficiency-gaining cuts. But it was not enough, and a series of scheduled and emergency budgets followed in 2008, 2009 and 2010, to try to arrest the slide towards a potential sovereign debt crisis. Rates of social welfare were cut for most categories of recipients. Public sector pay, which had risen rapidly for many employees during the 2000s, was cut on a tapered basis on two occasions, in 2009 and again in 2013. In 2011, almost one-third of current expenditure in the public service was accounted for by pay alone. Allowing for difficulties in comparing education levels and skill deployment across sectors, it was estimated that between 2003 and 2006 the relative overall gap (or pay premium) between public and private sector workers had risen from 14 to 26 per cent (Kelly *et al.* 2009). The EU-IMF progress report of March 2012 reported that as a result of the spending cuts, gross rates of public service pay were reduced by about 14 per cent cumulatively in 2009 and 2010.

In 2009, the Fianna Fáil-led government commissioned a report from economist Colm McCarthy on cutting public spending. This recommended reductions in the order of 17,300 personnel or approximately 5 per cent of the public service. An overall reduction of some 25,000 personnel (albeit on pre-crisis 2008 figures) by 2014 was agreed with the Troika in November 2010 as part of Ireland's bailout deal; these targets were met in 2013 through a combination of a hiring embargo and incentivised retirement. The profile of changes in the composition of spending can be seen in Figure 7.2.

The scale of the fiscal squeeze implemented in Ireland resulted in a fiscal consolidation that ranked third only after Iceland and Greece (OECD 2012: Annex Table 30). Bootstrapping out of a fiscal crisis in recessionary conditions is particularly painful. Despite the many tax increases imposed since the onset of the crisis, Ireland's total tax take relative to GDP was 28.9 per cent in 2011, down from 32.1 per cent in 2006, which made it 'the sixth lowest in the Union and the second lowest in the euro area' (Eurostat 2013). The profile of tax revenues is summarised in Figure 7.3.

The fiscal squeeze this time was undertaken in conditions that differed from the 1980s in important ways. The country was now richer, living standards had risen rapidly during the 2000s, and large cutbacks might now

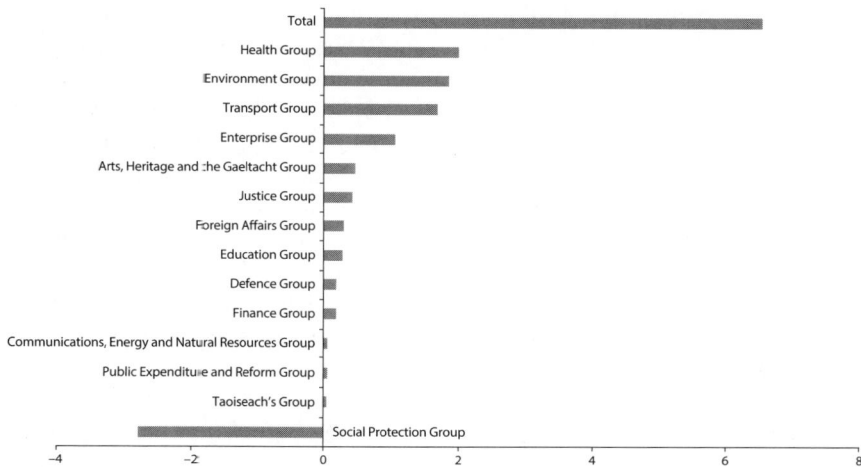

Figure 7.2. Impact of Irish spending cuts by category of public spending 2008–12 (€bn).
Source: Department of Public Expenditure and Reform (2013).

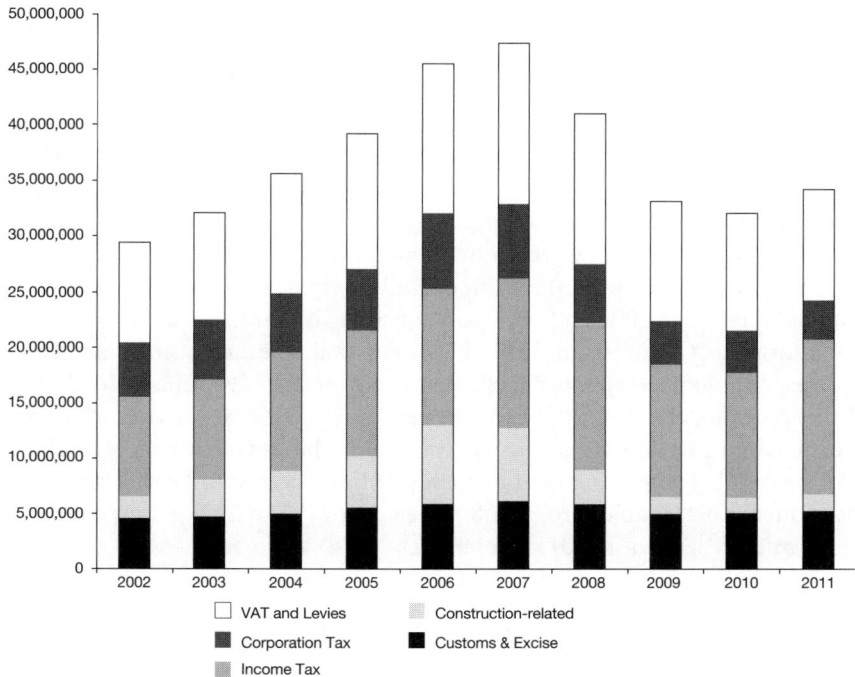

Figure 7.3. Actual outturn in revenue, Ireland 2002–11 (€bn).
Source: Department of Finance (2012b).

be expected to be more easily absorbed without causing major hardships. However, the constraints of EMU meant that any competitiveness gains could only be achieved through painful and unevenly experienced 'internal deflation', that is, by reducing real living standards. EMU member countries were all undergoing simultaneous deleveraging in the public sector, thereby intensifying the cumulative impact of parallel internal deflation. Notwithstanding their extensive public recapitalisation, banks sought to consolidate their balance sheets and still faced large unresolved issues of non-performing private sector loans and mortgages. This meant a dearth of lending activity, further squeezing the activities of firms in the private sector. Fiscal squeeze in these conditions has contractionary and not expansionary effects (De Grauwe 2013; De Grauwe & Ji 2013).

The effects of fiscal squeeze within a monetary union might therefore be expected to be experienced unevenly across different sectors of the population. Heavier tax burdens on income and on transactions may raise more revenue, but new revenue streams on items such as residential property, waste disposal and water were more visible. Public spending cuts were felt in shrinking pay packets and welfare payments, and in worsening health, education and other social services. But the costs in the private sector were most clearly felt in the form of unemployment, first in the devastation of the construction sector, then across a whole range of mostly domestically-owned enterprises that shed employees or simply went out of business.

The impact of fiscal squeeze on the disposable income available to households can be difficult to estimate accurately, in the light of the multiple effects of changes in income tax and indirect taxes, public sector pay and welfare entitlements. Some research findings suggest that while the impact of income tax, pay and welfare changes on household disposable income was more severe in Ireland than elsewhere, both the overall policy stance and the distributive outcomes between 2008 and 2012 had a progressive profile (Callan *et al.* 2012: 53; European Commission 2012: 17). That said, the increasing reliance on indirect taxation is regressive in effect, and different kinds of households were disproportionately affected. People dependent on welfare suffered most, and cuts to Child Benefit were particularly marked, whereas older people fared less badly overall. The proportion of the population deemed to be suffering 'deprivation' almost doubled from 11.8 per cent in 2007 to 22.5 per cent in 2010, and was 24.5 per cent in 2011 (Nolan *et al.* 2014).

Resistance, Protest and Fragmentation of the Party System

What, then, of the political costs of imposing fiscal squeeze this time round? Street protests against 'austerity' in Ireland were much less in evidence compared to the mass mobilisation that occurred in Spain, Portugal, Greece and Italy. Some public sector unions organised small-scale industrial action,

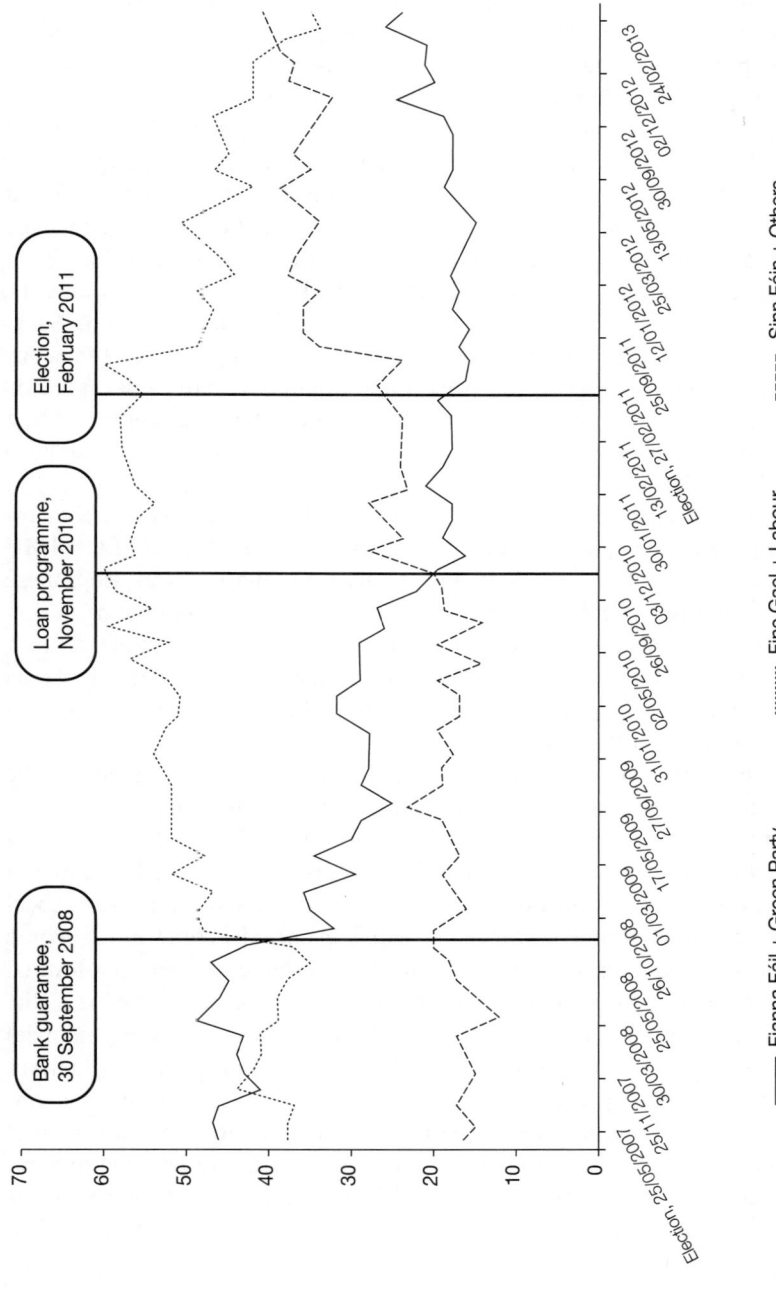

Figure 7.4. Opinion polls on support for parties, Ireland 2007–13.
Source: Elections Ireland (2013).

and in one early and quite successful rally, older people protested over medical entitlements. But negotiated agreements about the scale of pay cuts, concluded between both governments and the public sector unions, kept mass organised protest off the streets. Regular small-scale protests organised by various left parties made relatively little public impact.

The political effect of fiscal squeeze is seen most clearly in the electoral arena. Irish political life was transformed by the 'earthquake election' held in February 2011. Fianna Fáil, Ireland's historically dominant party, suffered devastating losses at the polls. It secured only 17 per cent of the popular vote, falling from 71 to 20 Dáil seats. Figure 7.4 illustrates a trend that had been apparent for quite some time, that is, that Fianna Fáil was deeply unpopular. Fianna Fáil was being punished not only for its implementation of fiscal squeeze after 2008, but also for its longer-term mismanagement of the economy. It was now also paying the price for its panicked bank guarantee of September 2008, and for the years of inadequate financial regulation that had led the domestic banks to the brink of meltdown, and the Irish economy to catastrophic collapse.

The Fine Gael–Labour coalition government that was formed in February 2011 recognised that it was bound by the conditions of the EC-ECB-IMF loan agreement. While voter dissatisfaction with Fianna Fáil ran deep, these two parties similarly held that the only feasible or realistic course of action was to continue with fiscal squeeze, modified a little where possible, at least until the term of the loan programme was finished and the fiscal deficit was sufficiently reduced. It is therefore striking that these two parties gained an additional 42 seats in the election.

But the extent and durability of electoral acquiescence should not be taken for granted. New institutions that had been set up to monitor the public finances resulted in some shifts in priorities, for example in capital spending and in labour market policy. But in Ireland as elsewhere in the Eurozone, it was unclear how long fiscal squeeze could be sustained without a clear expectation that better economic performance would eventually come about. Much of Europe suffered from a 'mutually reinforcing interaction between limited productivity gains, protracted deleveraging, weak banking sectors and distorted relative prices' (Darvas *et al.* 2013: 7). The commingling of financial crisis with sovereign debt crisis in Ireland, in the context of an all but stagnant European economy, appeared to point towards real problems of debt sustainability. It is surely a matter of some concern that Irish citizens' trust in their own government, always more contingent than the EU average, fell precipitously after the crisis began. It recovered in the context of anticipation of fresh elections and a change of government, but fell sharply again thereafter, as Figure 7.5 shows.

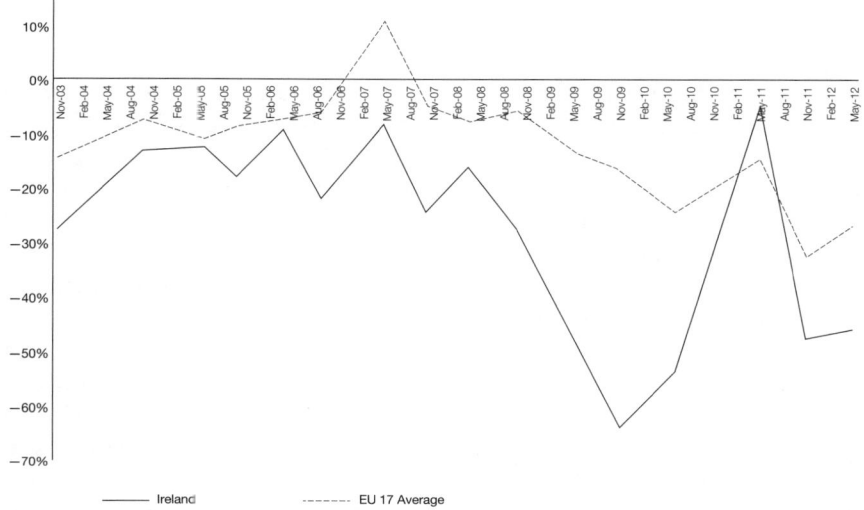

Figure 7.5.   Net trust in national government.
Source: Eurobarometer.

Weakening support for all the established political parties is also reflected in Figure 7.5. This shows that, while support for Fine Gael and Labour had been strong for over two years prior to the election, it peaked shortly thereafter. For as long as this government was implementing the more systematic fiscal squeeze required by the Troika, its popularity was shrinking. The biggest beneficiaries of this were a wide variety of small leftist parties and independent politicians. In September 2013, Fianna Fáil was reported to be making some comeback in the polls. But Sinn Féin was reported to be the third most popular party, with 21 per cent support, while the diverse array of 'others' (independents and small socialist parties) came in next with an aggregated support level of 18 per cent. Fine Gael dropped to 27 per cent of voters' support, while Labour fell back from the 19 per cent they had won in the election to about 10 per cent (Elections Ireland 2013). Meanwhile, new protest groups, organising around local issues to do with increased levies and service charges, prepared to contest local and European elections in 2014. Electoral volatility seemed to be considerable. Exit from the loan programme in December 2013 entailed little real change in tough budgets or in economic performance. It remained unclear whether or not Ireland was entering into a new phase of electoral realignment, or facing a sustained phase of potentially destabilising electoral dealignment.

Conclusion

While Ireland has been taken to be an exemplary case of successful growth-promoting fiscal retrenchment, many of the apparent lessons drawn from its experience turn out to be more complex upon closer inspection. The politics of fiscal squeeze is problematic on three counts: the framing of the decision to undertake fiscal consolidation, the composition of adjustment, and the electoral costs suffered by the parties who implement such measures.

During the 1980s, the decision to commit to fiscal squeeze was difficult for all parties, and this affected the consistency of political effort. These memories shaped governments' response to the economic crisis from 2008 on, when there was more ideological convergence over the inevitability of fiscal squeeze.

The policy mix during the 1980s relied on increasing taxes at first, followed by a bias towards spending cuts after 1987. But neither the politics of fiscal planning nor the design of the revenue system itself was subject to systematic institutional reform. The fiscal squeeze after 2008 entailed yet another episode of pro-cyclical fiscal correction. And without the option of devaluing, or of exploiting an international growth surge, the effects were harsh indeed.

The political costs of fiscal squeeze in the 1980s were somewhat ambiguous. Both Fine Gael and Labour lost seats, but Fine Gael suffered doubly because of its 'responsible' stance, supporting the new minority Fianna Fáil government externally. Fianna Fáil was unpopular for its spending cuts, but still benefited from the rebound by 1992. The political costs incurred by political parties after 2008 may be more far-reaching. Fianna Fáil suffered unprecedented collapse. The 2011 general election signalled a new phase in Irish electoral politics, with all the mainstream parties subject to challenge from less-organised contenders. What the significance might be for the profile of the Irish political system remained an open question.

References

Alesina, A., Carloni, D. & Lecce, G. (2011), *The Electoral Consequences of Large Fiscal Adjustments*, NBER Working Paper 17655 (Cambridge MA, National Bureau of Economic Research), http://www.nber.org/papers/w17655 (accessed 1 March 2013).

Bénétrix, A.S. & Lane, P.R. (2012), 'The Cyclical Conduct of Irish Fiscal Policy', *The World Economy*, 35(10): 1277–90.

Callan, T., Keane, C., Savage, M. & Walsh, J.R. (2012), *Distributional Impact of Tax, Welfare and Public Sector Pay Policies: 2009–2012* (Dublin, Economic and Social Research Institute).

Central Statistics Office (2012), National Income and Expenditure Data 2011.

Clarke, B. & Hardiman, N. (2012), 'Crisis in the Irish Banking System', in S. Konzelmann & M. Fouvargue-Davies (eds), *Banking Systems in the Crisis: The Faces of Liberal Capitalism* (Oxford, Routledge), 107–33.

Coffey, S. (2011), 'How Much Austerity Have We Had?', *Economic Incentives*, http:// economic-incentives.blogspot.ie/2011/11/how-much-austerity-have-we-had.html (accessed 1 March 2013).

Darvas, Z., Pisani-Ferry, J. & Wolff, G.B. (2013), *Europe's Growth Problem (and What To Do About It)*, Bruegel Policy Brief Issue 2013/03, April 2013 (Brussels).

De Grauwe, P. (2013), 'The Political Economy of the Euro', *Annual Review of Political Science*, 16: 153–70.

De Grauwe, P. & Ji, Y. (2013), *Panic-Driven Austerity in the Eurozone and its Implications*, http://www.voxeu.org/article/panic-driven-austerity-eurozone-and-its-implications (accessed 1 March 2013).

Dellepiane, S. & Hardiman, N. (2012), *The New Politics of Austerity: Fiscal Responses to the Economic Crisis in Ireland and Spain*, UCD Geary Institute Working Paper 2012/07 (Dublin).

Dellepiane, S., Hardiman, N. & Las Heras, J. (2013), *Building on Easy Money: The Political Economy of Housing Bubbles in Ireland and Spain*, UCD Geary Institute Geary Working Paper 2013/18 (Dublin), http://www.ucd.ie/geary/static/publications/workingpapers/gearywp201318.pdf (accessed 1 March 2013).

Department of Finance (2011), *Ireland: Stability Programme Update* (Dublin, Department of Finance).

Department of Finance (2012a), *Budgetary and Economic Statistics* (Dublin, Department of Finance).

Department of Finance (2012b), Department of Finance Databank, http://databank. finance.gov.ie/ (accessed 1 March 2013).

Department of Public Expenditure and Reform (2013), Department of Public Expenditure and Reform Databank, http://databank.per.gov.ie/ (accessed 1 March 2013).

Economic and Social Research Institute (2013), Irish Economy, http://www.esri.ie/ irish_economy/ (accessed 1 March 2013).

Elections Ireland (2013), Opinion Polls in Ireland, http://electionsireland.org/polls. cfm?show=table&year=all (accessed 1 March 2013).

European Commission (2010), *Public Finances in EMU 2010*, European Commission, Directorate-General for Economic and Financial Affairs (Brussels).

European Commission (2012), *The Economic Adjustment Programme for Ireland. Winter 2011 Review*, Directorate-General for Economic and Financial Affairs, European Economy Occasional Papers 93, March 2012 (Brussels).

European Commission (2013), Ameco Database, http://ec.europa.eu/economy_ finance/ameco/user/serie/SelectSerie.cfm (accessed 1 March 2013).

Eurostat (2013), *Taxation Trends in the European Union: Data for the EU Member States, Iceland and Norway* (Eurostat).

Hardiman, N. (2013), *Rethinking the Political Economy of Fiscal Consolidation in Two Recessions in Ireland*, UCD Geary Institute Working Paper 2013/17 (Dublin).

Honohan, P. (1992), 'Fiscal Adjustment in Ireland in the 1980s', *The Economic and Social Review*, 23(3): 285–314.

Honohan, P. & Conroy, C. (1994), 'Sterling Movements and Irish Pound Interest Rates', *The Economic and Social Review*, 25(3): 201–20.

Kelly, E., McGuinness, S. & O'Connell, P. (2009), 'Benchmarking, Social Partnership and Higher Remuneration: Wage Setting Institutions and the Public–Private Wage Gap in Ireland', *The Economic and Social Review*, 40(3): 339–70.

Kinsella, S. & Leddin, A. (eds) (2010), *Understanding Ireland's Economic Crisis: Prospects for Recovery* (Dublin: Blackhall Publishing).

Laeven, L. & Valencia, F. (2012), *Systemic Banking Crises Database: An Update*, IMF Working Paper 12/163 (Washington DC).

Lane, P. (2010), 'A New Fiscal Framework for Ireland', *Journal of the Statistical and Social Inquiry Society of Ireland*, 39: 144–65.

MacSharry, R. & White, P. (2000), *The Making of the Celtic Tiger: The Inside Story of Ireland's Boom Economy* (Dublin, Mercier Press).

Mair, P. (1987), *The Changing Irish Party System: Organisation, Ideology and Electoral Competition* (London, Pinter).

Mauro, P. (ed.) (2011), *Chipping Away at Public Debt: Sources of Failure and Keys to Success in Fiscal Adjustment* (Hoboken, NJ, Wiley).

Mulas-Granados, C. (2004), 'Voting Against Spending Cuts: The Electoral Costs of Fiscal Adjustments in Europe', *European Union Politics*, 5(4): 467–93.

Nolan, B., Calvert, E., Fahey, T., Healy, D., Mulcahy, A., Maitre, B., *et al.* (2014), 'Ireland: Inequality and its Impacts in Boom and Bust', in B. Nolan, W. Salverda, D. Checchi, I. Marx, A. McKnight, I.G. Tóth & H.G. van de Werfhorst (eds), *Changing Inequalities and Societal Impacts in Rich Countries: Thirty Countries' Experiences* (Oxford, Oxford University Press), 346–68.

OECD (2012), *OECD Economic Outlook*, OECD vol. 92, no. 2 (Paris).

Penniman, H. & Farrell, B. (eds) (1987), *Ireland at the Polls, 1981, 1982, and 1987: A Study of Four General Elections* (Durham, NC, Duke University Press).

Sinnott, R. (1995), *Irish Voters Decide: Voting Behaviour in Elections and Referendums Since 1918* (Manchester, Manchester University Press).

8

Fiscal Squeeze in Germany: Drifting Away from the Politics of the Switching Yard?

MARTIN LODGE AND KAI WEGRICH

IN THE LATE 1990s GERMANY WAS DESCRIBED AS THE 'sick man of the Euro' (*The Economist*, 3 June 1999). Germany was represented as a fossilised corporatist system that was saddled with high labour costs, a political system that was unable to reform, and a welfare state that was increasingly creaking at its seams. The political need to transfer resources to eastern Germany, especially during the first half of the 1990s, meant that the inflation-shy Bundesbank imposed high interest rates that were said to stifle economic development in the West. The transfers (approximately €1,600bn until 2009[1]) added tax burdens to the West and were blamed for destabilising the overall German economy.[2] During the early 2000s, Germany cheated on the provisions of the euro's Stability and Growth Pact. Academic observers shared the view of a stagnating system: 'Given Germany's painfully slow, incremental process of political and economic change, for some time there is likely to be a growing gap between rapid problem accumulation and slow problem-solving in existing political and economic institutions' (Kitschelt & Streeck 2003: 2).

As the Noughties turned into the Teens, the headlines changed: Germany was praised for its reforms that had kept its public finances in order, reduced real wages and seen a fall in unemployment rates. Germany witnessed export-led economic growth at time when most other European economies were, at best, stagnating (*The Economist*, 15 June 2013). Academic observers,

---

[1] http://www.seiten.faz-archiv.de/faz/20090822/fd1200908222386664.html (last accessed 28 June 2013).

[2] Initially, the financing of unification involved a 'solidarity surcharge' on income tax, and an additional increase in mineral oil tax. In 1998, a tax surcharge of 5.5 per cent was imposed on income, capital gains and corporate tax liabilities. The additional revenues were counted as federal revenue. In addition, the federal equalisation pact between the German Länder was enhanced. After 2004, the latter targeted structurally disadvantaged regions across the whole of Germany. Further measures included increases in VAT and other taxes, such as those on tobacco, mineral gas and insurance.

Proceedings of the British Academy, **197**, 161–183. © The British Academy 2014.

typical of stereotype, were less impressed, but did note considerable fiscal consolidation-driven change beneath the surface of existing welfare state institutions (see Howarth & Rommerskirchen 2013; Palier & Thelen 2010; Streeck & Mertens 2010).

Apparently successful fiscal squeezing should come as a surprise to observers of the German political system for at least three reasons. First, the German system of executive and cooperative federalism has long been seen as incapable of reform. Due to decision rules that require extra-large majorities to initiate or change concurrent intergovernmental policies, a 'joint decision trap' is said to exist: the pivotal voting power of actors likely to lose from cutting back programmes prohibits policy adaptation to changing circumstances (Scharpf 1988). Thus, the growth of federal spending programmes is difficult to reverse as veto-players in the political system are able to block any reform. Outright reform blockage was particularly noticeable during the final term of the CDU–FDP administration (1994–98; the coalition had been initially established in 1982) under Helmut Kohl, where the second chamber, the Bundesrat, opposed major reform attempts as it was dominated by Social Democrat-led governments.[3] This contrasted with earlier periods when individual Land governments could be 'bought off' in intergovernmental negotiations. In those areas where the centre-right government managed to introduce cost-containing elements (such as the introduction of a 'demographic factor' in pensions policy), the subsequent SPD–Green government (1998–2005) initially reversed or suspended these measures. More generally, despite attempts at reforming the system of fiscal federalism, the economic diversity of the Länder continued to increase, with economically declining areas faring considerably worse than more prosperous (southern) Länder. In addition, redistribution towards eastern Germany added a further dimension. Similarly, economic disparity explained why some local governments were facing considerable financial constraints given decreasing autonomous tax income and increasing demands for social benefit payments, whereas others were hardly affected.

Second, the German system of public finances has been characterised as a *Verschiebebahnhof* (a switching yard). The idea of the 'switching yard' suggests that German policymakers have used budgetary and organisational fragmentation as well as the federal system to shift around expenditures and revenues in order to fix short-term problems in non-transparent ways.

---

[3] The German bicameral system includes the Bundestag, composed of directly elected representatives which forms the federal government, and the second chamber, the Bundesrat. The latter represents the governments of the Länder. A clear dominance of one party (or block of parties) in the Bundesrat can lead to a reform blockage under specific conditions, namely when the party political adversarial logic outweighs the compromise-seeking logic of intergovernmental negotiations (Lehmbruch 2000).

Especially when it came to social matters, changes in taxes at the federal level shifted problems to areas where local governments had to pick up the pieces in administrative cost terms. In other words, one aspect of the politics of the federal switching yard involved the federal level (often in agreement with Land governments) burdening local governments with increasing financial obligations. Local governments responded by privatising and closing public services, by reducing investment into capital assets, and by engaging in derivatives markets. The latter came unstuck during the financial crisis of 2008, causing local governments to lose further discretion in their expenditures. Thus, local governments argued that their financial room for manoeuvre was increasingly constrained. Indeed, some local governments were under 'special supervision' from their Land government as they declared themselves unable to run a balanced budget as required constitutionally.

Third, the most prominent switching yard has traditionally been the German welfare state (Trampusch 2009). The complex nature of an insurance-based system coupled with a variety of schemes and budgets allowed policymakers to shuffle money around in order to fill short-term needs in non-transparent and blame-avoiding ways without having to address long-term developments.

However, from the viewpoint of 2014, all three of these blockages appear in a different light.

First, despite much scepticism and criticism, the reforms of the federal system included a *Schuldenbremse* (literally 'debt brake', but in the following translated as 'debt ceiling'). This rule-based constitutional provision required the federal and the Land governments to operate on the principle of balanced budgets. It was agreed in 2009 and replaced an earlier constitutional provision that had allowed for broader discretion.

Second, the intergovernmental switching yard paid increasing attention to local governments' claim that their financial position had been destabilised. Tasks that previously had been jointly or concurrently 'owned' by both federal and Land governments were returned to Land sovereignty. Furthermore, budgetary reforms paid increasing attention to relieving the financial plight of local governments.

Third, the financial pressures arising from the welfare state led to considerable labour market reforms in the mid-2000s (the so-called Hartz IV Reforms, discussed below). Partly these pressures arose from the continued need to subsidise the activities of the Employment Agency (then called Bundesanstalt für Arbeit). Partly, and more importantly, changes occurred because of the dire financial situations of many local governments.

The German case is an example of a domestic crisis that led to internal reforms; furthermore, it is a case that evolved over three decades and affected different aspects of the switching yard at different points. For connoisseurs of the German political system, the politics of fiscal squeeze represent either a story that emphasises the 'gridlock' of the political system as a mechanism that will lead to inevitable decline, or one that highlights the inherent flexibilities in the system that allows for incremental reform (Behnke & Benz 2009: 224). Such a pattern of build-up of cost pressures, incremental reforms to achieve cost containment, and subsequent pressures arising from these measures in other areas of this interlocking political system makes it difficult to suggest that squeezing went through distinct periods (for such an approach, see Breuer *et al.* 2011). In terms of consequences for political actors, fiscal squeezing was significant. The splits within the SPD over welfare state reforms and the need for the Red–Green coalition to rule in a continuous informal grand coalition with the CDU via the latter's majority in the Bundesrat from 2002 onwards (after a series of disastrous SPD election results at the Land levels), motivated then Chancellor Schröder to engineer an early election in 2005 under constitutionally questionable circumstances (Reutter 2012). The divisions within the SPD led to the rise of a socialist party (WASG: Arbeit und Soziale Gerechtigkeit—Die Wahlalternative) in 2004. This party, containing some former prominent Social Democrats (including Oskar Lafontaine, formerly SPD Land prime minister, federal finance minister and chairperson, and chancellor candidate in 1990), eventually merged with the remnants of the former East German governing Communist Party to form Die Linke. That party gained considerable success at the ballot box in western parts of Germany (it had maintained its electoral significance in the eastern parts).

The inconclusive 2005 election led to the formation of a grand coalition under Chancellor Merkel. This grand coalition further contributed to the rise of Die Linke and, subsequently, to the SPD's worst election result in post-1945 Germany in the 2009 general election.[4] In addition, the grand coalition also facilitated the liberal party, the FDP, which campaigned on an 'anti-state' platform (until it eventually entered government with the CDU after the 2009 elections). The FDP represented a 'protest vote' of disenchanted Christian Democrat voters who wanted not just to signal their dislike of the (median-voter-seeking) 'social democratisation' of their party, but also to pave the way for a CDU–FDP coalition. The failure of the FDP to enter the Bundestag after the 2013 election was largely due to its vote migrating mostly to the CDU or the anti-euro protest party, the AfD (Alternative für Deutschland). The opposition parties (SPD, Green and Linke) either lost or only gained

---

[4] The SPD lost 11.2 per cent of its vote and ended up on 23.0 per cent. Die Linke gained 11.2 per cent (up 3.2 per cent), the CDU received 33.6 per cent (a loss of 1.4 per cent), the FDP 11.6 per cent (a gain of 4.7 per cent) and the Greens achieved 10.7 per cent (a gain of 2.6 per cent). For analysis of the electoral punishment suffered by the SPD in 2009, see Bytzek (2011).

moderately, thereby suggesting an electorate that was keen on austerity in the domestic setting, and, most of all, austerity in the Eurozone. In other words, the politics of financial consolidation in post-unification Germany had considerable political implications, both in the way in which financial pressures at different points in the system triggered reforms, and in the way in which these reforms informed electoral politics.

The following looks first at the aggregate developments in terms of the size of the German state. It then illustrates developments in expenditure across federal ministries over the period 1991–2013 to investigate 'who lost where and how'. Finally, this paper turns to political reforms that were driven by concerns about fiscal consolidation.

The Overall Picture

Figure 8.1 notes a degree of consolidation after a temporary peak in 1995.[5] That peak can be explained by the one-off incorporation into the general budget of the Treuhandanstalt, the agency responsible for privatising the eastern Germany economy. However, even without this peak, there is an approximately 4 percentage points decline, mostly falling on public expenditure rather than the social insurance-related expenditures of the welfare state. The late 1990s also benefited from a mild economic upturn. Figure 8.1 represents annual developments from 1990 onwards, and five-year datapoints beforehand. This figure also points to one essential aspect, namely the relative shares of public expenditures as separated between the share of governmental spending and the share of spending by social insurance schemes. The fluctuation in the late 2000s reflects the federal government's response to the financial crisis.

In terms of share in overall debt, the patterns have been broadly stable over time. The federal government was responsible for about 60 per cent of the overall debt (62.5 per cent in 2007), the Länder accounted for about a third (32.1 per cent in 2007), and local governments for around 5 per cent (5.4 per cent in 2007). For local governments and Land governments revenue raising was not a major consideration when faced with calls for financial consolidation. This was because of their limited revenue-raising autonomy. Land governments could only raise approximately 8 per cent of tax on their own, local governments even less. Land governments were staff-heavy in terms of their expenditure and therefore had to rely on privatisation, outsourcing and related wheezes to reduce public expenditures. To increase revenue in any significant way, Land governments had to rely on negotiations

---

[5] All figures are taken from the official budgetary documentation published by the Federal Ministry of Finance.

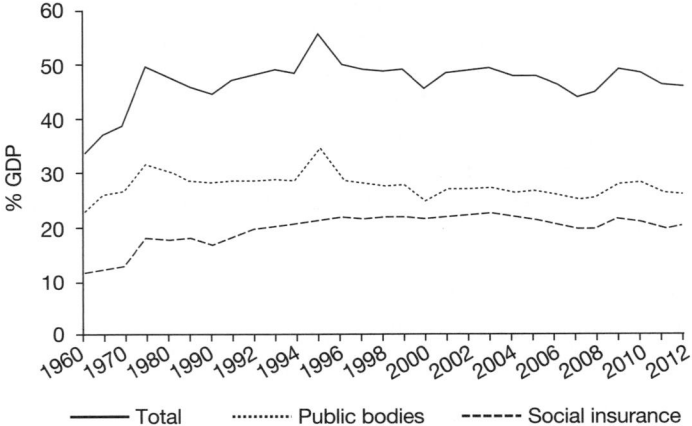

Figure 8.1. Share of public expenditure as % GDP, Germany 1960–2010.
Source: Official budgetary documentation, Federal Ministry of Finance.

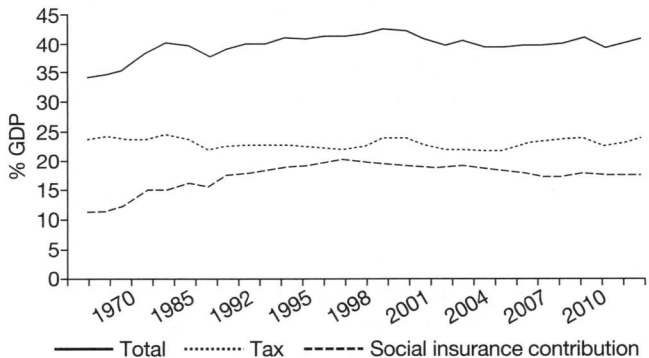

Figure 8.2. Revenue as % GDP, Germany 1960–2012.
Source: Official budgetary documentation, Federal Ministry of Finance.

with the federal government to increase their share of revenue drawn from federal taxation.

Figure 8.2 points to the contribution of tax and social insurance revenue as percentage of GDP. It highlights a politically engineered flatlining around 40 per cent since the 2000s, after a rise in the 1970s and 1980s. The rise in revenues is largely a result of increases in social insurance contributions (as noted below, largely because of rising unemployment). These contributions declined from 2000, whereas the tax income has remained broadly stable. Within the tax system, the period since 1990 has been characterised by a decline in direct and corporate tax and a rise in indirect taxation (such as value added tax (from 14 to 19 per cent), and taxes on tobacco and mineral

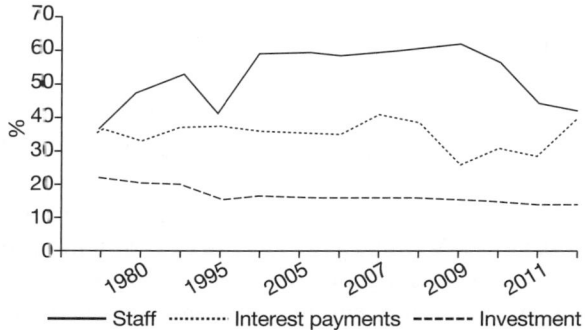

Figure 8.3. Share of particular expenditures in federal budget as %, Germany 1975–2010.
Source: Official budgetary documentation, Federal Ministry of Finance.

oil-related products) (BMF 2012). Again, the pre-1990 data are in five-yearly steps, while the data from 1990 reflect annual changes.

When major spending cutbacks are proposed, one of the key expectations is that squeezing will focus on large-expenditure items rather than ongoing running costs. Figure 8.3 looks at the three key federal expenditure items in terms of their share in the overall federal budget. It shows a decline in the share of personnel cost over the years, especially since unification. The period 1975–2005 is illustrated in five-year steps, and on an annual basis after 2005. Significantly, the patterns point to some variation in the share of investment-related expenditures, especially the reduction in the share of investment expenditure in the second half of the 2000s. The decline in share of interest payments has, partly, to do with the low-interest climate post-financial crisis and the overall reduction in state debt. Partly it reflects the growth in investment expenditure in response to the financial crisis in the late 2000s.

The overall picture points to a degree of containment in certain parts of the budget, broad stability in the overall 'state quota', but also some degree of incremental decline after a peak in the early 1990s which was caused by unification. This mixed picture is also illustrated when focusing solely on federal departments. The biggest loser among federal departments is defence, whereas ministries involved in social security-related expenditures gain. The growth in social expenditure reflected the shift of expenditures away from insurance schemes to direct federal subsidies. The agriculture portfolio witnessed a considerable reduction in transfer payments. In contrast, other ministries, such as environment, gain. The latter gains largely because of a growing emphasis on renewable energy as well as a growth in the budget for research and education. More broadly, there is also a broad growth in the share of mandatory over discretionary expenditures. As noted by Streeck & Mertens (2010: 16), the percentage of discretionary expenditures declined from 39.6 per cent in 1970 to 21.5 per cent in 2008. This could be largely explained by debt payments and the rise in social security payments.

Fiscal Squeeze at the Centre?

Among these developments which affected overall public spending, certain trends within executive government are noticeable. Post-unification, staff numbers were slimmed down. As redundancies were unlawful, this largely operated through a process of 'natural wastage': at most every second position was replaced. Departments relied on short-term positions staffed from civil service 'pools'. Squeezing also raised issues about how programmes could be administered. Politicians did agree on spending programmes for particular initiatives, but often 'forgot' to add administrative costs to their spending commitments. This partly encouraged the recruitment of external consultants for the running of programmes. Similar trends occurred at the Land level, while privatisation, corporatisation, and outsourcing of public services were particularly widespread in local government. Table 8.1 illustrates aggregate staff numbers according to different ranks. It also distinguishes between (*a*) staff numbers in federal departments (and the small number of staff working for parliament and the federal president), and (*b*) subordinate federal units. Despite increases in the years 2008–14, the overall trend since unification is one of ongoing decrease.

Across the federal bureaucracy running costs were to be capped, if not reduced. Again, this raised problems among those agencies that were exposed to fluctuations in, for example, electricity prices. One of the primary ways to cut staff costs, apart from not replacing retiring staff (leading to a rapid age-

Table 8.1.   Staff numbers in the German Federal Administration.

	B-posts		Higher posts		Total	
	a	*b*	*a*	*b*	*a*	*b*
1988	1,383	946	3,876	31,265	12,126	99,362
1992	1,642	1,128	5,192	41,274	15,918	131,825
1996	1,573	1,167	4,699	13,360	16,192	126,042
2000	1,539	1,171	4,261	12,731	14,433	124,299
2004	1,534	1,150	4,456	12,762	14,641	122,322
2008	1,511	1,134	4,570	12,504	13,979	120,078
2014	1,449	1,191	5,204	13,967	14,237	123,140

Note: B-posts represent senior civil service positions; higher posts are A16–A13; *a* denotes staff in federal departments; *b* denotes staff in subordinate federal units.
Source: BT11/700 (1988), BT12/1000 (1992), BT13/2000 (1996), BT14/1400 (2000), BT15/1500 (2004), http://www.bundesfinanzministerium.de/bundeshaushalt2008/html/index.html (2008), BT17/14300 (2014).

ing of the civil servant population), was to cut additional payments. In 2002, civil service rewards were changed, in that two extra payments (holiday and Christmas pay) were combined and their amount was reduced from one month's salary to 84 per cent (63 per cent in eastern Germany). This was reduced further between 2005 and 2010 (to 60 per cent). In terms of actual staff expenditure reductions, the ministry of defence witnessed the largest fall. The other two 'losers' were the ministry of finance and the ministry of the interior. All other ministries witnessed a pattern of stable decline due to the policy of 'natural wastage'.

Within the federal government, some different trends in altering spending priorities can be distinguished. One is the trend to reduce subsidy payments to particular industries, starting in 2004. Targets included, for example, subsidy payments for coal production once the traditional system that relied on price support (the 'Kohlepfennig') had been turned into a tax-funded subsidy programme. Other subsidy schemes that relied on co-funding with Land governments also suffered, especially as the Länder proved less willing to continue (and capable of continuing) co-financing arrangements.

The second theme was a system of targeted squeezing. Once the federal cabinet had agreed on an overall spending reduction target, this target was translated into targets for individual departments. The specific reduction target depended on a number of factors, one being the extent to which spending commitments were mandatory (due to legislative commitments) or not. A second factor influencing the intensity of the cutback requirements was whether the spending commitment reflected overall government priorities (namely, renewable energy, education and research). The result was that those ministries, such as the federal economics ministry, suffered more cutbacks because of their spending profile. A third theme was the reduction in investment in the mid-2000s. Whilst not directly noticeable in the investment-related expenditures of the federal departments themselves, the reduction in investment spending was more prominent in the wider departmental budgets.

Similar trends were noticeable at the Land level. The immediate period following unification was characterised by over-optimistic projections as to future economic and demographic growth profiles. By the mid-1990s, a concern with fiscal consolidation was noticeable. There was little scope to raise revenues, and staff costs represented a far higher share of public expenditure at the Land than the federal level. This meant that there was little leverage to reduce expenditure levels quickly. As at the federal level, staff costs were reduced through staff non-replacement. This meant that some Land administrations were slimmed down: for example, Hamburg (a city state) reduced its staff numbers by 30 per cent throughout the 1990s. Berlin cut its staff by 50 per cent over the period of 1991 to 2011 (through a hiring freeze) and cut wages by 10 per cent. Brandenburg reduced its administrative staff by 8,000 over a period of five years (1999–2004). As at the federal level, budgeting was conducted through the development of targets. More coercive means were applied where departments proved unwilling to squeeze. One such means was the 'lawnmower' approach, which required all budget lines to be cut by the same amount. At the same time, civil servants engaged in budget negotiations at the federal and Land level noted how spending departments increasingly showed a united front when seeking to challenge the finance ministry.

In general, therefore, the politics of public spending among federal and Land executive governments did not change fundamentally; however, it took place in a context in which staffing levels were slimmed down, and where there was an increasing willingness to tackle long-established subsidy payments. This occurred not just by capping spending, but also in the way in which spending was financed, with certain items moving from 'special budgets' to direct tax-funded budget lines.

Welfare State

Whereas expenditure consolidation by federal or Land ministries attracted little public attention, attempts to contain costs in different areas of the welfare state had considerable political consequences. Wage-based contributions to statutory insurance schemes have been a hallmark of the German welfare system. These schemes involved the areas of unemployment, health and pensions. In the 1990s, a further component, an insurance-based mechanism to finance old age care, was added to the system. As an insurance-based system, welfare benefits were financed from contributions by employers and employees. So-called contribution rates (i.e. the overall amount paid by employers and employees) were therefore critical in determining the overall cost of, and demand for, labour. They therefore were seen as directly related to the costs of unemployment (for extensive discussion, see Trampusch 2009).

The ability to use the various insurance-based schemes as a 'switching yard' meant that policymakers could utilise the welfare state to avoid difficult choices. From the 1980s, the politics of economic reform started to focus on the aggregate employer and employee contribution rate as a cause for rising unemployment. Starting from a rate of 25 per cent of gross income throughout the 1960s, contribution rates steadily increased from the mid-1970s onwards and, even more prominently, throughout the 1980s. This was largely attributable to rising unemployment. However, it was not just rising levels of unemployment that accounted for the growth in indirect labour costs, it was the actual policy response. That is, a subsidised 'early retirement' policy was established in order to reduce official unemployment rates. This early retirement policy pleased (nearly) all relevant constituencies: companies could cut down their workforces, trade unions protected their members from less generous redundancy packages, and the federal government could claim to be keeping unemployment rates down. However, as this scheme was financed through the unemployment and pension system, the social security contribution rates needed to be increased by 3.7 per cent over the 1980s (from 32.2 per cent in 1980 to 35.9 per cent in 1989). Some squeezing did take place, partly through cutbacks in eligibility (such as means-testing) and through rises in contributions. For example, in the area of pensions, there was a switch in adjusting pension levels by moving from a system that traced increases in the gross to increases in the net wage in 1989, thereby leading to reduced increases in pension payments. Furthermore, age of retirement provisions was equalised between women and men. There was, however, also some selective welfare state expansion, especially regarding family-related measures (Leibfried & Obinger 2003).

The economic and social impact of unification added considerable pressure on the German welfare state—and undermined the earlier, small-scale cost-containment measures. By the mid-1990s, the contribution rate had increased to 40 per cent of gross wages. Much of the social adjustment cost was shouldered by the insurance system rather than through tax-financed public expenditures. This conveniently reduced the potential tax burden and therefore also ensured that the CDU's election promise not to raise taxes was not directly broken. The early retirement device was widely applied to address the collapse of the eastern German economy.[6] This policy, however, proved increasingly unsustainable and was identified as a 'vicious cycle' (Streeck 2009: 60): contribution rates added to the non-wage labour costs, increasing rates were seen to trigger further growth in unemployment, and rising unemployment rates required even higher contribution rates.

In response, the then CDU–FDP government committed itself to keeping the contribution rate below 40 per cent. This meant that federal budgetary subsidies were used to beef up the affected insurance schemes. As a result, the federal budget became increasingly preoccupied by the concerns of the welfare state: by the early 2000s, social security was consuming approximately 35 per cent of the federal budget. The alternative, benefit cuts, was seen as politically unpalatable. Table 8.2 provides an overview of developments from

---

[6] Between 1993 and 2002, 675,944 employees in eastern Germany were retired early; the annual number of early retirements in the east peaked at 160,000 in 1995 (in the west, the total number for that year was 111,000) (Trampusch 2009: 110).

Table 8.2. Monthly pay-as-you-go rates contributing to German social insurance system (%).

	Health insurance	Pension fund	Old age care	Unemployment insurance	Aggregate
1990	12.6	18.7	0	4.3	35.6
1995	13.2	18.6	1	6.5	39.3
2000	13.5	19.3	1.7	6.5	41
2001	13.6	19.1	1.7	6.5	40.9
2002	13.98	19.1	1.7	6.5	41.28
2003	14.31	19.5	1.7	6.5	42.01
2004	14.22	19.5	1.7	6.5	41.92
2005	13.73	19.5	1.7	6.5	41.43
2006	13.31	19.5	1.7	6.5	41.01
2007	13.9	19.9	1.7	4.2	39.7
2008	14	19.9	1.95	3.3	39.15
2009	14	19.9	1.95	2.8	38.65
2010	14	19.9	1.95	2.8	38.65
2011	14.6	19.9	1.95	3	39.45
2012	14.6	19.6	1.95	3	39.15

Source: Official budgetary documentation, Federal Ministry of Finance.

1990. Figure 8.4 shows the increasing involvement of the federal government in the financing of the pension system alone.

Cost-containing efforts from the 1990s onwards led to a different type of switching-yard politics. It was the switching itself that started to cause additional 'pain', whereas in the past the switching around was largely used to alleviate temporary inconvenience. For example, the incremental reforms of pension and unemployment benefit schemes throughout the 1990s sought to contain, if not reduce, benefits. Tougher eligibility criteria and reduced generosity in benefit were intended to reduce the financial burden of the agency

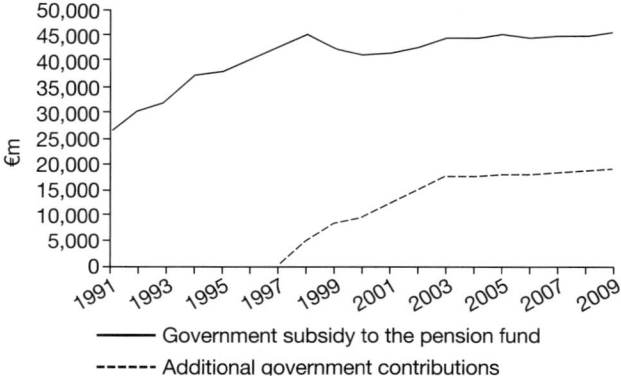

Figure 8.4.   Federal government contribution rates to pension system (€m).
Source: Official budgetary documentation, Federal Ministry of Finance.

responsible for unemployment benefits, the Bundesanstalt für Arbeit. However, this created a growing number of social benefit claimants, as individuals were no longer eligible for unemployment benefits. As local governments were responsible for social benefit payments and the actual delivery of social pro-grammes (such as social benefit payments, social housing, child and youth care), this policy development placed a considerable burden on local govern-ments. In response, local governments created secondary labour markets by establishing their own enterprises, so-called 'Beschäftigungsgesellschaften'. These locally owned companies offered time-limited employment opportuni-ties to recipients of social welfare payments. Unsurprisingly, the time-limited contracts were designed in a way that would make individuals eligible for unemployment benefits once their contract had ended (and thereby return them to the financial responsibility of the unemployment benefits system). The federal government responded by tightening eligibility criteria further. In addition, welfare state expansion added further strain on local govern-ment finances. For example, federal legislation granted every child the right to attend kindergarten. However, the financial cost to provide for additional kindergarten places fell on local governments.

Elsewhere, cost-containment measures taken in the 1990s, such as the introduction of a 'demographic factor' in the pension system, faced outright opposition from the then Social Democrat opposition and trade unions (Streeck 2009: 61; Leibfried & Obinger 2003). The demographic factor was to reduce pension levels from 70 per cent to eventually 64 per cent of the former net wage. Politically, it was the first time in post-1945 history that pension reforms were pushed through without the support of the opposition party (as well as business and trade union support). It also reflected public opinion (Haverland & Stiller 2010: 433): public opinion polls suggested that a later retirement age was less popular than increased contributions or reduced bene-fit levels. The 1998 SPD election manifesto promised a reversal of these cost-containment measures. The 'demographic factor' was 'suspended' for two years once the SPD–Green government had taken office in late 1998.

Dynamics of welfare state reform, and in particular the way in which cost containment affected the ability to use the politics of the switching yard, changed considerably by the mid-2000s. In 2002, public uproar over gamed job placement data by job centres (a consequence of target-driven perfor-mance management systems) provided the immediate context for a further exercise in labour market reform.[7] However, the wider context was constituted by the federal budgetary deficit that violated the criteria of the Stability and Growth Pact (despite the receipts of the 3G licence). A further condition was

---

[7] The gaming scandal involved the revelation that only 30 per cent of supposedly 'successful' placements had been correctly recorded (see 'Der Beton lebt', *Der Spiegel*, 18 February 2002).

the lack of reform initiatives that emerged from the corporatist Bündnis für Arbeit, which had been established to allow peak business and trade union organisations to negotiate a reform package to enhance employment (Streeck 2003). The collapse of this tried-and-tested device to deal with German welfare state problems can be partly explained by the changing labour market conditions that weakened the traditional power bases of business and trade unions alike. It was also due to the lack of party political consensus and party discipline (especially in the SPD) to motivate the 'social partners' to seek a consensual set of reform proposals. These three conditions motivated then Chancellor Schröder to abandon the corporatist tradition of welfare state negotiations and to establish an executive-driven inquiry to develop proposals for far-reaching reform of employment policy. This inquiry was chaired by former Volkswagen executive and confidant of Chancellor Schröder, Peter Hartz.

The so-called Hartz reforms (various packages were introduced between 2003 and 2005) included tightened eligibility criteria for the receipt of welfare and unemployment payments (such as reducing the duration of particular benefit payments[8]) and created so-called 'mini jobs' that did not require social insurance contributions. They also merged two tax-based funds, the (income-related) unemployment and the (flat-fee) social security schemes, into a general social assistance scheme (Weishaupt 2010). The merged scheme was no longer income-related. Instead, flat-rate benefits were paid at the level of social welfare payments, on a means-tested basis. In the area of pensions, the demographic factor (called 'sustainability factor') was reintroduced in 2003. The 'early retirement' policy itself was retired. These reforms marked a change away from a 'pay as you go' insurance system and from a payroll to a general tax-based system. The Hartz reforms were also predicted to release local governments from some of their financial constraints (BT15/1516).

Reforms of the 2000s also included growing incentivisation to encourage private provision by placing an emphasis on choice and individual 'responsibility'. For example, reforms in 2001 introduced old age protection that encouraged voluntary private arrangements. Similarly, the 2003 Health Care Modernisation Law emphasised the importance of individual responsibility in containing costs by reducing the burden on employers and the insurance scheme. This was done by changing certain insurance provisions (e.g. dentures had to be insured personally), increasing contributions in general and for particular medical services (e.g. visits to dentists), and removing certain services (e.g. spectacles for non-disabled adults). At the same time, the federal welfare state also expanded to reflect the governmental aim to make working

---

[8] From 32 to 12 months for the under 50-year-olds, to 15 months for those up to the age of 55, and to 24 months for those up to 58 years old.

life more child-friendly. This involved the expansion of kindergarten places as well as encouraging the development of all-day schools. In both cases the federal government was required to subsidise a considerable part of the administrative cost (which fell to the local and Land levels); in both cases this involved €4bn from the federal budget.

These reforms proved a significant change in the nature of the German welfare state. Furthermore, they proved politically very costly for the SPD–Green coalition government. They facilitated the split in the SPD and the triggering of a constitutional crisis by Chancellor Schröder to allow for early elections. In terms of squeezing, by increasing a direct link between federal budget and social welfare payment, they also reduced the scope for switching-yard politics between different welfare schemes in the future. The age of retirement was increased from 65 to 67, although this measure was to be phased in over a period of two decades.[9] They also proved cost-containing, at least in the medium term (because unemployment rates fell). More generally, contribution rates and government subsidies remained at a constant (albeit relatively high) level, as economic growth (and reduced unemployment) contained cost pressures on the welfare state.

In sum, the changing nature of the welfare state, especially in the context of unification, meant that the politics of the switching yard entered a new era. Given the political commitment to keep the overall contribution rate below 40 per cent, the federal budget became ever more involved in supporting the activities of the insurance funds. The federal budget therefore became ever more exposed to the vagaries of the labour market, encouraging further cost-containment-related reforms and more political interest in the traditional autonomously organised corporate interests that were at the heart of the German welfare state. Within the welfare state 'switching yard', the traditional corporatist negotiation patterns were abandoned. In terms of actual measures, the politics of welfare state austerity created a clear boundary line and labour market 'dualism' between (western German) insiders who continued to benefit from the (less generous) existing regime, and outsiders (mostly in eastern Germany) (Palier & Thelen 2010; Eichhorst & Marx 2011).

Fiscal Federalism

As noted, the developments affecting the financing of the welfare state had a direct impact on the second traditional switching yard, namely the fiscal transfers affecting the relationship between federal, Land and local governments.

---

[9] It was noticeable that the 'coalition agreement' between CDU–CSU and SPD in 2013 agreed on a partial moderation of these proposals due to SPD demands.

The German system of federalism has been defined as 'executive federalism', as it privileged the involvement of Land governments in federal law-making via the Bundesrat. Furthermore, the Land governments gave up policy autonomy in exchange for federal resources and joint voting-power at the federal level, thereby reducing the power of Land parliaments. The growing involvement of the Länder in negotiating and voting on federal legislation since the late 1960s was originally justified on the basis that the problems of contemporary society could only be solved with the resources of the federal government.

In addition, German federalism was also an 'administrative federalism', as Land and local governments were engaged in the implementation of federal legislation. The federal level was rarely involved in implementation. In addition, local governments, despite being constitutional creatures of the Länder, had the constitutional guarantee of 'local self-administration'. All levels of government, therefore, were supposed to be financially autonomous, but, in the case of the Land and local governments, depended on the federal government for their (administrative) wellbeing.

Local governments were particularly hit by federal switching-yard politics (see Hassel & Schiller 2010). One particular cause was retrenchment in terms of unemployment benefits: long-term unemployed were moved into the category of social benefit recipients. This meant that local governments had to find the resources to support social assistance in a variety of ways, such as in terms of subsidised housing and child support. The economic downturn after 1990 further added to the pool of the long-term unemployed, who were either 'retired' early or became social benefit recipients. Further reforms in the mid-1990s sought to relieve the financial difficulties faced by some local governments (especially those in economically deprived areas). This relief of the local government burden involved, for example, reforms of the financing of asylum seekers and the introduction of an insurance-based scheme to deal with old age care.

Apart from intentional switching-yard-type politics, local government finances were further stretched by unintended consequences. For example, the reform of the tax code introduced by the Schröder government in 2000 was mainly about reducing the burden on business. However, it also resulted in the collapse of one essential revenue source for local governments, the *Gewerbesteuer* (local corporate tax). Local governments' revenues fell from €19.35bn in 2000 to €15.29bn in 2003. Combined with rising costs for social benefits and services—not least triggered by the 'switching yard' policy of the federal government—local governments in the late 1990s and early 2000s witnessed increasing debt rates, cuts in investment and financing of administrative tasks from loans (*Kassenkredite*). According to Hassel & Schiller (2010:

109, quoting Jungfer 2005), the overall debt of the 127 largest German cities increased from €1.3bn in 1993 to €8.7bn in 2003.

Hassel & Schiller (2010) suggest that the proverbial window of reform that facilitated the Hartz IV reforms of 2005 was constituted by two problem streams, namely the depletion of local government finances and the realisation that the federal budget could no longer accommodate rising subsidy payments to insurance funds. Accordingly, the merger of two social benefits systems (unemployment and social assistance) and the move towards a means-tested flat-rate social assistance scheme were only feasible as financial resources were depleted. The concern with financial sustainability was further raised by Germany's violation of the 3 per cent deficit criterion set out in the Maastricht Treaty. Although the welfare state reforms did not solve the financial problems of local government, the 'nationalisation' of social assistance via Hartz IV had a number of cost-containing effects. First, it removed unemployment benefits from the politics of the switching yard as they became increasingly tied to the federal budget. Second, the decrease in the number of unemployed (from 11.7 per cent in 2005 to 6.8 per cent in 2012) also allowed for a reduction of federal subsidies to the labour agency (the Bundesagentur Arbeit[10]). However, cost containment had, as yet, not involved the pension system.

Besides the intergovernmental politics of the welfare state switching yard, there were also far-reaching initiatives in the area of intergovernmental relations (Renzsch 2010). The constitution required equivalent living conditions across all Länder. One of the key motivations to reconsider financial flows was that existing agreements to deal with the generous treatment of eastern Länder were set to end in 2019 (as set out in legislation). The initial 'Solidarity Pact' of 1995 (that was supposed to deal with the money flows across the different Länder) placed the major burden for supporting the eastern Länder on the federal government. It also changed the constitutional settlement regarding concurrent legislation (Art 72.2/3): the federal government was only to legislate in areas where federal legislation was seen as 'necessary' to achieve equivalence in living conditions (Wolf 2010).

The constitutional court played a significant role in changing the nature of intergovernmental financing. The initial Solidarity Pact was ruled out as unconstitutional by the Federal Constitutional Court in 1999 after a case had been taken against the Pact by the governments of Bavaria, Baden

---

[10] One aspect of the reform package was also a change in the organisational status of the employment agency, symbolised by the change from *Bundesanstalt* to *Bundesagentur*. This was to signal a more incentive-driven approach.

Württemberg and Hesse (all, at the time, governed by Christian Democrats).[11] The second Solidarity Pact of 2005 moved towards a more competitive understanding of federalism that no longer aimed at 'equal living conditions' across the Länder (by ensuring that all Länder would have at least 95 per cent of the economic 'strength' of the average of all Länder). Instead, the constitutional aim (Art 107.2 of the Basic Law) was to ensure that different economic performances across the Länder were to be 'appropriately compensated'. A joint commission of Bundestag and Bundesrat was established to reallocate responsibilities between federal and Länder level. The joint commission initially failed as the run-up to the 2005 election made an agreement between Christian Democrats and Social Democrats problematic. Some of the reform proposals were taken up after the 2005 election, although the overall reforms were considered a failure (Scharpf 2009). In particular, fiscal federalism remained outside the deliberations. However, the commission's work led to the prohibition of the direct imposition of federal tasks onto local governments. There were continued concerns (voiced by local governments) as to whether Land governments were using federal funds to support local governments, or used them for alternative spending priorities.

Earlier, in 1992, the Federal Constitutional Court had ruled that the dire financial position of Bremen and Saarland required a federal bailout.[12] In 2006, it also found that Berlin required help.[13] However, the Court also argued that the federal government and the Länder should develop a system that would put the finances of the Länder on a more sustainable basis. This ruling occurred in a favourable political climate. The federal government was keen to reduce its financial transfers to various Länder. The rich Länder demanded a system that reduced their transfer payments (in the complex system of horizontal fiscal equalisation, *horizontaler Länderfinanzausgleich*). The poor Länder were open to reform, but asked for more burden-sharing, especially in the area of social services. These background conditions influenced the deliberations of the so-called second 'federalism reform commission' that concentrated solely on fiscal relations and came to an agreement in 2009 (Heinz 2012).

Debates ensued as to whether a new system of fiscal relations should rely on tightened up constitutional provisions. According to (the old) Article 115, the federal government was not allowed to debt-finance expenditures beyond the level spent on investment over the course of a business cycle. This provision had

---

[11] Bundesverfassungsgericht, 11 November 1999, Az. 2 BvF 2, 3/98 and 1, 2/99; BVerfGE 101, 158 (http://www.bverfg.de/entscheidungen/fs19991111_2bvf000298.html, last accessed 2 September 2013).

[12] Bundesverfassungsgericht, 27 May 1992, Az. 2 BvF 1, 2/88 and 1/90, BVerfGE 86, 148 (http://www.servat.unibe.ch/dfr/bv086148.html, last accessed 2 September 2013).

[13] Bundesverfassungsgericht, 19 October 2006, Az. 2 BvF 3/03, http://www.bverfg.de/entscheidungen/fs20061019_2bvf000303.html, last accessed 2 September 2013).

been shown to be hardly effective; the criteria as to what constituted 'investment' were soft and there had been considerable creativity in defining the relevant business cycle in the past. The experience of Land and local government finances did not suggest that a tightening up was a viable policy option.

The alternative was to introduce a 'debt brake' (or ceiling) which would introduce provisions resembling the Maastricht criteria into the German constitution. These proposals were initially backed by the then SPD finance minister. The main opposition to these proposals emerged from the left-wing factions of the Social Democrats, economically weak Land governments and the Bavarian Christian Democrats. However, the opposition was overcome, again, placing most pressure on the SPD in terms of managing an overall agreement with a ceiling on public expenditure while accommodating concentrated opposition to such fiscal straightjackets.

According to the new Art 109 (and 115) of the Basic Law, German public finances, at the federal and Land level, were to respect a 'structural balanced budget' rule.[14] Land budgets were to be balanced from 2010. The federal government was to run a balanced budget as of 2016. However, the federal government was granted some leeway: governments could run a deficit of 0.35 per cent of GDP over a business cycle. Nevertheless, the provisions were said to be open to manipulation via devices such as private–public partnerships. Moreover, they could be suspended should some vaguely defined economic or natural emergency situations occur.

Monitoring was conducted by a 'Stability Council', consisting of the federal ministers of finance and economics as well as finance ministers of the Länder. In case of a diagnosed budgetary imbalance, the affected Land government had to agree on sets of corrective measures and to report on progress. In addition, five Länder were given additional payments to facilitate their transition to the changing constitutional landscape. These payments, amounting to €7.2bn in total, were provided on a co-financing basis between the federal government and 'rich' Länder. In terms of fiscal consolidation, the overall effect was uncertain. It was uncertain whether some Land governments would comply with the new fiscal rule (including Saarland and Bremen, but potentially also the largest Land, North Rhine Westphalia) (RWI 2013). However, the early monitoring system made the system more predictable for the federal government, and most Länder committed themselves to a policy of consolidation by, for example, including a 'debt ceiling' into their own constitution.

---

[14] BMF (n.d.), 'Compendium on the Federation's Budget Rule as set out in Article 115 of the Basic Law', http://www.bundesfinanzministerium.de/Content/DE/Standardartikel/Themen/ Oeffentliche_Finanzen/Schuldenbremse/2012-06-14-kompendium-en.pdf?__blob= publicationFile&v=3 (last accessed 2 September 2013).

The rise of the debt ceiling as a viable policy option has to be seen in the context of the federal government's response to the financial crisis. As the US financial market's credit crunch caught up with Europe, it was the German IKB bank that required the first bailout in Europe, in August 2007. This was soon followed by Sachsen LB. A further bailout was required to rescue the mortgage lender Hypo Real Estate in September 2008 (shortly after the Lehmann collapse) (see Zohlnhöfer 2012: 231–3). Widespread financial problems involving the (public) *Landesbanken* led to the resignation of a number of Land ministers who were accused of having neglected their oversight obligations. The federal government's response involved a punitive bank stabilisation package that led to some partial bank nationalisations, a facility to create a 'bad bank' for toxic assets and a loan facility for businesses to ensure their access to credit. In addition, the federal government issued an economic stimulus package that amounted to €54.3bn (2.1 per cent of GDP) and did not immediately respond to the constitutional court that ruled two tax increases unconstitutional (Zohlnhöfer 2012: 233). The perceived need to address financial market concerns about the extent of these stimulus packages facilitated calls for budgetary consolidation in general, and supported the move to a rule-based debt ceiling in particular.

Conclusion

The politics of fiscal squeezing in Germany hardly suggests an axing of expenditures. Significant changes to the settings of public expenditure did happen—within ministerial departments (through cost containment in administrative costs, especially staffing), within the welfare state (by changing policy settings and funding streams), and within the system of fiscal federalism (by introducing a debt ceiling). These changes emerged as a result of accumulated effects rather than as the consequence of one-off cutbacks. One major exception is the reform package involving the welfare state (Hartz IV). Overall, however, the politics of fiscal squeezing was a result of incremental change in a number of ways. First, squeezing throughout the past thirty years was a result of a gradual build-up of financial pressures that eventually could no longer be addressed through the conventional methods of the politics of the switching yard, as resources were depleted, or as governments had committed themselves to rules or targets that made it difficult to grant discretionary expenditures. For example, the perceived plight of some local governments could no longer be met by discretionary transfers or tax re-negotiations.

Second, squeezing was conducted in an incremental way. Partly this was a result of a highly interdependent system that required negotiated settlements that balanced winners and losers. Partly it was because of the legal restrictions that constrained the scope for scaling back administrative personnel and put an emphasis on 'natural wastage' in staffing. Partly, incremental change was a result of intended and unintended changes, such as the ones noted above on the changes to the welfare state and the tax system. Demands for financial consolidation led to partial changes in the type of welfare state that would influence spending over time rather than immediately.

Third, squeezing measures in the areas of fiscal federalism and the welfare state were of an incremental nature. Measures were taken that shifted revenue sources around (for example, by moving from pay-as-you-go contributions to indirect taxation) and by reducing the generosity of welfare schemes. However, the decision to change the policy settings of the welfare state on this basis could also be seen as a non-incremental decision.

The politics of financial consolidation also had significant effects on the political system itself. As noted, financial consolidation led to splits within the SPD and between the SPD and some trade unions, and thereby directly affected its decline in electoral fortune throughout the 2000s. However, the politics of financial consolidation also shifted the parameters of political debate (Streeck & Mertens 2010; Howarth & Rommerskirchen 2013). The initial attempts at budgetary consolidation in the 1980s were largely framed in the context of 'Standort Deutschland' (a debate about the viability of Germany as an economically viable location), namely in the way in which the costs of the welfare state were potentially impeding the wellbeing of the economy. This debate shifted to a different kind of argument in the 2000s because of the financial crisis, the bailout of other European governments, and a degree of disillusionment over the high costs of unification. The 'health' of the budget became a political football in itself, as did the lack of scope for elected governments to service little else but mandatory expenditures.

While there were the predictable outcries by concentrated interests in the case of proposed cutbacks, politicians (with the exception of Die Linke) were endorsing the importance of the *Schuldenbremse* (see Zohlnhöfer 2011). The electorate was similarly not opposed to reform per se. In short, while the consolidation of the German public finances was largely incremental, especially when seen in cost terms, the effects of these reforms in political terms were significant in hastening the decline of the Social Democrats while in federal government in particular. Whether these political consequences were to represent a continued pattern remains to be seen, as core support for the SPD and the Christian Democrats has continued to decline, while the electoral appeal of Die Linke has waned and support for the FDP has collapsed.[15]

---

[15] The CDU–CSU vote in the 2013 federal election saw a return to 41.5 per cent. However, whether this election represented a reversal of a long-term decline of the CDU–CSU remained to be seen.

References

Behnke, N. & Benz, A. (2009), 'The Politics of Constitutional Change between Reform and Evolution', *Publius*, 39(2): 213–40.

BMF (Bundesfinanzministerium) (2012), Übersicht über die Steuerrechtsänderungen, BMF, August 2012 (Berlin) http://www.bundesfinanzministerium.de/Content/DE/ Standardartikel/Themen/Steuern/Weitere_Informationen/zusammenstellung- der-steuerrechtsaenderungen-seit-1964-anlage.pdf?__blob=publicationFile&v=7

Breuer, C., Gottschalk, J. & Ivanova, A. (2011), 'Germany: Fiscal Adjustment Attempts With and Without Reforms', in P. Mauro (ed.), *Chipping Away at Public Debt* (Hoboken, NJ, Wiley/International Monetary Fund).

Bytzek, E. (2011), 'The Zero-sum Game of Governing Together? Effects of Merkel's Grand Coalition on the Results of the 2009 German Federal Election', *German Politics*, 20(2): 260–72.

Eichhorst, W. & Marx, P. (2011), 'Reforming German Labour Market Institutions: A Dual Path to Flexibility', *Journal of European Social Policy*, 21(1): 73–87.

Hassel, A. & Schiller, C. (2010), 'Sozialpolitik im Finanzföderalismus', *Politische Vierteljahresschrift*, 51(1): 95–117.

Haverland, M. & Stiller, S. (2010), 'The Grand Coalition and Pension and Health Care Reform', *German Politics*, 19(3): 429–45.

Heinz, D. (2012), 'Varieties of Joint Decision-Making: The Second Federal Reform', *German Politics*, 21(1): 109–15.

Howarth, D. & Rommerskirchen, C. (2013), 'A Panacea for all Times? The German Stability Culture as Strategic Political Resource', *West European Politics*, 36(4): 750–70.

Jungfer, K. (2005), *Die Stadt in der Krise: Ein Manifest für starke Kommunen* (Munich, Carl Hanser Verlag).

Kitschelt, H. & Streeck, W. (2003), 'From Stability to Stagnation: Germany at the Beginning of the 21st Century', *West European Politics*, 26(4): 1–34.

Lehmbruch, G. (2000), *Parteienwettbewerb im Bundesstaat* (Wiesbaden, Westdeutscher Verlag).

Leibfried, S. & Obinger, H. (2003), 'The State of the Welfare State: German Social Policy between Macroeconomic Retrenchment and Microeconomic Recalibration', *West European Politics*, 26(4): 199–218.

Palier, B. & Thelen, K. (2010), 'Institutionalizing Dualism: Complementarities and Change in France and Germany', *Politics & Society*, 38(1): 119–48.

Renzsch, W. (2010), 'Federal Reform under the Grand Coalition', *German Politics*, 19(3/4): 382–92.

Reutter, W. (2012), 'Yet another Coup d'État in Germany?', *German Politics*, 15(3): 302–17.

RWI (Rheinisch-Westfälisches Institut für Wirtschaftsforschung) (2013) *Projektbericht: Gesetz über die Feststellung des Haushaltsplans des Landes Nordrhein-Westfalen für das Haushaltsjahr 2014 (Haushaltsgesetz 2014)* (Essen, RWI), http://en.rwi-essen. de/media/content/pages/publikationen/rwi-projektberichte/PB_Stellungnahme_ Landeshaushalt_NRW.pdf

Scharpf, F.W. (1988), 'The Joint Decision Trap', *Public Administration*, 66(3): 239–78.

Scharpf, F.W. (2009), *Föderalismusreform* (Frankfurt am Main, Campus).

Streeck, W. (2003), *No Longer the Century of Corporatism. Das Ende des 'Bündnisses für Arbeit'*, MPIfG Working Paper 03/4, http://www.mpifg.de/pu/workpap/wp03-4/wp03-4.html

Streeck, W. (2009), 'Endgame? The Fiscal Crisis of the German State', in A. Miskommon, W.E. Paterson & J. Sloam (eds), *Germany's Gathering Crisis* (Basingstoke, Palgrave Macmillan), 38–63.

Streeck, W. & Mertens, D. (2010), *Politik im Defizit*, MPIfG Discussion Paper 10/5 (Cologne), http://www.mpifg.de/pu/dp_abstracts/dp10-5.asp

Trampusch, C. (2009), *Der erschöpfte Sozialstaat* (Frankfurt am Main, Campus).

Weishaupt, J.T. (2010), 'Germany after a Decade of Social Democrats in Government: The End of the Continental Model?', *German Politics*, 19(2): 105–22.

Wolf, H. (2010), 'German Unification Twenty Years Later', *German Politics & Society*, 28(2): 71–81.

Zohlnhöfer, R. (2011), 'The Federal Election and the Economic Crisis', *German Politics*, 20(1): 12–27.

Zohlnhöfer, R. (2012), 'Between a Rock and Hard Place: The Grand Coalition's Response to the Economic Crisis', *German Politics*, 20(2): 227–42.

9

Fiscal Squeeze in Sweden, 1990–1997: The Causes, the Measures, and their Short- and Long-Run Effects

ANDERS LINDBOM

> And then there's Sweden, the rock star of the recovery.
> *Washington Post*, 24 June 2011

SWEDEN'S POPULATION IS NOT EVEN A HUNDREDTH OF CHINA'S OR INDIA'S and the size of the economy is only about one-thirtieth of that of the United States Swedes who make longer trips abroad often discover that their home country is associated with cuckoo clocks and the Alps, in other words, that it is confused with Switzerland. However, among people who are interested in politics, the 'Swedish model' tends either to be a shocking example of big government or an inspiring role model. But in spite of what is commonly believed, high social spending is not really a central characteristic of Sweden. Instead the core of the Swedish welfare state is the idea that it must cater to middle-class interests in order to serve the working class best (Esping-Andersen 1990; Lindbom 2011; Steinmo 2010; Korpi & Palme 1998).

Historically, the Social Democratic Party has been the dominant party in Swedish politics. During the period 1932 to 2006, the party dominated the government for 66 out of 75 years. The proportional electoral system tends to generate minority governments, however, and hence the government needs to make deals with (parts of) the opposition. These political compromises tend to be possible because of the dominance of the socio-economic conflict dimension and the strong and centralised parties (Steinmo 2010). Sweden is a unitary country and that means that a few broad and centralised interest groups are dominant, such as the blue collar confederation (LO) and the Swedish Employers Association, which negotiate tripartite deals with the government (Swank 2002). This type of corporatism has mostly been developed in small export-dependent countries (Katzenstein 1985; cf. Hall & Soskice 2001). Sweden underwent a rapid industrialisation process about a hundred years ago when international demand for its natural resources grew.

Proceedings of the British Academy, **197**, 185–206. © The British Academy 2014.

Before industrialisation Sweden was one of the poorer countries in Europe, but by 1970 it was the fourth-richest country in the world.

What Prompted the Fiscal Squeeze?

During the late 1980s, the Swedish economy was booming: unemployment was around 2 per cent, whereas in many other countries within the OECD it approached 10 per cent, and the Swedish budget surplus was the largest in the OECD. Property prices were rising rapidly, partly due to low mortgage costs. But wage increases and inflation were getting out of hand. When international demand decreased, the Swedish export industry rapidly lost market share, which led to reduced employment.

Simultaneously, the Swedish housing bubble collapsed. German unification in combination with a domestic tax reform led to rapidly increasing real interest rates. This amplified the effect of overinvestment in commercial property and triggered a downward price spiral, resulting in large credit losses for banks and financial institutions (Englund 1999). In response, the government guaranteed all bank deposits and nationalised two of the major banks. Sweden spent around 4 per cent of its GDP to rescue its ailing banks, which is fairly comparable to what the US was expected to spend in the recent financial crisis (*New York Times*, 22 September 2008). This put further strain on an already bleeding budget.[1]

GDP declined in 1991–93 and unemployment increased by around 600 per cent during the same period. As a result of these changes, the central government's tax revenues were declining. Simultaneously, spending increased dramatically because of the generous social insurance schemes doing what they were supposed to, that is, acting as automatic economic stabilisers. Hence the budget deficit rapidly increased and became the largest in Europe (11.9 per cent) in relation to GDP (Prop. 2000/2001:100, appendix 5). A comparison with the deficits in 2009 in, for example, Greece (15.6 per cent) and the USA (11.9 per cent) illustrates the magnitude of this (OECD Economic Outlook No. 92).

The government needed to borrow money on the international financial markets in order to cover current expenditures. The dependence on financial markets, which probably saw the Swedish welfare state as an unduly expensive

---

[1] It has been argued, however, that the Swedish state later regained these costs when it sold its shares in the banks and that these measures should be a model for other governments, e.g. the US government in 2008 (*New York Times*, 22 September 2008).

institution that slowed economic growth by perverting the incentive structures of the markets, led to a strong pressure for political change. During the
1990s, it was commonly argued in political economy circles that globalisation
had fundamentally changed politics. It was therefore claimed that a country
like Sweden could no longer deviate from the policies implemented in other
countries (cf. Cerny 1996; Strange 1996; Greider 1997; Martin & Schumann
1997; Gray 1998; Lindbom 2001a).

Because of Sweden's earlier tendency to use devaluations to solve recur-
ring problems of international competitiveness, there was, on the one hand, a
broad political agreement that Sweden should stick to a disinflation policy
(Lindvall 2004; Bergh 2007). On the other hand, this policy lacked credibility
in the markets.

In late summer of 1992 interest rates exploded. On 16 September, the
central bank raised its interest rate to 500 per cent in order to sell its bonds.
Over a couple of weeks, two political agreements, on substantial cutbacks in
the public sector and tax increases, were struck. The agreements were supported by both the Social Democratic opposition and the four-party
centre-right government, and the overall effect was predicted to improve the
budget balance by 28 billion kronor in 1993 and 40 billion in 1997, which
would have equalled 2.5 per cent of GDP (*Tidningarnas Telegrambyrå*, 20
September 1992). These measures were in vain, however: shortly thereafter,
158 billion kronor poured out of the country during a single week thanks to
expectations of a forthcoming devaluation of the currency. These expectations became a self-fulfilling prophecy, and in November 1992 the krona was
allowed to float.

The entire Swedish political establishment had invested its prestige in
defending the krona's fixed exchange rate, but to no avail. The minister of
finance talked about 'a black day for Sweden' and the prime minister acknowledged 'the defeat' (Lindbom 2011). For Swedes, who were used to thinking of
their country as a role model for others, the situation was humiliating. But in
hindsight, this defeat was probably an important factor in Sweden's economic
recovery.

***

The foregoing shows how powerless the Swedish government seemed at this
low point. The economic decline was spectacular. This chapter goes on to
describe how the government made the necessary economic adjustments in
the regulation of production, and in particular in the reforms of the welfare
state. It then portrays the economic effects, the social effects and the political
effects of the reforms.

Economic Reform

Fiscal consolidation has not been all about fiscal squeeze. The floating currency helped to restore Swedish firms' ability to compete in world markets by lowering labour costs by around 20 per cent. But some structural reforms of the economy also deserve to be mentioned.

A number of tax reforms had been implemented and although the timing of the last and biggest one was unfortunate, just before the crisis exploded, it is likely that it decreased the incentives for firms as well as wage-earners to make certain economic decisions for tax reasons rather than for productive purposes (Steinmo 2010). Reforms to increase competition were conducted on a large scale. In the early 1990s, former monopolies were deregulated in the markets for electricity, mail, telecommunications, domestic flights, railways, and taxis. According to Gwartney & Lawson's index on economic freedom, the Swedish value increased spectacularly and matched the level of the United Kingdom and the USA in 2003 if we disregard their indicator 'size of government' (Bergh 2007).

The municipalities and counties, which are responsible for welfare services, were also deregulated and given much more freedom to organise their provision of welfare services on whatever basis they considered most rational (Montin 2007). Private production of publicly financed services increased rapidly. Simultaneously, vouchers were introduced for welfare services, both at the national level (for schools) and sometimes locally for other functions (Lindbom 2013). Last but not least, pension reform, which most probably saved the existing system from future bankruptcy, was implemented during the height of the crisis (Green-Pedersen & Lindbom 2006). While many of these reforms were implemented by the centre-right government (1991–94), it is noteworthy that some of them were already in the political pipeline. Others were not nullified when the Social Democrats regained power. Last but not least, some of the reforms were made by broad political majorities including both the Social Democrats and centre-right parties (cf. Bergh 2007). Swedish politics has a consensual trait.

How Was the Fiscal Squeeze Implemented?

The 1994 election returned the Social Democrats to power. The state had to borrow money in the international markets to cover deficits in the budget. Sweden's credit rating had been downgraded and the costs of interest on loans had been rising rapidly to become the third-largest expenditure item in the budget, amounting to more than 10 per cent of total expenditure in 1996

(SCB 2009: Table 2.1). In order to get the loans, the government had to accept the conditions stated by the financial markets: make cutbacks and restructure!

The Swedish government embarked on institutional change in budgeting procedures in order to increase budget discipline. Instead of starting with individual budget items and then adding them all up to form an aggregate, the procedure was changed, to begin by deciding an overall level of expenditure and then breaking it down into 20 or so expenditure areas and beyond that into individual budget items (Molander 2001).

But future budget discipline was not enough; the budget deficit had to be reduced in the short run. Pierson (1994) suggests a number of strategies to implement unpopular change: among them bundling cutbacks into a single package, broad political coalitions, and obfuscation. In the next paragraphs each of these is analysed in turn.

A comprehensive package (the convergence programme) was implemented between 1994 and 1998 (see Table 9.1). It was the result of negotiations between the Social Democratic minority government and the Centre Party (the former Agricultural party). The convergence programme permanently strengthened the public finances by 126 billion kronor (or 7.5 per cent of GDP). This package built on the measures of the earlier government and hence there will be no attempt here to separate the effects of centre-right and Social Democratic policies of fiscal squeeze.

Table 9.1. The Swedish convergence programme (effect in 1998, in billion kronor).

Cutbacks	
Transfers to households	34.6
Cuts in subsidies	8.1
Consumption (the state)	6.8
Investments in infrastructure	2.7
Subsidies for pharmaceutical/dental care	2.8
Education	4.1
Other	12.1
Total cutbacks	**71.2**
Tax increases	
Contributions to social insurance	23.7
Taxes on capital income	7.5
'Tax on high income earners' (*värnskatten*)	4.2
Taxes on production	6.1
Other	27.5
Total tax increases	**69.0**
Tax decreases	
Lowered VAT on food	7.6
Other	7.1
Total tax decreases	**14.7**
Total effect	**125.5**

Source: Prop. 2000/01:100, appendix 5.

The fiscal squeeze was divided roughly equally between cutbacks and tax increases. The income tax of 'high income-earners' was raised and while it only accounted for 6 per cent of the increased revenue, it has been argued that it was probably important for the political legitimacy of the reforms.

More often than not, a broad spectrum of parties backed the cutbacks. The Social Democrats while in opposition supported the emergency package in 1992 and the Centre Party supported the Social Democratic government's fiscal squeeze programmes over the years 1995–98. The other centre-right parties often voted for the measures as well. But why did they? Santesson-Wilson (2008) argues that parties sometimes think beyond the next election. By taking some vote losses in the short term, they can achieve long-term success. The Social Democrats were Sweden's default governing party at this time and were probably fairly sure that they would return to power soon (that is, in the election scheduled for 1994). Rather than having the entire problem in their own lap after the election, they therefore helped their opponents. The Centre Party's choice to support the fiscal squeeze can be explained by the party leadership's hope of winning political credibility and securing compensation from the Social Democrats on other issues (a deal on the continuing nuclear decommissioning and reducing VAT on food), both of which were probably popular with the party's grassroots (Santesson-Wilson 2008).

But in spite of theories about blame-avoidance (Pierson 1994), both the centre-right and the Social Democratic government at times appear to have made a point of drawing everyone's attention to the cutbacks (on a general level). Sometimes the cutbacks were exaggerated in the hope of impressing the international financial markets. The interest rate is probably an important explanatory factor. The budget deficit had to be financed by borrowing money and this led to increasing interest rates. According to the Social Democratic prime minister at the time, the rampant interest rates in turn affected the many households who were paying mortgages and hence they accepted public expenditure cuts (Carlsson 2003).

On the other hand, acceptance of cutbacks in general is a quite different thing from acceptance of a specific cut. Göran Persson, Social Democratic minister of finance 1994–96 and prime minister 1996–2006, says that arguing for cutbacks in individual programmes is often a hopeless cause: 'All groups have good reasons for why their area should be spared from cutbacks' (Persson 1997: 131 and 61). Instead he opted for saving on 'everything', not making any exceptions. The idea was not to single out the losers and to communicate that everyone—including the party's own constituency—was contributing to the effort (Henriksson 2007).[2]

---

[2] The Swedish model in the labour market does not allow direct intervention by the state. Hence wages of civil servants were not and 'could not' be cut by unilateral decisions by the government.

Table 9.2.   Percentage cutbacks of cash benefits in Sweden in 1998, compared with 1990.

Housing allowance	41
Retraining allowance	36
Work injury: sickness	23
Unemployment benefit	22
Sickness benefit	21
Child allowance	21
Support for single parents	17
Parental leave	14
Survivor's pension	13
Early retirement	9
Basic pension	7
Supplementary pension (ATP*)	6
Work injury: annuities	4

* Allmän tilläggspension.
Source: Lindbom (2007).

My analysis largely confirms that transparent cutbacks were about the same magnitude in different social policy programmes (Lindbom 2007; see, however, Lindbom (2001b) regarding housing construction subsidies). Untransparent cutbacks followed a different logic, however. Table 9.2 presents my estimates of the 'real' cutbacks, not the forecast effects presented in the parliamentary proposals.[3]

In spite of the cheese slicer being put to use, there is a rather large variation between the cutbacks. I argue that this primarily reflects the power of the Swedish pensioners' organisations and the possibilities to make opaque cutbacks by allowing inflation or wage increases to hollow out the real value of benefits. To a smaller degree, the variation can be explained by worries about work incentives. Principles of just distribution do not seem to have been so important. The housing allowance for low-income families, for example, was cut the most, whereas the housing allowance for the elderly was improved (Lindbom 2007). The two types of households, however, look for housing in the same housing market.

Obviously the political actors of the time did not talk about the obfuscation strategy directly, but one did argue that 'indexation of expenditures and wages is to be avoided at all costs' (Henriksson 2007: 24). Were there, in spite

---

[3] With the use of a database consisting of information regarding a large number of citizens, I have estimated what the expenditure for a particular programme would have been in 1998 if the old programme rules had been left unchanged and if the programmes had been indexed to prices or wages. A simple example: the maximum benefit in unemployment insurance was not raised between 1993 and 1998. I have data regarding the former wage of a large number of unemployed people and I use this to estimate how much money the government saved by not adjusting the maximum benefit in line with the general increases in wages between 1993 and 1998. See Lindbom (2007) for further details of how cutbacks have been estimated.

of what the government said, items that were spared from cutbacks? It is difficult to answer this question, if for no other reason than that the government stuck to its framing and did not explicitly—as far as I have seen—point out any such digressions from its own norms. Nor can I recall that the media exposed important exceptions. But as has already been mentioned, pensions clearly were cut less than other social policy programmes. This result is in line with the arguments and findings of the welfare literature: pension retrenchment is particularly unpopular (Giger 2011).

The Economic Effects of Fiscal Squeeze

After several years of fiscal squeeze, in 1998 the national budget again was showing a surplus. The welfare reforms account for about two-thirds of budget change (Lindbeck 1997: 68) and the rest is to a large extent the effect of Swedish industrial competitiveness being lifted by the depreciation of the krona and the decreasing level of interest rates. The depreciation of the currency had over time restored Swedish industry's competitiveness.

By around 2000 Sweden had had six years of economic growth averaging 3 per cent a year. Unemployment had dramatically decreased (see Figure 9.2, p. 198 below), the budget showed a surplus and the debt had decreased for a number of years. There was a trade surplus of more than 2 per cent of GNP (Prop. 2000/01:100, appendix 5).

By 2010, the debt of the Swedish public sector had declined from 73 per cent in 1996 to 40 per cent. During the same time period, in the United Kingdom it increased from 51 per cent to 80 per cent (Eurostat). Inflation had been a constant problem during the 1970s and 1980s. Around 1990 it was above 10 per cent. But during the crisis inflation fell dramatically and ever since 1994 it has only rarely broken the 2.5 per cent level. In terms of the long-run effects on the macro-economy, the fiscal squeeze of 1990–97 seems to have been a success.

But what were the effects of the fiscal squeeze on the Swedish welfare state, predominantly characterised as universal and generous? Was it transformed to a liberal welfare state, that is, meagre benefits that are primarily directed at the poor (cf. Esping-Andersen 1990)? Which groups were particularly affected by the cutbacks? These questions are answered in the next section.

The Social Effects of the Fiscal Squeeze

Macro-level Analysis

Did Sweden have to fundamentally restructure its welfare state in order to appease the financial markets (Lindbom 2011)? I use two components of Esping-Andersen's seminal work on welfare regimes to estimate whether the welfare system was changed: (1) generosity is measured by the net replacement rates of an average worker and (2) the coverage of the public schemes is measured by a number of different indicators.

As a first step, we describe how the Swedish welfare state changed compared to other countries by ranking countries' replacement rates. While many readers may have the impression that Sweden had a uniquely generous welfare system in 1980 (Esping-Andersen 1990), this is not quite true and hence the changes are easily exaggerated if this fact is not recognised. Unemployment benefit was in fourth place in 1980 as well as in 2000, while sickness benefit fell from fourth place in 1980 to sixth place in 2000 (Lindbom 2011). This is a first indication that the changes were rather modest, but we still need to examine the *size* of the change.

In order to examine this, Table 9.3 shows the replacement rates of certain types of households, both in 2005 (close to when the Social Democratic Party was replaced by a centre-right government in 2006) and in 2010 (the latest available data) in order to evaluate the recent changes made by the new government.[4]

Table 9.3 shows both the Swedish social insurance programmes included becoming less generous between 1980 and 2005. The replacement rate for an average worker declined by approximately 11 percentage points for

Table 9.3. Net replacement rates 1980–2010 (%).

	Unemployment benefit	Sickness cash benefit
Sweden 1980	79	92
Sweden 2005	68	80
Sweden 2010	55	75
17 OECD 2010	57	62

Source: Palme *et al.* (2012).

---

[4] The replacement rates have been calculated for the average of two types of households: a single person and a family consisting of two adults and two children. The beneficiary earns the equivalent of an average worker. Since benefits are taxed in some countries (including Sweden), net replacement rates are presented, i.e. net benefit compared to net wage. Means-tested supplements are not included. While they are important in some countries, such as the United Kingdom, they are not in Sweden. (For more specific information on the calculations, see Palme *et al.* 2012.)

unemployment benefit and about 12 percentage points for sickness benefit. It is, however, clear that the Swedish system in 2005 was still more generous than the average for the 17 other OECD countries, but the difference has declined compared to 1980 (Lindbom 2011). However, since 2006 the centre-right government has allowed unemployment benefit to be hollowed out, largely by not raising the maximum benefit at all in spite of increasing wages and by lowering taxes for the gainfully employed (Earned Income Tax Credit, EITC).

Parental leave is not among the programmes that have traditionally defined welfare regimes. During the time of the fiscal squeeze, marginal changes that lowered generosity were implemented (cf. Table 9.2), but data for 2000 show that the generosity of Swedish social insurance is highest among the 15 countries for which data are available (Ferrarini 2003). I would argue therefore that the Swedish welfare state did not lose its relatively generous character during the financial crisis of the 1990s (cf. Lindbom 2001a).

If we proceed to analyse the stratification, and try to compare the situation in 1980 with data assembled close to the Social Democratic election loss in 2006, we can see the result in Table 9.4. The means-tested programmes' share of social spending accounts for 4.7 per cent for Sweden and an average value for the other 17 countries of 19.5 per cent in 2003 (OECD/own calculations). It is also clear that the relative importance of private pensions is considerably lower in Sweden than in comparable countries. The private share of health expenditure has increased, but in 2006 it is still much lower than the average of the other 17 countries.

No drastic changes have occurred since the centre-right parties came to power in 2006. As we can see in Figure 9.1, the share of the population eligible for social assistance has not increased much in spite of the international economic crisis, and hence expenditure has not increased much either. The share of means-tested programmes therefore has not exploded. There are no data available for the development of the share of private pensions after 2003, but there is no reason to expect any dramatic change there. (Since 1998 there has been an agreement between the Social Democratic Party and the four centre-right parties that a consensus among the five is necessary in order to

Table 9.4.   Stratification: indicators of liberalism (shares of expenditure), %.

	Means-tested / total cash benefits	Private pension / total pension	Private healthcare / total health
Sweden 1980	4.6	5.5	7.5
Sweden around 2006	4.7 (2003)	12.9 (2003)	18.4 (2006)
Other 17 OECD	19.5 (2003)	31.5 (2003)[a]	25.2 (2006)[b]

[a] Data for USA, France, Ireland and Japan are missing.
[b] Data for Belgium and the Netherlands are missing.

Source: Lindbom (2011).

make any changes to the existing pension system.) The share of private health expenditure has continued to increase slowly, but only to 19 per cent (OECD Health Statistics).

The discussion above has, however, been entirely devoted to system-level variables. The next section will instead focus on the welfare of individuals.

Micro-level Analysis

Has the partial restructuring of the welfare state that was described above affected the effectiveness with which social policies are able to handle problems like poverty? As Figure 9.1 shows, the percentage of the population who are in *relative poverty* (60 per cent of the median income) rose during the period of Social Democratic rule, from just over 7 per cent in 1995 to more than 10 per cent in 2006. Interestingly, the development of *absolute poverty* (persons eligible for social assistance), on the other hand, shows a marked decline in recent years after rising significantly during the deep recession of the 1990s. Between 1996 and 2006, the proportion of absolute poor declined by 50 per cent and the reason is not that eligibility criteria for social assistance have been tightened. The trend for relative poverty to increase was strengthened

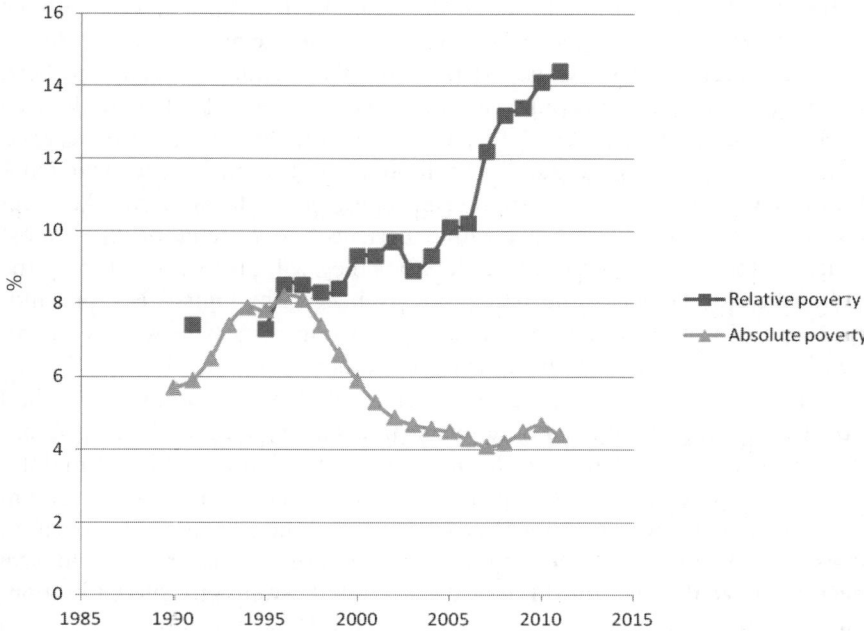

Figure 9.1. Absolute and relative poverty (% of Swedish population aged between 16 and 84). *Source:* Socialstyrelsen (2010).

under centre-right rule since 2006, whereas the absolute poverty level has not changed much in spite of the recession around 2010.

My interpretation of these seemingly contradictory trends is that Sweden, as a consequence of economic growth, experienced rising income inequality. Only people who were part of the labour market got a share of the wage increases. The income of the median voter rose, but a small but significant group of labour market outsiders did not receive a higher income and consequently 'relative poverty' increased. But the welfare state on an aggregate level managed to decrease the level of absolute poverty.

On a more disaggregated level, however, different groups experienced varying outcomes. It is difficult to identify winners in the fiscal squeeze measures. The measures taken were cutbacks of benefits and raised taxes rather than more generous policies towards groups. Moreover, there has been a strong societal transformation during the last twenty years and it is likely that, for example, globalisation is an important factor in explaining the changes in relative incomes. That said, it is clear that the income share of the top 1 per cent increased from around 4.5 per cent in 1990 to almost 7 per cent in 2010. Similarly, realised capital gains have increased (Roine & Waldenström 2010). When the squeeze impressed the financial markets, the lower interest rates benefited mortgage holders. Similarly, the fiscal squeeze, combined with devaluation and the structural reforms of the economy, may have had the indirect effect of making the Swedish economy prosper and the median income rise.

It is easier to identify the losers in the fiscal squeeze: single mothers, immigrants and young people were disproportionately affected by the cutbacks during the 1990s (SOU 2001). Given the way the cutbacks were carried out, this is not particularly surprising. Decremental cutbacks will particularly hit those who receive benefits from several different systems. Hence the effect on families: not only will this group experience the same cutbacks as most others if they are unemployed or sick, but they will also be affected by the reduced child allowance and parental leave benefit, by higher fees for childcare, and disproportionally by increasing housing costs (and will lack compensation for this through the housing allowance).

These 'losers' would have done considerably better if family policy had not been eroded. A typical household with a single parent and two children has lost a considerable amount due to the erosion of family policy: if maintenance support and child benefit had followed inflation, and the maximum wage-level of the housing allowance had followed the general wage-increases, disposable income after necessary consumption like food and rent would have been 14 per cent higher for this type of household (Swedbank 2010; Lindbom 2011).

The groups that experienced a worse than average development of their disposable income all share a lower than average propensity to vote (SCB

2012). Besides, only naturalised immigrants are entitled to vote in the national elections. All the losers furthermore share the trait that their participation in the labour market is lower than average. Relatively large shares of these groups do not even have the type of work history that would make them eligible for the unemployment benefit and they will therefore instead be supported by the much less generous social assistance scheme. In fact, Swedish unemployment benefit has *never* been universal, in spite of the tendency of many to understand Esping-Andersen (1990) that way. The Sweden that exists in the real world has never been identical to Esping-Andersen's ideal type (cf. Bergquist 1990). Ever since 1934, Swedish unemployment insurance has had eligibility criteria: to qualify for unemployment benefit, an unemployed person must have chosen to be a member of an unemployment insurance scheme and have satisfied certain work requirements. Since the benefit is voluntary, some abstain from paying the fee.[5]

To sum up, it is clear that employment is central to determining which groups of citizens are winners and which are losers in the fiscal squeeze. Moreover, it is argued here that unemployment is also central to understanding the long-term political effects of the Swedish economic crisis of the 1990s. The next section therefore describes the development of unemployment and of the active labour market policy.

Unemployment and Unemployment Policies

Since the point here is to follow the development in Sweden over time rather than to (try to) compare it to developments in other countries, Figure 9.2 shows the absolute numbers of unemployed.[6] The figure clearly illustrates how Sweden in the early 1990s experienced a skyrocketing increase in unemployment. Between 1990 and 1993, about half a million jobs—or 12 per cent of employment—disappeared. When the economy recovered, unemployment did decrease, but it has not returned to the earlier low levels. The fiscal squeeze is hardly the main reason for this. The Swedish economy is undergoing changes that make it increasingly difficult for people with low qualifications

---

[5] During the 1970s and the early 1980s, the percentage of the workforce that had membership of an unemployment fund was similar to that in 2013, i.e. around 70 per cent. Coverage gradually increased and peaked during the Swedish economic crisis, when the risk of becoming unemployed was widespread (87 per cent in 1998). Once the crisis was over, membership again declined (Lindgren 2013).

[6] During the 1970s and 1980s, the Swedish labour market appeared to be functioning well in international comparisons. The unemployment rate was around 2 per cent, while in other OECD countries it tended to be around 10 per cent (Rothstein 1986).

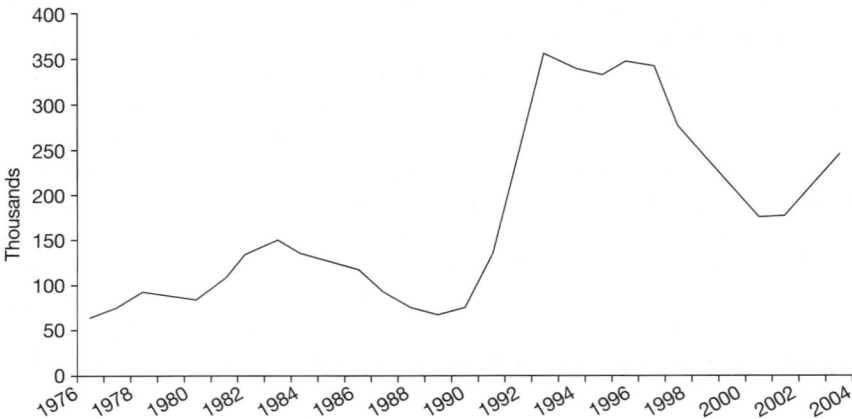

Figure 9.2.   Number of unemployed, Sweden (thousands).
Source: SCB (Swedish Bureau of Statistics), Labour Force Survey (AKU).

to find any job at all, but the relatively dramatic layoffs at the beginning of the crisis quickened that process.

The earlier situation of 'full employment' is, however, still the ideal to which the current conditions are compared and, as a consequence, labour market performance has been causing public discontent. The discontent has affected labour market policy, the bureau responsible for implementing it, and the party in government. The following sections describe this development.

Active Labour Market Policy

Traditionally, Active Labour Market Policy (ALMP) had provided small numbers of people with high-quality retraining in order to prevent bottle-necks. But in order to stop the unemployed from permanently being kicked out of the labour force, in the 1990s ALMP was changed to handle large numbers of unemployed.

The proportion of participants in ALMP that had become employed six months after finishing job-training decreased from 74 per cent in 1989 to a low of 25 per cent in 1993 (Prop. 1999/2000:98, p. 15). As a consequence, many unemployed people ended up in a feedback loop between 'passive' support from unemployment benefit and ALMP. As the quantity of people in training was given priority over the quality of the training, the reputation of ALMP deteriorated.

However, the effectiveness of labour market policy is, naturally enough, lower when there is low demand on the labour market. And it is likely that the earlier ALMP contributed to the very strong employment growth in 1998–2000 that was able to take place without accelerating inflation. Instead of being permanently excluded from the labour market, the long-term unemployed were often able to maintain their connection to it.

Still, the changing perception of ALMP had political implications. Public opinion polls in the late 1990s showed a growing dissatisfaction among citizens with active labour market policy. The Social Democrats changed their focus and increased the requirements on individual unemployed persons to actively search for jobs and to emphasise that unemployment benefit is not intended to be a permanent source of support but a help during the transition from one job to another (Lindvert 2006; Prop. 1999/2000: 98). A corresponding development also took place in sickness insurance (Johnson 2010). But the voters' evaluation of these changes seems to have been 'too little and too late'.

The Political Effects of the Fiscal Squeeze

The median voters have not suffered particularly from the fiscal squeeze. On average they do not really rely much on cash benefits for their support and therefore the cutbacks were less troublesome for them than for the losers: immigrants, young people and single mothers. However, if the median voters fall ill or lose their jobs, the changes in the social insurance system mean that they lose more than they would have done earlier (see Table 9.3 above). The effect on the median voter is hence rather one of drastically increased *risk* but only limited average loss.

Median voters do make use of the universal welfare services, however. State subsidies to local governments were largely excluded from cutbacks (in nominal prices), but municipalities still suffered from the crisis as their tax revenues fell due to rising unemployment, while their expenditure, for example for social assistance, increased. Many municipalities therefore both made cutbacks and tried organisational reforms with the market as a model for increasing operational efficiency (Montin 2007). These changes are probably part of the reason for the middle class opting out of municipal schools and using the school voucher to attend independent schools instead (Lindbom 2010). Once the fiscal squeeze was over, additional state subsidies (amounting to 21 billion kronor in 2000) were given to the municipal sector, with the intention that they would be used for welfare services. On the other hand, although some taxes were raised as part of the fiscal squeeze, there has been no trend of raising taxes as a share of GDP.

Short-Run Effects

By the election year 1998, fiscal squeeze had been replaced by a slight tendency to restore some of the welfare policies that had experienced cutbacks. In spite of these election promises, the two parties that had taken joint responsibility for the cutbacks were punished on election day. The governing Social Democratic Party suffered its worst electoral result since 1920 and gained only 36.4 per cent—a loss of almost 9 percentage points since 1994. The Centre Party lost almost a third of its votes from 1994. The informal governmental coalition as a whole lost 20.7 per cent of its seats in parliament.[7]

The Social Democrats were able to remain in power, however. The reason was that their disappointed former voters largely shifted to the Left Party, in itself a strong indication that they were protesting against the cutbacks. According to the measurement of Alesina *et al.*, the incumbent was therefore not punished. If we make a formalistic interpretation, Alesina *et al.* (2012) are not wrong: the Swedish government was not voted out. But in reality the election was the end of the informal majority coalition between the Social Democrats and the Centre Party. After the 1998 election, the Social Democrats normally relied on the support of the Left Party and the Green Party to achieve a parliamentary majority. Hence, there is a risk that Alesina *et al.*'s (2012) conclusion, that governments who quickly reduce budget deficits are not systematically voted out of office, stems from a lack of contextualisation of the dependent variable (cf. Lindbom 2014).

In the 2002 election, the Social Democrats partly recovered and won 39.9 per cent of the votes and continued ruling with the support of the Left Party and the Green Party. After that, however, their downward trend continued. In 2006, they received 35 per cent of the votes and a four-party centre-right Alliance gained power. After the 2010 elections, a weakened Alliance remained in power. The Social Democrats again had a historically bad electoral result: 30.7 per cent.[8]

Long-Run Effects: Issue-Ownership of Employment Policy

Although the fiscal squeeze is not more than one factor among others in explaining why unemployment has not returned to the pre-crisis levels, it is clear that citizens expect the government to do something about the situation and that the squeeze set limits to what sort of efforts the government could take.

After the squeeze was over, unemployment decreased for a number of years, but after 2003 the trend reversed (see Figure 9.2 above). The voters' perception of the importance of the issue for their vote decision varies accordingly: only 7 per cent said unemployment was an important issue in the election in 2002 but in the later elections that increased to 35 per cent (in 2006)

---

[7] www.val.se

[8] www.val.se

and 31 per cent (in 2010) (Oscarsson & Holmberg 2011: Table 21). Up to 2006, in all elections since 1982, the majority of the voters perceived the Social Democratic employment policies to be better than the policies of the centre-right parties. In the 2006 election, however, this changed, and the Moderates (the Liberal–Conservative party) gained ownership of the issue. In the 2006 election, 51 per cent of the voters considered that employment was a high-profile issue for the Moderates, whereas only 24 per cent thought that it was for the Social Democrats. The Moderate party's employment policies were on average seen as more credible than the Social Democratic proposals in both 2006 and 2010. Since the issue of employment was one of the voters' main concerns, this Social Democratic failure was a costly one, and a partial explanation for the fact that the Red–Green parties did not win the elections (Oscarsson & Holmberg 2011). While it is difficult to provide solid evidence for long-term effects of a fiscal squeeze (cf. Chapter 1 in this volume), my interpretation of the data is that voters would have been likely to punish the Social Democrats in the election in 2002 if the unemployment situation had been similar to 2006 or 2010.

The fiscal squeeze of the 1990s made it more difficult for the Social Democrats to win votes by arguing that their opponents might retrench the welfare state if they gained power, since the Social Democrats had implemented significant cutbacks themselves (Lindbom 2008). Like several other social democratic parties, some of the party's core voters had the perception that the Swedish Social Democratic Party had lost its soul when it engaged in third-way reforms of the welfare state. While the immediate effect in Sweden (in 1998) was smaller than in Denmark, Germany and the United Kingdom (Arndt 2013), probably thanks to the economic success of the fiscal squeeze and the fact that ALMPs were traditional policies in Sweden, the long-term effects probably were large.

The Social Democrats are still strong among young people, pensioners and the sick and unemployed. But according to a study published by the Bureau of Statistics (SCB), in 2010 the party only gained the same share of the votes as the Moderates (31 per cent) from people who had a job.[9] It has become increasingly difficult for the party to appeal to both labour market insiders and outsiders (Lindvall & Rueda 2011). In the words of their opponents in the Moderate party, the Social Democrats have transformed into a party for welfare beneficiaries rather than a party for 'workers'. Compared to the 2006 election, the Moderates in 2010 increased their share of votes among

[9] Other studies have even been widely—but at least partly falsely—quoted as showing that the Moderates are much stronger (32–22) in this group (*Aktuellt i politiken*, 20 May 2013). The 32–22 figures are unweighted data, but the Social Democrats tend to be under-represented among the people answering the survey on election night.

members of the blue-collar workers' union (LO) by 4.6 per cent to 15.7 per cent. The Social Democrats are still by far the highest among LO-voters, with a voting share of 50.7 per cent, but it is a concern for the Social Democrats that they—two elections in a row—have lost voters among the workers. In the 2006 elections the Social Democrats lost 6 per cent of the LO members and in the 2010 election they lost an additional 3.7 per cent (*LO-tidningen*, 20 September 2010).

To sum up, I argue that the perception of the Social Democratic Party changed as a long-term consequence of the fiscal squeeze. This is a partial explanation of why the perceived ideological differences between the major parties—the Social Democrats and the Moderates—have declined (Lindbom 2008). In recent elections, voters to a rapidly increasing extent instead have focused on parties' 'technical' ability to rule the country. In 2002, the competence to rule was one of the most important reasons for party choice for 31 per cent of the voters, but in subsequent elections its importance increased: to 42 per cent in 2006 and 51 per cent in 2010. The importance of this change can be illustrated by Moderate voters in the 2010 election: while only 39 per cent of these voters thought that the party had a good ideology, 77 per cent of them thought that they had competent persons able to rule the country (Oscarsson & Holmberg 2011: Table 18). Hence it is quite logical that in the 2014 election, the Social Democrats mainly seemed to focus on beating the incumbent centre-right government on the competence dimension, rather than to mobilise on class and ideology.

Conclusion

The Swedish economy showed a remarkable ability to recover. The national budget has been showing budget surpluses almost every year since 1998. The growth in GDP has been strong. There was a huge fall in 2009, but the recovery was swift. Moreover, the Swedish welfare state has not been going through radical retrenchment. While redistribution has declined, absolute poverty has declined too (at least until recently). The current Swedish centre-right government's ambitions to retrench the welfare state are more modest than right-wing governments tend to be in the Anglo-Saxon countries (Lindbom 2008).

All in all, the crisis management was an economic success and it was achieved without vicious social effects. Therefore we might expect the Social Democratic government to be rewarded for being able to balance the budget in 1998, but instead it seems it was punished, in the election of the same year, for the cutbacks it had implemented. The Social Democrats nonetheless managed to stay in power.

But the labour market never returned to the low pre-crisis levels of unemployment. Hence a significant part of the electorate no longer found the Social Democratic policy proposals regarding unemployment a credible solution to 'mass unemployment' in the election in 2006. In 2010, the Social Democrats again lost the election, partly because of the same issue. The long-run indirect effects of the fiscal squeeze seem to have cost the Social Democrats their traditional political dominance in Swedish politics. The party used to get 40–45 per cent of the votes, but in the election in 2010 they managed to get just over 30 per cent.

In Chapter 1 of this volume, Heald and Hood suggest a categorisation of fiscal squeeze with two dimensions: exogenous versus endogenous, and hard versus soft. Regarding the latter, it is clear that the Swedish fiscal squeeze on expenditure was *hard* rather than soft for the 1996–97 period (spending was reduced both relative to GDP and in absolute terms), even though over the longer 1993–2000 period considered in Chapter 2 it is a case of soft squeeze (see Table 2.2). Public spending was lower in constant price terms in 1998 than it had been in 1994 (SCB 2009: Table 2.1) and GDP had been growing since 1994 (SCB 2009: Table 2.3).[10] Consequently, over this period the loss imposition was absolute and hence relatively brutal and difficult.

Regarding the other dimension, *exogenous versus endogenous*, it is much more difficult to classify the development. Sweden is a small state and highly dependent on exports. For example, the first major fiscal squeeze was a reaction to exogenous forces that were speculating that the krona would go through a devaluation. But the underlying reason for that was that the export industry had lost its competitiveness because of excessive wage increases, which is clearly an endogenous process. We could continue tracing the process back in time in an infinite regress.

The framing of the problem is perhaps what matters. It is clear that George Soros and the international financial markets were not receiving much praise from Swedish politicians. But at the same time, the use of an outside scapegoat was not the dominant theme of the political discourse: Sweden joined the EU during the fiscal squeeze and the political establishment was unanimous in its support for entering the EMU, and even if a popular referendum crushed those plans, it shows that the elite remained as internationalist as ever. Instead,

---

[10] This underlines the point made in Chapters 1 and 2 that when discussing the periodisation of fiscal squeeze, it is important to recognise that there is often a systematic lag between one aspect of a fiscal squeeze (decisions) and another (observable effects in expenditure data). In terms of political decisions, the Swedish fiscal squeeze lasted from 1990 to 1997. From 1998 onwards, decisions tended to increase public expenditure. But in terms of expenditure outcome data, the fiscal squeeze occurred later: 1993–2000. Changes in other factors, such as unemployment, also distort the latter measurement of the political effort considerably.

the framing of the fiscal squeeze was to a large extent about being the masters of our own house. In a famous speech in parliament, the prime minister argued that 'He who is in debt is not free.' The meaning of this statement is not that others forced the government to make the cutbacks against its will, but that Sweden needed to make them in order to restore its pride and its self-determination and to save its societal model.

Hence I argue that Sweden is the type of case that this book considers particularly interesting, where the expenditure squeeze is hard and endogenous (for the period 1996–97). The question is, 'How, if at all, can incumbents in government pursuing endogenous hard-squeeze fiscal policies shift or share the blame for the losses they impose on voters?' Part of the answer is clearly that the Swedish political elite, with the exception of the Left Party, co-operated both when the centre-right parties were in government (1991–94) and when the Social Democrats returned to power (1994–98). This tendency to form a broad coalition on many issues helps to create legitimacy for reforms. This strategy is reinforced by the relatively high trust Swedish citizens have in the political elite. The political framing of the squeeze was, moreover, that 'we are all in this together': everything was cut and no exceptions were said to be given. Moreover, raised taxes and cut expenditure each contributed about half of the efforts to balance the budgets. In reality, the measures and their effects perhaps did not live up fully to this rhetoric, but at the same time the frame and reality are reasonably close.

The countries that are currently trying to handle large budget deficits and debts can probably learn a few things from Sweden: for example (1) that structural reform of the economy most likely has increased growth that helped to turn the budget deficits to surpluses, and (2) that broad political cooperation probably facilitates both these reforms and cutbacks of public expenditure. However, two factors may make it more difficult for other countries to pursue similar policies: (1) Swedes trust the state to a much higher degree than citizens of most other countries and, because of this, economic adaptation could occur without major disruptions from strikes and violent demonstrations, and (2) countries that are part of the Eurozone cannot imitate the depreciation of the exchange rate that was the effect of the international financial markets forcing the Swedish authorities to allow the krona to float. Moreover, in the current context, most countries around the world are going through a low in the business cycle. The situation during the Swedish crisis in the 1990s was different. Most of the country's largest trading partners were not experiencing a crisis. Hence there was a real possibility of increasing exports once the depreciation had restored the competitiveness of Swedish firms.

References

Alesina, A., Carloni, D. & Lecci, G. (2012), *The Electoral Consequences of Large Fiscal Adjustments*, NBER Working Paper 17655 (Cambridge MA, National Bureau of Economic Research).

Arndt, C. (2013), *The Electoral Consequences of Third Way Welfare State Reforms* (Amsterdam, Amsterdam University Press).

Bergh, A. (2007), *Den kapitalistiska välfärdsstaten* (Stockholm, Ratio).

Bergquist, C. (1990), 'Myten om den universella svenska välfärdsstaten', *Statsvetenskaplig tidskrift*, 93(3): 223–33.

Carlsson, I. (2003), *Så tänkte jag* (Stockholm, Hjalmarsson & Högberg).

Cerny, P. (1996), 'International Finance and the Erosion of State Power', in P. Gummett (ed.), *Globalization and Public Policy* (Brookfield, VT, Edward Elgar).

Englund, P. (1999), 'The Swedish Banking Crisis: Roots and Consequences', *Oxford Review of Economic Policy*, 15(3): 80–97.

Esping-Andersen, G. (1990), *The Three Worlds of Welfare Capitalism* (Cambridge, Polity Press).

Ferrarini, T. (2003), *Parental Leave Institutions in Eighteen Post-war Welfare States* (Stockholm, Institutet för social forskning).

Giger, N. (2011), *The Risk of Social Policy?* (Abingdon, Routledge).

Gray, J. (1998), *False Dawn: The Delusions of Global Capitalism* (London, Granta).

Green-Pedersen, C. & Lindbom, A. (2006), 'Politics within Paths', *Journal of European Social Policy*, 16(3): 245–58.

Greider, W. (1997), *One World, Ready or Not: The Manic Logic of Global Capitalism* (New York, Simon & Schuster).

Hall, P.A. & Soskice, D. (2001), *Varieties of Capitalism* (Oxford, Oxford University Press).

Henriksson, J. (2007), *Ten Lessons About Budget Consolidation*, Bruegel Essay and Lecture Series (Brussels, Bruegel).

Johnson, B. (2010), *Kampen om sjukfrånvaron* (Lund, Arkiv).

Katzenstein, P. (1985), *Small States in World Markets* (Ithaca NY, Cornell University Press).

Korpi, W. & Palme, J. (1998), 'The Paradox of Redistribution and Strategies of Equality', *American Sociological Review*, 63(5): 661–87.

Lindbeck, A. (1997), *The Swedish Experiment* (Stockholm, SNS).

Lindbom, A. (2001a), 'Dismantling the Social Democratic Welfare Model?', *Scandinavian Political Studies*, 24(3): 171–93.

Lindbom, A. (2001b), 'Dismantling Swedish Housing Policy', *Governance*, 14(4): 503–26.

Lindbom, A. (2007), 'Obfuscating Retrenchment', *Journal of Public Policy*, 27(2): 127–50.

Lindbom, A. (2008), 'The Swedish Conservative Party and the Welfare State', *Government and Opposition*, 43(4): 539–60.

Lindbom, A. (2010), 'School Choice in Sweden: Effects on Student Performance, School Costs, and Segregation', *Scandinavian Journal of Educational Research*, 54(6): 615–30.

Lindbom, A. (2011), *Systemskifte? Den nya svenska välfärdspolitiken* (Lund, Studentlitteratur).

Lindbom, A. (2013), 'Socialdemokraterna och privat drift i välfärden', in H. Jordahl *et al.* (eds), *Privatiseringarnas förklaringar* (Stockholm, SNS).

Lindbom, A. (2014), 'Waking up the Giant? Hospital Closures and Electoral Punishment in Sweden', in S. Kumlin & I. Stadelmann-Steffen (eds), *How Welfare States Shape the Democratic Public* (Cheltenham and Northampton MA, Edward Elgar), 156–80.

Lindgren, K.-O. (2013), 'Nya villkor för socialförsäkringarna', *Ekonomisk debatt*, 41(4): 18–31.

Lindvall, J. (2004), *The Politics of Purpose: Swedish Macro-economic Policy after the Golden Age* (Göteborg, Statsvetenskapliga institutionen).

Lindvall, J. & Rueda, D. (2011), 'Insider–Outsider Politics: Party Strategies and Political Behavior in Sweden', in P. Emmenegger *et al.* (eds), *The Age of Dualization* (Oxford, Oxford University Press), 277–303.

Lindvert, J. (2006), *Ihålig arbetsmarknadspolitik?* (Umeå, Borea).

Martin, H.-P. & Schumann, H. (1997), *Globaliseringsfällan: angreppet på demokrati och välfärd* (Stockholm, Östlings).

Molander, P. (2001), 'Budgeting Procedures and Democratic Ideals', *Journal of Public Policy*, 21(1): 23–52.

Montin, S. (2007), *Moderna kommuner* (Malmö, Liber).

Oscarsson, H. & Holmberg, S. (2011), *Åttapartivalet 2010* (Stockholm, SCB).

Palme, J. *et al.* (2012), *Sveriges socialförsäkringar i jämförande perspektiv* (Stockholm, Socialdepartementet).

Persson, G. (1997), *Den som är satt i skuld är inte fri* (Stockholm, Atlas).

Pierson, P. (1994), *Dismantling the Welfare State?* (Cambridge, Cambridge University Press).

Roine, J. & Waldenström, D. (2010), 'Top Incomes in Sweden over the Twentieth Century', in A.B. Atkinson & T. Piketty (eds), *Top Incomes: A Global Perspective* (Oxford, Oxford University Press).

Rothstein, B. (1986), *Den socialdemokratiska staten* (Lund, Arkiv).

Santesson-Wilson, P. (2008), 'Cutbacks as social investment', Paper presented at the Public Choice Society's Annual Meeting in Las Vegas.

SCB (Statistiska Centralbyrån) (2009), *Offentlig ekonomi 2009* (Stockholm, SCB).

SCB (2012), *Svensk valdeltagande under hundra år* (Stockholm, SCB).

Socialstyrelsen (2010), *Social Rapport 2010* (Stockholm, Socialstyrelsen).

SOU (Statens Offentliga Utredningar) (2001), *2001:79 Välfärdsbokslutet* (Stockholm, SOU).

Steinmo, S. (2010), *The Evolution of Modern States* (Cambridge, Cambridge University Press).

Strange, S. (1996), *The Retreat of the State: The Diffusion of Power in the World Economy* (New York, Cambridge University Press).

Swank, D. (2002), *Global Capital, Political Institutions, and Policy Change in Developed Welfare States* (Cambridge, Cambridge University Press).

Swedbank (2010), *Ensamstående förälder halkar efter i välfärd*, 16 March 2013, http://www.sparbankerna.se/web/page.aspx?refid=27&newsid=61243&page=45 (accessed 1 March 2014).

10

A Perfect Storm in Reverse: The 1994–1997 Program Review in Canada

DONALD J. SAVOIE

CANADA'S 1994–97 FEDERAL GOVERNMENT REVIEW PROCESS has been described at home as the turning point in managing the country's public finances. It has also been held up at the international level as the gold standard by which programme reviews should be measured. Ottawa's Program Review certainly led to a major re-orientation of Canada's public finances both within the federal government and also in provincial governments. In brief, the pain was widely shared.

By many accounts, the review was a resounding success. To be sure, the authors of the review have not been shy to trumpet its success. Jean Chrétien, the then prime minister, Paul Martin, his minister of finance, and Jocelyne Bourgon, the clerk of the Privy Council, have all accepted invitations in recent years to report on the review and its success (Bourgon 2009).

The success of the review was due in no small measure to political will on the part of the prime minister and his minister of finance and to the work of a handful of senior public servants. But there are other, no less important reasons. The review took place at a time when there was a kind of perfect storm in reverse. The economy was growing again after a short-lived but deep recession and the political environment had never before been as conducive to an ambitious programme review—nor, for that matter, has it been since. In addition, a significant part of the spending cuts was downloaded to provincial governments. It is also important to note that, though the federal government ran a budgetary surplus from 1997 to 2008, it is again struggling with a stubborn deficit. In brief, the success of the Program Review is due to strong political leadership; to the fact that opposition parties were either supportive of spending cuts or had little interest in the budget process; to pressure from the media on the government to get its fiscal house in order; and to an ability to download spending cuts in politically sensitive sectors to the provinces.

Proceedings of the British Academy, **197**, 207–227. © The British Academy 2014.

The Cuts

It is certainly the case that the Program Review generated substantial spending cuts. The authors of the review could and did make the point that the government of Canada's debt-to-GPD ratio dropped to 30 per cent from nearly 70 per cent in 1995–96—the best performance among G7 countries (Bourgon 2009: 1). Departmental spending was cut by $3.9 billion in 1995–96, $5.9 billion in 1996–97 and $7.2 billion in 1997–98 relative to what would have been the case in the absence of the Program Review exercise. The review also generated nearly $4 billion from new tax revenues (Canada, Department of Finance, n.d.). The number of federal public servants was reduced by 45,000 positions over three years, from 250,000 to 205,000 (Tables 10.1, 10.2 and 10.3). More to the point, the Canadian Program Review easily qualifies as a 'hard' squeeze, as described in Chapter 1 of this volume.

What Prompted the Cuts?

Jean Chrétien's Liberal Party came to power in 1993 after nine years of Tory rule under Brian Mulroney, who had inherited a difficult fiscal situation after the Trudeau years (1968–84).[1] The Trudeau government ran a sizeable deficit from 1975 to its last day in power. Indeed, we now know that from 1978 until the mid-1990s, the deficit of the government of Canada became 'structural' and 'chronic'. As early as 1982, the International Monetary Fund warned that Canada's deficit, as a percentage of GDP, was much too high in relation to other industrialised countries, except for Italy (IMF 1980). In brief, Canada had, from 1975 to 1984, gone from having 'one of the best to one of the worst fiscal performances among G7 countries' (Bourgon 2009: 7).

The Mulroney government pledged to restore fiscal health and launched an ambitious Program Review, in which private sector executives were included. The review urged the government to cut programme spending, privatise crown corporations and make changes to the machinery of government. The government, however, had to deal with a tenacious opposition to any spending cuts from both of the left-of-centre political parties that made up the opposition and, in the end, implemented precious few of the recommendations. All in all, the savings amounted to no more than $500 million over two years (Savoie 1990). The cost of servicing the growing federal debt shot up and, by the early 1990s, it consumed over 30 per cent of total federal government revenues (ibid.).

---

[1] Joe Clark's Progressive Conservative Party won a minority mandate on 4 June 1979 and served in government until 3 March 1980.

Table 10.1. Expenditure as % of GDP: Government of Canada.

Year	Major transfers to persons	Major transfers to other levels of government	National defence	Other	Total programme expenses	Public debt charges	Total expenditure
1986–87	5.2	3.8	1.8	6.4	17.1	5.6	22.7
1987–88	4.9	3.7	1.7	6.7	17.0	5.6	22.6
1988–89	4.7	3.6	1.7	6.1	16.1	5.8	21.9
1989–90	4.6	3.6	1.7	5.9	15.8	6.3	22.1
1990–91	5.1	3.4	1.7	5.9	16.0	6.6	22.6
1991–92	5.7	3.6	1.6	5.8	16.7	6.4	23.1
1992–93	5.9	3.8	1.5	6.3	17.4	5.9	23.3
1993–94	5.8	3.7	1.5	5.8	16.8	5.5	22.3
1994–95	5.2	3.4	1.4	6.0	16.0	5.7	21.7
1995–96	4.8	3.2	1.2	5.7	14.9	6.1	21.0
1996–97	4.6	2.6	1.1	5.0	13.3	5.6	19.0
1997–98	4.4	2.3	1.0	5.2	13.0	4.9	17.9
1998–99	4.4	2.8	1.0	4.6	12.7	4.7	17.5
1999–2000	4.1	2.4	1.0	4.6	12.1	4.4	16.5
2000–01	4.0	2.3	0.9	4.9	12.1	4.1	16.2
2001–02	4.1	2.4	0.9	4.8	12.3	3.6	15.9
2002–03	4.2	2.7	1.0	4.9	12.7	3.2	16.0
2003–04	4.1	2.4	1.1	5.1	12.7	2.9	15.6
2004–05	4.0	3.2	1.1	5.3	13.7	2.6	16.3
2005–06	3.8	3.0	1.1	4.9	12.8	2.5	15.2
2006–07	3.8	2.9	1.1	5.1	13.0	2.3	15.3
2007–08	3.8	3.0	1.1	5.1	13.0	2.2	15.2
2008–09	3.8	2.9	1.2	5.1	13.0	1.9	14.9
2009–10	4.5	3.7	1.4	6.4	16.0	1.9	17.9
2010–11	4.2	3.2	1.3	6.0	14.7	1.9	16.6
2011–12	4.0	3.3	1.3	5.4	14.0	1.8	15.8

Source: Canada, Fiscal Reference Table, Department of Finance, Ottawa, October 2012, p. 16.

Table 10.2. Details of programme expenditure in nominal terms (actual spending in $bn): Government of Canada.

Year	Transfers to persons	Transfers to other levels of government	Other transfers	Total transfer payments	Crown corporation expenses	National defence	Other departments and agencies	Total programme expenses	Total programme spending in constant price terms (2001–02=100)
1986–87	26,423	19,569	14,649	60,641	3,549	9,143	14,537	87,870	120,210
1987–88	27,400	20,518	16,800	64,718	4,344	9,708	16,239	95,009	124,390
1988–89	28,780	22,145	16,820	67,745	3,201	10,206	17,612	98,764	123,690
1989–90	30,501	23,417	16,157	70,075	3,530	10,982	19,197	103,784	125,980
1990–91	34,343	22,928	15,787	73,058	4,596	11,323	19,573	108,550	127,980
1991–92	38,900	24,865	17,712	81,477	4,445	10,759	17,863	114,544	133,290
1992–93	41,002	26,544	18,499	86,045	4,901	10,780	20,447	122,173	140,150
1993–94	42,407	26,947	18,789	88,143	2,770	11,087	20,304	122,304	138,710
1994–95	40,280	26,313	20,437	87,030	3,230	10,580	22,398	123,238	136,680
1995–96	39,121	26,076	18,578	83,775	7,666	9,817	19,598	120,856	131,900
1996–97	38,826	22,162	17,978	78,966	3,237	8,807	20,317	111,327	120,060
1997–98	38,952	20,504	22,099	81,555	2,578	9,087	21,565	114,785	124,320
1998–99	39,884	25,523	16,208	81,615	3,925	9,308	21,590	116,438	123,950
1999–2000	40,157	23,243	19,140	82,540	3,318	10,113	22,795	118,766	121,410
2000–01	43,354	24,724	22,070	90,148	3,448	9,744	27,226	130,566	131,990
2001–02	45,880	26,600	19,430	91,910	4,175	10,443	29,703	136,231	136,230
2002–03	48,011	30,640	22,657	101,308	4,572	11,803	28,996	146,679	142,010
2003–04	50,022	29,370	25,059	104,451	4,474	12,869	31,882	153,676	144,190
2004–05	51,307	41,927	27,553	120,787	6,835	14,318	34,422	176,362	160,180
2005–06	52,609	40,757	27,070	120,436	5,076	15,034	34,667	175,213	154,990
2006–07	55,582	42,481	28,979	127,042	5,109	15,732	40,386	188,269	161,400
2007–08	58,147	46,119	29,220	133,486	5,185	17,331	43,496	199,498	164,270
2008–09	61,586	46,476	32,438	140,500	5,859	18,770	42,728	207,857	174,510
2009–10	68,579	56,940	42,970	168,489	7,400	20,863	48,032	244,784	199,640
2010–11	68,135	52,787	39,967	160,889	7,584	21,273	49,846	239,592	188,930
2011–12	68,418	56,794	34,513	159,725	8,198	22,783	49,691	240,397	187,090

Source: Canada, Fiscal Reference Table, Department of Finance, Ottawa, October 2012, p. 20, actual spending. GDP deflator figures used to compute constant price spending (last column) taken from World Economic Outlook, IMF, October 2012.

Table 10.3.   Impact of the 1994–97 Canadian Program Review exercise ($bn).

Year	Revenue	Programme expenses + debt charges	Budget surplus or deficit
1992–93	124,486	163,505	−39,019
1993–94	123,873	162,403	−38,530
1994–95	130,791	167,423	−36,632
1995–96	140,237	170,263	−30,006
1996–97	149,889	158,608	−8,719
1997–98	160,864	157,905	+2,959
2011–12	245,203	271,413	−26,220

Source: Canada, Fiscal Reference Table, Department of Finance, Ottawa, October 2012, p. 9.

In the 1993 general election campaign, both major parties pledged to attack the deficit. The Liberal Party produced a 'Red Book' of promises, one of which committed the party to reduce the deficit to 3 per cent of GDP by the end of its third year in power. The Red Book, however, also contained a series of new spending commitments. The then governing Progressive Conservative party (PC) pledged to go further and eliminate the deficit within five years simply by eliminating waste and cutting government operating costs. However, the PC party was devastated in the election, holding on to only two seats in the Commons. Two new parties were born—one, the Bloc Québécois, with a goal of taking Quebec out of Canada, and the Western-based right-of-centre Reform Party. The Reform Party proposed to eliminate the deficit in only three years by cutting both programmes and government operations (Brooks 1996).

The day that the Chrétien government was sworn into power, the government's debt had reached 67 per cent of GDP and the cost of servicing it consumed over 30 per cent of federal government revenues. Still, the government made little reference to either the deficit or the growing debt in its first Speech from the Throne. While its first budget touched on the deficit, it had little to offer by way of solution (Canada, Department of Finance 1994) and consequently the budget came under heavy criticism over the government's lack of commitment to deal with the issue, a matter that was increasingly being raised in the media (Bourgon 2009).

All Hell Broke Loose

As the minister of finance and his department were working on the 1995 budget, the Mexican peso went into free fall. The *Wall Street Journal* ran an editorial which stated that 'Mexico isn't the only US neighbor flirting with the financial abyss'. The editorial was entitled 'Bankrupt Canada?' and argued that 'if dramatic action isn't taken in the next month's federal budget, it's not inconceivable that Canada could hit the debt wall and have to call in the International Monetary Fund to stabilize its falling currency' (quoted in Aucoin & Savoie 1998: 3). It sent shock waves throughout the Canadian media and inside government. David Dodge, the then deputy minister of finance, later described it as a 'seminal event' in the politics of the 1995 budget (Greenspon & Wilson-Smith 1996: 236). The balance between guardians and spenders shifted, with the guardians firmly gaining the upper hand for several years.

On the government side, politicians who only months earlier had been highly critical of the previous government's restraint measures became the new zealots in the hunt for cuts in government spending. Doug Young, who was now a senior minister in the Chrétien cabinet, had, while sitting in opposition, declared his firm intention to stand tall against the Mulroney government's plan to cut spending in several programmes. He offered to organise public hearings to enable voters to demonstrate publicly their opposition to the plan (Savoie 1999: 337). Now, fast forward to Chrétien's first mandate where Doug Young turned all his energy to fiscal concerns. He led the charge both in government and in public to implement substantial spending cuts to the very same programmes that the Mulroney government had earmarked for spending reductions (Bakvis 1998).

The time was ripe for the Chrétien government to launch its own Program Review. The *Wall Street Journal* editorial was an important catalyst, but there were other factors at work as well. Politicians on the opposition benches were, for the most part, either preoccupied with making the case for Quebec to leave the Confederation or were neo-conservatives highly critical of government intervention in the economy. The Reform Party would, if anything, be pushing the Chrétien government for more extensive cuts, not fewer. In addition, the Chrétien government also benefited from some fortuitous developments in the economy, notably increases in international grain prices that enabled the elimination of transportation subsidies to Western farmers (Kroeger 1998). Grain prices would continue to fluctuate in the years ahead but the die had been cast and there was no turning back. Thus, the political environment was far more welcoming to spending cuts in Chrétien's first mandate than had been the case for the Mulroney or even the Trudeau years.

The Government Is Returned

In the immediate aftermath of the Program Review exercise, the Chrétien government won a majority mandate in the 1997 general election. Chrétien won 155 seats, the right-of-centre Reform Party won 60 and became the official opposition, the sovereignist Bloc Québécois won 44, the left-of-centre New Democratic Party (NDP) won 21 seats and the Progressive Conservatives won 20 seats. Once again, the Reform and PC parties split the right-of-centre vote (some 19.3 per cent for Reform and 18.8 per cent for the PC), which enabled Chrétien to secure a majority mandate (Frizzell & Pammett 1998).

Chrétien's Liberal Party fought the 1997 election campaign, at least in part, on its ability to implement fiscal discipline in government. Neither the Reform nor the PC parties were about to criticise Chrétien for bringing the deficit under control, both having campaigned on the need to eliminate it. The Bloc Québécois campaign, meanwhile, had again focused on securing a better deal for Quebec and posed no threat to Chrétien outside of that province, given that the party only ran candidates in Quebec.

Public opinion was, or at least became, supportive of the government's efforts to deal with the deficit. The Department of Finance made full use of public opinion research in managing the Program Review exercise. David Herle, who designed most of the public opinion surveys for the minister and department of finance between 1994 and 2000, explains: 'The research itself was a kind of public consultative exercise in which respondents were asked to make the very trade-offs and choices that the government was facing.' He adds that 'important principles for deficit reduction were derived from public opinion research: more spending cuts than tax increases, but a mixture of the two; the federal government infrastructure itself should bear the greatest share of spending cuts; and every sector of the economy and walk of life should feel the cuts equally' (Herle 2007: 20).

The Results in Detail

The largest spending cuts were made in transport, industrial and regional support programmes and defence spending. In transport, the minister responsible made Program Review exercise his top priority and instructed the department to produce substantial spending cuts. Few other ministers followed his lead but in transport his directive worked. The government decided no longer to own, operate or subsidise large parts of Canada's transportation system, focusing its efforts instead on its core policy and regulating functions. The control of airports (all 25) was devolved to local airport authorities. With the transfer came 'all' financial responsibility both for operating the airports and for any capital improvements. The local airport authorities were not-for-profit corporations and governed by boards of directors, while airport staff were employed by local authorities and were no longer federal public servants (Canadian Airports Council, n.d.). Responsibility for operating Canada's ports was similarly devolved to local authorities. The 17 port authorities pointed out that they were 'commercially viable enterprises' (Bakvis 1998: 99–142). In brief, user fees rather than parliamentary appropriations now supported the operations of both Canadian ports and airports. All in all, full-time equivalents at Transport Canada fell from 19,881 in 1993–94 to 4,258 in

1998–99, and departmental spending fell by over 50 per cent, from $3.9 to $1.5 billion (Bakvis 1998: 99).

In the economic development field, the prime minister, the minister of finance and central agencies earmarked subsidies to business for substantial cuts. They were reduced by 60 per cent over three years. The remaining assistance was largely limited to loans, loan guarantees and repayable contributions (Canada, Department of Finance 1995: 34). Defence spending was to be reduced by $1.6 billion between 1994 and 1998 (ibid.).

The 1995 Budget Plan contained 21 pages of specific cuts. These covered virtually all areas of government activities. They included replacing the $2 note with a $2 coin; bringing greater administrative efficiencies to government departments and various programmes; reducing the subsidy paid to dairy producers by 30 per cent; having regional development agencies rely on loans and repayable contributions rather than on direct subsidies; reducing subsidies to cultural industries by 8 per cent; terminating freight rate assistance; and reducing international assistance spending by 21 per cent. In addition, the Program Review eliminated 73 agencies, commissions, boards and advisory bodies, generating about $10 million in savings annually (ibid.: 30–75).

The Program Review also generated new cost-recovery and user fees. Fees for food and meat inspections, drug approvals, fisheries inspections, fishing licences and marine services were introduced. A new immigration fee of $975 was also introduced and the Department of Foreign Affairs and Trade was instructed to incorporate new cost-recovery measures tied to some of the services it provided. The Department of the Environment and the Department of Indian Affairs and Northern Development were also asked to introduce measures to recover some of the cost of their services. All in all, cost-recovery measures were expected to generate $450 million in the first year alone. The government made it clear that if departments were to fall short of their cost-recovery estimates, then further spending cuts would be made to make up the difference (ibid.: 38–41).

The size of the public service was cut by 16 per cent or 45,000 positions. It is important to note that some 6,000 of the positions eliminated were actually transferred to the private sector or local airport or port authorities. The bulk of the remaining 39,000 positions were eliminated through attrition and financial packages to public servants to entice them to leave the public service.

The federal government took advantage of its Program Review to rethink its transfers to the provinces and territories and to individuals (see Table 10.4). Ottawa has a long history of transfer payments to the provinces to share the cost of healthcare and social services (ibid.: 49–51). In addition, the government of Canada, going back over 50 years, has an equalisation programme which provides funds to have-less provinces to enable them to offer comparable levels of public services at reasonably comparable levels of taxation. The

Table 10.4.   Sharing the pain: components of Canadian federal expenditure (% of total).

Year	Major transfers to persons	Major transfers to other levels of government	Total programme expenditure
1986–87	22.7	16.8	75.4
1992–93	25.1	16.2	74.7
1993–94	26.1	16.6	75.3
1994–95	24.1	15.7	73.6
1995–96	23.0	15.3	71.0
1996–97	24.5	14.0	70.2
1997–98	24.7	13.0	72.7
1998–99	25.0	16.0	72.9
1999–2000	24.8	14.3	73.2
2000–01	24.9	14.2	74.8
2009–10	25.0	20.8	89.3
2010–11	25.2	19.5	88.6
2011–12	25.2	20.9	88.6

Source: Canada, Fiscal Reference Table, Department of Finance, Ottawa, October 2012, p. 17.

programme is based on a complex formula measuring a province's ability to raise revenues (Canada, Department of Finance 2011).

The federal government introduced two changes to its transfer payment programmes: provincial governments would enjoy greater freedom to spend the transferred funds on their priorities but less federal funding would be made available to the provinces. It reduced transfers to the provinces by $2.5 billion in 1996–97 and by another $4.5 billion in 1997–98. Total federal transfers in 1996–97 would amount to $35 billion and in 1997–98 to $33.9 billion (Canada, Department of Finance 1995: 34). The thinking in Ottawa was that if federal departments and agencies had to take a hit then so should the provincial governments. The thinking squared with Prime Minister Chrétien's view that everyone should contribute to the review and everyone should share the pain.

The federal government is the principal source of funding for the Northern Territories. Territorial transfers had never before been subject to federal spending restraints. The Program Review exercise would change that—transfers to the territories were reduced by $14 million in 1995–96, by $79 million in 1996–97, and by $81 million in 1997–98 (Canada, Department of Finance 1995: 64).

Singing Its Praise

Shortly after the Program Review came to a close, the prime minister, ministers and senior public servants congratulated themselves on the process they had put in place. Marcel Massé, one of the ministers responsible for the review, in a special report in 1997 called *Getting Government Right*, maintained that 'these achievements in meeting the government's fiscal objectives result from a fundamental rethinking of priorities, programmes and relationships through Program Review' (Canada, Treasury Board 1997: 7). Jocelyne Bourgon wrote in one of her annual reports to the prime minister that 'program review made a significant contribution to redefining federal roles and to deficit reduction' (Canada, PCO 1995: 20). She added that the Program Review was necessary because it had become clear that 'past efforts to address pressure on public finances which took the form of across-the-board cuts and efficiency improvements' were no longer effective (ibid.: 19). A year later she was even more direct. She wrote: 'The magnitude and nature of the transformation underway and the period of time over which the transformation is occurring are unprecedented since World War II ... it is clear that an exceptional story about reinventing the role of government is being written in Canada today' (Canada, PCO 1997: 3). Still later she described the review as 'an example of cabinet government at its finest' (Bourgon 2009: 24). Paquet & Shepherd (1996: 7) offer a different perspective. They write that 'senior departmental officials tended to underscore flaws in the Program Review process while senior central agency officials were more disposed to declare Program Review a success although they were quite vague when asked what criteria they used to arrive at such an assessment.'

Bourgon credits the success of the Program Review to the full participation of public servants in identifying the cuts, rather than relying on outside consultants or outside expertise. She adds that the 'program review was a collective exercise of reform in which ministers, with the help of their departments, led their own reviews and were the architects of their own reform. Central agencies were the guardians of the process, ensuring that a consistent approach was used and that the underlying principles of the Review were sustained' (Bourgon 2009: 20). A former Privy Council Office (PCO) official who worked directly in the review wrote that 'the program review has transformed the traditional approach to reform, and the results have been significant' (Charette 1997: 20).

The Process

The crisis atmosphere created by the *Wall Street Journal*'s editorial led Prime Minister Chrétien and finance minister Paul Martin, together with central agencies, to take charge and drive both the process and the spending cuts. In hindsight, it is now clear that the prime minister 'never lost control of the steering wheel' (Savoie 1999: 184). He decided that the process would be 'designed and managed ... by three central agencies of the federal government: the Privy Council Office, the Department of Finance, and the Treasury Board Secretariat' (Aucoin & Savoie 1998: 2). The centre also established a Steering Committee of Deputy Ministers to guide the work of the review.

Another group, made up of media-savvy and high-profile regional ministers (CGM: Coordinating Group of Ministers), was set up as an informal committee to advise the prime minister and the finance minister and to sell the exercise to Canadians.

Early in the exercise, the Privy Council Office put together a series of tests against which the programmes would be assessed. The office came up with six questions and circulated them to all departments. They were:

Public Interest Test:	Does the program or activity continue to serve a public interest?
Role of Government Test:	Is there a legitimate and necessary role for government in this program area or activity?
Federalism Test:	Is the current role of the federal government appropriate, or is the program a candidate for realignment with the provinces?
Partnership Test:	What activities or programs should or could be transferred in whole or in part to the private or voluntary sector?
Efficiency Test:	If the program or activity continues, how could its efficiency be improved?
Affordability Test:	Is the resultant package of programs and activities affordable within the fiscal restraint? If not, what programs or activities should be abandoned?

While the Privy Council Office was developing the six questions, the Department of Finance was busy determining the amount that needed to be cut from the expenditure budget. Once this was established, it then set out to break the total amount into notional targets for each department. The finance minister was directly involved in establishing these targets.

By most accounts, the three central agencies (PCO, Finance, and Treasury Board Secretariat) were able to work well in developing and managing the Program Review exercise. That said, there were disagreements. Initially, PCO officials wanted to avoid establishing notional targets, arguing that financial targets would come to dominate the discussions. Finance officials resisted, insisting that 'notional government' or priority-setting exercises had been tried many times in the past and they had all failed (Savoie 1999: 178). Finance won the day.

A number of line ministers and their departments did not, at least initially, take the notional spending cuts seriously. Some felt that they were politically unrealistic and fully expected that the government would not go through with them. But by the end of June, it was a different story. At the last cabinet meeting before the summer break, Prime Minister Chrétien left 'no doubt whatsoever that he was four square behind Martin' (Savoie 1999: 179).

Though the prime minister did not participate directly in the work of the CGM, he was always fully aware of its deliberations. Two senior staff, members from his office, and the clerk of the Privy Council attended CGM meetings, and they regularly briefed the prime minister on the status of the Program Review. In addition, it had been agreed early on in the process that no decisions would be considered final until the prime minister had 'signed off on them'.

The prime minister stood firm at all times when ministers came calling to ask that he overturn Martin's decision on the proposed cuts for their own departments or to plead for a special project. One by one, ministers came to accept that Chrétien would not allow any light between himself and his finance minister. Indeed, ministers came to recognise that the notional targets were not simply Martin's targets, they were also Chrétien's. And in many ways they were. After Finance had come up with the targets, PCO reviewed them and made some relatively minor adjustments to them on behalf of the prime minister. John Manley (2005: 24), the then industry minister, explains: 'There could be no appeals, no minister, interest group or region could be spared from the effects of Program Review. One minister tried early on to appeal directly and openly to the Prime Minister. It was in a cabinet meeting. My colleague never had a chance to complete his sentence. No meant no.'

The prime minister's standing firm was a critical factor in the review's success. Many observers insisted that it was far more significant than the six test questions that the Privy Council Office put out to guide the process. The six questions were process-driven and did not in themselves generate decisions. Decisions were generated by the prime minister's determination to make the review exercise work.

The Consequences

The timing of the 1994–97 Program Review exercise was fortuitous. The global and, in particular, Canadian economies were expanding and so the cuts had limited impact on both Canada's employment rate and GDP. Canada saw 231,000 jobs created in 1995, 368,000 in 1997 and another 453,000 in 1998. Canada outpaced the rate of job creation in any other G7 country in the mid to late 1990s (Canada, Department of Finance 1999: 6). Canada's GDP growth averaged between 3 and 4 per cent annually from the mid-1990s to 1999 and some 1.3 million jobs were created between 1996 and 2000 (Canada, Department of Finance 2000: 24). The impact of Mulroney's 1989 Free Trade Agreement with the United States began to be felt. As Bourgon (2009: 24) explains, 'it created strong external demand for Canadian exports. This, combined with a weak dollar, replaced domestic demand and facilitated adjustment.'

But the same cannot be said about the process. Notwithstanding politicians and officials singing its praise, the process came to an end once it was decided that the job was done. In short, it was an ad hoc process. Arthur Kroeger, at the request of the Canadian Centre for Management Development, prepared a study of the role of central agencies in the Program Review exercise. He carried out numerous interviews with Finance officials and, on the issue of notional targets for line departments, he concluded that 'it is universally acknowledged by those who participated that this process was *utterly unscientific*. The reductions were broadly divided into three categories of across-the-board cuts: large, being 25 per cent or in some cases more; substantial—15 per cent; and token—5 per cent. The assigned reductions were to be implemented over a period of three years' (Kroeger 1998: 14–15). Kroeger (ibid.: 15) explains why the 'rough and ready' approach was adopted: 'There was not much alternative ... there was no time for elaborate evaluation studies.' In brief, the process was driven by the traditional approach of across-the-board cuts.

The machinery of government was also found wanting. Attempts to promote horizontal coordination and to break down 'departmentalism' and organisational 'silos' failed. The best that could be achieved was that the deputy ministers' committee that served to advise departments helped to minimise the number of surprises.

It quickly became clear that line ministers and their senior officials were not able to promote horizontal coordination within ministerial portfolios themselves. Agencies, crown corporations and departments essentially operated on the basis of 'every man for himself'. There were essentially four reasons for the lack of success on this front: 'Non-departmental organizations within portfolios operated at arm's-length from each other and from the department, and were not inclined to cooperate with anyone other than the minister; there had been few attempts at portfolio management prior to Program Review and there were few, if any, appropriate structures or forums for the coordination and integration of portfolio-based responses; there was no strategic framework that made sense for some portfolios; and, lines of accountability were not always clear and/or consistent with a portfolio-based management approach' (Charette 1997: 9).

Though federal government politicians and public servants with a direct hand in the Program Review make no mention of it, federal transfers to the provinces were subjected to nearly $6 billion in cuts between 1994 and 1997. Provincial governments hold jurisdictional responsibility for healthcare, post-secondary education and social services, but historically they have and continue to benefit from federal transfers to fund their programmes. The cuts had a profound impact on provincially delivered programmes: British Columbia, for example, saw federal transfers decline from 32 per cent in 1986 to 14 per cent of its spending on health, post-secondary education and income assistance in 1997 (Canadian Encyclopedia, n.d.). In 1980 federal transfers (both in cash and tax points) for healthcare represented about 44 per cent of provincial health expenditures but this fell to 29.3 per cent by 2000 (Banting 2007: 154). Provincial politicians made the case that while the Chrétien government was claiming full credit for getting its fiscal house in order, it was left to the provinces to actually implement the cuts in the politically sensitive areas of healthcare, social services and education programmes (see Tables 10.5 and 10.6).

To be sure, the 1994–97 Program Review had a profound impact on the government's expenditure budget and on its ability to eliminate the deficit. The previous Mulroney government's decision to introduce a Goods and Services Tax (GST) in 1991 was also a key factor (it generated 13 per cent of total government revenues for 1995). The GST replaced a hidden 13.5 per cent manufacturers' sales tax. The government maintained that the new tax would be revenue-neutral. The Chrétien Liberal Party broke its campaign promise to get rid of the tax or to replace it shortly after coming to office in 1993. Yet, neither Chrétien nor Bourgon, the clerk who had overseen the Program Review, ever mentioned the tax as a contributing factor when lauding the government's success in eliminating the deficit by the late 1990s.

The substantial resources and efforts poured into the programme evaluation function since the mid-1970s in the government of Canada also had very little impact on the decision-making process tied to the Program Review. Program evaluation units operated at a different level, uncertain of its practical value to policy and to decision-makers and, as could be expected, morale in government departments plummeted (Savoie 2003). The units essentially stood on the sidelines as the review exercise ran its course.

The Program Review also provided a ready-made target for provincial governments and federal government managers to take aim at when things went wrong or to engage in the blame avoidance game in the post-Program Review period. Senior government officials, including Jocelyne Bourgon, argued that cuts in key groups had weakened the capacity of public servants to produce strong policy advice. Alex Himelfarb, clerk and cabinet secretary under Chrétien and Martin, claimed that the Program Review cuts in the public service were one of the reasons for the sponsorship scandal. The sponsorship scandal dominated the Canadian media for several years and ultimately brought down the Liberal government.[2] He argued that there ought to have been more public servants occupying oversight functions in such areas as internal audit or financial management, but that they became easy targets for elimination under the Program Review (Canada, House of

---

[2] 'A Closer Look at the Sponsorship Scandal', *The Globe and Mail*, 22 July 2011, p. A3.

Table 10.5. Major transfers to other levels of government ($bn).

Year	Fiscal transfers*	Insurance and medical care	Education support	Canada Assistance Plan
1986–87	6,679	6,607	2,232	4,051
1992–93	8,664	8,307	2,887	6,686
1993–94	10,101	7,232	2,378	7,236
1994–95	8,870	7,691	2,486	7,266
1995–96	9,822	7,115	2,365	7,191
1996–97	9,863	–217	–41	105
1997–98	10,464	162	5	24
1998–99	12,121	2	n/a	8
1999–2000	11,254	n/a	n/a	56
2000–01	13,016	n/a	n/a	n/a
2009–10	16,789	n/a	n/a	n/a
2010–11	17,577	n/a	n/a	n/a
2011–12	19,188	n/a	n/a	n/a

* Certain comparative figures have been reclassified to conform to the current year's presentation.

Source: Canada, Fiscal Reference Table, Department of Finance, Ottawa, October 2012, p. 19.

Donald J. Savoie

Table 10.6. Revenues, Government of Canada (% of total).

Year	Personal income tax	Corporate income tax	Non-resident income tax	Other taxes and duties including GST	Total tax revenues	Employment insurance premiums	Other revenues
1986–87	42.3	11.2	1.6	24.3	79.4	11.1	9.5
1992–93	46.9	5.7	1.0	21.5	75.0	14.1	10.9
1993–94	44.5	7.3	1.2	21.7	74.9	15.6	9.6
1994–95	46.4	8.4	1.3	21.0	77.0	14.0	9.0
1995–96	45.7	11.0	1.3	19.4	77.4	13.6	9.0
1996–97	45.2	10.8	1.8	19.5	77.3	13.3	9.4
1997–98	46.6	13.2	1.2	19.4	80.4	12.0	7.7
1998–99	47.1	12.8	1.3	19.2	80.4	11.5	8.1
1999–2000	48.2	12.5	1.5	18.9	81.1	10.6	8.3
2000–01	47.7	14.6	1.5	18.4	82.2	9.6	8.2
2009–10	47.6	13.9	2.4	18.6	82.4	7.7	9.9
2010–11	47.9	12.6	2.2	18.1	80.8	7.4	11.9
2011–12	48.6	12.9	2.2	17.6	81.3	7.6	11.1

Source: Canada, Fiscal Reference Table, Department of Finance, Ottawa, October 2012, p. 13.

Commons 2004: 5). Ironically, on the one hand senior public servants applaud their work in shaping the Program Review exercise, while on the other they point to it to explain why things went off the rails later in both the policy advisory and programme implementation functions.

Senior government managers also long argued that the Program Review had a negative impact on their policy advisory role. Don Drummond, a senior Finance official who had a direct hand in shaping the Program Review, approved of Jocelyne Bourgon's decision to strengthen policy units in departments after they had been 'weakened' in the Program Review (Drummond 2011: 346). Cuts in the public service were made in all departments and at all levels, from the assistant deputy minister level down to front-line service delivery workers. Front-line workers and regional and local offices, however, assumed a larger share of the cuts (Savoie 2013).

The sponsorship scandal had everything to do with senior public servants breaking the rules and ignoring the Financial Administration Act and, more to the point, committing fraud. Charles Guité, a director-general-level official who received highly positive performance reviews from his supervisors, was convicted of all five charges of 'defrauding the federal government' (CBC News 2006). One could argue that the sponsorship scandal pointed to a breakdown of values and ethics in some quarters of the public service rather than to a lack of oversight bodies.

Still, the Program Review process enabled provincial governments and senior public servants to engage in the blame game for several years. Provincial governments insisted that responsibility for cuts in healthcare should be laid at the door of the federal government whenever a service or a hospital had to be reduced or eliminated.

Provincial premiers made the case that, given cuts in transfer payments, they had no choice but to close or merge hospitals. The Mike Harris Ontario government announced the closure of three hospitals in 1997, including the Montfort hospital. Montfort serves the francophone minority community in the National Capital Region and the announcement led to a heated political exchange between Harris and Prime Minister Chrétien. The local francophone community took the matter before the courts and won. The federal government subsequently announced a $10 million infusion of funds to Montfort (Montfort Hospital, n.d.).

Looking Back

For those looking to impose fiscal discipline in government, the mid-1990s in Canada constituted a kind of perfect storm in reverse. The *Wall Street Journal* editorial sounded the alarm that the government of Canada was close to hitting the debt wall and it sent a political shock wave throughout the media, political circles and the federal bureaucracy.

The Chrétien government had a relatively free hand politically to tackle the deficit. The Bloc Québécois, the official opposition, had little interest in Canada's fiscal woes, primarily concerned as it was with taking Quebec out of the federation. Two other parties—the Reform and Progressive Conservative parties—had themselves campaigned on eliminating the deficit. Public opinion surveys were also supportive of the government's efforts to tackle the deficit.

The Program Review generated $29 billion in savings over a three-year period and eliminated 45,000 positions in the broadly defined federal public service. Some $4 billion came from new tax revenues and $6 billion from cuts in transfers to the provinces and the territories. As noted above, Transport Canada's budget was cut by nearly $1.5 billion and it lost 6,000 positions. However, the tax burden and public service positions were actually transferred to users via local airport and port authorities. The budgets of Industry Canada and its agencies, together with regional development agencies, were reduced by $2 billion over the three-year period. This was done by shifting from business subsidies and cash grants to repayable loans. Defence spending was cut by $1.5 billion and foreign assistance by $500 million.

The Chrétien–Martin Program Review had a number of strengths. It was a timely response and it got the job done. It was a pragmatic approach that took full advantage of a political environment that enabled the government to impose a fiscal squeeze. Chrétien had a strong majority mandate, the media stressed the need for greater fiscal discipline, and the opposition, if anything, urged the government to cut spending further and to deal with the deficit.

However, the exercise was an ad hoc initiative. Once it got the job done, the machinery reverted to its old ways. Chrétien himself dismissed the review's 'Federalism Test' question when he made the scholarship fund his pet project a few years after the Program Review was finished. This fund provided financial assistance to university students, despite the fact that education falls clearly within provincial jurisdiction (Savoie 2003). Paquet & Shepherd (1996: 11) argue that both the 'federalism test and the partnership test would appear to have been essentially removed from the Program Review objectives' by the fall of 1995.

The government machinery, at both the political and bureaucratic levels, began to push for new spending the day the review exercise came to an end. The same can be said about provincial governments. For example, the federal government signed a ten-year healthcare agreement with the provinces in 2004 that provided for an annual increase of 6 per cent, no matter the state of the national economy (Ivison 2011).

The federal public service also went on a growth spurt in the immediate aftermath of the Program Review (Figure 10.1). The bulk of the new positions were created at senior levels, in policy, coordination and evaluation units, in the national capital region rather than in regional or local offices. By

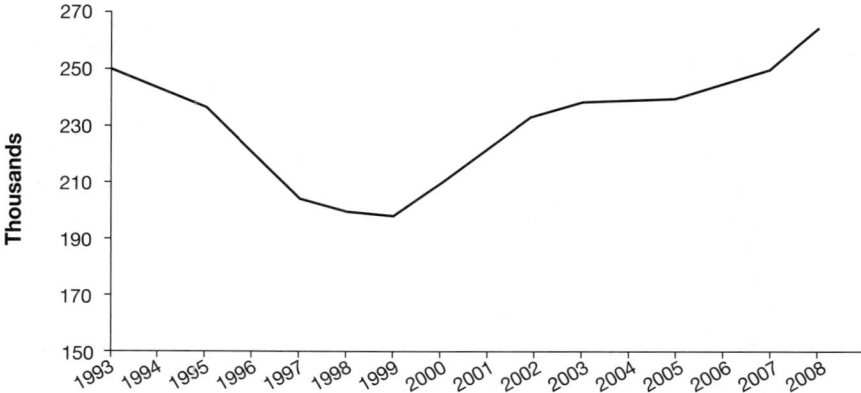

Figure 10.1. Total public service employment, Government of Canada, 1993–2008.
Source: Treasury Board of Canada Secretariat.

2013, some 43 per cent of federal public servants worked in the national capital region compared to only 27 per cent 30 years before (Savoie 2013).

The Harper government launched its own Program Review in 2011 to deal with a growing deficit and, once again, to reduce the size of the federal public service, which had added 70,000 positions since 1998.

In brief, the Chrétien–Martin Program Review exercise was successful in that it dealt with a growing fiscal problem in a timely and pragmatic manner. Its success, however, was limited to a specific period. The moment the prime minister, the minister of finance and the guardians in central agencies took their eyes off the ball, the machinery of government went back to its old ways, with the spenders quickly gaining the upper hand. Pressure to increase spending came from all policy sectors, all departments and agencies, and all provincial governments.

Looking Ahead

What about lessons learned for the future? What about lessons learned for other jurisdictions? There are some fairly obvious ones.

A programme review exercise needs strong political will at the very top. Chrétien and Martin provided it. Martin made clear his political commitment when he said that he would defeat the government's deficit 'come hell or high water', which became one of the most-quoted phrases in Canadian politics and the title of the book he published after his tenure as prime minister (Martin 2008).

But political will in a vacuum is not sufficient. At the risk of sounding repetitive, the political and economic environment of the mid-1990s in Canada was a kind of a perfect political storm in reverse. In Chapter 2 of this volume, Rozana Himaz and Christopher Hood distinguish between exogenous and endogenous forces fuelling programme reviews. In Canada, pressure from outside the government and outside the country shaped the 1994–97 Program Review. The foreign media rang the alarm bell that Canada was about to hit a major fiscal crisis and the two opposition parties in parliament were either calling for deeper spending cuts or for a break-up of the country. The economy was also rebounding, the private sector was creating jobs by the thousands, and provincial governments came in handy as recipients of some of the spending cuts. It is unlikely that such a perfect storm in reverse could surface again in Canada, let alone in other countries. Indeed, the recent Harper government Program Review drew little inspiration from the 1994–97 review. To sum up, the exercise was a one-off, pragmatic response to a difficult fiscal situation that cried out for attention.

References

Aucoin, Peter & Savoie, Donald J. (eds) (1998), *Managing Strategic Change: Learning from Program Review* (Ottawa, Canadian Centre for Management Development).

Bakvis, Herman (1998), 'Transport Canada and Program Review', in Aucoin & Savoie (1998), 99–142.

Banting, Keith (2007), 'The Three Federalisms: Social Policy and Intergovernmental Decision-Making', in Herman Bakvis & Grace Skogstad (eds), *Canadian Federalism: Performance, Effectiveness and Legitimacy*, 2nd edn (Don Mills, Ontario, Oxford University Press), 137–60.

Bourgon, Jocelyne (2009), *Program Review* (London, Institute on Governance).

Brooks, Stephen (1996), *Canadian Democracy: An Introduction*, 2nd edn (Toronto, Oxford University Press).

Canada, Department of Finance (1994), *Budget Speech* (Ottawa).

Canada, Department of Finance (1995), *Budget Plan* (Ottawa).

Canada, Department of Finance (1999), *Maintaining Sound Economic and Financial Management* (Ottawa).

Canada, Department of Finance (2000), *Budget Plan* (Ottawa).

Canada, Department of Finance (2011), *Equalization Program*, available at www.fin.gc.ca

Canada, Department of Finance (n.d.), *The Budget in Brief 1995–3* (Ottawa).

Canada, House of Commons (2004), Transcript of Testimony before the Public Accounts Committee, author's transcript (Ottawa).

Canada, PCO (Privy Council Office) (1995), *Third Annual Report to the Prime Minister on the Public Service of Canada* (Ottawa).

Canada, PCO (1997), *Fourth Annual Report to the Prime Minister on the Public Service of Canada* (Ottawa).

Canada, Public Works and Government Services Canada (1998), *Annual Financial Report of the Government of Canada 1997–98* (Ottawa).

Canada, Treasury Board (1997), *Getting Government Right* (Ottawa, Treasury Board of Canada Secretariat).

Canadian Airports Council (n.d.), 'Ownership and Management of Canada's Airports', available at www.cacairports.ca

Canadian Encyclopedia (n.d.), 'Provincial Government', available at www.thecanadianencyclopedia.com

Charette, Janice (1997), *Program Review: Lessons Learned and Challenges Ahead*, report (Ottawa, Canadian Centre for Management Development).

CBC News (2006), 'Chuck Guité found guilty of fraud', 6 June 2006, available at www.cbc.ca.

Drummond, Don (2011), 'Personal Reflections on the State of Public Policy Analysis in Canada', in Fred Gorbet & Andrew Sharpe (eds), *New Directions for Intelligent Government in Canada: Papers in Honour of Ian Stewart* (Ottawa, Centre for the Study of Living Standards), 337–52.

Frizzell, Alan & Pammett, Jon H. (eds) (1998), *The Canadian General Election of 1997* (Toronto, Dundurn).

Greenspon, Edward & Wilson-Smith, Anthony (1996), *Double Vision: The Inside Story of the Liberals in Power* (Toronto, Doubleday).

Herle, David (2007), 'Poll-driven Politics: The Role of Public Opinion in Canada', *Policy Options*, May 2007: 19–25.

International Monetary Fund (1980), 'Data Indicate Deepening Trend in Government Budget Deficits' (Washington DC, IMF Survey).

Ivison, John (2011), 'Tories Push Cap on Federal Health Funding', available at www.nationalpost.com

Kroeger, Arthur (1998), 'The Central Agencies and Program Review', in Aucoin & Savoie (1998), 11–38.

Manley, John (2005), 'How Canada Slayed the Deficit Dragon and Created the Surplus', *Policy Options* (October): 21–6.

Martin, Paul (2008), *Hell or High Water: My Life in and out of Politics* (Toronto, McClelland & Stewart).

Montfort Hospital (n.d.), 'Our History', formerly available at www.hopitalmontfort.com/our-history.cfm

Paquet, Gilles & Shepherd, Robert (1996), *The Program Review Process: A Deconstruction*, Working Paper 26/15, University of Ottawa (Ottawa).

Savoie, Donald J. (1990), *The Politics of Public Spending in Canada* (Toronto, University of Toronto Press).

Savoie, Donald J. (1999), *Governing from the Centre: The Concentration of Power in Canadian Politics* (Toronto, University of Toronto Press).

Savoie, Donald J. (2003), *Breaking the Bargain: Public Servants, Ministers, and Parliament* (Toronto, University of Toronto Press).

Savoie, Donald J. (2013), *Whatever Happened to the Music Teacher? How Government Decides and Why* (Montreal & Kingston, McGill-Queen's University Press).

11

Budget Politics in Really Hard Times: Fiscal Squeeze During and After Argentina's Great Depression

SEBASTIÁN DELLEPIANE-AVELLANEDA

Introduction

IN 1991, THE ARGENTINE GOVERNMENT sought to defeat the country's chronic inflation by implementing a convertibility regime, which firmly tied the peso to the dollar (in a form of currency board). This change, together with sweeping neo-liberal reforms, brought about an unprecedented period of price stability and economic growth. However, in the late 1990s, a combination of negative external shocks (the East Asian crisis, the Russian default, and most significantly the Brazilian devaluation of January 1999) and accumulated domestic imbalances (current account and fiscal deficits) started challenging the macroeconomic viability of Argentina's 'economic miracle'. The Argentinian elites were committed, though, to confronting the mounting economic disequilibria within the strict boundaries of convertibility. But the multiple efforts made to save the hard peg proved insufficient. Argentina's convertibility experiment ended tragically in December 2001.

Argentina's most recent financial meltdown, widely constructed as the worst crisis in the country's history, captured the imagination of many. The story is remarkable: in 1998, the Argentine president addressed the IMF–World Bank Annual Meeting as the champion of neo-liberal reforms; a few years later, the country declared the largest sovereign default in history. Between 1999 and 2002, the Argentine economy shrank by almost 25 per cent of GDP. This speedy transition, from poster child to basket case, of one of the emerging markets' darlings has naturally received a great deal of academic and journalistic attention. The Argentine experience has been extensively revisited to discuss alternative monetary and exchange rate regimes (including ultra-hard pegs), the role of the IMF, the working of globalisation, and even novel forms of political protest. Interest in the Argentine case strongly re-emerged in the wake of the global financial meltdown of 2008, when

Proceedings of the British Academy, **197**, 229–253. © The British Academy 2014.

comparisons with countries like Greece became frequent. Yet, strikingly, relatively little systematic research has been conducted on the logic and determinants of the key budget decisions taken before, during and after the financial collapse of 2001, let alone on the political implications of such decisions. This chapter seeks to fill this gap.

This chapter provides an intensive analysis of the politics of fiscal squeeze during Argentina's Great Depression (1999–2002) and subsequent economic recovery (2003–07). It offers a detailed assessment of (1) the profile of fiscal policymaking during and after the recession, with focus on the timing, size and composition of deficit-cutting measures; (2) the political process of budget control, including the strategies adopted by governments to restore credibility and legitimise austerity; and (3) the economic, political and social consequences of the spending and tax decisions taken during the squeeze. Our analysis of fiscal policy in Argentina in the period 1999–2007 is informed by two academic literatures: the political economy of fiscal consolidations and the politics of economic policy (for details, see Chapter 1 of this volume).

Argentina may be a 'substantively interesting case' (Goertz & Mahoney 2012) of fiscal squeezes as political effort. For one thing, the Argentine experience illustrates the dynamics of budget control under different conditions: hard and soft currency, internal and external devaluation, pre- and post-default. For another, the case speaks to debates about the gaps between announced and implemented consolidation, the right mix between spending cuts and tax increases, and the plausibility of expansionary fiscal contractions. Above all, it offers key insights into the political viability of budget adjustment in really hard times. Argentina provides a counterpoint to the dilemmas governments are currently facing, mainly in the European periphery, to weather the politics of austerity. The case study builds on both quantitative and qualitative data. We want to capture the economic picture, but also the narratives behind the numbers. We draw insights from macroeconomic indicators provided by official agencies and qualitative sources, including the testimonies of the key protagonists of this historical process.

The chapter proceeds as follows. It firstly locates the evolution of Argentina's public finances in historical and comparative perspective. Secondly, it analyses the various fiscal efforts aimed at saving convertibility (2000–01). Thirdly, it explains the dynamics of fiscal policymaking in the aftermath of default and devaluation. Fourthly, it accounts for the pattern of fiscal consolidation during the economic recovery (2003–07). Lessons from the Argentine case are discussed in the last section.

Argentina's Public Finances in Perspective

Argentina's economic history is 'the story of a decline unparalleled in modern times' (Della Paolera & Taylor 2001: 3). It is debatable whether fiscal fragility has been the cause or the consequence of this secular economic decline (probably both). What is clear, though, is that the Argentine government has been chronically in deficit. Successive governments, democratic or authoritarian, progressive or conservative, Peronist or non-Peronist, have consistently struggled to adjust spending commitments to funding sources. From a fiscal sociology perspective, the country has never developed the fiscal capacity required to finance the early development of its welfare state, let alone its further expansion. Pervasive fiscal imbalances have been the rule, triggering long spells of inflation, and in the extreme, chaotic episodes of hyperinflation. The long-term fiscal trajectory of Argentina has been inextricably linked to underlying macroeconomic developments (Cetrángolo & Jimenez 2003; Cetrángolo & Gómez-Sabaini 2007). Large fiscal deficits have coincided with revenue collapses during major macroeconomic crises (e.g. 1975, 1981–83, 1989–90). On the other hand, precarious instances of fiscal solvency have been associated with tax windfalls generated in the context of successful stabilisation plans (e.g. post-1976, post-1985, post-1991). Fiscal adjustment processes have generally proved to be unsustainable, leading to new cycles of crisis and consolidation.

At face value, it is hard to disagree with the proposition that Argentina has suffered 'a permanent fiscal problem' (Tanzi 2007). In the period 1961–2001, balanced budgets were exceptionally attained in 1993, and then only marginally (CEPAL 2008). Indeed, consistent evidence of fiscal prudence was not even observed in the golden age of Argentine development, the 1910s and 1920s (Gerchunoff & Llach 2010). The conventional view is that suboptimal fiscal policy outcomes have been rooted in weak economic and political institutions, including the famously problematic federal–fiscal pact (Braun 2006; Spiller & Tommasi 2009). However, these explanations overlook the fact that the country has been actually experiencing a substantive long-term fiscal adjustment (Cetrángolo & Jimenez 2003; Cetrángolo & Gómez-Sabaini 2007). Figure 11.1 shows that since the critical juncture of 1975, when the overall deficit reached a record 14 per cent of GDP, Argentina's public finances have been evolving towards a zero-deficit equilibrium. It has been a very bumpy road to fiscal consolidation, of course. Episodes of fiscal adjustment were punctuated by deep crises, which left a new (often lower) deficit equilibrium. The crisis-consolidation event of the period 1999–2007 should be treated as yet another episode (a quite significant one) of this long fiscal game.

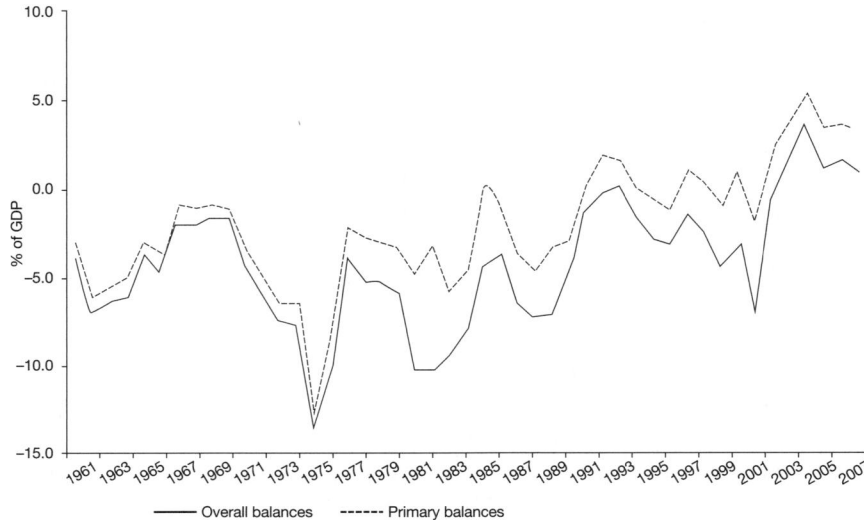

Figure 11.1.   Overall and primary budget balances (as % of GDP), Argentina 1961–2007.
Note: Fiscal data used in this chapter refer to Argentina's non-financial consolidated (including both the federal government and the provinces) public sector. Indicators are based on national accounts following the so-called 'international methodology'. Fiscal developments are measured on an accrual basis. This methodology is described in detail in MECON (2005). Some of the data have been kindly provided by Daniel Vega from the Oficina CEPAL, Buenos Aires.
Source: Own elaboration based on Cetrángolo and Jiménez (2003), CEPAL (2008) and Oficina de la CEPAL en Buenos Aires (www.cepal.org/argentina/).

In comparative perspective, the Argentine state has been relatively large by Latin American standards but small in relation to OECD countries. Argentina has developed a relatively comprehensive welfare system which can be traced back to high levels of urbanisation, a sizeable literate middle class, the early extension of the franchise, a strong civil society and militant unions, and the later inclusion of the working-class movement under Peronism (Haggard & Kaufman 2008). These evolutions have not been matched by the development of reliable revenue-raising capacities. The Argentine tax state is still fairly underdeveloped. As in many other emerging countries, the tax structure is skewed towards the collection of indirect and payroll taxes, with little participation of direct taxation on income and wealth. In the period 1991–2001, for example, VAT accounted for around 40–50 per cent of total revenues.

Another characteristic that Argentina shares with other emerging countries is that financial crises can occur at relatively low thresholds of deficits and debt. One of the ironies is that Argentina's public accounts nearly met the Maastricht rules in the run-up to the crash of 2001. In stark contrast with the daunting fiscal imbalances observed in the European periphery following the financial crash of 2008, Argentina approached the crisis with an overall deficit of 'only' 3.8 per cent (largely explained by interest payments) and a consolidated public debt of 50.8 per cent (Krueger 2002). An IMF Staff Report, produced in May 2001, projected a primary surplus of 1.6 per cent, an overall deficit of 3.1 per cent and a consolidated debt of 53 per cent of GDP respectively for 2001 (from Mussa 2002). This fiscal outlook is very important to contextualise the dilemmas policymakers were facing, and the choices they eventually made, during the crisis. Two issues are worth mentioning. Firstly, in this unstable equilibrium relatively small budget imbalances could trigger the imposition of a fiscal squeeze. Secondly, marginal deviations from specified fiscal targets could explain the difference between success and failure, between debt sustainability and default. Operating under the strict rules of convertibility, and without a lender of last resort (besides the IMF), the government needed to send strong signals to market actors that debt dynamics would be sustainable. These signals had to be credible enough. If not, financial actors would start wondering about Argentina's actual capacity to either fund or correct any fiscal gap, potentially activating a self-fulfilling financial crash.

High Political Effort without Consolidation (1999–2001)

This section focuses on the budget policy dynamics associated with the virtually impossible game of saving convertibility during the long two years of Alianza rule.[1] It profiles the successive fiscal efforts made by the coalition government to pull the economy out of recession and bring back financial sustainability. It also explains the political logic of fiscal squeeze at the end of the convertibility era.

The convertibility system, implemented in 1991, imposed not only a new monetary regime, but also a new fiscal constitution. Essentially, the convertibility rules prohibited the monetisation of public deficits (i.e. inflation tax), which had hitherto been a fixture in Argentina's political economy. In principle, the institutional reform should have enforced, almost mechanically, fiscal discipline. This was hardly the case. Although better fiscal outcomes were effectively achieved, mainly during the 1991–94 boom, public finances remained fragile (Cetrángolo & Jimenez 2003). Moreover, the credibility gained through the successful strategy of self-binding led to a peculiar process

---

[1] In this chapter, 'Peronist' governments / leaders refers to administrations led by / leaders of Partido Justicialista (PJ). For a summary of Argentine presidents, economy ministers, and parties in power in the period 1991–2007, see Table 11.1.

Table 11.1. Summary of Argentine governments, 1991–2007.

Period	President	Economy ministers	Ruling party
1991–99	Carlos Menem (in office July 1989 to Dec. 1999; re-elected 1995)	Domingo Cavallo (Feb. 1991 to Aug. 1996) Roque Fernandez (Aug. 1996 to Dec. 1999)	Partido Justicialista (PJ)
1999–2001	Fernando de la Rúa (assumed power Dec. 1999; resigned Dec. 2001)	José Luis Machinea (Dec. 1999 to Mar. 2001) Ricardo López Murphy (5–20 Mar. 2001) Domingo Cavallo (Mar. to Dec. 2001)	Alianza: coalition between Unión Cívica Radical (UCR) and Frente por un País Solidario (FREPASO)
2002–03	Eduardo Duhalde (elected interim president by Congress Jan. 2002; left power July 2003)	Jorge Remes Lenicov (Jan. to Apr. 2002) Roberto Lavagna (Apr. 2002 to Jul. 2003)	Partido Justicialista (PJ)
2003–07	Néstor Kirchner (in office July 2003 to Dec. 2007; replaced by Cristina Kirchner)	Roberto Lavagna (July 2003 to Nov. 2005) Felisa Miceli (Nov. 2005 to July 2007) Gustavo Peirano (July to Dec. 2007)	Partido Justicialista (PJ)

Note: The brief interim government of Adolfo Rodríguez Saá (22–30 Dec. 2001), also PJ, has not been included.

of market-led indiscipline (Dellepiane-Avellaneda 2005). While convertibility precluded inflationary finance, it did not prevent (and indeed induced) externally funded public deficits, at both national and provincial levels. This anomaly proved to be fatal. By increasingly borrowing in foreign currency, the country became vulnerable to a 'sudden stop' in international capital flows. The Russian default, the Brazilian devaluation and the global appreciation of the dollar (Argentina's monetary anchor) provided the perfect storm. See Table 11.2.

The Peronist government responded to the devaluation of Argentina's main trading partner, which caused an economic contraction of 4.4 per cent of GDP in 1999, by delaying stabilisation. With presidential elections scheduled for October, which would eventually be won by a newly created progressive coalition, the Alianza, the incumbents faced few incentives for enforcing budget-control measures. Yet, a pivotal Fiscal Responsibility Law was approved by the Congress in September. By setting visible deficit ceilings (a balanced budget would be secured by 2003), the reform was meant to strengthen the fiscal foundations of convertibility. Regardless of this institutional innovation, the reality is that President Menem 'gifted' Fernando de la Rúa a fiscal deficit of up to 4 per cent of GDP. More crucially, he left behind the makings of a poisonous political economy cycle. The incoming Alianza

Table 11.2. Key public finance and macroeconomic indicators, Argentina 1991–2007.

	Total revenues	Total expenditures	Primary balance	Overall balance	Public debt	Interest payments	GDP growth	Inflation (CPI)	Unemployment
1991	20.7	22.1	0.0	−1.4	38.8	1.4	9.1	84.0	6.5
1992	23.0	23.4	1.7	−0.4	32.9	2.1	8.1	17.5	7.0
1993	25.5	25.6	1.4	0.0	32.8	1.4	4.3	7.4	9.6
1994	24.4	26.1	−0.2	−1.7	35.1	1.5	4.5	3.9	11.5
1995	23.4	26.3	−0.9	−2.9	39.2	2.0	−4.0	1.6	17.5
1996	22.2	25.4	−1.2	−3.2	39.8	1.9	4.3	0.1	17.2
1997	23.5	25.0	0.8	−1.5	38.1	2.3	6.9	0.3	14.9
1998	23.3	25.8	0.2	−2.4	41.3	2.6	2.7	0.7	12.9
1999	24.0	28.5	−1.1	−4.5	47.4	3.4	−4.4	−1.8	14.3
2000	25.0	28.3	0.8	−3.3	50.8	4.1	−1.8	−0.7	15.1
2001	23.6	30.7	−2.0	−7.0	64.1	5.1	−5.4	−1.5	17.4
2002	23.8	24.6	1.8	−0.8	184.4	2.7	−11.7	41.0	19.7
2003	26.8	25.2	4.0	1.6	156.9	2.4	7.8	3.7	17.3
2004	28.7	25.2	5.2	3.5	143.3	1.7	8.0	6.1	13.6
2005	29.0	27.9	3.3	1.1	87.6	2.2	8.1	12.3	11.6
2006	29.9	28.6	3.5	1.4	76.3	2.1	7.4	9.8	9.8
2007	32.4	31.7	3.2	0.8	66.7	2.4	7.6	8.5	8.5

Note: Fiscal data are presented as % of GDP. Growth is the annual variation in GDP per capita (in 2000 dollars). Inflation refers to annual variations in the consumer price index. Unemployment is the percentage of unemployed people in Argentina's big cities.
Source: Fiscal data are from Cetrángolo and Jiménez (2003) and MECON (2005). Growth, inflation and unemployment data are from CEPAL database (www.cepal.org).

government, a loose and untested coalition between the UCR and FREPASO, which had been elected on a platform committed to addressing the institutional and social deficits of Menem's 'neo-liberal decade', was forced to rapidly recalibrate its economic policy priorities. In the following two years, de la Rúa's government attempted to restore financial sustainability by implementing a series of budget adjustment programmes.

The first move was on the revenue side. After just weeks in office, the economic team, led by José Luis Machinea, enacted a sizeable tax package, with strong focus on personal income and wealth taxes (IMF 2000). This basically implied the reduction of tax-free thresholds as well as increases of rates and cuts in deductions for very high earners. The tax reform, maliciously called by the local media the *impuestazo* (big tax hike), was supposed to raise additional resources worth 1.8 per cent of GDP (Cetrángolo & Gómez-Sabaini 2007: 29). Months later, reacting to a perceived revenue shortage in the face of weaker-than-expected economic activity, the government introduced a round of spending cuts, including an across-the-board 12–15 per cent cut in the salaries of civil servants earning more than Arg\$1,000 per month (IMF 2000). These fiscal savings achieved a marginal improvement in public accounts (IMF 2000; Cetrángolo & Jiménez 2003). However, the budget consolidation strategy failed to ease concerns about the sustainability of Argentina's spiralling public debt. On the contrary, market uncertainty escalated in the second semester, driven by the deepening of the recession and the resignation of Vice-President Alvarez (the leader of the coalition's junior partner). Technically, the attempted fiscal squeeze had a progressive make-up (the tax reform targeted high-income groups and a large proportion of civil servants earned less than \$1,000). Still, both the tax hike and the spending cuts were politically very costly for the Alianza, negatively affecting the public mood and hurting the professional middle classes, who were core supporters of the ruling coalition.

Argentina's next move was to seek external help. In December 2000, a huge IMF assistance package (the *blindaje*) was formally announced. In exchange, the Argentine government promised to renew its drive towards consolidation. Interestingly, the policy conditionalities attached to the *blindaje* contained not only deficit-reduction measures, but also measures aimed at stimulating the fragile economy. Specifically, the IMF allowed a flexible interpretation of the fiscal targets established by the Fiscal Responsibility Law in order to create much-needed fiscal space (Burgo 2011). This nuanced strategy—a subtle blend of fiscal orthodoxy and moderate Keynesianism— also failed to restore market confidence (and turmoil in Turkey did not help). As a result, the first economic team of the Alianza administration resigned. In March 2001, Argentina's austerity game took a dramatic twist. In a typical Argentine-style hyperbole, a new economic team, led by 'Chicago boy'

Ricardo López Murphy, announced an ultra-orthodox consolidation plan, which sought to tackle the 'structural sources' of the public deficit. The measures included deep cuts in the sensitive education budget, the reduction of transfers to the provinces and regional subsidies, the elimination of up to 40,000 public sector jobs, and the abolition of tax breaks (*Clarín*, 17 March 2001). The neo-liberal experiment ended before it even started. Lacking political support (key members of the cabinet resigned on the very night the plan was announced), López Murphy had to resign in a matter of weeks.

De la Rúa responded with yet another bold move. Following intense negotiations among the coalition partners, Domingo Cavallo, hero of the 1990s reforms and iconic figure of the Menem times, was called in in a last bid to save convertibility (his very own creature). Strikingly, Cavallo diagnosed that Argentina was not facing a fiscal crisis, but a competitiveness one. In this context, he signalled a flexibilisation of convertibility by announcing that in future the peso would be backed by a basket of currencies (including the euro). On the fiscal front, he was all over the place. He implemented an emergency tax on financial transactions (April), a market-friendly mega-swap of Argentina's public debt (May), and a de facto fiscal devaluation aimed at compensating exporters and taxing importers (June). As the markets remained unconvinced, or indeed growingly concerned, the fiscal game switched back towards orthodoxy. In July 2001, Cavallo made a reckless attempt to restore credibility by announcing a draconian 'zero-deficit rule', which effectively prescribed the subordination of spending commitments to current revenues (from day one, without any period of grace). This cold-shower, spending-based consolidation effort implied a further reduction in public wages and pensions of around 13 per cent (on the back of the cuts enforced in 2000, and more cuts were on the line in the face of declining tax collection). Not surprisingly, this desperate attempt to buy credibility by signalling toughness was widely regarded as incredible. Almost inevitably, the fiscal contraction plunged the economy further into depression. Both the economy and state revenues plummeted in the second semester of 2001.

By the end of 2001, influential external actors started suggesting that Argentina had 'had enough' of convertibility (Dellepiane-Avellaneda 2005). Still, the government stayed irrevocably committed to maintaining the cornerstone of the economic regime and the consensual basis of the political system. Despite this strong commitment, the two-level game that the government was playing with external creditors, on the one hand, and domestic groups, on the other, exploded in December 2001. In November, the IMF decided to pull the plug (the government was obviously not meeting deficits targets), activating an unwelcome chain of events: capital flight and deposit withdrawals, the collapse of the banking system, the imposition of a freeze on deposits and capital controls, the spread of social unrest across Argentine cities, and the removal of latent support by key economic and political groups. Having exhausted all its legitimacy, the Alianza administration, which was elected to deliver progressive convertibility (i.e. convertibility with a social face) in the context of 'the normalization of Argentine politics' (Levitsky 2000), left power in rather dramatic fashion—a remarkable twist of events.

The choice of fiscal consolidation strategies aimed at saving convertibility was framed by a powerful set of political incentives. An IMF Staff Report captured the essence of the economic policy gamble:

> The authorities reaffirmed their belief that, within the framework of the convertibility regime, the resumption of sustainable economic growth depends crucially on a credible commitment to, and evidence of, fiscal consolidation and structural reforms ... an alternative strategy of attempting to sustain demand through fiscal expansion would, in all likelihood, further undermine market confidence (IMF 2000: 15).

From a political economy standpoint, this mystical 'credible commitment' was not easily forthcoming. The adjustment process was seriously constrained by the need to accommodate pervasive financial market pressures in the context of an increasingly difficult domestic political environment (Bonvecchi 2002). The government was playing an impossible consolidation game, as neither revenue-based nor expenditure-based measures succeeded in restoring fiscal sustainability and/or pulling the economy out of recession. Moreover, at every step of the process, the economic conditions worsened, the fiscal targets moved further away, and the political challenges escalated. Still, the government confronted the mounting disequilibria within the boundaries of the convertibility paradigm, which was endorsed by a wide coalition of social actors and Argentine citizens at large (Dellepiane-Avellaneda 2005). Public support for convertibility remained very high (above 70–80 per cent) until the end, even after the collapse of the regime. This strong consensus around convertibility, linked to collective memories of hyperinflation, has always mystified external observers. Yet, devaluation was a non-starter. As one of de la Rúa's closest advisers allegedly claimed: 'the president who abandons convertibility would have to go and we would see three or four presidents before the situation stabilises' (cited in Burgo 2011; translated by the author). There was a cognitive dissonance, though: voters supported convertibility, but not the policies aimed at sustaining it. In the end, Argentina's resilient defence of convertibility proved to be futile. While the exit costs of breaking the peso–dollar peg were prohibitive, both the economic and political costs required to save the economic regime became unbearable as well.

By any standards, the Alianza sought to impose, and indeed imposed, a harsh fiscal squeeze. However, budget consolidation was not actually achieved. Having improved marginally in 2000, the fiscal gap opened widely in the second half of 2001. The successive economic teams attempted a range of fiscal consolidaticn strategies: an early tax hike, cuts in public wages, an IMF assistance programme and a debt mega-swap, both aimed at reducing the short-term interest bill, a tax on financial transactions, and a draconian zero-deficit rule which implied further cuts in wages and pensions. The problem was that, using the language of Giavazzi & Pagano (1990), the fiscal contraction was not expansionary. On the contrary, the policies deepened the recession, leaving the government chasing moving targets. Hence, this is a paradigmatic case of a politically costly fiscal squeeze, which involved the imposition of highly visible tax rises and spending cuts, and several Nixon-goes-to-China gambles, but did not result in budget consolidation. In macro-economic jargon, the *ex ante* fiscal adjustment proved to be inefficient, leaving a higher *ex post* deficit. Politically, this is a seminal example of how governments can actually go bankrupt.

Fiscal Adjustment in the Economic Abyss (2002)

This section focuses on fiscal adjustment in the critical year 2002. The declaration of sovereign default (23 December 2001) and the formal demise of convertibility (6 January 2002) led to a period of chaotic policymaking. The economic system was broken; the very question of governance was at stake. In this context, public budgeting in particular and economic policy in general were never more political.

In hindsight, we underestimate the fact that anything might have happened in Argentina during those critical months. This was not a mere economic crisis, but a crisis that threatened the country's political regime. The notion of Argentina potentially facing a civil war was an exaggeration. Yet, for several months the country 'teetered on the brink of anarchy' (Levitsky & Murillo 2003: 152). Most economists were predicting hyperinflation, followed by the return of either convertibility or de facto dollarisation. Some observers were even advocating another round of fiscal squeeze enforced by foreign-hands control over budget policy (Caballero & Dornbusch 2002). However, the Peronist-led interim government, led by Eduardo Duhalde, and supported by a different political coalition, consciously promoted a 'paradigm shift' (Hall 1993) in economic policymaking. The orthodox path to economic recovery was decisively rejected; a heterodox exit strategy from the crisis was chosen.[2] Defying dominant expectations, hyperinflation was avoided, not least because

---

[2] Radical heterodox solutions were also rejected. On Duhalde's economic strategy, see Amadeo (2003), Lamberto (2003), and Duhalde (2007).

the sharp devaluation of the peso imposed 'one of the major adjustments in Argentine history' (Lamberto 2003: 64, translated by the author).

To claim that this was a case of policymaking in hard times is an understatement. This was fiscal policy in the worst possible conditions. The 2001 fiscal year had closed with overall and primary deficits of 7 per cent and 2 per cent of GDP respectively (MECON 2005; CEPAL 2008). More worryingly, despite the zero-deficit rule, public accounts had heavily deteriorated in the last months of the year, and were bound to deteriorate even further given the severity of the economic meltdown. Without any external help (indeed Argentina made net payments for around US$4,000 million to multilaterals in 2002), the compliance with a de facto zero-deficit rule was imperative. Having broken the corset of convertibility, the government could in principle have relied on the inflation tax to cover the remaining fiscal gap. Yet inflationary finance was constrained by the credible threat of hyperinflation. It should be recalled that Argentina suffered two big hyperinflation episodes in 1989–90, which explain overwhelming public support for convertibility. Unlike the path to fiscal consolidation pursued by European countries following the 2008 crisis, balanced budgets had to be secured immediately, with the economy in free fall (GDP contracted by 12 per cent in 2002). Despite this daunting scenario (or maybe because of it), Duhalde's first economic team, led by Jorge Remes Lenicov, targeted a primary surplus of 1.5 per cent of GDP (Lamberto 2003). Against all the odds, Argentina pulled off a 1.8 per cent primary surplus in 2002. How was this unexpected fiscal outcome achieved?

The economic policy dilemma was how to reap the fiscal benefits of the huge devaluation without descending into hyperinflation. Regarding the budget process, the authorities ignored modern econometric techniques, relying instead on the principles of good housekeeping (Lamberto 2003: 46). Unable to estimate economic trends, they adopted a cash-based budget rule (money in, money out). On the spending side, the government anchored expenditures by maintaining the *nominalidad* (nominal value) of budget commitments. On the revenue side, the economic team ruled out the return of *ajuste por inflación* (adjustment for inflation). Policymakers crucially realised that allowing adjustment for inflation would be fatal, undermining tax collection and fuelling inflation expectations. The positive effects of inflation on revenue collection (the fiscal drag) had to outweigh the negative ones (the Tanzi effect). In the event, the mega-devaluation and concomitant inflation facilitated the transition towards a balanced budget. As some observers put it: 'The Argentine experience showed once more the virtues of inflation in reducing real public expenditure' (Levy-Yeyati & Valenzuela 2007: 220, translated by the author).

While monetary and fiscal rigour was ruthlessly imposed to avoid hyperinflation, other key unorthodox policy choices were made to build fiscal capacity and strengthen the political foundations of the recovery. Most crucially, the government levied significant export taxes (known in Argentina as *retenciones*). In March 2002, minister Remes Lenicov announced that, given the exceptional circumstances, agricultural exports would be taxed at 10 per cent and industrial exports at 5 per cent; oil exports would keep paying 20 per cent (*La Nación*, 5 March 2002). By 'temporarily' reintroducing *retenciones*, a policy choice which would have been anathema years before, the government extracted a portion of the windfall profits made by exporters as a result of the massive devaluation. Also crucially, the government explained that the revenues generated by export duties would be largely allocated to social programmes.

And indeed, the fresh funds were directly applied to finance a wide-reaching social programme called Plan Jefas y Jefes de Hogar Desocupados (Programme for Unemployed Male and Female Heads of Households), launched simultaneously. The Plan Jefas y Jefes, which provided direct cash transfers to more than two million households situated at the bottom of the income distribution, was perceived as vitally important for partially mitigating the social costs of adjustment. It should be borne in mind that in the first months of 2002 Argentina was facing a 'Polanyi moment'.[3] Economic adjustment could certainly lead to social breakdown. Unemployment soared to more than 20 per cent; 50 per cent of Argentines were living below the poverty line. Let's also remember that automatic stabilisers have limited effects in developing countries. In other words, the social safety net was dangerously weak. This plan became the flagship social policy of the Duhalde government and arguably one of the most important strategic decisions taken during the crisis. The expert consensus is that, though the programme was very probably undermined by implementation issues, clientelism and corruption, it did 'partially compensate many losers from the crisis and reduced extreme poverty' (Galasso & Ravallion 2004).

What was the combined effect of these orthodox and heterodox fiscal measures? From a policy design view, economic authorities were walking a tightrope. On the expenditure side, they maintained a strict control of nominal public expenditure, but also extended the social safety net. On the income side, they sought to compensate for the fall in revenues associated with the economic crash by regaining fiscal capacity. They achieved that by banning adjustment-for-inflation accounting and resorting to extraordinary taxation. Public finances remained fragile in the first quarter, but began to recover swiftly thereafter. The turning point came in May, when tax revenues showed the first increment against the previous year. Overall, the fiscal savings in 2002

---

[3] Polanyi ([1944] 2002) famously argued that market-led economic change would be inherently unstable without compensatory measures aimed at protecting societies against those changes.

resulted mainly from a large reduction in spending as a proportion of GDP (from 2003, this composition reversed on the back of solid tax collection). Spending cuts primarily arose from a reduction in the real value of public sector wages, pensions and interest payments (Cetrángolo & Gómez-Sabaini 2007: 15). Stunningly, a primary surplus was achieved despite the severe economic slump and the creation of a new social programme to deal with the social costs of the crisis (Levy-Yeyati & Valenzuela 2007: 337).

The politics of fiscal squeeze in the post-convertibility period, despite some apparent continuities, operated differently. The banking crisis of December 2001, which forced a temporary freeze of people's deposits and the widespread rupture of economic contracts, led to the renegotiation of both rules and coalitions. This process was anything but smooth; it was highly contested. Important interests, including the main banks and large internationalised economic conglomerates, fought hard to maintain the main pillars of the neo-liberal model, supporting a move towards dollarisation. Other powerful economic groups, mainly exporters and economic sectors highly indebted in dollars, advocated the demise of convertibility, devaluation, and the (strategic) 'pesification' of both credits and debts. In the event, the balance of power tilted towards a soft currency regime, not least because that choice was consistent with the survival of key political elites, including many provincial party bosses. The adoption of a new political economy model, predicated upon the rejection of the neo-liberal paradigm, shaped the politics of budget adjustment in 2002.

In addition, the financial meltdown changed the blame game. While de la Rúa's government attempted to legitimise their hard choices by arguing that the country was 'close to the edge', Duhalde's peddled the narrative that they were pulling the country 'from the abyss' (Amadeo 2003; Duhalde 2007). The Alianza, having strongly endorsed progressive convertibility, had little room for playing the politics of blame avoidance. Duhalde's government, on the other hand, enjoyed more space for deploying blame-avoidance strategies. They could argue that they did not 'kill' convertibility, but that the regime was already 'dead' due to the policy failures of the previous government(s). The socially constructed idea that convertibility had been 'an illusion' progressively made ground in post-crisis Argentina (Levy-Yeyati & Valenzuela 2007). More generally, the government built on the trauma of the crisis to question the neo-liberal model, including the exit strategy to the crisis proposed by the IMF and orthodox groups. The transformed political landscape was a fertile ground for policy experimentation and the refocusing of priorities. President Duhalde believed that, in crisis management, politics had to lead, and sometimes trump, economics (Duhalde 2007). The social dimension played a crucial role as well. As Roberto Lavagna, Duhalde's second finance minister, remarked in his first public statement, 'economic and social policies are indivisible ... the social question would be at the core of program design' (Lavagna 2011: 24).

That said, legitimacy remained an issue over the whole period, not least because the politics of 'loss imposition' continued in the context of fragile governability. The Argentine government was walking a tightrope not only economically, but also socially and politically. After years of economic malaise, and with further pain down the road, the political class was completely discredited. The popular cry was 'Que se vayan todos' (Everybody out!). Economic policies were not only contested in the streets, but also by influential economic and institutional actors (the interests linked to the dollarisation project, important Peronist and opposition leaders, the Supreme Court, the IMF, the media). In this volatile situation, as suggested above, anything might have happened. The irony is that, despite the *fin de siècle* political mood, it was one of the legacies of convertibility, the fear of hyper-inflation, that played the key role in disciplining political and social actors in post-default Argentina.

The size of the fiscal effort, following debt default and devaluation, should not be underestimated, most notably during 'the worst one hundred days' (Lamberto 2003). In the first quarter of 2002, the government was forced to squeeze budgeted spending by around 20 per cent, in an already critical situation (Burgo 2011: 312). Figure 11.2 shows that the nominal value of key budget components, including wages and pensions, remained virtually constant in 2002 despite the mega-devaluation and the inflationary bout.

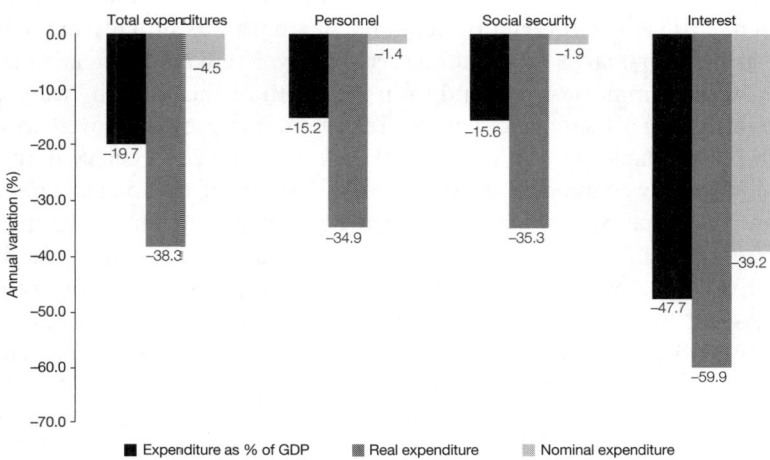

Figure 11.2. Variation in Argentine public expenditures on key budget components, 2002 vs 2001.
Source: Own elaboration based on MECON (2005).

Although the situation eased in the second semester, fiscal caution prevailed. The 2003 budget, presented in September 2002, planned a record fiscal surplus of 2.2 per cent of GDP, with an estimated inflation rate of 22 per cent and growth of around 3 per cent. Notably, in contrast with previous experiences, this ambitious fiscal target would be met without discretionary tax increases and high-profile spending cuts (Lavagna 2011: 165). The fiscal target was eventually overachieved, not least because economic growth rebounded to more than 8 per cent and current revenues registered an annual increase of almost 90 per cent. All in all, the critical year 2002 is key for understanding Argentina's transition from Great Depression to Great Recovery.

Budget Consolidation with Low Political Effort (2003–07)

This section looks at the sudden reversal of fiscal fortunes during Argentina's Great Recovery. It discusses the policy and political implications of the massive turnaround in public finances. It argues that the pattern of fiscal adjustment observed can be understood from the perspective of budget consolidation with low political effort.

Since the second semester of 2002, but more steadily from 2003, Argentina experienced a surprising and unexpected recovery. The feared 'lost decade', which according to gloomy predictions would follow sovereign default and the abandonment of convertibility, never materialised. As Anne Krueger recognised in one interview, 'to the surprise of everyone, including myself, Argentina has returned to growth, without falling into hyperinflation' (cited in Lavagna 2011). The reversal of economic fortunes was initially met with scepticism. The first signs of economic recovery were talked down as a mere *veranito* (short summer) or rebound from the depth of the crisis (a 'dead-cat bounce' in Krueger's sarcastic words). Yet, economic growth proved to be solid and sustainable. In the period 2003–07, it averaged 8 per cent (pre-depression levels were crossed in 2005), leading to one of the longest growth cycles in Argentine history. The swift recovery benefited from the boom in commodity prices, but also from a new growth model based on a stable and competitive real exchange rate (Frenkel & Rapetti 2007; Cetrángolo *et al.* 2007). As for the government budget, a substantial fiscal consolidation episode was observed (see Figure 11.3). The overall balance, which had sunk to −7.0 per cent of GDP in 2001, reached a positive 3.5 per cent in 2004. The primary surplus was above 5 per cent, the highest ever registered in the country (CEPAL 2008). What were the fundamentals of this impressive fiscal turnaround?

Regarding the underlying model of political economy, the election of President Néstor Kirchner in 2003 further accentuated the role of the state in

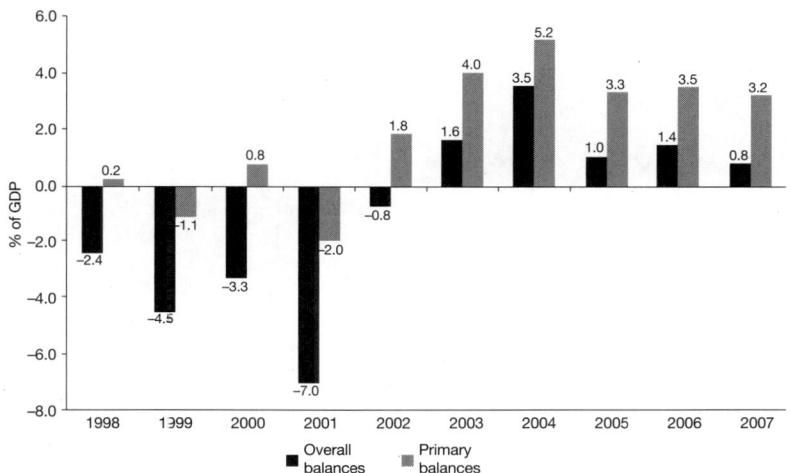

Figure 11.3.   Overall and primary budget balances, Argentina 1998–2007 (% of GDP).
Source: CEPAL (2008) and Oficina de la CEPAL en Buenos Aires (www.cepal.org/argentina/).

the economy. The so-called *modelo K* was predicated upon the idea that markets should be decisively governed by state authorities. However, the new framework fell short of a paradigm shift, mainly in relation to Duhalde's economic policies. Indeed, *Kirchnerismo*, at least in the initial phase, was characterised by a strategy of 'bending and moulding' the existing political institutions and economic model (Wylde 2012). Elements of populism and neo-liberalism were interwoven to create a new form of 'new developmentalism' (*neodesarrollismo*) (Grugel & Riggirozzi 2007). The permanence of Lavagna as finance minister assured continuity in economic management. The policy fundamentals were maintained: a high and stable exchange rate, twin fiscal and trade surpluses, monetary activism, debt deleveraging, a distant relationship with the IMF, and a tough stance towards international creditors (Lavagna 2011). According to Levy-Yeyati & Valenzuela (2007), the pillars of the evolving economic model were 'a high dollar, financial autonomy and fiscal solvency'.

Fiscal solvency indeed. The economic recovery led to a spectacular, and also largely unexpected, fiscal turnaround. The post-crisis, post-convertibility fiscal outlook was highly exceptional for Argentina. Public accounts had been in deficit ever since the 1920s (with the only exception of 1992–93, when they were in equilibrium, only marginally). In the period 2003–07, the country achieved unprecedented primary and overall surpluses of 3.8 per cent and 1.7 per cent of GDP respectively (CEPAL 2008). Regarding its composition, the fiscal effort switched, progressively, from the expenditure to the revenue side (see Figure 11.4). In 2002, the burden of adjustment had fallen on

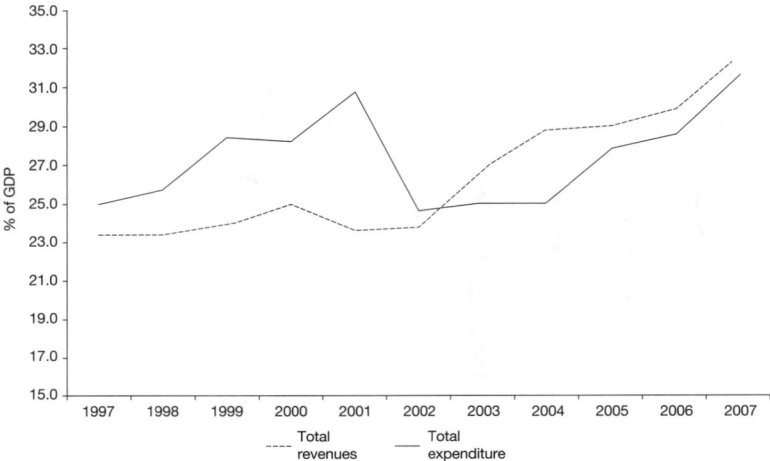

Figure 11.4. Total expenditure and revenue (% of GDP), Argentina 1998–2007.
Source: Own elaboration based on MECON (2005), CEPAL (2008) and Oficina de la CEPAL en Buenos Aires (www.cepal.org/argentina/).

inflation-driven reductions in real spending; from 2003, tax revenues started growing at higher rates than both economic output and public spending (Cetrángolo & Gómez-Sabaini 2007: 15).

The reaction of public revenues was impressive. The new economic model delivered 'the highest tax burden in Argentine history' (Cetrángolo & Gómez-Sabaini 2007). Total tax revenues solidly recovered from the depression levels of early 2002, rising by around ten points of GDP in a matter of five years.[4] The tax burden, which oscillated around 20–22 per cent of GDP during the convertibility era, reached a higher plateau of around 25–27 per cent. Very strikingly, the frontiers of the tax state were extended without major discretionary revenue-raising measures, let alone a comprehensive tax reform. Actually, the positive budget balances achieved between 2003 and 2007 largely built on the emergency taxes implemented during the crisis: the tax on financial transactions introduced in April 2001 and the export duties levied in March 2002. Taken together, these two extraordinary (for tax experts, also distortive) sources of revenue raised almost 4 per cent of GDP between 2003 and 2006, explaining virtually all the primary surpluses obtained in that period (Levy-Yeyati & Valenzuela 2007: 290–1; Cetrángolo & Gómez-Sabaini 2007). The rest of the job—the steady improvement of VAT, income and

---

[4] *Current* revenues were booming. By mid-2003, VAT and income tax were increasing 89 per cent and 122 per cent respectively against the previous year; total revenues were up 80 per cent (Lavagna 2011: 303–4).

payroll taxes—was done by the growth model itself. We can classify this process as growth-led fiscal consolidation.[5]

On the expenditure side, despite the anti-adjustment rhetoric, the Kirchner government kept public spending under control (mainly under Lavagna, who resigned in 2005). In the backdrop of solid growth, public wages and pensions rose in nominal terms from the base values of 2002. The three key budget components—public wages, pensions, and interest payments—sharply declined in real terms during the post-crisis period, only returning to pre-crisis levels by 2008 and 2009 (CEPAL 2008). As the fiscal effort mainly consisted in not accommodating inflation, the result was an across-the-board squeeze in public spending, equally affecting most budget functions. It was broadly recognised, even in orthodox quarters, that Lavagna imposed fairly tight fiscal policies (*The Economist* 2005). The trajectory of public wages illustrates the logic of adjustment under soft money conditions as opposed to the logic of internal devaluation under hard currency. By the end of 2002, Lavagna was able to announce the reversal of the 13 per cent spending cuts imposed in 2001 (he even issued a bond to compensate public workers and pensioners for the losses accumulated between July 2001 and December 2002).[6] The 2004 budget contemplated a 1.9 per cent nominal increase in public wages, with an estimated inflation of 10.5 per cent, implying a *real* adjustment of 7.8 per cent (CIPPEC-Grupo Sophia 2003). So, even though real wages were still below pre-recession levels, the government could start selling good news and building political support by allowing *nominal* increases of salaries and pensions. Regarding the blame game, Kirchner was extremely well positioned: the 'dirty job' had been done by others; he could only claim the credit.

The fiscal evolution between 2003 and 2007, as far as political economy was concerned, responded to the logic of fiscal squeeze without high political effort. The fiscal effort was more associated with the smart management of inertia strategies (full accommodation of growth-led tax increases; partial accommodation of repressed spending demands) than with the unpleasant politics of loss imposition. According to the standard econometric-based literature, this event should be categorised as an episode of fiscal consolidation, a big one indeed, given the observed improvement in primary and overall fiscal balances. Yet, the irony is that, from the perspective advocated by Mauro (2011), the period is not associated with any major (planned) consolidation programme. On the contrary, the rhetoric of adjustment was

---

[5] Yet fiscal solvency was a pillar of the growth model. So causality was going both ways.
[6] This decision responded to a previous Supreme Court ruling which deemed unconstitutional the 2001 zero-deficit rule (Lavagna 2011: 136). Alianza's income tax reform was also reversed later on.

completely alien to the discourse and practices of *Kirchnerismo*. Indeed, Kirchner advocated an expansionary economic strategy that would precisely replace the 'model of permanent adjustment' (Kirchner 2003). If anything, adjustment policies belonged to the infamous neo-liberal era, the Washington consensus, the nasty 1990s. Yet, solid balanced budgets were achieved due to a curious combination of factors: the path-dependent effects of measures taken by previous governments, the fiscal spillovers of the underlying growth model, and Kirchner's own *fiscalista* perspective. The president believed that fiscal accumulation was the real source of financial and political independence. As he observed in his inaugural speech, 'the wise rule of not spending more than what we collect should be observed. The fiscal equilibrium should be protected' (President Néstor Kirchner Inaugural Speech, 25 May 2003, translated by the author).

Argentina's public finances in the post-crisis period reflect continuity and change. The model of political economy introduced by President Duhalde in 2002, and consolidated over the governments of Néstor and Cristina Kirchner, has changed the economic policy game. The (re)introduction of *retenciones*, the (re)emergence of the inflation tax and the reversal of central bank independence, the (re)nationalisation of private pensions, the substantive expansion of the tax and welfare states (see Table 11.2 and Figure 11.4), are policy options that clearly deviate from the orthodox blueprint. Yet, many of the 'emergency' policy choices made in previous crises were maintained. Argentina still has a VAT rate of 21 per cent (increased by Cavallo during the Mexican crisis in 1995) and a tax on financial transactions (introduced also by Cavallo in 2001). Perhaps more importantly, neither Duhalde nor the Kirchners attempted to correct the regressive bias of the tax system, which is heavily oriented to indirect taxation. Personal income taxes (broadly perceived in Argentina as a tax on 'wealth') still deliver less than 2 per cent of GDP. Barely a progressive outcome.

Lessons From (and For) Argentina

For a long time, great fiscal crises accompanied by market and political turmoil were perceived to be the domain of emerging countries (Mauro 2011). This is no longer the case. In this context, the Argentine experience may have comparative merits, not least because both the economics and the politics of fiscal consolidations are currently on trial. Yet, we should be careful about Argentina. For some, this volatile country is an extraordinary economic laboratory (Tanzi 2007); for others, it is the ultimate outlier, 'the weirdest country on earth' (Przeworski 2007). Lessons from Argentina should be drawn, but cautiously.

The *analytical* lessons of this study are worth considering. First, this work confirms the relevance of Mauro's (2011) arguments: we should distinguish between designed and observed consolidation; we should focus on both successful and unsuccessful attempts. In relation to the core themes of this book, the Argentine case is a paradigmatic example of high political effort (loss imposition) without consolidation, in the convertibility era, and consolidation with low political effort (inertia strategies), in the post-default era. Second, this work underlines the value of studying budget adjustment as a process as opposed to a set of discrete episodes. Pathways to fiscal consolidation are long and bumpy roads (Dellepiane & Hardiman 2010). A process approach is crucial for capturing motivations and beliefs, political economy constraints, the range of available options, the choices made, and the intended and unintended effects. Third, the case suggests that budget consolidation should be examined in the light of underlying monetary regimes (and indeed growth models). Fiscal adjustment under convertibility (hard currency) and fiscal adjustment post-convertibility (soft currency) were different games, economically and politically.

The *policy* lessons, regarding what works and doesn't work in fiscal consolidation, are less obvious. Debates about the failed attempts to save convertibility are based on untested counterfactuals. A popular argument is that Machinea's early tax hike killed the recovery. For others, he should have moved first with spending cuts. But a counter-argument can be raised. The strategy should have aimed at dragging resources from convertibility's winners (privatised utilities, banks), sacrificing market credibility in exchange for fresh money and legitimacy. Similarly, variations in Cavallo's inconsistent efforts could have tilted the fiscal equilibrium. Another argument is that debt should have been restructured earlier. In orthodox accounts, the non-implementation of López Murphy's shock therapy marked the end of convertibility (Mussa 2002). Yet that event epitomises our core argument that there is no policy without politics. Duhalde's extension of the social safety net in the depth of the crisis provided a counter-example. It seemed to defy fiscal orthodoxy; it made political sense. What would have happened without the Plan Jefas y Jefes or export taxes? We will never know, but all these counterfactuals deserve further scrutiny. An important point should be made, forcefully. Nothing was inevitable. There were always (constrained) options along the road. Politicians actually made choices.

Above all, the Argentine case speaks to a pivotal issue in the political economy of fiscal squeezes, namely the importance of announcing a credible plan. Credibility is an elusive concept. It is, to an extent, about restoring macroeconomic balances. Yet, it is also about the *politics* of budget choices. Market credibility is a chimera without political legitimacy. When countries are facing a Polanyi moment ('more markets' might destroy the social fabric, and hence markets) both credibility and legitimacy concerns should be accommodated in the design of crisis management strategies. The multiple gambles to save convertibility showed that the relationship between budget policies and market sentiment is problematic (Dellepiane-Avellaneda 2005). The idea that credibility can simply be bought by signalling toughness should be reassessed. The collapse in confidence following the announcement of the zero-deficit rule suggests that doing the hard thing is not always the good thing. The issue is taking the politics of adjustment (and credibility) seriously. Mauro (2011: 258) concludes that 'public support for fiscal adjustment' is a key determinant of successful consolidations. But the notion that fiscal squeezes would be supported, assuming a proper 'communication campaign', is naïve. In hard times, this consensus is hardly forthcoming; political support is squeezed to the limits. Survival is the name of the game (Bonvecchi 2002).

The causes and implications of the Argentine crisis have typically been analysed through polarising (ideological) lenses. While orthodox commentators blamed politicians' profligacy and fiscal imbalances, heterodox observers focused on competitiveness issues and monetary rigidities. In the last years, the debate has twisted, but stayed polarised. Whereas heterodox observers are now referring to Argentina to sell the magic of devaluation (and sometimes default), orthodox commentators are still using the case to preach the old truths of fiscal conservatism. These arguments mirror debates about the merits and viability of the euro. The reality was more nuanced, though. Both accounts involve critical anomalies. The orthodox narrative has to face the realities that Argentina's fiscal problems have been largely on the revenue side and that the country actually crashed following a series of attempted fiscal squeezes (the 'party' had ended a long time ago). Heterodox accounts, correspondingly, need to accept that the adjustment imposed following default was probably harsher than the one implied in Cavallo's demonised zero-deficit programme. They should also live with the fact that 2002 is crucial for understanding Argentina's Great Recovery. And getting 2002 by design is not a very appealing proposition.

What about the lessons *for* Argentina? The Great Recovery has not eliminated the country's propensity to fall into perverse political economy cycles. The record surpluses achieved in 2004 and 2005 have progressively vanished, even in the context of sustained growth. Rising spending commitments have been funded with unreliable, one-off sources and increasingly with inflationary finance. The considerable fiscal squeeze imposed during and after the depression was not accompanied by comprehensive tax reform. Among other problems, the 'temporary' taxes introduced in successive crises remain in place (not even the 1995 VAT increase was ever reversed); the collection of income taxes is still extremely weak; the inefficient and unfair federal–fiscal pact remains unreformed. Most crucially, a sustainable fiscal contract is lacking. In this scenario, new episodes of fiscal crisis and fiscal squeeze are highly likely. As Vito Tanzi (2007: 150) predicted: 'sooner or later, the fiscal cycles are likely to re-establish themselves'. I do really hope we have learnt a thing or two from previous experiences.

References

Amadeo, Eduardo (2003), *La Salida del Abismo* (Buenos Aires, Planeta).

Bonvecchi, Alejandro (2002), 'Estrategias de Supervivencia y Tácticas de Disuasión: Los procesos políticos de la política económica después de las reformas estructurales', in Marcos Novaro (ed.), *El Derrumbe político en el ocaso de la convertibilidad* (Buenos Aires, Norma), 107–93.

Braun, Miguel (2006), 'The Political Economy of Debt in Argentina, or Why History Repeats Itself', paper presented at the Conference on Sovereign Debt and Development: Market Access Countries, Washington DC, The World Bank, 12–13 October 2006.

Burgo, Ezequiel (2011), *7 Ministros* (Buenos Aires, Planeta).

Caballero, Ricardo & Dornbusch, Rudi (2002), *Argentina: A Rescue Plan That Works*, Working Paper (Boston, Massachusetts Institute of Technology).

CEPAL (2008), *Panorama Gráfico Fiscal* (Buenos Aires, Oficina de la CEPAL).

Cetrángolo, Oscar & Gómez-Sabaini, Juan Carlos (2007), *Política Tributaria en la Argentina: Entre la solvencia y la emergencia*, Serie Estudios y Perspectivas 38 (Buenos Aires, Oficina de la CEPAL).

Cetrángolo, Oscar & Jiménez, Juan Pablo (2003), *Política fiscal en Argentina durante el régimen de convertibilidad*, Serie Gestión Publica 35 (Santiago de Chile, Oficina de la CEPAL).

Cetrángolo, Oscar, Heymann, Daniel & Ramos, Adrián (2007), 'Macroeconomía en recuperación: la Argentina post-crisis', in Bernardo Kosacoff (ed.), *Crisis, recuperación y nuevos dilemas: La economic argentina 2002–2007*, CEPAL Coleccion de Documentos de Proyectos (Santiago de Chile, Naciones Unidas), 27–61.

CIPPEC-Grupo Sophia (2003), *Informe sobre la Ley de Presupuesto Nacional 2004* (Buenos Aires).

Della Paolera, Gerardo & Taylor, Alan (2001), *Straining at the Anchor: The Argentine Currency Board and the Search for Macroeconomic Stability, 1880–1935* (Chicago: University of Chicago Press).

Dellepiane, Sebastián & Hardiman, Niamh (2010), *Fiscal Politics in Time: Pathways to Budget Consolidation 1980–2000*, DEI Working Paper 10/2 (Dublin, UCD Dublin European Institute).

Dellepiane-Avellaneda, Sebastián (2005), 'The Political Economy of Institutional Credible Commitments: The Case of Argentina's Convertibility Law, 1991–2001', PhD dissertation, University of Essex.

Duhalde, Eduardo (2007), *Memorias del Incendio: Los primeros 120 días de mi presidencia* (Buenos Aires, Sudamericana).

Frenkel, Roberto & Rapetti, Martin (2007), *Argentina's Monetary and Exchange Rate Policies After the Convertibility Regime Collapse*, Working Paper, Center for Economic and Policy Research (CEPR), April 2007 (Washington DC).

Galasso, Emanuela & Ravallion, Martin (2004), 'Social Protection in a Crisis: Argentina's Plan Jefes y Jefas', *World Bank Economic Review*, 18(3): 367–99.

Gerchunoff, Pablo & Llach, Lucas (2010), *El Ciclo de la Ilusión y el Desencanto. Un siglo de políticas económicas argentinas* (Buenos Aires, Emece).

Giavazzi, Francesco & Pagano, Marco (1990), 'Can Severe Fiscal Contractions Be Expansionary? Tales of Two Small European Countries', *NBER Macroeconomics Annual*, 5: 75–111.

Goertz, Gary & Mahoney, James (2012), *A Tale of Two Cultures: Qualitative and Quantitative Research in the Social Sciences* (Princeton, Princeton University Press).

Grugel, Jean & Riggirozzi, Pía (2007), 'The Return of the State in Argentina', *International Affairs*, 83(1): 87–107.

Haggard, Stephan & Kaufman, Robert (2008), *Development, Democracy, and Welfare States* (Princeton, Princeton University Press).

Hall, Peter (1993), 'Policy Paradigms, Social Learning, and the State: The Case of Economic Policymaking in Britain', *Comparative Politics*, 25(3): 275–96.

IMF (2000), 'Argentina: IMF Staff Country Report No. 00/164', December 2000 (Washington DC, International Monetary Fund).

Kirchner, Néstor (2003), 'Discurso del Señor Presidente de la Nación, Doctor Néstor Kirchner, ante la Honorable Asamblea Legislativa', Buenos Aires, 25 May 2003. Casa Rosada, Presidencia de la Nación, http://www.presidencia.gob.ar/discursos-2007/11020 (accessed 22 February 2014).

Krueger, Anne (2002), 'Crisis Prevention and Resolution: Lessons from Argentina', Conference on the Argentina Crisis, Cambridge, 17 July 2002, http://www.imf.org/external/np/speeches/2002/071702.htm (accessed 22 February 2014).

Lamberto, Oscar (2003), *Los Cien Peores Días: El fin de la convertibilidad* (Buenos Aires, Editorial Biblos).

Lavagna, Roberto (2011), *El Desafío de la Voluntad: Trece meses cruciales en la historia argentina Abril 2002–Mayo 2003* (Buenos Aires, Sudamericana).

Levitsky, Steven (2000), 'The Normalization of Argentine Politics', *Journal of Democracy*, 11(2): 56–69.

Levitsky, Steven & Murillo, Maria Victoria (2003), 'Argentina Weathers the Storm', *Journal of Democracy*, 14(4): 152–66.

Levy-Yeyati, Eduardo & Valenzuela, Diego (2007), *La Resurrección: Historia de la Poscrisis Argentina* (Buenos Aires, Editorial Sudamericana).

Mauro, Paolo, ed. (2011), *Chipping Away at Public Debt: Sources of Failure and Keys to Success in Fiscal Adjustment* (Hoboken NJ, Wiley).

MECON (2005), *Sector Publico Argentino No Financiero. Cuenta Ahorro-Inversión-Financiamiento, 1961–2004* (Buenos Aires, Ministerio de Economia y Producción).

Mussa, Michael (2002), *Argentina and the Fund: From Triumph to Tragedy* (Washington, DC, Institute for International Economics).

Polanyi, K. ([1944] 2002), *The Great Transformation* (New York, Beacon Press).

Przeworski, Adam (2007), 'Capitalism, Democracy, and Science', in Gerardo Munck & Richard Snyder (eds), *Passion, Craft, and Method in Comparative Politics* (Baltimore, Johns Hopkins University Press), 456–503.

Spiller, Pablo & Tommasi, Mariano (2009), *The Institutional Foundations of Public Policy in Argentina* (Cambridge, Cambridge University Press).

Tanzi, Vito (2007), *Argentina: An Economic Chronicle: How One of the Richest Countries in the World Lost its Wealth* (New York, Jorge Pinto Books).

The Economist (2005), 'After Lavagna, an Uncertain Tilt towards Populism', 1 December 2005.

Wylde, Christopher (2012), 'State, Society and Markets in Argentina: The Political Economy of *Neodesarrollismo* under Nestor Kirchner, 2003–2007', *Bulletin of Latin American Research*, 30(4): 436–52.

Part III
Conclusion

12

Politics In and After Fiscal Squeeze

DAVID HEALD, ROZANA HIMAZ AND CHRISTOPHER HOOD

Introduction

IN CHAPTER 2, WE EXAMINED WHAT COULD BE SAID about the politics of fiscal squeeze by comparing the available statistics on spending and revenue for the nine cases we have explored in this book and relating them to other more or less readily documented features of those cases, particularly their forms of government, the political parties involved in the 'squeeze' episodes and electoral outcomes. The nine chapters that followed took a more nuanced and in-depth look at the numbers and the politics behind them as seen by experts on each of those country cases of fiscal squeeze. So this chapter briefly puts together what answers to the questions about the politics of fiscal squeeze set out in Chapter 1 can be gleaned from combining the comparative statistical analysis of Chapter 2 with those qualitative case studies in Chapters 3 to 11. It then offers some reflections on the implications of this study for future studies of the politics of fiscal squeeze, and concludes by setting out some of the what-to-do policy conclusions that flow from this book.

We begin by repeating what was said in Chapter 1, that this is an exploratory study of the politics of fiscal squeeze, not a randomised controlled trial, and that it comprises insufficient cases for tests of statistical significance to be meaningful. That does not mean that such a study is of no value, far from it, but rather that we have to be careful in specifying what can be concluded from it. This sort of inquiry cannot be used to confirm a general hypothesis, and we do not claim to have done that, but it can be used for two very important purposes.

One is to *disconfirm* hypotheses about what is presumed to be always or usually the case—on the basis that (to take a rather hackneyed methods-textbook example used by philosophers at least since John Stuart Mill (1840: 204–6) and revived with the more recent appearance of 'black swan theory' (Taleb 2007)) we only need to identify one black swan to disconfirm the hypothesis that all swans are white. We shall develop that point in the next

Proceedings of the British Academy, **197**, 257–272. © The British Academy 2014.

section because there are several greyish, if not black, swans that come out of this study.

The other use that can be made of this kind of study is to help develop theory, concepts and/or methodology, by framing better or clearer hypotheses informed by a limited in-depth study and thus establishing more clearly what 'we know we don't know'. After all, a key test of scientific progress is to be able to develop better or more precise questions about a subject of study, and to move from what has been called 'systemic' to 'parametric' uncertainty (Green, Tunstall & Fordham 1991: 228)—or in plainer language, made famous by former US Defense Secretary Donald Rumsfeld (2011)—move from what we don't know we don't know to 'known unknowns'.

Revisiting Our Opening Three Questions

In Chapter 1, we raised three main questions about the politics of fiscal squeeze, which the chapters exploring the triggers, processes and consequences of fiscal squeeze in the nine cases considered here were intended to illuminate. One was the idea that there is something inherently different about the politics of fiscal squeeze, as something especially challenging and difficult for political leadership in modern democracies. Another, closely related to the first, was the idea that fiscal squeeze presents incumbent political parties and leaders with high blame risks, particularly where squeezes are 'hard' and more or less endogenous. A third is the idea that fiscal squeezes are high-consequence, never-the-same-again events in democratic politics and government that leave a long shadow as a result of the changes they bring about. Chapter 2 examined what could be gleaned from aggregate statistical analysis about these questions, particularly the second one. Table 12.1 (in which, as in Chapter 2, 'hybrid' means a squeeze that is hard on one fiscal element (revenue or expenditure) but soft on the other) repeats some of the main conclusions from that chapter. What can the qualitative accounts add to—or subtract from—that analysis?

The Distinctiveness of Fiscal Squeeze Politics

A systematic answer to the question of whether there is something inherently different about the politics of fiscal squeeze as compared to periods of fiscal stasis or expansion—for example, whether it is indeed a nastier, less rewarding and more difficult environment for politicians in democracies—would need to be based on a careful comparison of those different financial circumstances, and this study has focused only on squeezes. Even so, these nine cases suffice

Table 12.1. Summary of conclusions from previous chapters.

Case study[a]	Type of squeeze (policy mix)	Type of trigger	Estimated political effort	Political context at start of squeeze		Short-term political consequences	
				Strong government	Veto points	Planners lost office	Implementers lost office
USA 1838–43	Single (expenditure) hard squeeze	Exogenous	High	No	Yes	Yes (1840) Yes (1844)	Yes (1840) Yes (1844)
UK 1923–25		Endogenous	High	Yes	Yes	Yes (1923)	Yes (1923) Yes (1924)
Netherlands 1983–89	Double soft squeeze[b]	Endogenous	Medium	Yes	Yes	Yes (1986)	Yes (1986) No (1989)
Sweden 1993–2000		Endogenous	Medium	No	Yes	Yes (1994)	Yes (1994) No (1998)
New Zealand 1992–97	Hybrid squeeze (soft tax/hard spending)	Endogenous	High	Yes	No	No (1993) Partly (1996)	No (1993) Partly (1996)
Ireland 1987–89		Endogenous	High	Yes	Yes	Yes (1987)	Partly (1989)
Germany 1996–2000		Endogenous	Medium	Yes	Yes	Yes (1998) No (2002)	Yes (1998) No (2002)
Canada 1993–97		Endogenous	High	Yes	No	No (1997)	No (1997)
Argentina 2003[c]	Double hard squeeze[c]	Exogenous	1999–2002: Medium/High; 2003: Low	Yes	Yes	Yes (1999)	n/a

[a] For more details on the periodisation of the squeeze episodes, see Chapter 2, pp. 28–33.
[b] As shown in Chapter 2, the categorisation of the Swedish case depends on the time period chosen; it is a hybrid squeeze (soft tax, hard spending) for the period 1996–97.
[c] Conclusions in columns 4, 7 and 8 are based on outcomes for the qualitatively defined episode (1999–2003) rather than just the quantitative (2003), as they differ. The incumbents in 2003 were an interim government appointed in 2002.

to show that fiscal squeeze in a democracy is not invariably prompted by external *force majeure*, does not automatically reflect a standard set of economic and financial conditions (as we showed in Chapter 2), does not necessarily produce deep political crisis or political violence, and is not necessarily marked by political turning-points in the form of the 'Nixon-goes-to-China' phenomenon that we noted in Chapter 1. We have at least one 'black swan' to show for each of these propositions.

First, the idea that we referred to in Chapter 1, that modern democracy is an environment that leads inexorably to long-term public spending growth unless the irresistible political force of pressures for extra spending meets an immovable object in the form of constitutional, legal or other obligations to balance budgets, by no means fits all the cases considered here, as Table 12.1 indicates. Of course the degree of 'exogeneity' is contestable in many cases, given that those who want to change fiscal course can always play up threats of crisis, as plainly happened in Canada after the Mexican peso crisis. Nevertheless, there are several cases in our collection for which it could not plausibly be said that fiscal squeeze was a response to an immediate threat to the currency or an inability to borrow on international capital markets. The Netherlands in the 1980s, which repositioned itself from a Scandinavian-type to a Northern European-type fiscal profile by holding back public spending while GDP grew, is perhaps the blackest swan in our set for the idea that democratic governments only practise fiscal squeeze when the international markets force them to do so.

A second possible element of political distinctiveness is the idea that fiscal squeeze is likely to remove the financial glue that holds societies and political systems together and thus is likely to produce political crisis in some form and even to cause politics to shift from peaceful debate to violence. Such an idea is far from implausible, and indeed was part of the background for the IMF's '1 per cent a year' rule of thumb for the practical limits of fiscal squeeze that we mentioned in the opening chapter, but the cases in our set suggest that those effects by no means occur in all cases of fiscal squeeze. If political crisis is reflected by developments such as abrupt changes in leadership, sudden collapse of governments, suspension of normal institutional or constitutional rules and at a deeper level by a significant descent into political violence, such effects occurred to a marked degree in only a minority of the episodes considered here (notably the United States and Argentina). Post-unification Germany's fiscal squeeze is just one of several distinctly 'black swans' for that proposition.

A third possible element of political distinctiveness about fiscal squeeze, as discussed in Chapter 1, is the idea that such circumstances are likely to provoke political turning-points and political cross-dressing, notably in Nixon-goes-to-China moments where policy reversals are championed by leaders previously opposed to spending cuts and/or tax increases. In most of the nine cases considered here, there was indeed some evidence of such effects, for example when the Social Democrats implemented the spending squeeze initiated by the (centre-right) Moderates in Sweden or when Fianna Fáil implemented the squeeze planned by Fine Gael in Ireland. Moreover, there were numerous instances of parties who had opposed major new taxes in opposition continuing with those taxes when in government, as with the Goods and Services Tax in Canada. New Zealand—whose 1990s fiscal squeeze was both planned and implemented by a right-wing government—is perhaps the blackest swan in this set for the idea that fiscal squeeze will always lead to policy switches of that type (though even there the Bolger/Richardson squeeze involved jettisoning the National Party's election pledge to scrap the politically salient superannuation tax imposed by its predecessor).

Fiscal Squeeze as a Blame Trap or Credit Magnet

A second issue about the politics of fiscal squeeze raised in Chapter 1, closely related to the first, was the idea that fiscal squeeze presents incumbent political parties and leaders with high blame risks, particularly where squeezes are 'hard' and more or less endogenous, and therefore likely to pose a severe test of political blame-avoidance skills.

Chapter 2 showed that parties planning or implementing expenditure squeezes lost office in subsequent elections in over half of our cases, but we cannot say from this analysis how such a casualty rate relates to that applying to non-fiscal squeeze politics. The argument of Alberto Alesina and his colleagues, to which we referred in Chapter 1, that parties in government can improve economic conditions by expenditure-led fiscal adjustments linked with changes in regulation designed to improve competitiveness, which may in turn lead to electoral credit rather than blame, may well apply to some of the cases considered here (Canada and Argentina might be seen as examples). However, those who planned spending cuts wholly or partly lost the subsequent elections nine times out of twelve in the cases considered here.

Within this set of cases there is some hint that the casualty rate of parties implementing fiscal squeezes planned by their predecessors might be lower than that of parties who both plan and implement fiscal squeezes (two out of four as against seven out of ten, as calculated using Table 12.1), in line with the 'inertia politics' analysis we referred to in Chapter 1. But we cannot rate it as more than a hint, and certainly the tactic of avoiding electoral blame for a squeeze by pinning responsibility onto an earlier government was not invariably successful for avoiding loss of office. The blackest swan in this collection for the idea that planning and executing expenditure-led fiscal squeeze is a short route to electoral perdition is that of Canada, in the very peculiar political circumstances described by Donald J. Savoie in his account of the famous Program Review. Clearly fiscal squeeze is not invariably a 'blame magnet' for incumbents and at least in that instance it may have served as a credit-claiming opportunity, following Alesina's analysis.

Three other propositions about the link between fiscal squeeze and political blame can be shown to be contingent rather than universal even from this set of nine cases. One is the apparently common-sense hypothesis that we tentatively sketched out in the opening chapter, that blame would tend to stick to incumbents when squeezes are unambiguously triggered by endogenous factors or are 'hard' in terms of expenditure and/or taxation. That remains broadly plausible, but even then such squeezes do not seem to be an automatic route to electoral annihilation. After all, the New Zealand National Party managed to squeak back into office (admittedly by a hair's breadth) in 1993, and the UK Conservative Party, co-planner of the 'Geddes Axe' expenditure squeeze and subsequent implementer, seems to have suffered only short-term electoral damage in 1923, in sharp contrast to the Liberal Party, its coalition partner at the time the cuts were planned.

A second is a variant of the proposition put forward by Alesina and others that expenditure-led fiscal adjustments are always less costly than tax-led adjustments. By that such commentators mean that the economic costs incurred are lower, but if we consider the proposition that fiscal squeezes that were purely or largely expenditure-based invariably have lower political costs (in terms of avoidance of loss of office at subsequent elections) than fiscal squeezes that were a hybrid of tax rises and spending cuts, that does not seem to apply in these cases. The black swan here is the UK in 1923 (and possibly the USA, for the federal-level counterpart of the state-level fiscal squeezes analysed by Alasdair Roberts), where incumbents lost office after implementing expenditure-only squeezes. For the corollary, that costs would be higher for fiscal squeezes putting more emphasis on tax increases, the black swans are Canada and New Zealand, where incumbents retained office after planning and implementing hybrid tax-expenditure squeezes.

Finally, if fiscal squeeze is expected to be electorally toxic, we might expect the process of implementing such squeezes to be dominated by blame-avoidance strategies, and here the accounts given of those processes in the case-study chapters provide important evidence. If blame-avoidance strategies dominated the process, we might expect fiscal squeeze politics to emphasise the following: presentational strategies such as pinning the blame on the profligacy or incompetence of predecessors in office or on implacable market forces; agency strategies such as delegation of unpopular choices to technocrats, bureaucrats or lower-level governments; policy strategies such as grand coalitions; and the sort of cheese-paring approaches that cut spending or raise taxes by technical or small-print changes that make it harder for opponents to draw a line in the sand and mount last-ditch defences of the status quo that will command public sympathy.

The preceding nine chapters indeed showed examples of many of those processes accompanying the politics of applying fiscal squeeze, and the rhetoric of irresistible market forces does seem to have been a widespread tactic used by the squeezers. It does not seem to have invariably been the case that cutbacks were imposed disproportionately on lower-level governments (the UK in the 1920s is again a 'black swan' for that proposition) or that the poisoned chalice of deciding what to cut was handed over to technocrats (indeed, that seems to have been fairly rare). From the accounts given in the preceding country chapters, cheese-paring seems to have been widespread, for instance in public service salary cuts or freezes which invariably seemed to accompany fiscal squeeze. However, in some cases major 'cliff-edge' cutbacks were made, for instance in the abolition of transport subsidies in Canada and the scrapping of plans for the extension of post-14 education in the UK. None of the cases involved a formal grand coalition of all the major political parties. Trying to dodge the blame may be a universal in politics, but it does not seem to have played out in the same way in all of the cases considered here.

The Consequentiality of Fiscal Squeeze: Never the Same Again?

The third issue about the politics of fiscal squeeze raised in Chapter 1 concerned its consequentiality or otherwise. Consequentiality could mean that the changes made during periods of fiscal squeeze tend to be irreversible or at least highly 'sticky' in the medium term: for example, that new taxes or higher tax rates once imposed as part of a fiscal squeeze tend to become a fixture, or that old subsidies or other spending items once removed or reduced tend to be gone for good. It could mean that fiscal squeeze has palpable and clear-cut effects on the working of government and politics, as a once-and-for-all 'critical juncture' that disrupts path dependence and, possibly irreversibly, reshapes institutional and policy development. Examples include reshaping the state or altering the relative power of major political and institutional players (such as lower levels of government relative to federal or central governments). Even more broadly—as the high-consequentiality rhetoric of fiscal squeeze politics tends to imply, for example with claims that it will lead to a 'lost generation'—fiscal squeeze could have palpable consequences for the society more broadly.

Table 12.2. The consequentiality of fiscal squeeze.

Case study	Fiscal and economic effects	Constitutional and institutional effects	Effects on location of effective power	Effects on societal values	Effects on social order	Overall: was it a critical juncture?
USA 1838–43	H: introduction of new taxes and a shift towards financing state expenditure from taxes rather than loans and land sales	H: balanced budget rules in state constitutions remain in place 18 decades later	H: strengthened federal power, particularly at the executive level	H: contributed to continuing suspicion of big government after phase of entrepreneurial state government led to defaults	H: extensive rioting, the incidence of which contributed to the establishment of bureaucratic policing	Yes: enduring legacy in reliance on constitutional limitations and emphasis of state-level self-sufficiency
UK 1923–25	M: fiscal squeeze was part of policy outlook that led to ill-fated return to the gold standard in 1925			M: halt in post-WWI reconstruction policies may have contributed to disillusionment of key voters		No: other events in the interwar period had more important legacies
New Zealand 1992–97	H: led to a decade of strong fiscal performance protected by transparency reforms but effects on economic performance less clear	H: likely to have contributed to the introduction of MMP, reducing chances of single-party majority in unicameral parliament	M: offsetting effects of strengthening Treasury's reputation and policy control yet electoral system led to coalition-forming deals	H: may have contributed (along with demographic change) to weakening of egalitarian values and policy shift to market-based policies		Yes; pioneering welfare state leads move to smaller state (neo-liberal) policies
Netherlands 1983–88	M: tighter fiscal control continued, OECD public expenditure/GDP ranking henceforth lower		L: seems to have been associated with increased role of technocrats and managers at local level	L: may have contributed to populist challenges to technocratic and managerial policymaking		(Yes): led to lasting change in spending/GDP ratio; may have helped to spark new populist/right politics
Ireland 1987–89	H: misleadingly became the poster child for 'expansionary fiscal contraction'. Celtic Tiger period led to real economic gains but spectacular crash later			L: significant changes in Irish society not attributed to fiscal squeeze, more to decline in religious affiliation, and to effects of immigration and emigration		No: represented a missed opportunity to address issues that would have to be addressed in the later fiscal squeeze after 2008

Germany 1996–2000	H: in aftermath of unification (e.g. fiscal transfers to new eastern Länder), 'internal devaluation' made Germany super-competitive within the Eurozone	M: highly symbolic constitutional reforms in debt brake, being echoed at Länder level, designed to lock in benefits of period of fiscal squeeze	L: continuing Federal leadership of the federation, with countervailing Länder influence via the Bundesrat	L: fiercely competitive party system but two big parties often operating on shared societal values	(No): critical juncture was unification in 1990. However, allegedly inflexible political system showed agility in negotiating reforms
Sweden 1993–2000	H: economic recovery helped by crisis being standalone, by devaluation and later protected by status outside Eurozone; strong fiscal performance backed by transparency			L: continuing acceptance of welfare state and big government; has avoided collapse of trust in government. Capacity of governments and oppositions to compromise on fiscal measures and pension reform	(Yes): public expenditure/GDP ratio is now less detached at the top of OECD rankings. Decline of the once-dominant Social Democrats
Canada 1993–97	M: continued efforts in terms of maintaining trends in revenue and expenditure; consolidated Goods and Services Tax		M: Shift of greater fiscal responsibility to provinces, through unfunded or partially funded mandates		No: though it gave Canada 'poster child' status elsewhere after 2008
Argentina 2003	M: devaluation in 2002 led to rapid rise in GDP and consequent growth. Tax reforms instituted in early 2000s helped revenue increase			H: protests linked to economic crisis of 1999–2002 and consequent political effort to squeeze	No: contributed to remarkable recovery after 1999–2002 crisis, but fiscal improvement was not sustained

Notes: The evidence base for judgements is Chapter 2 and the relevant country chapter.
L = Low, M = Medium and H = High, the scale relating to the strength of the effect rather than directly to the quality of supporting evidence. Blank cells indicate that the study has produced no relevant evidence. Brackets around coding in the final column indicate weaker statements.

As we noted in Chapter 1 and as the nine case studies have shown, such questions are easier to ask than to answer, even for country experts with the benefit of hindsight. Table 12.2 attempts to sum up what consequences can be attributed to the nine fiscal squeezes discussed in this book on five aspects of politics and society, with an overall 'critical juncture' column on the right of the table. Each country case is a row and the five analytic items and the summary judgement are the columns. These categories are drawn from the literature discussed in Chapter 1 and the scores come from the comparative analysis of Chapter 2 and the editors' interpretation of the evidence presented in the nine case studies. Where effects have been identified, they are scored as Low (L), Medium (M) or High (H). Where no evidence is presented in this book, the cell is left blank. This scoring of effects in Table 12.2 is to be distinguished from the scoring of political effort devoted to fiscal squeeze in Table 12.1. The final column then indicates whether the fiscal squeeze episodes should be regarded as critical junctures: the scoring options are Yes, (Yes), (No) and No, bracketing indicating a more qualified response. That scoring is an overall qualitative judgement, not based on counting Ls, Ms and Hs.

The picture presented in Table 12.2 and the case study chapters also suggests black or at least greyish swans for the idea that fiscal squeeze is clearly and invariably a high-consequentiality affair, in terms of irreversibility of tax and spending changes; for long-term political impact, in terms of major party-system upsets or constitutional change; and for lasting social effects of a broader kind. Taking those in reverse order, Canada appears to be the blackest swan in our set for the idea that fiscal squeeze invariably prompts major social change of a 'lost generation' kind. As for the middle item, in most cases our country experts detected some evidence of fiscal squeeze having non-trivial impacts on party politics in the short or medium term, but only in one or two cases were there constitutional or major institutional changes (for example, in the balance between local and central government) that are unambiguously attributable to fiscal squeeze. As for the first item (irreversible change), we see evidence in several cases of fiscal squeeze introducing or serving to consolidate new unpopular taxes (such as the Goods and Services Tax in Canada), reflecting Peacock & Wiseman's (1961) famous comment that 'it is harder to get the saddle on the horse than to keep it there'. However, Argentina appears to be the blackest swan in our collection for the idea that expenditure cuts invariably tend to be once-and-for-all, and it is notable how temporary was the slimming effect on the Canadian federal bureaucracy of the much-lauded-at-the-time Program Review.

Where To From Here?

This book takes a step towards a fuller analysis of the politics of fiscal squeeze, but there is of course further to travel. At least three new questions arising from this study demand some attention in future analyses of this phenomenon.

As we have shown, the politics of fiscal squeeze is not readily reflected in the numbers reported in cross-national economic datasets. Political pressure, the central element in our definition of fiscal squeeze, is not necessarily reflected by reported changes in primary balances, yet it is the latter that the dominant literature tends to concentrate on. Moreover, the political impact of fiscal squeeze will include 'announcement effects' as well as the effects of enacted changes in tax and spending, yet it is the latter that most quantitative studies focus on. Outcome-based economic data can therefore be distracting as well as illuminating. Measurement, even conceptualisation, of 'political pressure' is in its infancy, and though Chapter 1 developed an indicative scheme, the analysis here relies heavily on qualitative judgement. So how can we get closer to assessing or measuring the 'political effort' going into fiscal squeeze? Must it remain one of those 'known unknowns', such as would be needed to disconfirm the Second Law of Thermodynamics (which can be stated but still not measured)?

Second, as we said in Chapter 1, our nine fiscal squeeze cases can only serve to disconfirm propositions about what might be claimed to apply to all cases of fiscal squeeze, and as we have shown in the previous section, numerous 'black swans' emerge from this study. Those who believe (for instance) that democratic governments will never cut spending unless faced with strong external pressure, that fiscal squeeze will always produce political crises, that it will invariably lead to annihilation of incumbents at the polls or have deep and irreversible consequences, will find this study suggests otherwise. But if we want to turn from disconfirmation to the more positive task of confirming what might be distinctive about fiscal squeeze politics, we need both more cases (for example, by combining country comparisons with over-time comparisons) and a comparative strategy that matches cases of fiscal squeeze with control cases of 'unsqueezed' politics.

Third, this study has only covered a sub-set of all the possible kinds of fiscal squeeze in democracies. We began by defining fiscal squeeze as political effort put into reining in public spending and/or raising taxes, and that means fiscal squeeze can vary in the relative emphasis placed on cutting spending as against raising taxes. Table 12.3, developing Table 2.1 in Chapter 2, classifies the nine country case studies according to 16 possible combinations of revenue/spending and hard/soft introduced earlier. The nine cases cluster into 4 out of the 16 cells representing all the possible combinations of revenue

Table 12.3.   Types of fiscal squeeze.

Revenue	Expenditure			
	No fall	Fall only in constant prices	Fall only as % of GDP[a]	Fall as % of GDP and in real terms
No rise	1 No squeeze	2 Single (expenditure) soft squeeze	3 Single (expenditure) soft squeeze	4 Single (expenditure) hard squeeze **Cases: USA, UK**
Rise only in constant price terms	5 Single (revenue) soft squeeze	6 Double soft squeeze	7 Double soft squeeze **Cases: Netherlands, Sweden**[b]	8 Hybrid squeeze **Cases: New Zealand, Ireland, Germany, Canada**
Rise only as % of GDP[c]	9 Single (revenue) soft squeeze	10 Double soft squeeze	11 Double soft squeeze	12 Hybrid squeeze
Rise as % of GDP and in real terms	13 Single (revenue) hard squeeze	14 Hybrid soft/ hard squeeze	15 Hybrid soft/ hard squeeze	16 Double hard squeeze **Case: Argentina**

[a] Fall as of % GDP: cut-off points as defined for Table 2.1.
[b] For period defined in Chapter 2: Sweden is a case of hybrid squeeze for the period 1996–97.
[c] Rise as % of GDP: cut-off points as defined for Table 2.1.

rises and spending falls. Two of our specimens are single (spending-only) 'hard' squeezes (USA and UK in cell 4). One (Argentina, 16) is a double hard squeeze (revenue plus spending), while the other six cases bunch into 'hybrid' cell (8) and one double soft squeeze cell (7). Developing the study of the politics of fiscal squeeze requires both comparing more cases within those populated cells (in particular the double hard squeeze category) and exploring the unpopulated cells in Table 12.3, in particular the revenue-only type of hard squeeze. How rare are those unpopulated cells and what political effects do they have?

What Should Policymakers Take Away from this Study?

Flashforward—The Next Great Crash

Picture the scene, at some indefinite point in the future. The global economy has recovered after the previous financial crash. Pressures on public finances have eased, with governments in many developed countries able to run primary surpluses and to congratulate themselves on the political effort they have put into the future sustainability of their public finances. Social tensions linked to unemployment and increased inequality have been contained in most countries, despite warnings about the effects of increased income inequality on the social fabric and on economic performance (Dorling 2011; OECD 2011). The narrative of 'strivers and shirkers' has proved its electoral value as heresthetic in many countries and (in spite of a few dogged dissenters in highbrow, low-circulation blogs and publications) blame for the 2008 financial crisis has been pinned squarely on the excessive welfare spending and incompetent financial regulation of feckless governments during the decade prior to the 2008 crisis. The banking and financial sectors have boomed to new heights, and international agencies such as the IMF and OECD have concluded that prudential regulation is now well designed and effective.

Then comes the next Great Crash. One Sunday evening, out of the blue, the US president personally telephones the leaders of all G8 countries to warn them that Wall Street will be closed on Monday until further notice. Massive US financial institutions are being declared bankrupt, ahead of liquidation. The crisis has been sparked by rogue trading, false accounting, bad investments in property, outright corruption in several countries and massive exposure to misunderstood risks in others. The scale of defaults means that many financial institutions across the world are likely to be brought down on Monday by counterparty risk. After these tense phone calls, the president attends a specially convened meeting of his Council of Economic Advisers, to consider what fiscal and monetary steps to take in these bleak circumstances, and equivalent what-to-do discussions are about to start across much of the rest of the world.

***

We do not claim any gifts of prophecy. Economists have been defined as people who can tell you tomorrow why yesterday's prophecy failed to fit today's events (McCloskey 1985: xix) and political science is also littered with failures to foresee the future. However, if anything like the scenario painted above comes about, what lessons can policymakers take from this comparative study of historical cases of fiscal squeeze?

First, on the basis of past experience, those who have to grapple with the next generation of fiscal squeeze decisions are likely to be struggling with problematic economic and fiscal data, possibly exacerbated by measures to cut costs in previous fiscal squeezes. Reflecting on the contribution which public finances had made to country vulnerability in 2008, the IMF (2012) stressed the role of inadequate data quality and weak fiscal transparency in contributing to policy errors. In grappling with the data, these future fiscal squeezers will encounter some more or less technical problems arising from more fragmented public services delivery (complicating the scoring of public spending) and the effects on the economy of globalisation, financialisation and electronic transactions (recording GDP, including estimation of the shadow economy). They are also likely to face data problems that are more behavioural in origin, for example where governments have restrained measured public expenditure by the use of policy instruments (such as off-balance sheet Public–Private Partnerships and government guarantees) that do not show up in reported numbers (Heald 2012). When engaged in cross-national comparisons, they are likely to struggle to reconcile budgetary and financial reporting data, since government accounting practices vary across countries in a way that private sector practices no longer do. Simply being able to establish the current position, and what happened even in the recent past, is more fraught than many decision-makers realise.

Second, on the basis of past experience, policymakers in the next set of fiscal squeezes are likely to find themselves grappling with those difficult data problems within a highly compressed time period. Policymakers rarely have the luxury of a lengthy period of reflection before they have to implement fiscal squeeze measures. When crises hit, decision-making time can be minimal, leading to policy errors. There is not likely to be a 'level playing field', either in terms of how markets react (note that Argentina's default came when it would have met the Maastricht deficit criteria) or of how international/supranational institutions respond to countries in fiscal difficulties (for example, Ireland was severely criticised by the European Commission in 2002 for breaching the Excessive Deficit Procedure, whereas the rules were rewritten when they were later breached by France and Germany).

Third, in the middle of grappling with problematic data under extreme time pressure, policymakers will find themselves having to assess the policy panaceas that are on offer to show what they should do. These proposals are often put forward by key actors from previous crises proclaiming their success and generalising from highly contingent circumstances; such actors from New Zealand, Canada and Sweden were prominent after 2008. Our country chapters make it clear that judgements about success, even in these celebrated cases, have to be nuanced, but under the kind of pressures noted above often are not. Cartwright & Hardie (2012) stress the crucial difference between 'Did it work *somewhere?*' and 'Will it work *here?*', and policymakers will find themselves struggling to decide how much to discount claims of 'transferability' and 'best practice' where contextual factors are uncertain. Of course they will not be passive actors in the process: academic and other experts aim to influence the course of public policy, but policymakers will also find themselves shopping for those research results that buttress their preferred choices.[1]

---

[1] In his defence of Reinhart & Rogoff (2010) (after criticism that they had made data errors), Summers (2013) squarely put the blame on policymakers shopping for evidence.

Fourth, a key aspect of the judgements about context that these future decision-makers in the next generation of fiscal squeezes will need to make concerns the state of the world economy, and particularly whether major trading partners have comparable fiscal difficulties. That element is often neglected in accounts of economic recovery after periods of fiscal squeeze. For example, the 'success stories' of Ireland in the 1980s and Canada and Sweden in the 1990s were all cases where fiscal squeeze took place in a far more buoyant international economy or with policy instruments that were not available to the Eurozone countries in the 2010s.

Fifth, the dog that did not bark is the absence of revenue-led fiscal squeezes. The three revenue squeeze cells (5, 9 and 13) in Table 12.3 are all unpopulated. There are several possible explanations that invite future research. This result might have technical origins, in that however hard governments work on raising tax rates and expanding tax bases, the trajectory of GDP prevents revenue increasing either in real terms or as a percentage of GDP (the automatic stabilisers playing a role). However, possible deeper causes are that such a result is a characteristic of capitalist democracies and an indication of the effects of globalisation on the tax-revenue-generating capacities of their economies. A pragmatic lesson is that governments should fix their tax systems, particularly their tax bases, during periods of prosperity: Argentina and Ireland stand out in the way they demonstrate the fiscal risks attached to a narrow tax base in general and to heavy reliance on transaction taxes in particular.

Finally, future policymakers grappling with the next round of fiscal squeezes are likely to be making decisions whose consequences they may not be able to foresee. At the time when decisions have to be taken, it can be unclear whether a critical juncture has been reached and, if so, what would be the direction of change. The 2008 global financial crisis, which some commentators had expected to mark the end of neo-liberalism (Crouch 2011), might alternatively lead to intensification. As the preceding discussion of consequentiality showed, not all fiscal squeezes seem to have high long-term consequentiality, but some certainly do. For example, the US states' constitutional provisions that followed the 1830s state defaults may possibly have contributed to less government growth than elsewhere, but have certainly accentuated the marked pro-cyclicality of sub-national public expenditure in the United States. New Zealand's change of electoral system in the 1990s seems to have been motivated in part by a reaction against strong governments imposing far-reaching institutional and fiscal changes without serious challenge. Of course in many cases the consequences of fiscal squeeze are likely to be subtle and contestable, such as in changes in the relative power of central and sub-national governments (more likely in unitary states than in federations), and in the consequences of substituting technocratic expertise for the legitimacy of democracy (Barber 2011).

Whenever the next set of major pressures on government spending and revenues comes, such decisions—about problematic data, uncertain consequences, contestable lessons, and perplexing contextual judgements, all made under severe time pressure—are likely to be as central to the politics of the next fiscal squeeze as they have been in the past.

References

Barber, T. (2011), 'Policymakers Relegate Democracy at their Peril', *Financial Times*, 29 September.

Cartwright, N. & Hardie, J. (2012), *Evidence-Based Policy Making: A Practical Guide to Doing It Better* (Oxford, Oxford University Press).

Crouch, C. (2011), *The Strange Non-Death of Neoliberalism* (Cambridge, Polity Press).

Dorling, D. (2011), *Injustice: Why Social Inequality Persists* (Bristol, Policy Press).

Green, C., Tunstall, S.M. & Fordham, M. (1991), 'The Risks from Flooding: Which Risks and Whose Perception?', *Disasters*, 15(3): 227–36.

Heald, D. (2012), 'Why is Transparency about Public Expenditure so Elusive?', *International Review of Administrative Sciences*, 78(1): 30–49.

IMF (2012), *Fiscal Transparency, Accountability and Risk* (Washington DC, International Monetary Fund).

McCloskey, D.N. (1985), *The Rhetoric of Economics* (Madison WI, Wisconsin University Press).

Mill, J.S. (1840), *A System of Logic, Ratiocinative and Inductive* (London, Longmans).

OECD (2011), *Divided We Stand: Why Inequality Keeps Rising* (Paris, OECD).

Peacock, A.T. & Wiseman, J. (1961), *The Growth of Public Expenditure in the United Kingdom* (Princeton NJ, Princeton University Press).

Reinhart, C.M. & Rogoff, K.S. (2010), 'Growth in a Time of Debt', *American Economic Review*, 100(2): 573–8.

Rumsfeld, D. (2011), *Known and Unknown: A Memoir* (New York, Sentinel).

Summers, L. (2013), 'The Buck Does Not Stop with Reinhart and Rogoff: Political Leaders Pushing Austerity Made Their Choice, Then Cast About for Intellectual Buttresses', *Financial Times*, 6 May.

Taleb, N.N. (2007), *The Black Swan: The Impact of the Highly Improbable* (New York, Random House).

Index